CLEMATIS
THE GENUS

Christopher Grey-Wilson

A COMPREHENSIVE GUIDE FOR GARDENERS, HORTICULTURISTS AND BOTANISTS

TIMBER PRESS

PORTLAND, OREGON

Text, illustrations and photographs (except where otherwise credited)
© Christopher Grey-Wilson 2000

Volume copyright © B T Batsford Ltd 2000

First published in North America in 2000 by
Timber Press, Inc.
The Haseltine Building
133 S.W. Second Avenue, Suite 450
Portland, Oregon, 97204, U.S.A.

Reprinted 2000

A catalog record for this book is available from the Library of Congress.

ISBN 0-88192-428-8

Designed by Simon Rosenheim

Printed in Hong Kong

Table of Contents

Preface

This book is essentially about *Clematis* species. It has been written with the gardener, as well as the horticulturist and botanist in mind. I have tried to keep the botanical jargon to a minimum, while at the same time attempting to include as much detail as possible. Gardeners will, I hope forgive me for putting much important detail, especially measurements of leaves and flower parts, into rather formal species descriptions. With 297 species to fit into the text any other form would have proved impossible. As it is, some of the details, especially for the lesser-known species, are extremely brief. To do otherwise would have overburdened the text and made the book far too expensive to produce.

At the same time, I trust that my botanical colleagues will forgive me for straying from a more traditional botanical approach. I have reclassified the prime divisions of the genus while working through the species over the past few years. I have also attempted to give as full a synonymy of the genus as possible; not an easy undertaking as those who have ever looked at the genus will undoubtedly understand. Throughout the main part of the text, identification is aided by botanical keys which stray from the more normal approach found in monographs. Instead the divisions of the keys are dispersed amongst the text. They may prove useful to those trying to name a plant, especially a species new to cultivation. Although the key statements include useful information on groups of species, or individual species, it is not essential to use them in order to understand the species text.

In some instances it has not been possible, for the sake of brevity, to include all the known botanical information on particular species. For instance, details of fruit characters are sparingly presented, except where such details are of great importance in accurate identification.

I am extremely grateful to those who have helped me during the preparation of this book, particularly Chris Brickell, Dick Brummitt, Phillip Cribb, Jack Elliott, Raymond Evison, Mike Gilbert, John Grimshaw, Roy Lancaster, Martyn Rix and Mike Smith. To my wife Christine, many thanks for reading the text and for putting up with my absences for many hours while I shut myself in the office in order to complete this work.

Introduction

Clematis have never been as popular as they are today. The range available is astonishing and just about every garden centre can be guaranteed to have a varied assortment. This availability has been made possible by specialist clematis growers and the mass production of plants, particularly the large-flowered cultivars, which gardeners can usually purchase at very reasonable prices. As a result, clematis today rates as one of the most popular of all garden flowers. Amongst climbing plants it scarcely has a rival with the exception of honeysuckle, wisteria and climbing roses.

It is the infinite variety found in clematis that beckons the gardener. From modest alpines to herbaceous perennials, from delicate scramblers to rampant climbers, both deciduous or evergreen 'which can develop a woody trunk as thick as a man's wrist in time' the genus offers the gardener plenty of scope. The flowers can be intriguing, from simple flat or cupped blooms, to bell-, urn- or tubular-shaped, or even those in which the 'petals' recurve in the form of a Turk's-cap. Some have delightfully scented flowers and the range of flower colour virtually fills the spectrum, from white, yellow and blue, to green, brown and many shades of red.

The foliage is rarely outstanding, although the lustrous evergreen leathery foliage of *C. armandii* is very handsome. The majority of species are deciduous and bear foliage in various shades of green, sometimes with a pleasing bronze or purplish flush, especially when they are young. Autumn colour is rare, although some species turn yellow before the leaves fall. Autumn interest is provided in many species by attractive silky or fluffy seedheads that can be white or silvery, sometimes flushed with pink, purple or yellow. The fruitheads can be solitary or bunched together and can make a fascinating study in the absence of flowers. Like the flowers they make wonderful subjects for the photographer.

In recent years there have been a number of books written about clematis. Most of these are very fine but they primarily deal unashamedly with the numerous cultivars, especially the large-flowered kinds. In 1997 Magnus Johnson of Södertälje near Uppsala published his *magnum opus* on the genus 'Släket Klematis' which deals fully with most of the species and the majority of cultivars. Unfortunately, this book, which is almost 900 pages long, is only in Swedish and as such the information is practically unavailable to the majority of clematis enthusiasts and gardeners around the world, unless an English translation is forthcoming.

I have been working on the genus *Clematis* for a number of years with the ultimate intention of writing a monograph. At the same time it seemed to me that a condensed overview of the genus would make an interesting book, highlighting the species in cultivation but, at the same time providing some details on the numerous species yet to be brought into cultivation. Today, there is an increased interest in *Clematis* species and more and more are appearing in cultivation as a result of recent expeditions to places such as western China, the Himalaya and Korea. The species have a great deal to offer the gardener, in flower size, form and colour, as well as habit.

Familiar species in cultivation

A number of species have been cultivated for many years and have become an essential part of the garden; for example *C. alpina, C. armandii, C. cirrhosa, C. flammula, C. heracleifolia, C. integrifolia, C. macropetala, C. montana, C. tangutica* and *C. viticella.*

What do the species offer the gardener?

Although few *Clematis* species are as large-flowered or as brazen in size and colour as many of the large-flowered cultivars, the genus has plenty to offer the gardener. The wild forms of *C. alpina, C. macropetala, C. montana,* and *C. tangutica* are just as good as their cultivated counterparts, and are showy garden plants. Seeing *C. montana* adorning bushes in Nepal or Yunnan in the spring, its shoots wreathed in bloom, is a memorable sight and they will respond just as well in our gardens. *Clematis* species can offer a wide range of colour and form to suit many situations in the garden from walls, fences and pergolas to bushes and trees. The more vigorous species are excellent in the wild garden or for clambering up lofty trees, while the herbaceous types are excellent and fascinating subjects for the herbaceous border. In addition, some of the smaller non-climbing species are desirable plants for the alpine garden.

Besides the great range of form and flower type, many clematis bear attractive, even exciting, displays of fluffy fruitheads to continue interest into the autumn and early winter. One only has to think of the tresses of Old Man's Beard, *C. vitalba*, one of the most vigorous of species, adorning an autumn hedgerow, to realize such decorative potential. If that were not enough, many species have scented flowers. *C. montana* is noted for its fragrance and this delightful vanilla scent has been passed from the species to some of the cultivars ('Elizabeth' and 'Mayleen' for instance). *C. heracleifolia* has a rich hyacinth-like smell, whereas the little pale yellow bells of the charming *C. rehderiana* are scented of the finest cowslips, *C. turkestanica* has a jasmine scent, *C. armandii* smells of Hawthorn, *C. flammula* of vanilla, while the New Zealand *C. forsteri* has the fragrance of lemon verbena. Other species which have a notable fragrance include *C. aethusifolia*, *C. apiifolia*, *C. aristata*, *C. brachiata*, *C. buchananiana*, *C. chinensis*, *C. cirrhosa*, *C. connata*, *C. crispa*, *C. denticulata*, *C. elizabethae-corolae*, *C. fasciculiflora*, *C. finetiana*, *C. foetida*, *C. gouriana*, *C. grata*, *C. graveolens*, *C. integrifolia* (some forms), *C. koreana* var. *fragrans*, *C. ligusticifolia*, *C. mandschurica*, *C. marata*, *C. meyeniana*, *C. microphylla*, *C. orientalis* (some forms), *C. paniculata*, *C. parviflora*, *C. recta*, *C. serratifolia*, *C. smilacifolia*, *C. songarica*, *C. terniflora*, *C. trichotoma*, *C. tubulosa*, *C. uncinata*, *C. veitchiana*, *C. virginiana* and *C. vitalba*.

Using this book

This book is laid out in three main sections. First comes cultivation, then the botany and classification of the genus *Clematis* follow. The remainder of the book consists of a survey of all the known species. These are arranged according to the classification of the genus outlined on pp.24-31. Each species is given a number, starting from 1 and ending with 297, which represents the total world-wide number of species currently recognized. In a book of this size it has proved impossible to give each species a full description; however, it is hoped that enough salient features are given to enable the reader to distinguish between species, subspecies and varieties. Important and well-known species, especially those in cultivation, are given more comprehensive coverage, with the inclusion of significant cultivars and hybrids. Under each species there will also be found details of the plant's known distribution in the wild,

its habitat and flowering time and, when possible, details of altitude.

An important aspect is the inclusion of a comprehensive synonymy together with the author's names for each recognized species and the synonym.

The species are arranged according to their subgenera and sections. This means that closely allied species come together in the text. As an additional aid to identification, keys are presented throughout to help the reader distinguish a particular plant. These are scattered throughout the text and work in couplets like many botanical keys. Thus each couplet consists of contrasting statements preceded by a symbol which is doubled for the second entry for each couplet. The species which apply to each half of the couplet follow in brackets, by number. e.g.

▼ Leaves pinnate; flowers white (species 57–65)
▼ ▼ Leaves ternate; flowers yellow (species 66 & 67)

The two halves of a couplet may be well separated in the text; the essential thing is to look for the second half of the couplet if the species does not fall under the first; this is indicated by the double symbol of the first.

There may be a number of such couplets within any particular subgenus or section (each couplet with its own unique symbol), especially when they contain a large number of species. Thus in the above example all the species with pinnate leaves and white flowers (i.e. species 57–65) are found after the symbol ▼, but before ▼ ▼. In contrast, those with ternate leaves and yellow flowers (species 66 & 67) are to be found after ▼ ▼ and up to the end of that particular section of the book.

I have endeavoured throughout to use as little technical jargon as possible so that the text is, I hope, accessible to gardeners, horticulturists and the botanists. Some technical terms like 'pinnate', 'cyme', 'dioecious' and 'achene' have had to be used, and such terms are explained in the glossary at the end of the book.

Codes

I have endeavoured to minimize the number of codes used in the main text, but the following will be found in order to save space: three key codes are used under the species:

An '*' after the species name or cultivar name, indicates that the species in question is in cultivation and available at the time of writing.

An 'H'-symbol followed by a number indicates the hardiness rating of the species in question. Thus plants rated as hardiness zone H5 are known to be hardy to

–29°C (–20°F), while those in H11 are intolerant of any frost whatsoever. See p.15 for hardiness zones. A 'P'-symbol indicates the pruning group for a particular species, and immediately follows the hardiness rating. There are three main groups P1, P2 and P3, see p.12.

Obviously when a species is not in cultivation (this applies to almost a half of all those known) then none of these symbols will appear.

No attempt has been made to indicate hardiness ratings or pruning categories unless they have been established. However, they can be deduced fairly accurately for species new to cultivation by looking at their close allies that are already established in cultivation.

Awards

Three types of award are indicated in the main text and they are given to the plant in the past by the Royal Horticultural Society:

Award of Merit (AM) is given to meritorious plants that have been exhibited at the Society's shows, including the Chelsea Flower Show. This, like the following award, is given to the plant (species, form or cultivar) as exhibited.

First Class Certificate (FCC) is a higher award than the AM and is only given to plants that are outstanding at exhibition.

The Award of Garden Merit (AGM) is wholly different and not related to the above awards. It is a more useful indicator to gardeners and highlights plants of outstanding garden excellence.

Societies to join

British Clematis Society, 4 Springfield, Lightwater, Surrey, GU18 5XP, UK.
International Clematis Society, 115 Belmont Road, Harrow, Middlesex, HA3 7PL, UK.

Cultivation

At the time of writing there are just over 100 species of clematis available in the horticultural trade. Others are grown in specialist and private collections. Furthermore, additional species are coming into cultivation all the time as a result of seed collecting expeditions to various parts of the world, most notably to China in recent years. Added to these are the numerous subspecies, varieties, and selected forms (cultivars) of the species, which add enormously to the plants available to horticulturists and botanists.

It would be foolish to say that all clematis species are desirable in the garden, for there are quite a few with small greenish or whitish flowers which are scarcely worth considering, except if you are an avid collector of species and want all that are available. On the other hand, there are plenty of exciting and garden-worthy species to attract attention and they enrich our gardens with a subtlety and elegance that many modern clematis cultivars, brash and brazen in their sumptuous blooms, have singularly lost. Of course there is a place in the garden for both the species and the large-flowered cultivars and this is witnessed by the huge and growing popularity of the clematis today.

The species have much to offer from attractive foliage and flowers, to rash displays of fluffy fruits and in some there is the added bonus of scent.

There are advantages to confining yourself to growing only the wild species rather than garden cultivars, for they are generally less fussy to grow and, once established, are often long-lived and flower well each year. In addition, apart from one or two, they do not suffer from the dreaded clematis wilt that afflicts so many of the large-flowered cultivars, much to the chagrin of gardeners.

I could go on extolling the virtues of the wild species but will resist the temptation. Suffice it to say that they are great fun to grow and offer the garden a wide range of possibilities.

Selection

It is important to site clematis species carefully in the garden. Many are vigorous climbers, some invasively so, and no amount of careful training and pruning will keep them properly under control. Placed in the wrong position, they will quickly overrun their allotted space and escape into the neighbour's garden, smother surrounding bushes or venture unhindered over the rooftop. But even these thugs have their place in the garden. Choosing the right plant for the right place is critical.

The majority of the climbing species like their roots in the cool shade, but with their 'heads' reaching upward into the light and sunshine. Remember that they are predominantly plants of forests, woodlands and bushy places and will scramble up from the shade into the sunlight. A position where their roots can enjoy shade, at least during the hot hours of the day, is ideal. Naturally there are exceptions: the southern European *C. flammula* is perfectly at home in full sunshine, indeed thrives on it, and members of the Orientalis Group (e.g. *C. tangutica* and *C. tibetana*) are certainly more drought-tolerant than most species and will thrive in hotter and drier places in the garden than the majority of their cousins.

Tropical and subtropical species are mostly not frost-hardy and require very sheltered warm places in the garden, although many are excellent conservatory subjects; they should certainly be tried more in Mediterranean and subtropical gardens!

Soil type

Like most plants clematis enjoy a free-draining yet moisture-retentive soil. They will not tolerate poorly aerated heavy soils or those that ever become waterlogged. For many of the temperate species, high temperatures resulting in soil desiccation will at least slow down both root and shoot growth and cause stunting, or may even stop growth all together. The ideal soil is a good deep loam. Heavy soils can be improved by adding a generous helping of sharp sand or fine grit and digging it in thoroughly. Poorer lighter soils can be greatly enhanced by incorporating as much humus as possible in the form of well-rotted manure or, better still, good garden compost. The site chosen needs to be well dug over and any weeds, particularly perennial types, carefully removed. *Clematis* species, particularly some of the less vigorous ones, can be successfully grown in containers. For instance, a large urn with *C.*

macropetala tumbling out of it can look very splendid. Other species which respond to container planting include *C. alpina, C. florida* and *C. viticella* and their cultivars. A good humusy loam is essential and containers must never be allowed to dry out.

Where to plant

Clematis can in fact be planted in many positions in the garden. The base of walls and fences, trees, pergolas and arches or amongst shrubs can be selected for many of the climbing types, although some like the white-flowered *C. flammula* can look very effective when allowed to straddle a retaining wall or simply form an entanglement on a sunny bank. Most of the non-climbing herbaceous species are good subjects for the flower garden, looking equally effective in the herbaceous border as well as amongst low shrubs. The smallest make interesting additions to the rock garden while alpine species such as *C. marmoraria* and *C. tenuiloba* can create a point of interest on raised beds or in troughs amongst other choice alpine plants.

The soil at the base of supports, especially walls, fences and trees, is generally very dry. It receives less direct rain than areas further away and more in the open, and in any case tends to dry out more quickly. It is by no means the best place to plant moisture-loving clematis; south- and west-facing walls and fences are generally the worst, unless they are part-shaded. So the rule is to plant well away from the base and to lead the plant into its intended support as it grows. Even so the planting spot should be shaded at the base, especially during the height of summer, and the soil moist and humusy. If planting close to trees and bushes it is advisable to plant on the shade side, ideally facing north.

Clematis can look very effective on walls and fences. However, the base of the plant can often look gaunt with all the exciting growth and flowers borne at the top; this is in the very nature of clematis in the wild! This can be overcome by planting clematis amongst wall shrubs and other climbers that will mask the unsightly base of the clematis. They can look fine in association with a wide range of other plants such as roses, honeysuckles, ceanothus, cotoneasters, pyracanthas, deutzias and philadelphus. For instance in my garden I have a purple variant of *Clematis viticella* clambering through *Euonymus europaeus* 'Red Cascade', the two working in perfect harmony.

Clematis can also be grown in association with one another and it is sometimes exciting to contrast species and cultivars; for instance C. 'Jackmannii' with its large velvety-purple blooms is a wonderful foil for the dainty white sprays of *C. flammula* which appear at the same time.

Selecting plants

It perhaps goes without saying that only strong and healthy plants should be purchased in the first instance. Old, tired and pot-bound specimens, or any that show any sign of pests or disease, should be left well alone. Many garden centres today, and even supermarkets, sell very young, small, single-shooted plants with soft growth and pale foliage at a very modest price. These will succeed but need to be nurtured into stronger more substantial plants before they are placed in the garden. They can be potted on and fed for a few weeks until they are more robust. Planted as bought, they often succumb to wind or frost damage or, worse still, to the depredations of slugs and snails. It is better to pay more for a really good plant in the first instance, multi-stemmed and with an existing woody framework. These may cost four times the price but they are more likely to succeed and will give years of lasting pleasure. Best of all is to visit a nursery that specializes in climbing plants, or solely in clematis, and select the plants yourself. The proprietor will only be too keen to offer advice and help make a suitable selection. Many nurseries have more mature plants on display and one can often have the added pleasure of seeing then in flower or fruit. Selecting plants can be an absorbing pastime.

Planting out

Today nearly all clematis are available as container-grown plants. In essence this means that they can be purchased throughout the year and planted at any time, weather permitting. Undoubtedly the best time to plant out hardy species is in the late summer and autumn providing it is not too hot and dry. Under average conditions planting at this time of the year will allow the plants to put on some growth, especially root growth before winter arrives. Spring and summer planting is fine provided plants are given a good and regular supply of water. Mulching around the base of plants will help conserve moisture, while at the same time keeping the vital base and roots of the plants cooler.

The less hardy species are best planted in the late spring or early summer when the danger of damaging frosts has past.

It is important to emphasize soil preparation again, for a clematis once planted will be in position for many years to come and time allocated to soil preparation in the first instance is time well spent.

Poor, stony or clay soil is best removed and replaced by good loam, incorporating well-rotted manure or garden compost at the same time, as well as a handful of bonemeal. Prepare an area larger than that required, say 50 cm (20 in) across and deep, then dig out a hole large enough to receive the rootball. Container plants should be soaked for half an hour prior to planting to ensure that the rootball is thoroughly wet; this is best done by placing the container in a bucket of water.

It is widely recommended that clematis be planted deeper than they are in their container, a practise I have always followed. This comes as a bit of a shock when one has been brought up, like so many gardeners, to plant at the same depth, a practise important in establishing trees and shrubs. Forget this when it comes to clematis. The reason is simple; by deep planting most clematis will produce a 'crown of buds' below the soil surface and these will come into growth should the top growth die down for one reason or another (this is especially important for the large-flowered cultivars which succumb to the dreaded clematis wilt; the below-ground buds will grow out to replace wilted top-growth). Deep planting gives the plants a better long-term survival strategy.

The extra depth of planting is not critical but the top of the rootball should be 6–10 cm (2.4–4 in) below the final soil surface. Climbing as well as herbaceous clematis respond well to this treatment.

Shade can be created, if necessary, around the base of the plant by placing low-growing plants or small shrubs close by on the south side; these should not be deep-rooted plants that would compete too much with the clematis for water. Alternatively, pieces of flat rock such as slate or old tiles placed around the base of the plant will also help to keep the base of the plant cool and moist.

Replanting

Most herbaceous clematis will replant quite successfully and this includes the *C. viticella* types. Replanting is best carried out before growth commences in late winter. Plants should be removed with as much soil and rootball intact as is practical and replanted in their new site as soon as possible. Careful watering and after-care are essential and even then some losses are to be expected. For most climbing species my advice is not to try and move them once they are established; it will only lead to a lot of frustration and disappointment. It is much better to collect some seed or, better still, to propagate fresh stock from cuttings. There is nothing more annoying than seeing a fine specimen ruined as it is dug, for more often than not the roots snap off and the rootball,

with the essential fibrous roots, necessary to sustain the plant, break away.

Propagation

Clematis are, on the whole, not particularly difficult to propagate, although of course there are exceptions. Propagation from cuttings or layerings is essential if a good form or variant of a species is to be maintained in cultivation, for it is unwise to rely on seed-raised plants being identical to their parent or parents. On the other hand, raising species from seed can be both exciting and rewarding and there is always the chance that an especially good form may arise in a batch of seedlings. Propagating plants can be great fun with the added bonus that extra plants can be given away as presents to friends or taken along to plant sales or charities.

Seed

The seed of clematis is short-lived and it is always best sown the moment it is ripe or as soon afterwards as possible. Getting fresh seed is not always easy, except when home-grown. Certainly seed collected in the wild should be sown at the earliest opportunity and as long as it has been treated well, and the delay between gathering and sowing not too prolonged, then good results can be expected. Most clematis seed is endowed with a fluffy (plumose) tail which aids in wind dispersal. When ripe the seedheads break up into their individual one-seeded components (achenes), each with its own tail, and these are quickly wafted away by the slightest breeze. The seed needs to be collected shortly before this happens. Seed matures at different times of the year: the early flowerers such as *C. alpina*, *C. cirrhosa* and *C. macropetala* will be ripe by mid-summer, while those of the later-flowering species such as *C. flammula* and *C. viticella* will not ripen until the autumn. The autumn- and winter-flowering species will often abort seed set, particularly if the weather is too cold or wet as the young fruits develop. However, as long as the fruits are reasonably mature and the seed plump, then if the weather turns too unfavourable, the seed clusters can be cut off and dried in an airy, cool place.

If seed cannot be sown immediately then it is best placed in dry packets in airtight boxes in a refrigerator until required. Some success can be had with sowing semi-mature green seed, although mature seed will always give better results.

To tail or not to tail seed. I have never found any appreciable difference in the germination of seed sown with their tails attached or removed. It is much quicker to sow untreated seed, especially if many packets are involved. However, if seed is sown too thickly then the fluffy tails may well start to mould and this could cause problems to the germinating seedlings. In any case, thin sowing is essential for the best results. Removing seed-tails is a slow and laborious and fiddly business, but where a particularly rare or valuable species is involved then the time spent is probably well worth while.

For the average gardener only small quantities of seed will be involved. They can be sown in pots (standard plastic pots are perfect for the job). Fill the pot to within 2.5 cm (1 in) of the rim and firm down gently with the base of another flowerpot. Place the seeds evenly and thinly over the surface. Thick sowing will result in a mass of seedlings appearing, the over-congestion will at the worst lead to damping-off problems and at the least make seedlings difficult to separate. Finally cover the seeds with a thin layer of the same compost and top up the pot with fine grit and water thoroughly. It is important to label each pot clearly with the name of the species and the date of sowing; otherwise confusion is certain to occur.

Place the sown pots in a cool position in the garden and never allow them to dry out; a shaded cold frame or under the greenhouse benching are good spots! Regular inspection is essential to ensure that the pots remain moist and to watch for signs of germination.

Seed varies in its germination time from species to species. *C. tangutica* and *C. serratifolia* and many others of the Orientalis Group can germinate in two or three weeks, but many species will not germinate until the spring after sowing. Not all the seed may germinate at the same time and it is not unknown for some to wait for a further twelve months, so do not be too eager to throw out ungerminated pots of seeds.

The seedlings usually first appear with their two small seed leaves or cotyledons. Once seedlings have developed two or three true leaves (some have paired young leaves, others are alternate) they can be pricked out into individual pots. Pots of seedlings should be watered first then knocked out carefully and the seedling prized apart, trying not to damage the vulnerable root systems. Pot on individually into 5- or 7.5-cm (2- or 3-in) pots using a standard potting compost such as John Innes No. 2, and grow on the young plants in a cold frame or on the greenhouse bench until they are large enough to plant out; usually at the beginning of the second season, although slow-growing species will take longer.

Regular feeds of weak liquid fertilizer will help to keep young plants growing vigorously. They may need to be potted on into larger pots (up to 23 cm (9 in)) as the season progresses. Pinching out growing tips will help to promote strong bushy plants. Plants can be grown on in their containers until they flower. In this way only the best need be retained for planting in the garden. Some species will flower rapidly from seed (*C. tangutica* will sometimes flower in the second season from a sowing the previous summer, while the cultivar 'Helios' can flower within four months of sowing), others will take longer, some as much as four years before the first blooms can be expected.

Division

Division is really only possible for clump-forming herbaceous clematis such as *C. heracleifolia*, *C. integrifolia* and *C. recta*. Division can be attempted any time from the mid-autumn until the early spring, before growth recommences and providing the weather is mild. The entire plant needs to be dug up, removing the roots and crown as intact as possible. The clump can be prized apart using two garden forks back to back for large mature crowns. Small crowns can often be pulled apart by hand, although tough crowns may need to be partly dissected with a sharp knife. Each division should have a portion of crown with accompanying buds and sufficient root to sustain it until new roots develop. Replant the divisions in their new site as soon as possible and as the spring advances ensure that (as the shoots emerge) the plants are never allowed to dry out.

Cuttings

Cuttings provide one of the best ways of ensuring that good forms and varieties of species are promoted in cultivation. However, whereas species like *C. alpina*, *C. macropetala*, *C. montana*, *C. tangutica* and *C. viticella* and their kin are relatively easy from cuttings, many others are not and species like *C. aethusifolia*, *C. armandii* and *C. florida* test the most skilled propagators.

Clematis are best rooted from internodal cuttings. These should be semi-mature (i.e. the stem firm but not hard, certainly not soft). Strong healthy leafy shoots of the current season should be selected, chopping out single-node pieces of the right maturity. When prepared each should have a pair of leaves with a short 5 mm (0.2 in) piece of stem above and 3–4 cm (1.2–1.6 in) of stem below. One leaf of the pair can be removed and if the remaining leaf is large it can be cut down by a half. This will help prevent the cutting from desiccating by reducing water loss.

Always handle the cuttings by the node to avoid damage to stem or leaves. The lower cut end of the cutting can be dipped into a hormone rooting powder and the cuttings placed in pots or trays of a suitable cuttings compost (one of equal parts loam, perlite or peat (or peat substitute) and sharp sand is ideal). Remember to label each batch of cuttings clearly with the name of the clematis and the date the cuttings were taken. Containers of cuttings can be placed in a shaded cold frame or in a propagator to root. Small batches in pots can be sealed in polythene bags and placed on a light but shaded windowsill in the house. Cuttings root best in moist, warm conditions, with temperatures between 20–25°C (68–77°F) being ideal. Too low or too high a temperature will slow down the process or prevent rooting altogether, while desiccation will ruin batches of cuttings.

Under ideal conditions many clematis can be expected to root in four or five weeks, but beware, others may take far longer. Once rooted, cuttings can be lifted and prized apart gently and potted on and really treated in a similar fashion to seedling plants.

Layering

Clematis species, except for the herbaceous types, can be increased from layering and this can be a useful method of increasing those that are otherwise difficult from cuttings, or those that rarely produce viable seed. One-year-old stems with good pairs of buds should be selected in early spring. Choose a suitable node with a good pair of active buds midway along the stem and with a sharp knife cut a slit up the stem for about 2 cm (0.8 in) upwards to the base of the node. Dust the cut with hormone rooting powder. Peg down the node to the soil with a hooked stick or bent wire, or preferably inserted into pots buried to their rims and filled with cuttings compost. Cover with compost and weigh the stem down with a small rock to ensure that it does not lift. Trim back the stem above the node to two or three nodes and tie it to a cane to prevent it waving about too much. Keep the layer moist at all times by ensuring the pot or soil is kept watered, especially during hot weather. By the autumn the layer will have rooted and can be severed from the parent plant. Top growth can then be reduced, the layer lifted and potted on as for cuttings. This is a rather slow and laborious method but when only one or two new plants of a rare species are wanted then it is well worthwhile.

Pruning

The pruning of clematis has often vexed gardeners unnecessarily. It is basically fairly simple, once the growth and flowering time of the plants are ascertained. As far as species are concerned pruning is reasonably straightforward, indeed many species can thrive quite happily without any pruning other than to keep plants in check and to remove weak or diseased growth. Three pruning groups can be recognized:
Group one (P1 in the main text). All the early-flowering deciduous species such as *C. alpina, C.*

macropetala, C. montana and their allies, as well as early-flowering evergreen species such as *C. cirrhosa* and *C. armandii* and their allies are included here. These all flower from the nodes of the previous year's shoots. Any pruning that is carried out should be done immediately after flowering ceases, thus ensuring that plants put on as much new growth during the season to bear the flowers for the next year. Any pruning late in the season will reduce potential flowering shoots and spoil the display to come. Pruning, if necessary at all, can usually be carried out in May, its main aim to reduce the bulk or extent of the plant, especially those that have outgrown their allotted space.

Group two (P2 in the main text). This includes the numerous species that flower on the current season's shoots from mid-summer onwards. The semi-herbaceous *C. viticella* and *C. viorna* belong here, as do the more woody climbers such as *C. flammula, C. tangutica,* and *C. vitalba.* The former including the fully herbaceous species (e.g. *C. recta* and *C. integrifolia*) can be pruned down to ground level in the late winter or early spring. With some semi-herbaceous kinds, especially many of the *C. viticella* cultivars, prune back to a strong pair of buds up to 50 cm (20 in) above the soil surface. With the majority of the species in this group which develop woody stems, either no pruning is required (especially for those allowed to clamber into large shrubs or trees) or the bulk can be reduced by pruning the woody stems back by up to two-thirds of their bulk. Any weak or damaged shoots can be removed at the same time. Species climbing over shrubs can become heavy and bulky in time and it may be necessary to prune them every two or three years to reduce the growth, otherwise they may well eventually pull down their host.

Old plants often become very entangled and pruning can become a major operation. Long strands can be severed and pulled out of the host plant. To avoid too much damage to the clematis and its host it is advisable to cut out unwanted growth in reasonable-sized portions instead of dragging a large mass of cut stems through the host.

Group three (P3 in the main text). Very few species belong to this group but it includes numerous early and mid-season-flowering large-flowered cultivars. These flower from lateral buds produced and ripened the previous season. *C. lanuginosa* and *C. patens* belong here but very few other species. Pruning consists of removing dead or weak growth in the early spring and reducing the remainder down to the strongest pair of lateral buds. These fat buds are clearly visible at this time of the year and they will carry the flowers later in the season (generally from late spring to mid-summer).

Training

The climbing species require little training except to guide the direction of growth. Shoots often become congested and tangled and will clasp around one another with their leaf-stalks. Once this happens they are almost impossible to separate without damaging the brittle young shoots. Training from early on is necessary, especially for plants trained on walls and fences, to ensure even coverage. Shoots can be spaced out and tied in lightly to their support.

Clematis grown up shrubs or trees are more difficult to guide and as long as they seem to be going in the right direction they are probably best left to their own devices.

Feeding

Clematis are gross feeders. They like plenty of nutrients. It can be argued that vigorous species such as *C. montana* do not need the encouragement of feeds, which will make them even more vigorous. However, for most, feeding during the growing season, especially during the summer months can be beneficial. This can be applied as a liquid feed (there are many suitable flower feeds available on the market) or as a fertilizer. Bonemeal lightly dug in around the plant or even rose fertilizers are excellent. Foliar feeds can be useful, especially for plants showing obvious pale-green leaf characteristics.

A mulch placed around the plant can help feed it as well as keep the roots moist. Well-rotted manure, garden compost, peat or bark chippings (the latter two are unlikely to add much in the way of nutrients) are all useful. They are best placed within a few centimetres of the plant base but not right up to it.

Clematis grown in containers or young pot-grown plants require regular feeds to keep them growing vigorously and healthily.

Pests and diseases

Clematis are remarkably pest- and disease-free. For gardeners growing the large-flowered cultivars, clematis wilt may cause problems, sometimes considerable problems, but this major disease rarely attacks the species. Always choose sprays for control with care, selecting the type of spray that suits your gardening regime.

Aphids. Young growth may be afflicted with aphids, especially in the spring, and flowerbuds can be overwhelmed. Severe infestations will cause mottling and distortion of both foliage and flowerbuds. Any proprietary spray available at garden centres will soon cure the problem.

Birds. Developing buds can be damaged by birds in the spring (*C. alpina* and *C. montana* are particularly at risk from the advances of bullfinches and sparrows) but it is rarely a major problem and rarely happens year after year. Netting or black cotton or some sort of bird scarer may help but they are generally troublesome to use.

Caterpillars. The caterpillars of various moths can prove troublesome by chewing at expanding buds, this in turn reducing the growth and flowering potential. They are rarely a problem but winter moths sometimes infest early-flowering clematis such as the *C. alpina* and *C. montana* types. By the time the damage has been noted it is generally too late and infestations may not occur every year. If the problem is suspected, then a spray of Derris as the buds begin to expand will provide an immediate remedy.

Clematis wilt. This is rarely a problem with species clematis or with the *C. viticella* cultivars; however, both *C. armandii* and *C. texensis* are known to suffer sometimes. A soil-borne fungus, *Phoma clematidina*, which attacks at ground level, entering the plant stem through a wound or crack, causes the problem. It then infests the stem and prevents the uptake of water and nutrients. The first sign the gardener sees is the sudden and complete collapse of a stem, sometimes the entire plant; this can happen overnight from a seemingly totally healthy plant. Wilted stems should be removed at once as close to the base of the plant as possible and burnt. Control consists of drenching the base of the plant and the surrounding soil with Bio Supercarb (carbendazim) at the rate recommended by the manufacturer. Deep-planted clematis (as advised on p.10) will have formed a crown of dormant buds below ground and when the top growth is destroyed by wilt they will grow out as replacement shoots.

If a plant repeatedly succumbs to wilt then it is best dug up and destroyed, treating the soil with Bio Supercarb at the same time.

Earwigs. These little critters can be very troublesome, especially to clematis growing close to walls and fences. The damage is done mainly at night, the earwigs attacking the young foliage and buds and cutting holes in them. They can completely ruin a potential display of flowers and make the plant look very unsightly. Various proprietary sprays are available but old fashioned earwig traps are equally effective to the diligent gardener.

Mice and voles. Both can be very irritating and can ruin a clematis very quickly by biting out lengths of stem close to the ground for nesting material, leaving all above to wilt and die. The plant will not be killed but will usually resprout from below the ground, but it may take some time to recover, although the result may be a stronger and bushier plant. Young plants are especially vulnerable. The cure is to use mousetraps or, as I did, get yourself an energetic cat or two; they can be remarkably successful in keeping down the rodent populations in the garden.

Mildew. Few species are subjected to attacks of powdery mildew. However, various members of the *C. viorna* group can be affected. The white powdery infection generally attacks the leaves and flowerbuds and can look very unsightly. A spray used for controlling rose mildew is very effective provided it is applied before the mildew takes hold. Plants known to succumb are best sprayed at fortnightly intervals at the onset of the growing season, preferably before any sign of the disease has appeared.

Rabbits and hares. These can be very damaging and can completely remove the top growth of clematis. Fortunately, they are often more interested in other plants in the garden. Plants trained up through 60 cm (24 in) long tubes (e.g. plastic drainpipe or better still, land drains) or encased at the base in fine-mesh wire netting will be better able to withstand attacks. Better still, get another cat or buy a gun.

Red spider mite. This is generally a problem of plants grown under glass, but during hot dry summers outdoor clematis may sometimes be affected, especially those growing against sunny walls. The minute mites cause pale blotching and dulling of the leaf surface. Turn the leaf over and you will see (use a x10 hand-lens) numerous minute pinkish mites and the infected parts of the plant may become covered in a fine web. High humidity can control this pest but infestations can build up alarmingly quickly. Some proprietary pesticides are available but not always a hundred per cent effective and repeated applications are necessary. A good measure of control can be had under glass by using a predatory mite, *Phytoseiulus persimilis*. Frequent spraying of the plants with plain water will also help to control the pest as they greatly dislike a humid atmosphere.

Scale insects. These are very occasionally a problem and attack mainly evergreen species grown under glass. *C. armandii* and its close relatives are particularly prone. The scale can infest stems and leaves (particularly underneath) and, like aphids, puncture the plant in order to reach the sap within. Severe infections can cause distortion to leaves and buds and will look very unsightly, and weaken the plant. Worse still, they make the infected parts of the plant very sticky (from honeydew secreted by the insects) and this in turn invites in sooty moulds that make the plant look even worse. Light infestations can be controlled by going over the plant systematically with a small brush dipped in soapy water and 'spotting' the scales. However, this is impractical for large plants and more severe infestations when it is better to resort to a chemical control; sprays that contain Malathion or Permethrin are equally effective controls, although repeat applications may well be necessary.

Slugs and snails. Both will eat young tender growth, especially when it develops in the early spring and in bad years they can devastate a plant. Various controls are available from beer traps to surrounding the base of the plant with coarse abrasive material or even soot. Slug pellets or liquid baits should be used with great caution for they are detrimental to various friends in the garden, especially frogs and toads, as well as hedgehogs and cats. Some of the slug killers available are harmless but their effect is often short-lived. Half grapefruits, once the contents have been eaten, placed hollow side down in shade close to the base of plants also act as a good slug trap; the entrapped slugs can be removed at intervals and disposed of.

Vine weevils. These hateful little beetles munch the leaf-margins and may even have a go at the young flowerbuds. Fortunately, they are not too often a major problem although I have a corner in my garden where they are rife. Unfortunately, the amateur gardeners have few effective chemicals at their disposal and the most effective control is probably a biological one; a nematode predator, *Heterorhabditis* sp. is now readily available.

Whitefly. This is primarily a pest of some clematis grown under glass, especially in conservatories. The little white-winged flies can build up to considerable numbers, especially in hot dry summers, and are to be located primarily on the underside of the leaves. The slightest disturbance of the foliage will make them fly out in clouds. Affected foliage becomes sticky and covered in an unsightly sooty mould. Various chemical controls are available but, better still, go biological and use a little parasitic wasp, *Encasia formosa* (now widely available) to help you out.

Hardiness

The hardiness of the species in this book is indicated whenever possible. Unfortunately, the hardiness of some species is uncertain, while other species are not in cultivation and there is no real way of telling how hardy they are likely to be, except by making comparisons with other species within their geographical region. Hardiness zones were developed by the United States Department of Agriculture (ASDA) and are based on the average annual minimum temperatures for each zone. In this book hardiness zones are indicated by the letter 'H'. For instance H5 indicates –29 to –23°C (–20 to –10°F) which means that the species in question will tolerate temperatures as low as indicated but not lower. This will give a good clue as to which species are likely to be hardy in your area. Hardiness ratings should not be taken as gospel for each area has its own particular microclimates and areas around buildings and walls can provide a significantly milder climate, allowing species to be grown that would otherwise perish in the open garden. Added to this is the fact that the true hardiness of some species has not been properly tested and the only way to really find out is to plant them and find out. Hardiness of plants is a complex subject with temperature playing only a part. Exposure, soil type and other factors are also influential. In addition, some forms of a species, particularly those from higher altitudes, may prove to be hardier in the garden than others. The hardiness zones are as follows:

H1: below –46°C (–50°F)
H2: –46 to –40°C (–50 to –40°F)
H3: –40 to –34°C (–40 to –30°F)
H4: –34 to –29°C (–30 to –20°F)
H5: –29 to –23°C (–20 to –10°F)
H6: –23 to –18°C (–10 to 0°F)
H7: –18 to –12°C (0 to +10°F)
H8: –12 to –7°C (+10 to +20°F)
H9: –7 to –1°C (+20 to +30°F)
H10: –1 to +4°C (+30 to +40°F)
H11: above +4°C (above +40°F)

Botany of Clematis

The clematis plant is essentially a woody vine or climber, some modest and weak-stemmed and reaching just two or three metres (six to ten feet) tall. Others are more massive with stems 30 m (100 ft) long or more which become very thick and heavy with age. The vast majority of species fit into this later category. They are plants of forests and woodlands, of bushy places and shrubberies in the wild, occasionally tumbling over rocks or scrambling up cliffs. In older plants the stems become interlaced and very woody, generally bare below and with all the new growth and flowers borne on the higher, younger parts of the plants. In clematis, the stems although woody are very flexible, the wood never becomes dense, hard and self-supporting as it does in many trees. Interestingly, *Clematis* is the only genus in the Buttercup Family, the Ranunculaceae, to develop woody stems and the evolution of this phenomenon in the family must be seen as an adaptation to life in shaded habitats such as forests and shrubby places. The climbing species have been equipped with twining leaf-stalks or petioles that clasp onto supports and act as anchorage for the clambering stems. They can be deciduous or evergreen, the latter primarily, but not exclusively, from the warmer subtropical and tropical regions of the world.

The clematis of more open habitats such as grassland, swampy places, cliffs or rocky slopes, are generally shrubby or herbaceous in character, in the latter case with the stems dying down to ground level annually. These are generally plants up to about 1.5 m (5 ft) in height, occasionally taller, and do not possess twining leaf-stalks; the stems are either self-supporting or are held upright by the surrounding vegetation. If no support is at hand the plants will simply sprawl on the ground or form a self-supporting mound. Naturally, in any genus there are exceptions. Some species (notably *C. viticella, C. viorna* and *C. texensis)* are basically herbaceous perennials with climbing stems, a sort of halfway version between the two major growth types, with slender, rather weak stems and clinging leaf-stalks. The stems in fact may become slightly woody towards the base and only die partway down to ground level in the autumn! This is especially true of cultivated plants; whereas the wild counterpart, growing under more exacting and often harsher conditions will often behave in a wholly herbaceous

manner. *C. integrifolia* is truly herbaceous, but this characteristic is not particularly common within the genus. Several species are adapted to the harsh environment of high mountain rocks, above the tree line. They are small ground-hugging plants which nestle into rock crevices and bear very reduced leafy stems as little as 20 cm (8 in) long, but expand laterally by means of short underground stolons or suckers. Both the North American *C. tenuiloba* and the New Zealand *C. marmoraria* fit into this category and represent the two smallest species of clematis known. Interestingly, both are clearly related to, and have undoubtedly evolved from, climbing species inhabiting lower-altitude habitats. In addition, *C. tenuiloba,* like the other members of the *C. alpina* group, is a deciduous species, whereas the very distantly related *C. marmoraria* is pronouncedly evergreen.

In a few species the stems are more or less smooth and round, but in the vast majority the stems are clearly ridged or grooved to some extent. As in most climbing plants the stems elongate rapidly ahead of the developing leaves which anchor themselves securely before the leaf-blades expand, thus supporting the increasing weight of the stems as they mature.

Leaves

With the exception of just the Himalayan *C. alternata*, which has strictly alternate leaves as its specific name implies, clematis bear opposite, occasionally whorled, leaves. The leaves can be simple or compound. Compound leaves can be ternate or pinnate or biternate or bi-pinnate or sometimes tri-pinnate, although in many species pinnate leaves may have ternate or tri-lobed secondary divisions.

The leaves or leaflets can be evergreen or deciduous, papery, fleshy or leathery. They vary enormously in shape and size from species to species and sometimes even within the same species. The leaf- or leaflet-margin can be untoothed (entire) or toothed, or variously lobed and toothed. The veins are simple and netted (reticulate) or there may be several main veins from the base of the leaflet to the apex, or partway to the apex, with a network of lesser veins in between. All these features are important diagnostic features when it comes to accurate identification of the species.

The leaves are generally stalked but in some species unstalked; it is the stalk or petiole that is capable of twining around adjacent supports. Leaflets may also be stalked or unstalked and secondary petioles (petiolules) are also capable of twining. A few species are remarkable in having articulated or jointed petioles (e.g. *C. uncinata* and its allies).

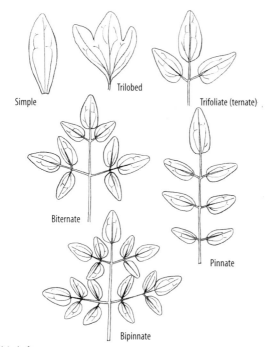

Simple
Trilobed
Trifoliate (ternate)
Biternate
Pinnate
Bipinnate

Major leaf types

The leaves, like the stems, can be variously ornamented with hairs, especially on the young stems and leaf undersurfaces. The hairs may be thin and straight, or curled, sparse or dense, silky, woolly or downy. Only occasionally are glandular hairs present and these generally impart a stickiness to stems and leaves.

In clematis seedlings there is a pair of seed leaves or cotyledons which appear above ground, or slightly below, shortly after germination. In some species the first true leaves are alternate but these are soon followed by opposite leaves. In other species the first true leaves are strictly opposite from the start. The seedling characteristics have long been held of importance in subdividing the genus and the major, despite the fact that the seedling characteristics of many species are unknown.

Bracts and bracteoles

Bracts vary enormously from species to species, but when present they are always paired. They can be large and leaf-like, compound or simple. In quite a number of species they are rather small and inconspicuous, often lanceolate or scale-like. Bracteoles are usually present in species with cymose or compound inflorescences. Both bracts and bracteoles are absent from some species with solitary flowers (*C. montana* and its allies, for instance) but in *C. viorna* and its allies, which also generally bear solitary flowers there is often a small pair of bracts partway along the apparent pedicels (flower-stalks).

Inflorescence

The majority of *Clematis* species bear flowers in a formal inflorescence, although certain species (for instance *C. alpina* and its allies (Section Atragene) and *C. montana* and its allies (Section Cheiropsis Subsection Montanae) bear solitary or fascicled (clustered) flowers. In its simplest form the inflorescence is a 3-flowered cyme (strictly a dichasial cyme) with a terminal flower which opens first and a later lateral flower on each side. More complicated compound cymes are frequent, often with the central axis of the inflorescence extended and multi-branched to form a panicle-like structure (sometimes condensed and corymb-like). True racemes or panicles are not found in the genus, although in describing the inflorescence such terms are often used.

The inflorescence or individual flowers can be lateral in some species while terminal in others, or sometimes both on the same plant.

Flowers

The *Clematis* flower is basically simple and symmetrical, like many members of the Ranunculaceae. Flowers may be upright, ascending to fully nodding. Species with upright or ascending flowers tend to have blooms that are rather flat, star or saucer-shaped, while species with nodding flowers favour deep cup-shaped, bell-shaped, urn-shaped or tubular flowers, but there are exceptions (for instance some of the New Zealand and Australian species have fairly flat nodding, or half-nodding, flowers). It is quite remarkable how such a relatively simple assemblage of basic flower parts can take on so many different shapes, although the shape is always strictly symmetrical (actinomorphic).

The flowers are primarily hermaphrodite (bisexual), but they may be unisexual in some groups (in the latter more complicated situations can arise in which some plants may have bisexual flowers and others may be purely male; androdioecious).

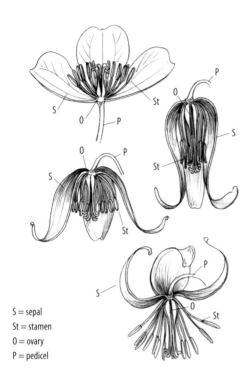

S = sepal
St = stamen
O = ovary
P = pedicel

Clematis half-flowers showing relative positions of flower parts

Sepals

These, which are sometimes wrongly called tepals (a generic term which encompasses the sepals and petals, or perianth parts, when they cannot be distinguished), are always present and often 4 in number, sometimes 5–8 (many more in some cultivars). In the vast majority of species the sepals meet along their edges in bud and are said to be valvate, while a few species, especially those of Subgenus Pseudoanemone (formerly the genus *Clematopsis*), bear partly overlapping or imbricate sepals, but the latter character is not restricted to Pseudoanemone. In the valvate-sepalled types the sepals are usually held together in bud by a dense felt or down of tiny hairs which acts like velcro holding the sepals tightly together, but the sepals are finally forced apart by expansion as the flowers open.

The sepals may be thin and papery, or thick and rather fleshy as they are in many of the species of the *Clematis orientalis* Group (Section Meclatis).

The sepals provide visually the most obvious and dramatic part of the flower and, as in most flowers, they serve to attract pollinating insects. Many species have white, greenish-white or cream sepals. True yellows (buttercup-yellow to deep ochre-yellows) are confined to Section Meclatis much to the chagrin of the

horticulturist who would like to see such colours extended into some of the other groups of clematis. Pinks in all shades, blues, purple and purple-red, mauve, lilac and various reds are all found in the species, giving a wide spectrum of possibilities in the garden.

The sepals can be glabrous, but they are more often adorned with hairs on one or both sides; these hairs are sometimes confined to a central strip down the outside.

The sepal shape varies from narrow-oblong to lanceolate, oval or almost rounded, the tip pointed to

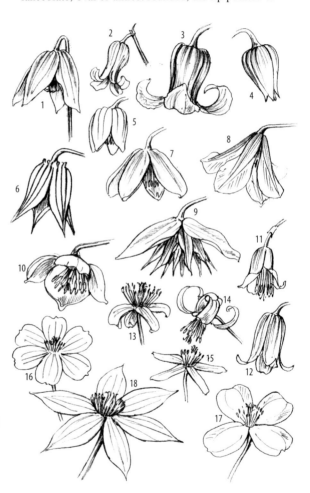

Clematis flower types

1. *C. alpina*	10. *C. villosa*
2. *C. heracleifolia*	11. *C. napaulensis*
3. *C. crispa*	12. *C. japonica*
4. *C. versicolor*	13. *C. vitalba*
5. *C. grandiflora*	14. *C. orientalis*
6. *C. chiisanensis*	15. *C. flammula*
7. *C. tibetana* subsp. *vernayi*	16. *C. potaninii*
8. *C. viticella*	17. *C. montana*
9. *C. macropetala*	18. *C. patens*

blunt, or even shallowly notched, straight or
variously recurved.

Petals

In reality petals are absent in *Clematis* but petal-like
structures are to be found in some species, most
noticeably in the members of the *Clematis alpina*
Group (Section Atragene). The petal-like structures are
modified stamens or staminodes and are transitions
between them and true stamens can often be easily
observed. Staminodal petals can be scarcely larger than
the stamens or considerably larger, sometimes almost
as large as the sepals, and vary from spoon- or spatular-
shaped to elliptical or oblong. They may be coloured
like the sepals or whitish, rarely a different colour. In
C. macropetala and its close allies the flowers appear
to be double because of the elaborate development of
staminodal petals. In the unrelated *Clematis florida* var.
plena the whole centre of the flower is taken over by
numerous petal-like staminodes. In *C. florida* var.
sieboldiana the staminodes form a prominent central
pompom of purple which contrasts markedly with the
outer white sepals.

Stamens (Androecium)

Except in the relatively few species with unisexual
flowers, all clematis flowers possess a boss of stamens.
These can be pressed close together as they are in the
species with tubular or narrow bell-shaped flowers, or
they may spread widely apart, especially as the flower
matures, in species in which the sepals are also wide-
spreading. The stamen details vary a good deal and are
characteristic of the various sections and other divisions
within the genus. In the simplest form the stamens are
glabrous with slender thread-like filaments (stamen
stalks) with no extension of the connective (the central
portion of the anther that links its two halves). In others
the filaments and sometimes the anthers are adorned with

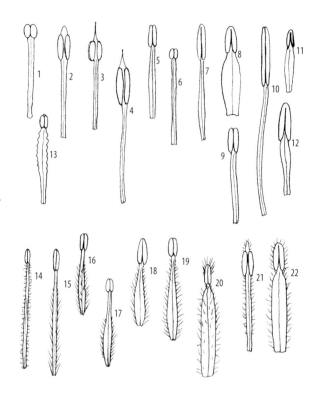

Stamen types

1. *C. vitalba*	12. *C. brachyura*
2. *C. potaninii*	13. *C. crassifolia*
3. *C. papuasica*	14. *C. alternata*
4. *C. aristata*	15. *C. grewiiflora*
5. *C. cirrhosa*	16. *C. wightiana*
6. *C. fasciculiflora*	17. *C. hirsuta*
7. *C. armandii*	18. *C. orientalis*
8. *C. viticella*	19. *C. tangutica*
9. *C. recta*	20. *C. barbellata*
10. *C. lanuginosa*	21. *C. texensis*
11. *C. phlebantha*	22. *C. integrifolia*

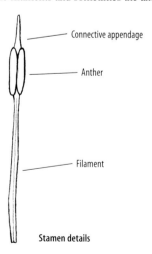

Stamen details

hairs of various sorts, this sometimes thick and silky or
even furry to look at, the hairs covering everything or
confined to a part of the stamen (sometimes to the centre
or just the margins of the filaments). In addition, the
filaments may be very slender or broad and ribbon-like,
or greatly expanded, especially towards the base.
Similarly the connective may sometimes extend
characteristically beyond the anther to form a small, yet
noticeable point or projection.

The outer stamens mature first and, in the more
open flower types they spread outwards (often folding
back against the sepals) allowing the inner whorls of

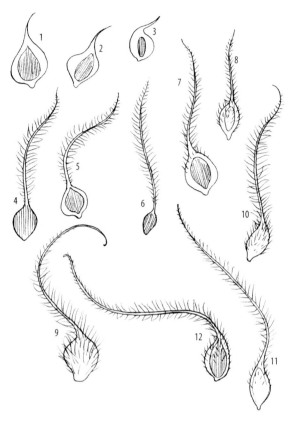

Achene types

1. *C. viticella*
2. *C. crispa*
3. *C. brachyura*
4. *C. potaninii*
5. *C. montana*
6. *C. paniculata*
7. *C. integrifolia*
8. *C. angustifolia*
9. *C. canescens*
10. *C. grewiiflora*
11. *C. hirsuta*
12. *C. napaulensis*

stamens to develop. The pollen is usually white, cream or yellow. The stigmas are generally fully receptive by the time the first stamens have shed their pollen.

In some species the stamens are nectariferous. Specialized nectaries are not differentiated as specific organs in the clematis flower. However, in some species (notably Subgenus Viorna) some cells on the inward-facing surface of the filaments are differentiated into nectar-secreting cells. This requires a fuller investigation.

Ovaries (Gynoecium)

The clematis ovary consists of a tight cluster of numerous carpels that are basically single-ovuled, although extra rudimentary ovules can be observed in the carpels of some species. The carpels can be glabrous or variously hairy and are attached to a swollen rounded receptacle. Each carpel is drawn out at the top into a straight, curved or hooked style that can also be glabrous or variously hairy. At pollination and fertilization the style generally begins a rapid elongation, attaining as much as 8 cm (3.2 in) in some species, occasionally even longer.

Fruit

The clematis fruit is an achene (a single-seeded, non-dehiscent structure which falls from the plant in one piece). In most species the achene is adorned with an attractive hairy, often feathery (plumose) style which aids the seeds to be wind-dispersed. In a few species the style is reduced to a short non-plumose hook, as in *C. viticella* and its allies. The achene can be rounded or flat (compressed) in cross-section, smooth, bristly or hairy, according to the species, and variously ornamented with ridges or pits, sometimes with a broadened and thickened margin. The plumose tails of the achenes are usually sleek and silky at first but by the time the achenes have matured they have become more woolly or fluffy in appearance. At this point the achenes are readily detached from the receptacle; in nature they are dislodged by the wind and carried off, some eventually finding their way to a suitable habitat for germination, although many will be wasted.

Scent

It is not generally realized that many, but by no means all, clematis species are scented, this is especially true of those species with white or pale flowers. As far as cultivation goes the presence of scent can be an added bonus. As an example, many members of the *C. armandii* (Subsection Meyeniana), *C. montana* (Subsection Montanae) and *C. flammula* (Subsection Flammula) bear scented flowers, whereas species related to *C. orientalis* (Section Meclatis), *C. alpina* (Subsection Atragene) and *C. viticella* (Subsection Viticella) are generally unscented.

As a guide to gardeners, those species in cultivation that are well scented include the following: *C. aethusifolia*, *C. armandii*, *C. chinensis*, *C. cirrhosa*, *C. crispa*, *C. flammula*, *C. forsteri*, *C. heracleifoia*, *C. integrifolia*, *C. montana* (some forms) and *C. rehderiana*.

The Clematis Family

Clematis belongs to the large and diverse buttercup family, the Ranunculaceae, a family generally considered by botanists to belong to one of the most primitive groups of flowering plants, characterized by being primarily herbaceous plants with the gynoecium (the female part of the flower) basically multi-carpelled. The flower and fruit characteristics of the members of the Ranunculaceae are extremely important and diagnostic. The flower is basically simple with all the flower parts separate from one another. The buttercup flower serves as a useful example in which there are distinct whorls of sepals (the outermost organs of the flower) and petals, followed towards the centre of the flower by several whorls consisting of many stamens, then, in the centre of the flower, a cluster of numerous small carpels. The carpels may be pod-like and contain several to many ovules, or they may be single-ovuled structures: in the former the fruits that develop are follicles which split along one side to release the seeds, whilst in the latter the fruitlets are achenes, each one-seeded and not splitting when mature. It can be demonstrated that the single-ovuled type has been derived from the many-ovuled type through evolution by simple reduction in the numbers of ovules; in several species of *Anemone* and *Clematis*, for instance (both genera with single-seeded achenes), extra rudimentary ovules can be observed in the early development of the carpels.

The range of flower types found in the buttercup family is a result of modification of the basic type and it is common for various organs to be modified, reduced or to be absent altogether. A common characteristic, and one that greatly perplexes gardeners, is the fact that in quite a few genera the sepals become large, colourful and petal-like, while the petals are either absent altogether, or modified into smaller, often less obvious, nectaries. At the same time, the outer stamens may become modified into sterile staminodes, which may sometimes mimic petals. Thus in familiar genera such modifications can be easily observed: in *Adonis, Callianthemum* and *Ranunculus* there are both sepals and petals, the latter two with nectaries at the petal bases; in *Anemone* and *Pulsatilla* the buttercup flower type is obvious, but there are no petals; in *Eranthis* and *Helleborus* the petals are modified into a whorl of small cup-shaped nectaries; in *Nigella* the petals are modified into a whorl of small bilobed structures; in *Delphinium* the petals are extended backwards into a single prominent spur, whilst in *Aquilegia*, each of the five petals is modified into a spur.

Clematis fits into the simple petal-less flower type in which the sepals are large and showy, there are plenty of stamens and the ovules develop into single-seeded achenes. In some species modified stamens or staminodes are present and, in some instances, these are elaborated into petal-like organs. The genus belongs to the same tribe as such familiar garden genera as *Anemone, Hepatica* and *Pulsatilla*, but it is immediately distinguished by its markedly woody stems which bear opposite pairs of leaves. In addition, most of the species of *Clematis* have valvate rather than imbricate (overlapping) sepals and a plumose tail to the achenes. Even the minority of *Clematis* that are herbaceous bear opposite leaves and plumose fruits and they could scarcely be confused with other genera in the family.

Inclusion within *Clematis*

Various allied genera have been treated in different ways by authors over the years.

The genus *Archiclematis*, which contains a single Himalayan species, is sometimes regarded as a distinct genus based solely on having undivided alternate leaves, but in other characters it closely matches *Clematis* and it undoubtedly belongs in that genus and, with the exception of Michio Tamura, that is where most modern authors place it.

The genus *Atragene* has been singled out in the past on account of possessing 'petals' (petaloid staminodes) as well as sepals. But such a character is not unique to *Atragene* and, although the species clearly belong to a distinctive group, they are included within *Clematis* by nearly all modern authors as Section Atragene, which contains familiar species such as *C. alpina* and *C. macropetala*.

The genus *Clematopsis* is slightly more controversial and modern authors are not altogether agreed on the distinctiveness of the genus. *Clematopsis* was described by John Hutchinson in

1920 on account of its distinctive imbricate sepals. However, although all the species of *Clematopsis* are confined to Africa and neighbouring Madagascar and form a rather natural grouping, it is difficult to uphold the genus on the sepal characteristics as a number of species, including the New Zealand species of *Clematis* as well as the Japanese *C. williamsii* have imbricate sepals, although these species can in no way be considered to belong to *Clematopsis*. Magnus Johnson and some other modern authors have accepted *Clematopsis* as a distinct section within *Clematis*, using the sectional name Pseudoanemone under which Prantl had included the species in 1888. One has to admit that not everyone will agree on the inclusion of *Clematopsis* but the lack of defining characters and the fact that several species of *Clematopsis* have been crossed quite readily with *Clematis* in recent years, makes one question the validity of the genus. In this work I follow Magnus Johnson in including it within *Clematis*, but as a subgenus.

Where I cannot go along with Johnson is in the inclusion of the tropical genus *Naravelia* into *Clematis*. *Naravelia* is quite remarkable in having flowers with distinct petals that are drawn out into a whip-like or knob-like elongation, longer than the sepals, while at the same time the leaves are terminated by tendrils instead of leaflets. Evolutionarily *Naravelia* can be seen to have been derived from *Clematis* and Tamura considered the genus to be the most advanced genus in the subtribe Anemonae, which contains *Anemone, Clematis, Pulsatilla* and *Hepatica*, besides other less familiar genera.

The genus *Viorna* is characterized by possessing erect sepals and hairy stamens and includes primarily North American species. Despite being a rather distinctive group of plants, most modern authors have included them within the genus *Clematis* as Section Viorna, based on their overall characters. Familiar species in this section are *C. pitcheri, C. texensis* and *C. viorna* itself.

Any classification of the genus *Clematis* is fraught with difficulties. The problem with *Clematis*, and indeed many genera in the Ranunculaceae, is the lack of good and consistent characters and the fact that such characters as there are often appear to be incredibly variable. As a result many classifications, including the present one, use botanical characters in close conjunction with geography in order to gain a realistic interpretation.

Various authors have attempted a classification in the past and each has been markedly different. Thus in 1818 de Candolle recognized four sections, Atragene, Cheiropsis, Flammula and Viticella. Spach in 1839 recognized six separate genera, *Atragene, Cheiropsis,*

Flammula, Meclatis, Viorna and *Viticella*, regarded by most subsequent authors as subgenera or sections within *Clematis*. Edgeworth added the section Bebaeanthera in 1851 and Tamura 1968 added several other sections, his classification being the most thorough and comprehensive this century.

There is not room in this present work to discuss at length the various classifications made by botanists and horticulturists over the years. I can do no better than recommend the comprehensive historical review published by Magnus Johnson in 'Släktet Klematis' in 1997. In his own classification Johnson divides the species up into two major groups based on the possession of either alternate or opposite leaves in the seedling plants, although he does not indicate whether these groups should be considered subgenera or not. He adds Tamura's genus *Archiclematis* as a section of *Clematis*, at the same time including the genus *Clematopsis* (as Section Pseudoanemone) and the genus *Naravelia* as Section Naravelia, both previously proposed by Prantl in 1888. In addition, he describes several new sections and subsections: Section Novae-Zeelandiae; Subsections Aethusifoliae, Africanae, Fasciculiflora, Fuscae, Lanuginosae, Phlebanthae, Potaninianae and Williamsiae. Unaccountably, he places the Subsection Africanae in the wrong section (in Section Clematis), whereas it is clearly most closely allied to Section Meclatis (both included in Subgenus *Campanella* Section Meclatis in the present account!).

Mention has to be made of the comprehensive nineteenth-century overhaul of the genus made by Otto Kuntze 'Monographie der Gattung Clematis' of 1885. This work was extremely liberal in its interpretation of species and at times wholly bizarre and few have taken much note of it in the intervening years. However, Kuntze has left a legacy of complex taxonomy and synonymy which has in fact hindered research and confused accurate identification of some taxa ever since.

Michio Tamura (1995) in his systematic review of the Ranunculaceae takes a subgeneric approach to *Clematis*, defining four prime subgenera (*Campanella, Clematis, Flammula* and *Viorna*). This seems to me the most logical approach and it is one that I have followed to some extent. It seems illogical to me to include such distinctive groups as *Archiclematis, Atragene, Cheiropsis, Clematopsis* and *Tubulosae* in the existing framework and these have also been accorded subgeneric rank. This, I trust, will make the classification easier to comprehend, whilst at the same time preserving well-known and much cherished and distinctive groups within the clematis 'umbrella'. Of course, I do not in any way pretend that this is a final statement on the classification of the genus and I doubt if any two botanists will ever agree on the subject. As a friend put it to me recently 'one can go on fiddling with the classification for evermore and never come out with the same result consecutively.' What is needed to clarify the position is an in-depth analysis of the species from an anatomical and cytological point of view. This, linked with the extensive morphological knowledge already gained, should help to resolve problems of affinities within the genus and come up with a more scientifically-based classification. Unfortunately, the genus is an extensive one and any comprehensive study would involve a lot of work, a number of researchers and various disciplines. Enough species are now in cultivation to make this a meaningful and possible proposition. In addition, there is a great deal of fieldwork needed to resolve problems of interpretation in subgenera such as *Atragene, Cheiropsis* and *Pseudoanemone*.

Classification

KEY TO SUBGENERA

1. Stamens glabrous – 2
    Stamens hairy, at least in part – 4

2. Leaves opposite in seedlings:
    Subgenus Three *Flammula*
    Leaves alternate in seedlings – 3

3. Flowers borne in lateral or terminal cymes, rarely
    reduced to a single flower, always bracteate,
    hermaphrodite to unisexual:
    Subgenus One *Clematis*
    Flowers solitary, ebracteate, mostly from axils of
    winter buds, always hermaphrodite:
    Subgenus Two *Cheiropsis*

4. Sepals imbricate; non-climbing subshrubs;
    inflorescence or solitary flowers always terminal:
    Subgenus Eight *Pseudoanemone*
    Sepals valvate; climbers, subshrubs and
    herbaceous perennials – 5

5. Flowers tubulose with sparsely hairy filaments;
    inflorescence terminal; subshrubs or herbaceous
    perennials: **Subgenus Seven** *Tubulosae*
    Flowers flat to urn- or bell-shaped with densely
    hairy filaments; inflorescences primarily lateral,
    occasionally solitary flowers terminal – 6

6. 'Petals' present: **Subgenus Six** *Atragene*
    'Petals' absent – 7

7. Leaves opposite, even in seedlings:
    Subgenus Nine *Viorna*
    Leaves alternate in seedlings – 8

8. Mature plants with strictly alternate simple leaves:
    Subgenus Four *Archiclematis*
    Mature plants always with strictly opposite,
    ternately to pinnately compound leaves:
    Subgenus Five *Campanella*

KEYS TO SECTIONS

(Subgenera *Archiclematis*, *Atragene*, *Pseudoanemone*
and *Tubulosae* are without further division)

SUBGENUS ONE *CLEMATIS*

1. Sepals imbricate; flowers always unisexual:
    Section Novae-Zeelandiae
    Sepals valvate; flowers hermaphrodite or unisexual
    – 2

2. Anthers with the connectives projecting above as a
    small appendage – 3
    Anthers without a projecting connective – 4

3. Flowers unisexual: **Section Aspidanthera**
    Flowers hermaphrodite: **Section Narveliopsis**

4. Flowers hermaphrodite, borne on the upper part of
    the current year's shoots: **Section** *Clematis*
    Flowers unisexual, borne towards the base of
    shoots of the current year: **Section Lasiantha**

SUBGENUS TWO *CHEIROPSIS*

1. Flowers erect, rather flat to saucer-shaped;
    pedicels' without bracts: **Section Montanae**
    Flowers nodding, campanulate; 'pedicels' with or
    without bracts – 2

2. Pedicels' with bracts (in the centre or towards the
    top); flowers solitary or two per leaf-axil:
    Section Cheiropsis
    Pedicels' without bracts; flowers in clusters of up
    to 8:   **Section Fasciculiflora**

SUBGENUS THREE *FLAMMULA*

1. Achenes strongly compressed and winged, beaked
    and without a plumose tail: **Section Pterocarpa**
    Achenes not or slightly compressed, unwinged and
    usually with a feathery tail (except in some
    members of Subsection Viticella) – 2

2. Shrubby plants with woody erect to ascending stems: **Section Fruticella**
   Climbers, if erect perennials then herbaceous except for the woody base – 3

3. Flowers generally white, greenish or yellowish, generally less than 50 mm (2 in) across, few to many per inflorescence: **Section Flammula**
   Flowers generally blue, pink, lilac or purple, rarely white, often more than 60 mm (2.4 in) across:
   Section Viticella

SUBGENUS FIVE *CAMPANELLA*

1. Flowers solitary, borne in the axils of winter bud-scale or in the leaf-axils at the base of a shoot; campanulate with the sepals not diverging:
   Section Bebaeanthera
   Flowers in cymose inflorescences, rarely solitary (then usually bracteate), borne on the upper part of shoots of the current year – 2

2. Flowers narrow-campanulate to campanulate, the sepals not or scarcely diverging; stamens with strap-shaped to filiform filaments, the anthers often hairy along the connectives:
   Section Campanella
   Flowers broad-campanulate, the sepals often diverging, often widely so; stamens dilated towards the base, the anthers glabrous:
   Section Meclatis

SUBGENUS NINE *VIORNA*

1. Plants climbing (bushy in *C. addisonii*); leaves with twining petioles and petiolules; bracts generally present: **Section Viorna**
   Plants perennial, sometimes herbaceous; stems upright, the leaves without twining petioles or petiolules; flowers without bracts – 2

2. Sepals markedly diverging and expanded in the upper half; leaves often simple:
   Section Integrifoliae
   Sepals not markedly diverging or expanded in the upper half; leaves compound:
   Section Hirsutissima

CLASSIFICATION OF CLEMATIS BY SUBGENERA, SECTIONS AND SUBSECTIONS

Note: Species numbers correspond to numbers in the main text.

SUBGENUS ONE *CLEMATIS*

Climbers, primarily deciduous with the leaves alternate in the seedling stage. Leaves ternately or pinnately compound, occasionally simple, the leaflets usually toothed. Inflorescence few- to many-flowered, often very well developed, lateral from shoots of the same, or occasionally the previous, year. Flowers flat with wide-spreading valvate sepals, often white, greenish-white or yellowish. Stamens with rounded to elliptic anthers (small and generally 1.2–2.2 mm (0.05–0.09 in) long) and filiform glabrous filaments, sometimes slightly dilated towards the base; connective not projecting. Petals absent. Achenes usually pubescent and with a plumose tail. (species 1–65)

Section Clematis

(syn. Section Clematis Subsection Euvitalbae Prantl, Section Vitalba Spach Subsection Vitalbae Prantl). Climbers or scramblers usually with well-developed woody stems and twining petioles. Inflorescences borne on the current year's shoots. Flowers small, few to many, erect, opening flat, hermaphrodite or unisexual. Sepals usually 4. (species 1–51)

- **Subsection Clematis:** Flowers hermaphrodite with 4 sepals, generally rather small (often 15–25 mm (0.6–1 in) across), and many per inflorescence; filaments filiform, narrower than the anthers. Achenes hairy. (23 species) *C. apiculata, C. apiifolia, C. argentilucida, C. brevicaudata, C. burmanica, C. chingii, C. formosana, C. ganpiniana, C. gouriana, C. grandidentata, C. grata, C. gratopsis, C. heynei, C. javana, C. mollissima, C. multistriata, C. peterae, C. sasakii, C. subumbellata, C. taiwaniana, C. tamurae, C. tsaii, C. vitalba.* Europe; India & Himalaya; China; Korea; Japan; SE Asia. (species 1–23)

- **Subsection Pierotianae (Tamura) Tamura (syn.** Series Pierotianae Tamura): Flowers hermaphrodite, with 4 sepals, generally moderately large (30–50 mm (1.2–2 in) across) and few, often 3 per inflorescence; filaments slightly dilated towards the base. Achenes hairy. (8 species) *C. mashanensis, C. parviloba, C. pierotii, C. pinnata, C. puberula, C. tinghuensis, C. wissmanniana, C. zemuensis.* E Himalaya; China, Japan. (species 24–31)

- **Subsection Potaninianae M. Johnson:** Flowers hermaphrodite, with 6 sepals, relatively large (30–70 mm (1.2–2.8 in) across) and 3–7 per inflorescence; filaments filiform. Achenes glabrous (excluding the plumose tail) (2 species) *C. potaninii, C. trichotoma*. W China; South Korea. (species 32–33)

- **Subsection Dioicae (Prantl) Tamura:** Flowers unisexual, plants often dioecious or androdioecious, mostly 4-sepalled, small and in large inflorescences; filaments filiform. Achenes hairy. (18 species) *C. alborosea, C. bonariensis, C. campestris, C. catesbyana, C. coahuilensis, C. denticulata, C. dioica, C. drummondii, C. grossa, C. haenkeana, C. ligusticifolia, C. millefoliata, C. peruviana, C. seemannii, C. stipulata, C. subtriloba, C. uruboensis, C. virginiana*. North & South America. (species 34–51)

Section Lasiantha Tamura

Flowers unisexual (plants dioecious and androdioecious), 4-sepalled, borne in lateral fascicles on the previous year's shoots; filaments filiform. Achenes hairy. (2 species) *C. lasiantha. C. pauciflora*. SW USA; Baja California. (species 52–53)

Section Naraveliopsis Hand.-Mazz.

Climbers with woody stems and twining petioles which are sometimes connate at the base. Leaves simple, ternate or pinnate. Inflorescences lateral, borne on the current year's shoots, few- to many-flowered; flowers hermaphrodite. Sepals 4 usually, sometimes 6, white, yellowish or purplish inside, white, green or brownish outside. Stamens with filaments dilated towards the base and with the connective projecting beyond the anther (often by 2 mm (0.08 in) or more); outer stamens often transformed into linear staminodes. (17 species) *C. antonii, C. bourdillonii, C. crassipes, C. filamentosa, C. fulvicoma, C. herrei, C. korthalsii, C. loureiriana, C. macgregorii, C. menglaensis, C. mentuoensis, C. papillosa, C. petelotii, C. pianmaensis, C. smilacifolia, C. tashiroi, C. theobromina*. India & E Himalaya, S China, S Japan, Vietnam, SE Asia. (Species 54–71)

Section Aspidanthera Spach

Climbers mostly with woody stems, sometimes partly herbaceous, usually with twining petioles. Leaves ternately or pinnately compound, occasionally simple. Inflorescence lateral with few to many flowers, borne on the current year's shoots, or on the previous years; flowers usually erect and rather flat, occasionally half-nodding and campanulate, unisexual, dioecious or androdioecious. Sepals 4–6, occasionally 8, white, greenish or yellowish. Stamens with filiform or slightly dilated filaments, with a pronounced projection of the connective beyond the anthers. (species 72–84)

- **Subsection Aspidanthera** (syn. Section Aristatae Prantl): Leaflets generally toothed or lobed, or leaves simple. Lateral branches of inflorescence not contracted; bracteoles present. Sepals valvate, occasionally slightly imbricate. Anthers with a pronounced projection of the connective. (8 species) *C. aristata, C. clitorioides, C. fawcetii, C. gentianoides, C. gilbertiana, C. glycinoides, C. microphylla, C. pickeringii**. Australia & Tasmania; *SE Asia; Java & Celebes to New Guinea & N Australia. (species 72–78)

- **Subsection Papuasicae Hj. Eichler:** Leaflets with an entire margin. Lateral branches of inflorescence contracted (inflorescence appearing raceme-like); bracteoles absent. Sepals valvate. Anthers with a pronounced projection of the connective. (6 species) *C. archboldiana, C. clemensiae, C. papuasica, C. stenanthera, C. phanerophlebia, C. tenuimarginata*. Sulawasi east to New Guinea and the Solomon Is. (species 79–84)

Section Novae-Zeelandiae M. Johnson

(syn. Section Hexapetalae Prantl) Climbers or dwarf alpine plants with primarily ternately compound leaves. Leaflets mostly toothed or lobed. Lateral branches of inflorescence not contracted; bracteoles present. Flowers basically unisexual. Sepals imbricate. Anthers without a pronounced projection of the connective. (11 species) *C. afoliata, C. australis, C. cunninghamii, C. foetida, C. forsteri, C. hookeriana, C. marata, C. marmoraria, C. paniculata, C. petriei, C. quadribracteolata*. New Zealand. (species 85–95)

SUBGENUS TWO *CHEIROPSIS* (DC.) PETERM.

(syn. Section Cheiropsis DC.; Series Montanae (Schneid.) Rehder & Wilson; Subsection Montanae Schneid.) Climbers with well-developed woody stems and twining petioles. Leaves alternate in the seedling stage. Leaves basically ternately compound, rarely pinnate. Flowers solitary, borne in the axils of winter buds on the previous year's shoots, or in the lower axils of young shoots early in the season, often appearing to be fascicled due to contraction of the internodes of lateral shoots, relatively large, nodding to erect, campanulate to broad saucer-shaped, hermaphrodite. Sepals usually 4, occasionally 6, white, cream, greenish or pink. Stamens with filiform or slightly dilated glabrous filaments, the connective not projecting. (species 96–108)

Section Montanae (Schneider) Grey-Wilson

(syn. Section Cheiropsis Subsection Montanae Schneider)
Flowers half-nodding to erect, opening more or less flat, without a pair of bracts midway along the pedicels. Sepals valvate. (9 species) *C. acerifolia, C. brevipes, C. chrysocoma, C. glabrifolia, C. gracilifolia, C. montana, C. spooneri, C. tongluensis, C. venusta.* N India & Himalaya; China. (species 96–104)

Section Cheiropsis

Flowers nodding, campanulate, with a pair of bracts midway along, or towards the top, of the 'pedicels'. (species 105–107)

• **Subsection Cheiropsis:** Sepals valvate. (2 species) *C. cirrhosa, C. napaulensis.* Mediterranean region; Himalaya & SW China. (species 105–106)

• **Subsection Williamsianae M. Johnson:** Flowers nodding, campanulate, with a pair of bracts midway along the pedicels. Sepals imbricate. (1 species) *C. williamsii.* Japan. (species107)

Section Fasciculiflora (M. Johnson) Grey-Wilson

(syn. Section Flammula Subsection Fasciculiflora M. Johnson)
Flowers clustered, nodding, campanulate, the pedicels without bracts. (1 species) *C. fasciculiflora.* SW China; Myanmar; N Vietnam. (species 108)

SUBGENUS THREE *FLAMMULA* DC.

Predominately climbers, sometimes subshrubs or herbaceous perennials, with ternately or pinnately compound leaves which are always opposite, even in the seedling stage; leaflets often unlobed. Inflorescences few- to many-flowered, generally lateral. Flowers flat or almost so, with the 4, sometimes 5–6 sepals, spreading widely apart.

Stamens with oblong to linear anthers and filiform or somewhat dilated glabrous filaments; connectives not projecting or only slightly so. Achenes usually with a long plumose tail. (species 109–162)

Section Flammula

As for the subgenus; plants usually climbing, occasionally herbaceous. Flowers small to medium, not more than 50 mm (2 in) across; sepals usually white, cream, greenish-yellow or occasionally pinkish. (species 109–141)

• **Subsection Flammula:** Leaves pinnately compound, deciduous; leaflets lobed or unlobed, usually untoothed. Flowers hermaphrodite, erect, white or cream. Stamens without projecting connectives. (12 species) *C. akoensis, C. dilatata, C. elisabethae-carolae, C. flammula, C. kirilowii, C. mandshurica, C. papuligera, C. pseudoflammula, C. recta, C. sichotealiinensis, C. taeguensis, C. terniflora.* Europe, Russia & Central Asia, China & Japan. (species 109–120)

• **Subsection Meyenianae (Tamura) M. Johnson** (syn. Series Meyenianae Tamura): Evergreen climbers with usually ternate, occasionally pinnate or simple, leaves. Flowers hermaphrodite, produced mainly from lateral buds on the previous season's shoots. Sepals white, rarely greenish-yellow. Stamens with connectives slightly projecting. (12 species) *C. armandii, C. baominiana, C. chekiangensis, C. finetiana, C. hastata, C. hedysarifolia, C. jialasanensis, C. lingyunensis, C. meyeniana, C. quinquefoliata, C. vanioti, C. zygophylla.* China; S Japan; N India; Laos; Taiwan; Vietnam. (species 121–132)

• **Subsection Chinenses (Tamura) M. Johnson** (syn. Series Chinenses Tamura): Deciduous or partly evergreen climbers. Plants (leaves and flowers especially) blackening on drying. Leaves pinnately compound; leaflets with entire margins. Flowers borne on the current season's shoots. Flowers white or cream, hermaphrodite or unisexual to some degree. Stamens without projecting connectives. (6 species) *C. anhweiensis, C. chinensis, C. fujisanensis, C. kyushuensis, C. obscura, C. shensiensis.* China & Japan. (species 133–138)

• **Subsection Uncinatae (Tamura) Magnus Johnson** (syn. Series Uncinatae Tamura): Evergreen climbers similar to Subsection Meyenianae but leaves pinnate or bipinnate, with a distinct articulation on both petioles and petiolules. (1 species) *C. uncinata*. China; S Japan; Taiwan; N Vietnam. (species 139)

• **Subsection Angustifoliae Tamura:** Perennials or subshrubs with non-climbing erect stems and pinnately lobed leaves. Inflorescences terminal. Sepals 6, white. Stamens with slightly projecting connectives. (1 species) *C. hexapetala*. N China; Japan; Korea; Mongolia; SE Russia. (species 140)

• **Subsection Crassifoliae (Tamura) Tamura** (syn. Series Crassifoliae Tamura): Evergreen climbers with ternate, untoothed leaves. Flowers white, borne in lateral or terminal inflorescences on shoots produced earlier in the season. Stamens with wrinkled (rugulose) filaments, the anthers without projecting anthers. Winter-flowering. (1 species) *C. crassifolia*. SE China; S Japan; Taiwan. (species 141)

Section Viticella (Moench) DC.
(syn. Viticella Moench)

Semi-herbaceous and deciduous climbers with ternately or pinnately compound leaves; leaves opposite, even in seedlings; leaflets lobed or unlobed, usually entire. Flowers hermaphrodite large, terminal or lateral, with 4–8 dilated, valvate, sepals which spread widely apart, white, pink, purple or blue, occasionally cream. Stamens with somewhat dilated (especially in the upper half) hairless filaments and linear anthers; connectives not or slightly projecting. Achenes with or without a plumose tail. (species 142–152)

• **Subsection Viticella:** Leaves pinnate. Flowers 30–60 mm (1.2–2.4 in), nodding or half-nodding, solitary at axils of current year's shoots, with a pair of bracteoles present; sepals usually 4. Achenes with a short beak, without a plumose tail. (5 species) *C. cadmia, C. calabrica, C. campaniflora, C. huchouensis, C. viticella*. S Europe, Himalaya & China. (species 142–146)

• **Subsection Floridae (Prantl) Tamura:** Like the previous but flowers terminal to lateral branches borne on the previous season's shoots, generally larger (to 10 cm (4 in)), ascending to erect; sepals usually 6. Achenes with a long plumose tail. (4 species) *C. courtoisii, C. florida, C. hancockiana, C. longistyla*. C, E & S China; NE India; Myanmar; N Vietnam. (species 147–150)

• **Subsection Patentes Tamura:** Leaves ternate or trilobed. Flowers large, 8–15 cm (3.2–6 in), erect, borne on short leafy shoots (generally with 2–3 pairs

of leaves) from the previous year's wood, with 6–8 sepals; bracteoles absent. Achenes with a feathery tail. (1 species) *C. patens*. NE China; Korea. (species 151)

• **Subsection Lanuginosae M. Johnson:** Flowers large, to 25 cm (10 in), erect, borne on the current season's shoots; bracteoles present; sepals 6. Achenes with a long plumose tail. (1 species) *C. lanuginosa*. E China. (species 152)

Section Pterocarpa Tamura

Semi-herbaceous plants, woody at the base, with ternate leaves and entire leaflets. Inflorescence 1–3-flowered, terminal and lateral. Flowers hermaphrodite. Sepals 4–5, somewhat dilated towards the tip, valvate. Stamens with oblong anthers; filaments filiform, glabrous. Achenes markedly compressed and winged, with a short non-feathery beak. (1 species) *C. brachyura*. South Korea. (species 153)

Section Fruticella Tamura

Shrubs or subshrubs with entire or pinnately lobed leaves, without twining petioles. Flowers hermaphrodite, solitary, terminal, or in terminal cymose inflorescences, hermaphrodite, erect or nodding, white or yellow. Sepals 4–7, valvate, half- to wide-spreading. Stamens with oblong anthers and filiform to somewhat dilated, glabrous filaments; connectives not projecting. Achenes with a feathery tail. (species 154–162)

• **Subsection Fructicella:** Bushes with small pinnately lobed or unlobed, leathery leaves. Flowers 1–3 usually, nodding or half-nodding; sepals 4, yellow or white, ascending. (4 species) *C. canescens, C. delavayi, C. fruticosa, C. nannophylla*. N & W China; Mongolia. (species 154–157)

• **Subsection Songaricae Serov** (including Subsection Ispahanica Serov): Subshrubs with part-herbaceous erect to ascending stems. Leaves simple to pinnately lobed. Flowers erect or ascending, borne in terminal cymes, generally of 5 or more; sepals 4–6, white, sometimes pink-tinged, spreading widely apart. (4 species) *C. asplenifolia, C. ispahancia, C. lancifolia, C. songarica*. C Asia, W Pakistan; NW China (species 158–161)

• **Subsection Phlebanthae M. Johnson:** Shrub with arching or spreading stems. Leaves pinnate, white-downy beneath. Flowers usually solitary, erect, relatively large (25–45 mm (1–1.8 in) across), white,

5–7-sepalled; sepals with grooved veins. (1 species)
C. phlebantha. W Nepal. (species 162)

SUBGENUS FOUR *ARCHICLEMATIS* (TAMURA) GREY-WILSON

(syn. *Archiclematis* (Tamura) Tamura; *Clematis*
Section Archiclematis Tamura)
Climbers with woody stems. Leaves always alternate,
with twining petioles. Flowers lateral, solitary or two,
borne on the current year's shoots, nodding, narrow-
urn-shaped; sepals 4, valvate in bud. Petals absent.
Filaments filiform, hairy; anthers and connectives
glabrous. (1 species) *C. alternata.* C Nepal. (species
163)

SUBGENUS FIVE *CAMPANELLA* TAMURA

(syn. Section Campanella Tamura, Section Connatae
(Koehne) M. Johnson; Section Viorna Subsection
Connatae Koehne; including Subsection Aethusifoliae
(Serov) M. Johnson)
Predominantly climbers, occasionally subshrubs or
partly herbaceous climbers. Leaves alternate at the
seedling stage, later strictly opposite; leaflets usually
toothed. Flowers hermaphrodite, nodding or half-
nodding, usually campanulate, with the 4 (occasionally
5–6) valvate sepals, not- or wide-spreading, valvate;
petals absent. Stamens with hairy filaments, at least in
part, rarely glabrescent; anthers glabrous, the
connectives not projecting. Achenes compressed or
half-compressed, generally hairy, with a plumose tail.
(species 164–240)

Section Campanella Tamura

(Syn. Viorna Subsection Connatae Koehne; Clematis
Section Connatae (Koehne) M. Johnson)
Climbers with woody stems, rarely herbaceous.
Leaves with twining petioles, ternately or pinnately
compound, rarely simple. Flowers borne on shoots of
the current season, generally in lateral inflorescences,
more rarely solitary or terminal, nodding to half-
nodding, often narrow-campanulate, sometimes more
open, hermaphrodite. Filaments filiform or strap-
shaped, generally with dense long hairs, the
connectives and anthers often also hairy. (43 species)
*C. acuminata, C. acutangula, C. aethusifolia,
C. buchananiana, C. chiupehensis, C. clarkeana,
C. confusa, C. connata, C. dasyandra, C. grandiflora,
C. grewiiflora, C. hainanensis, C. henryi,
C. hupehensis, C. jingdungensis, C. jinzhaiensis,
C. kakoulimensis, C. kilungensis, C. kweichowensis,
C. lasiandra, C. leschenaultiana, C. loasaefolia,
C. nukiangensis, C. otophora, C. pinchuanensis,
C. pogonandra, C. pseudootophora,*

*C. pseudopogonandra, C. qingchengshanica,
C. ranunculoides, C. rehderiana, C. repens, C. roylei,
C. rubrifolia, C. siamensis, C. shenlungchiaensis,
C. subfalcata, C. urophylla, C. veitchiana, C. wattii,
C. yui, C. yuanjiangensis, C. yunnanensis.* China,
Himalaya, N India, SE Asia; two (*C. grandiflora* and
C. kakoulimensis) in tropical Africa. (species 164–206)

Section Bebaeanthera Edgew.

(syn. Section Paratragene Tamura)
Climbers with woody stems, generally with twining
petioles. Leaves ternate. Flowers solitary, lateral, borne
in the axils of bud scales or new leaves of condensed
axillary shoots (often appearing to be fasciculate),
campanulate, hermaphrodite. Sepals usually 4, valvate.
Petals absent. Filaments dilated, short-hairy; anthers
often hairy. (3 species)
C. barbellata, C. japonica, C. tosaensis. Japan; W
Himalaya. (species 207–209)

Section Meclatis (Spach) Tamura

(syn. Meclatis Spach)

Climbers or subshrubs with woody stems, occasionally
partly herbaceous. Leaves pinnate or bipinnate,
occasionally ternate, usually with twining petioles.
Flowers hermaphrodite, borne on shoots of the current
year, usually in lateral inflorescences, occasionally
solitary or terminal, nodding or half-nodding, often
campanulate but sometimes wide open or with
reflexed sepals. Sepals usually 4, generally yellow or
greenish-yellow, occasionally whitish. Stamens
slightly to markedly dilated, hairy at least in part;
anthers oblong, glabrous. (species 210–240)

• **Subsection Africanae M. Johnson:** Sepals
thinnish, whitish, greenish or greenish-yellow, wide-
spreading to somewhat recurved. Stamens with
filiform or slightly dilated filaments, hairy in part
(especially towards the base), and glabrous anthers.
(16 species) *C. brachiata, C. commutata,
C. djalonensis, C. dolichopoda, C. hirsuta,
C. ibarensis, C. laxiflora, C. mauritiana,
C. microcuspis, C. oweniae, C. simensis,
C. thalictrifolia, C. tibestica, C. triloba, C. viridiflora,
C. welwitschii.* Africa; Madagascar & Mascarene Is.,
S India (species 210–226)

• **Subsection Meclatis:** Sepals often thick and fleshy,
scarcely spreading to wide-spreading. Filaments
markedly dilated towards the base, hairy, or
puberulous, especially along the margin, the
connectives and anthers glabrous. (14 species):

C. akebioides, C. caudigera, C. corniculata,
C. graveolens, C. hilariae, C. intricata, C. ladakhiana,
C. orientalis, C. pamiralaica, C. sarezica,
C. serratifolia, C. tangutica, C. tibetana,
C. zandaensis. E Europe, C Asia, NW & W China,
W Himalaya. (species 227–240)

Subgenus Six *Atragene* (L.) Grey-Wilson

(syn. *Atragene* L.; *Clematis* Section Atragene (L.)
DC., Subsection Atragene (L.) Prantl)
Climbers with woody stems and twining petioles, more
rarely dwarf and non-climbing. Leaves ternate to
biternate, alternate in the seedlings but later strictly
opposite. Bracts absent. Flowers hermaphrodite, usually
solitary and terminal on short lateral shoots (with 1–2
leaf pairs) borne on the previous season's wood, nodding
or half-nodding, campanulate. Sepals 4, valvate. 'Petals'
present, white, cream, blue, purple or mauve; either
staminodal or like the sepals, often spatulate. Stamens
with dilated and densely hairy filaments. Achenes with
plumose tails. (18 species) *C. alpina, C. chiisanensis,*
C. columbiana, C. crassisepala, C. dianae, C. fauriei,
C. fusijamana, C. iliensis, C. koreana, C. macropetala,
C. moisseenkoi, C. nobilis, C. occidentalis,
C. ochotensis, C. robertsiana, C. sibirica, C. tenuiloba,
C. turkestanica. Much of the temperate northern
hemisphere. (species 241–258)

Subgenus Seven *Tubulosae* (Decne) Grey-Wilson

(syn. Section Viorna Subsection Tubulosae (Prantl)
Schneid.)
Herbaceous perennials with stems only woody at the
base, without twining petioles. Leaves usually ternate,
rarely biternate. Flowers terminal or lateral, few to
many in regularly branched inflorescences, rarely
solitary, borne on current year's shoots, nodding,
tubular-campanulate, hermaphrodite or bisexual (then
often dioecious). Sepals 4, rarely 5, valvate, generally
purplish, bluish or whitish. Petals absent. Filaments
filiform or dilated, hairy at least near the top, the
connectives and anthers glabrous. (8 species)
C. heracleifolia, C. psilandra, C. speciosa, C. stans,
C. tatarinowii, C. tsugetorum, C. tubulosa,
C. urticifolia. N & E China, Korea, Mongolia, Japan,
Taiwan. (species 259–266)

Subgenus Eight *Pseudoanemone* (Prantl) Grey-Wilson

(syn. *Clematopsis* Hutch.; *Clematis* Section
Pseudoanemone Prantl)
Subshrubs or herbaceous perennials, with the stems at
least woody towards the base. Leaves ternate or
pinnate, occasionally 3-lobed or simple, opposite in all
but the seedlings, without coiling petioles. Flowers
terminal on main stem or lateral branches, solitary or
2–5, nodding or half-nodding, campanulate,
hermaphrodite. Sepals 4, occasionally 5–6, imbricate,
white or cream, often flushed with pink or purple.
Petals absent. Filaments dilated, hairy to puberulous.
(8 species) *C. bojeri, C. chrysocarpa, C. grandifolia,*
C. homblei, C. spathulifolia, C. teuczii, C. uhehensis,
C. villosa. Africa and Madagascar. (species 267–274)

Subgenus Nine *Viorna* Tamura, non Reichb.

(syn. Section Viorna A. Gray, Section Viorna sensu
Prantl, non Reichb., Section Urnigerae Levallée)
Climbers, or perennials, sometimes herbaceous, with
leaves always opposite, even at the seedling stage.
Leaves simple to ternately or pinnately divided.
Flowers nodding, urn-shaped to campanulate, or
tubular-campanulate, solitary or few, lateral or
terminal, with or without bracts. Sepals 4–5, held
closely together (connivent) in at least the lower half,
spreading to recurved towards the tip. Stamens with
hairy linear to strap-shaped filaments, not dilated, and
with hairy connectives and often anthers as well;
connectives not extended beyond the anther. Achenes
slightly to markedly compressed, often rimmed,
usually, but not always, with a plumose tail. (species
275–297)

Section Viorna

(syn. Subsection Viorna Ericks. ex M. Johnson)
Climbers with rather woody stems (*C. addisonii* is
bushy) and pinnate or ternate leaves, with twisting
petioles and petiolules. Flowers in lateral 1–few-
flowered cymes, or solitary and terminal; bracts
present. Sepals thick and leathery, with their margins
held closely together for most of their length. Achenes
relatively large, rimmed, with or without a plumose
tail. (species 275–286)

• **Subsection Viorna:** Sepals not expanded towards
the tip, glabrous or appressed pubescent outside.
Achenes relatively large, with a distinct rim and a
plumose or occasionally non-plumose tail. (9 species)
C. addisonii, C. beadlei, C. glaucophylla,
C. morefieldii, C. pitcheri, C. reticulata, C. texensis,
C. versicolor, C. viorna. C, S & E USA. (species
275–283)

• **Subsection Crispae Prantl p.p.** (syn. Subsection
Viticellae Ericks.): Flowers terminal on stem or lateral
shoots; bracts absent. Sepals held closely together in

the lower half, recurving, expanding and frilled in the upper half. Achenes relatively large, weakly rimmed, the tail slightly hairy but not plumose. (1 species) *C. crispa*. C & E USA. (species 284)

• **Subsection Fuscae M. Johnson:** Flowers solitary, lateral or terminal; bracts present. Sepals thick and fleshy, held closely together for three-quarters of their length, then somewhat diverging and slightly recurved, but not expanded near the tip, downy to shaggy with hairs on the outside, or subglabrous. Achenes rimmed, with a plumose tail. (2 species) *C. fusca, C. ianthina*. E & SE Siberia, NE China, Korea, Mongolia, Japan. (species 285–286) `

Section Integrifoliae Serov p.p.

(syn. Subsection Integrifoliae Ericks. ex M. Johnson) Erect perennials often woody towards the base, sometimes herbaceous, with simple or compound leaves, generally only a few pairs per stem; petioles short, sometimes absent. Flowers campanulate, solitary or 2–3 at the shoot tips; bracts absent; sepals recurved and expanded towards the top. (species 287–294)

• **Subsection Integrifoliae Ericks. ex M. Johnson p.p.** (syn. Section Integrifoliae Serov. p.p.): Erect perennials with stems generally somewhat woody below. Leaves simple and usually with an entire margin. Sepals rather thin, held closely together in the lower third to half but diverging, recurving and somewhat expanded in the upper half or two-thirds, usually slightly downy outside. Achenes relatively small and scarcely rimmed, usually with a plumose tail. (6 species) *C. albicoma, C. coactilis, C. fremontii, C. integrifolia, C. ochroleuca, C. viticaulis*. C & E USA, Europe, W & C Asia. (species 287–292)

• **Subsection Baldwinianae Ericks. ex M. Johnson:** Herbaceous perennials with erect stems and deeply lobed or pinnately lobed leaves, occasionally simple and then narrow. Flowers terminal and solitary or 2–3; bracts absent. Sepals narrow, held closely together in the lower half but diverging, recurving and expanded in the upper, glabrous outside apart from the margin. Achenes rimmed and with or without a plumose tail. (2 species) *C. baldwinii, C. socialis*. SE USA. (species 293–294)

Section Hirsutissima (Ericks. ex M. Johnson) Grey-Wilson

(syn. Subsection Hirsutissimae Ericks. ex M. Johnson).

Erect herbaceous perennials, the stems sometimes becoming somewhat woody at the base. Leaves pinnately divided, with narrow segments. Flowers solitary and terminal; bracts absent. Sepals rather narrow, held closely together in the lower two-thirds, spreading and somewhat recurved, but not expanded, in the upper third, softly downy outside. Achenes small, scarcely compressed and thin-rimmed. (3 species) *C. bigelovii, C. hirsutissima, C. palmeri*. North America; concentrated on the Rocky Mts. (species 295–297)

Trends within the Genus (Some technical details)

Seedlings

Germination is either epigeal (with the two cotyledons or seed leaves appearing above the ground) or hypogeal (the cotyledons remaining below ground so that the first sign of germination is the appearance of the first true leaf). Thus the epigeal state is primarily restricted to species from warm temperate and subtropical regions of the world, whereas species from colder regions possess hypogeal germination. Subgenera *Archiclematis, Campanella, Cheiropsis, Clematis* and *Pseudoanemone* possess seeds with primarily epigeal germination, whereas subgenera *Flammula* and *Viorna* tend to have hypogeal germination. This is not altogether clear-cut: Tamura, Mizumoto and Kubota in 1977 stress that the hypogeal germination character appears to be an adaptation from warmer to cooler regions and they point out that in one species at least, *C. terniflora*, plants in the warmer southern part of the species distribution possess epigeal germination, while those to the north reveal hypogeal germination.

Phyllotaxy

The position of the leaves on the stem is very interesting in *Clematis* and has affected the classification of the genus to a marked extent. It was studied by both Haccius (1939, 1942 & 1950) and Tamura (1980). In the present classification subgenera *Archiclematis, Atragene, Campanella, Cheiropsis, Clematis, Pseudanemone* and *Tubulosae* possess seedlings with alternate leaves, but as they develop (in all but Subgenus *Archiclematis*) the leaves become strictly opposite. In subgenera *Flammula* and *Viorna* the seedlings, like the mature plants, have strictly opposite leaves. There is a marked tendency for those subgenera with epigeal germination to also possess seedlings with alternate leaves, while those with hypogeal germination bear opposite leaves in the seedling stage.

Stamen characters

The possession of hairy stamens (the filament usually, but sometimes the anther connective or the anther itself) is also specific to subgenera. Thus subgenera *Archiclematis, Atragene, Campanella, Pseudanemone, Tubulosae* and *Viorna* possess hairy stamens, whereas subgenera *Cheiropsis, Clematis* and *Flammula* possess glabrous stamens. Interestingly, with one or two exceptions, all the species with flat or saucer-shaped flowers have glabrous stamens, with the flowers pointing upwards. In contrast, virtually all the species with urn-, tubular- or bell-shaped flowers possess hairy stamens and in these the flowers are nearly always pendent. Exceptions to the rule are seen in Subgenus *Cheiropsis* Section *Cheiropsis (Clematis cirrhosa, C. napaulensis* and *C. williamsii)* and Section Fasciculiflora (*C. fasciculiflora*), where the species bear pendent or semi-pendent bell-shaped flowers but have glabrous stamens.

Parallelism

Some characters although specific to certain groups within the genus appear to have arisen independently and have to be viewed as examples of parallel evolution.

Aestivation. Of these the best known is seen in the aestivation of the sepals. In Subgenus *Pseudanemone*, Subgenus *Cheiropsis* Subsection Williamsianae and in Subgenus *Clematis* Section Novae-Zeelandiae the species possess imbricate sepals; that is with the sepals overlapping one another in bud to some extent. These groups are not related phyletically. All the other subgenera and sections posses species with valvate sepals, that is with the sepal margins in bud held against one another but not overlapping.

Flower development. Another interesting example of parallel evolution is in the development of the shoots and flowers. In the majority of species the vegetative development of that year takes place prior to flowering

and may continue on afterwards. In these, the vast majority of species, the flowers or inflorescences are borne laterally, or sometimes terminally on the current year's shoots (often from mid-summer onwards). However, in Subgenus *Atragene*, Subgenus *Campanella* Section Bebaeanthera, Subgenus *Cheiropsis* and Subgenus *Clematis* Section Lasiantha, which represent different phyletic groups, the flowers are produced early in the season from the axils of winter-bud-scales borne on the previous year's shoots, with the main vegetative development taking place after flowering.

Dioecism. In the majority of species in the genus the flowers are bisexual (hermaphrodite) with both male and female organs in the same plant. However, in Subgenus *Clematis* Section Aspidanthera, Section Clematis Subsection Dioicae, Section Lasiantha and Section Novae-Zeelandiae the plants are dioecious with the male and female organs separated out onto different plants. In addition, some species in Subgenus *Tubulosae* and Subgenus *Flammula* Subsection Chinenses also show a trend towards dioecism. Dioecism in clematis can be quite complicated. Whereas in some species the sexes are strictly separated, in others partial separation occurs so that within the same species strictly male plants can occur alongside plants which are essentially female but with some or all the flowers may bear some fertile stamens, although these are often reduced in number. In some dioecious species male flowers may possess rudimentary, non-functional female organs in the centre of the flower. Likewise, female flowers may often possess rudimentary male organs, which are generally represented by a whorl of stamen-like staminodes.

Anther appendages. The possession of anther appendages is another case in point and appears to have arisen independently on several occasions during the evolution of the genus. The anther appendage is an extension beyond the anther of the connective. It is apparent in Subgenus *Clematis* Sections Aspidanthera and Narveliopsis, and in various species in Subgenus *Clematis*, Subgenus *Tubulosae* and Subgenus *Viorna.*

Genus Clematis
Subgenus One Clematis

SECTION CLEMATIS
SUBSECTION CLEMATIS
(THE VITALBA GROUP)

This is primarily a group of 21 species most of which are little known in cultivation although one, the European native *C. vitalba*, is familiar to many. They originate primarily from the Himalaya, China and Taiwan, but *C. javana* has a wide distribution in south-eastern Asia. The species are characterized by having large panicle-like inflorescences of rather small white, greenish or cream 4-sepalled flowers with slender hairless filaments to the stamens. The flowers are borne on shoots of the current season. Those in cultivation tend to be vigorous plants suitable for large screens and fences or for clambering into trees; *C. vitalba,* in particular, can become very large, woody and heavy in time. *C. brevicaudata,* in its best forms, can be a very beautiful climber bearing masses of cream flowers during the summer. The flowers are small with wide-spreading or somewhat reflexed sepals,

MAP ONE

Subgenus *Clematis*

Section Clematis

    subsection Clematis ••••••••••••

    subsection Pierotianae ------------

    subsection Potaninianae +++++++

Section Narveliopsis ————

but the lack of size is more than adequately
compensate by the wealth of bloom that is followed
by an equally heavy display of fruit. Unfortunately,
the majority of species are not in cultivation.

▼ **Leaves primarily ternate to biternate (species 1–10)**
◆ **Stems 12-ribbed (species 1 & 2)**

1. *Clematis apiculata* Hook. f. & Th.
(syn. *C. apiifolia* subsp. *apiculata* (Hook. f. & Th.)
Kuntze, *C. apiifolia* (Hook. f. & Th.) var. *apiculata*
Honda, *C. gouriana* forma *trifoliata* in mss!)

DESCRIPTION. A slender climber with 12-ribbed stems,
appressed hairy when young. Leaves ternate; leaflets
ovate to elliptic, often 2–3-lobed, 25–80 mm (1–3.2
in) long, 8–60 mm (0.3–3.2 in) wide, with 3–7 veins
from the base and an entire to slightly toothed margin.
Flowers borne in lateral and terminal panicles up to 30
cm (12 in) long, each flower small, 10–13 mm
(0.4–0.5 in) across. Sepals 4, white, oblong to narrow-
ovate, 4–7 mm (0.16–0.28 in) long, 1–3 mm
(0.04–0.12 in) wide, wide-spreading, downy outside
but glabrous inside. Stamens two-thirds to almost as
long as the sepals. Achene ovate, 4–6 mm (0.16–0.24
in) long, hairy, with an almost appressed-hairy tail to
60 mm (2.4 in) long.

DISTRIBUTION. NE India (Assam); 910–1225 m
(3000–4000 ft).

2. *Clematis burmanica* Lace

DESCRIPTION. A deciduous climber with 12 ribbed
stems with appressed hairs and ternate leaves. Leaflets
oval to ovate with a rounded or heart-shaped base, to
18.5 cm (7.3 in) long and 5.5 cm (2.2 in) wide, with
an entire to crenate margin, hairy, especially on the
veins beneath, and with 5 or 7 main veins from the
base. Flowers borne in leafy panicle-like
inflorescences to 30 cm (12 in) long, sometime longer,
each flower 18–30 mm (0.7–1.2 in) across. Sepals 4,
white, narrow-oval, 8–15 mm (0.32–0.6 in) long, 3–6
mm (0.12–0.24 in) wide, spreading widely apart,

downy outside but practically hairless inside. Stamens
about half the length of the sepals. Achenes ?

DISTRIBUTION. C Myanmar (Burma); c. 900 m (3000 ft).

HABITAT. Woodland margins and shrubberies;
July–Sept.

◆ ◆ **Stems 4–6-ribbed (species 3–10)**
✽ **Leaflet margins entire; untoothed (Species 3 & 4)**

3. *Clematis formosana* Kuntze

DESCRIPTION. A deciduous herbaceous climber or
scrambler with 4–6-ribbed olive-green stems that are
densely white-downy (puberulous) when young.
Leaves membranous, ternate, the leaflets lanceolate to
narrow-ovate, to 74 mm (2.9 in) long and 34 mm (1.3
in) wide, often smaller, unlobed to 2–3-lobed (the
lobes narrow-oblong to almost linear), with a broad
wedge-shaped base and an entire margin, glabrous or
slightly puberulous above, sparsely puberulous
beneath, with 3 main veins from the base. Flowers in
small 3–5-flowered lateral cymes or in larger terminal
panicles, flat, 15–25 mm (0.6–1 in) across. Sepals 4,
white, narrow-oblong, spreading, with an acute, often
mucronate, tip, velvety beneath, otherwise glabrous.
Stamens two-thirds the length of the sepals, glabrous;
filaments slightly thickened at the top. Achenes ovate
to elliptic, 3–5 mm (0.12–0.2 in) long, pubescent, with
a yellowish plumose tail to 40 mm (1.6 in) long.

DISTRIBUTION. C & S Taiwan (Hualien, Kaosiung,
Pingtung) and adjacent islets; to 800 m (2600 ft).

HABITAT. Forest margins, bushy places and limestone
rocks; Nov–Jan.

Rather similar in general appearance to *C. gouriana*
and differing primarily in its strictly ternate leaves
which are rather narrowly lobed, but untoothed, and
somewhat hairier, and in the few-flowered
inflorescences.

4. *Clematis sasakii* Shimizu

DESCRIPTION. Very similar to *C. formosana*, but
leaflets more papery, lanceolate and entire, hairy but
not densely down beneath; flowers larger, c. 20 mm
(0.8 in) across, the sepals 10–11 mm (0.39–0.43 in)
long and 4–5 mm (0.16–0.2 in) wide. Achenes with
tails to 25 mm (1 in) long.

DISTRIBUTION. SE Taiwan (Mt Daixwanzan).

HABITAT. Forest fringes and shrubberies; Nov–Jan. The new 'Flora of China' includes this species as a synonym of *C. formosana*. However, the two have a distinct geographical range on Taiwan and differ in various details: most notably are the larger inflorescences and smaller flowers of *C. formosana* but, in addition, the filaments of *C. sasakii* are noticeably linear-lanceolate, broadest in the lower third, whilst those of *C. formosana* are linear and somewhat thickened at the top. The affinity of *C. sasakii* is probably closer to *C. bartlettii*, but clearly this requires further investigation. Both species have some ornamental value but they are unlikely to be particularly hardy; however, their winter-flowering habit may be of value in subtropical or Mediterranean gardens.

❀ ❀ **Leaflet margin toothed (species 5–10)**
❀ **Flowers white (species 5–8)**

5. *Clematis apiifolia* DC.*
(syn. *C. apiifolia* subsp. *normalis* Kuntze, subsp. *franchetii* Kuntze & subsp. *niponensis* Kuntze, *C. aquifolia* Steud., *C. virginiana* sensu Lour., non L.)

DESCRIPTION. A vigorous deciduous climber to 3–6 m (10–20 ft), with slender, somewhat downy, 5–6-ribbed stems and ternate leaves. Leaflets rather thin, ovate to ovate-lanceolate or more or less triangular, to 90 mm (3.5 in) long and 70 mm (2.8 in) wide, often shallowly 3-lobed, with a tapered to heart-shaped base, deeply incised-dentate (with 1–5 teeth on each side), sparsely puberulous all over. Flowers borne in lateral and terminal cymes, each with 7 or more flowers, together making large panicles up to 15 cm (6 in) long, each flower flat and star-like, 12–20 (–28) mm (0.5–0.8 (–1.1) in) across, occasionally larger, faintly scented. Sepals 4, dull white, spreading, oval to oblanceolate, 5–10 mm (0.2–0.4 in) long, to 3.2 mm (1.3 in) wide, downy on both surfaces, velvety above. Stamens two-thirds the length of the sepals, glabrous. Achenes egg- to spindle-shaped, 3.5–4.5 mm (1.4–1.8 in), with a plumose style to 15 mm (6 in) long.

DISTRIBUTION. S & E China (S Anhui, N Fujian, S. Jiangsu, NE Jiangxi, Zhejing), Japan, Korea; generally up to c. 900 m (3000 ft).

HABITAT. Generally in mixed evergreen/deciduous forests and shrubberies, but also on grassy stream banks; late Aug–Oct.

Cultivated in Britain for about 100 years, this species is quite closely related to *C. vitalba* but it is not so exciting in flower and can scarcely compare with that species in fruit, although better forms may exist in the wild. It often grows with other familiar climbers in the wild, e.g. *Ampelopsis brevipedunculata* and *Vitis flexuosus*.

H7; P2

6. *Clematis argentilucida* (Lévl. & Vant.) W. T. Wang
(syn. *C. apiifolia* var. *argentilucida* (Lévl. & Vant.) W. T. Wang and var. *obtusidentata* Rehd. & Wils., *C. grata* sensu Maxim., non Wall., *C. g.* var. *argentilucida* (Lévl. & Vant.) Rehd., *C. g.* var. *lobulata* Rehd. & Wils., *C. obtusidentata* (Rehd. & Wils.) Hj. Eichler, *C. vitalba* var. *argentilucida* Lévl. & Vant., *C. v.* var. *grata* Finet & Gagn.)

DESCRIPTION. Very similar to *C. apiifolia* but leaflets larger, to 13 cm (5.1 in) long and 9.5 cm (3.7 in) wide, with rounded or somewhat cuneate base and a coarsely toothed and rather uneven margin, grey-downy (velvety puberulous), especially beneath. Sepals 4, occasionally 5, white, widely spreading, narrow-oblong, 10–18 mm (0.4–0.7 in) long, downy beneath only. Achene with a plumose tail to 27 mm (1.1 in) long.

DISTRIBUTION. C, W & S China (S Anhui, N Guangdong, N Guangxi, Guizhou, S Henan, Hubei, Hunan, S. Jiangsu, Jiangxi, S Shaanxi (= Shensi), Sichuan, SE Yunnan); 200–2300 m (650–7550 ft).

HABITAT. Forests, shrubberies and stream margins; June–early Sept.

Included in the new 'Flora of China' as a variety of *C. apiifolia*.

7. *Clematis javana* DC.
(syn. *C. biternata* DC., *C. gouriana* sensu Miq., non Roxb., *C. g.* var. *malaiana* Miq., *C. grata* sensu Miq., non Wall., *C. indica* Blume, *C. javana* sensu Thunb., *C. junghuhniana* de Vriese, *C. leschenaultiana* sensu Spanoghe, non DC., *C. vitalba* sensu Bak. f. , non L., *C. v.* subsp. *cumingii* Kuntze, *C. v.* subsp. *brevicaudata* Kuntze, *C. v.* var. *biternata* (DC.) Boerlage, *C. v.* var. *javana* (DC.) Kuntze)

DESCRIPTION. A moderately vigorous climber 2–6 m (6.5–20 ft), generally with 6-ribbed stems. Leaves biternate; leaflets narrow- to broad-ovate, 50–110 mm (2–4.3 in) long, 20–70 mm (0.8–2.8 in) wide, with a rounded to heart-shaped base and coarsely toothed, sometime irregularly lobed, or entire margin. Flowers numerous, borne in lateral or terminal cymes or panicles, each flower 14–23 mm (0.55–0.9 in) across. Sepals 4, white, oblong to narrow-elliptic, 7–12 mm

1. *Clematis brevicaudata*, Jie-tai Temple, near Beijing
Photo: Christopher Grey-Wilson

(0.28–0.47 in) long, 2–4.5 mm (0.08–0.18 in) wide, wide-spreading, downy outside. Stamens slightly shorter than the sepals. Achene ovate to elliptic, hairy, with a whitish plumose tail to 40 mm (1.6 in) long.

DISTRIBUTION. SE Asia (Bali, Flores, Java, Lombok, Madura, New Guinea, Philippines, Sumba, Sumbawa, Timor); to 1600 m (5250 ft).

HABITAT. Open forests and forest fringes, scrub and grassy places, occasionally clambering over rocks.

In the Philippines, perhaps elsewhere in south-eastern Asia, wounds have been treated traditionally using the juice squeezed from the leaves of *C. javana*.

8. *Clematis mollissima* (**Hallier**) **H. Eichler**
(syn. *C. vitalba* L. var. *mollissima* Hallier)

DESCRIPTION. Similar to *C. javana*, but stems and leaves covered with soft pale brownish hairs, the leaflets often 3-lobed. The white flowers are somewhat larger, 18–26 mm (0.7–1 in) across.

DISTRIBUTION. Celebes; 400–1500 m (1300–4950 ft).

HABITAT. Similar habitats to *C. javana*.

❦ ❦ **Flowers basically cream, greenish or yellowish (species 9 & 10)**

9. *Clematis brevicaudata* **DC.***
(syn. *C. apiifolia* var. *biternata* Makino, *C. thalictroides* sensu Horan, non Steud., *C. vitalba* subsp. *brevicaudata* (DC.) Kuntze)

DESCRIPTION. A vigorous deciduous climber to 15 m (50 ft), although generally 5–10 m (16–33 ft), with 5–6-ribbed stems which are often finely pubescent when young and purple-flushed. Leaves generally biternate but sometimes pinnate with 5–7 segments; leaflets ovate to lanceolate, 15–60 mm (0.6–2.4 in) long, 7–35 mm (0.28–1.4 in) wide, occasionally 3-lobed, thin, glabrous or somewhat puberulous on both surfaces, the base rounded to somewhat heart-shaped, the apex acuminate to caudate, the margin with up to 5 coarse teeth on each side. Bracteoles small and subulate, not leaf-like. Flowers borne in lateral and terminal cymes (with up to 25 flowers), which are rather shorter than the leaves, 12–20 mm (0.47–0.8 in) across. Sepals 4, white flushed with green or yellow, oblong to obovate, 6–12 mm (0.24–0.47 in) long, 2–5 mm (0.08–0.2 in) wide, finely downy on both surfaces. Stamens slightly shorter than the sepals. Achenes elliptic, 2.5–3 mm (0.1–0.12 in) long, puberulous, with a plumose tail to 20 mm (0.8 in) long (often 10 mm (0.4 in) or less).

DISTRIBUTION. N, NE & W China (E Qinghai eastwards to Heilongjiang & Jilin, and southwards to Henan, Shaanxi, Sichuan, NW Yunnan & E Tibet), N Korea, Mongolia and the neighbouring part of Russia; 460–2800 m (1500–9200 ft).

HABITAT. Open forest, shrubberies and rocky places, riverbanks; July–Oct.

A very fine and vigorous species which is widespread in northern and north-eastern China, where it puts on a fine display of bloom in late summer and autumn. It is much-underrated in gardens, for it is quite the rival of the closely related *C. vitalba* in floriferousness, hardiness and vigour. In the best forms the flowers wreath the stems in panicle-like masses and although the flower colour varies the finest forms are a charming creamy-yellow. The species is common in the hills around Beijing, especially in the vicinity of the Great Wall, but the best forms seem to come from further west in Qinghai and Gansu provinces. Seed and young plants have recently been introduced from

Qinghai so it is to be hoped that some superior forms will now become established in our gardens.

In the garden it requires plenty of space and it looks particularly effective when allowed to roam over a wall or fence, or allowed to scramble over shrubs. The late butterflies are attracted to the blooms, as are bees and various other insects.

H5; P2

10. *Clematis ganpiniana* (Lévl. & Vant.) Tamura
(syn. *C. brevicaudata* DC. var. *ganpiniana* (Lévl. & Vant.) Hand.-Mazz., var. *leiophylla* Hand.-Mazz. and var. *lissocarpa* Rehd. & Wils., *C. parviloba* Gardn. & Champ. var. *ganpiniana* (Lévl. & Vant.) Rehd. and var. *labrescens* Finet & Gagn., *C. pierotii* sensu Finet & Gagn., non Miq., *C. vitalba* L. var. *ganpiniana* Lévl. & Vant.)

DESCRIPTION. A deciduous climber to 5 m (16.5 ft) with bipinnate or biternate leaves, more rarely pinnate. Leaflets ovate, to 98 mm (3.9 in) long and 50 mm (2 in) wide, often much smaller, unlobed to 3-lobed, the margin entire to dentate, sparsely pubescent, or practically glabrous beneath. Flowers mostly in 9–many-flowered lateral or terminal cymes, 15–24 mm (0.6–0.95 in) across; sepals cream, spreading, oblong to narrow-obovate, 7–12 mm (0.28–0.47 in) long, the apex acute to obtuse, velvety on the margin beneath. Stamens about two-thirds the length of the sepals. Achenes glabrous, compressed and rather rounded, 3.5–5 mm (0.14–0.2 in) long, with a plumose tail to 35 mm (1.4 in) long.

DISTRIBUTION. China (Shaanxi to S Anhui southwards to Yunnan, Guangxi and Guangdong, including E Xizang); to 3300 m (10,800 ft).

HABITAT. Woods, shrubberies and streamsides; July–Oct.

Sometimes confused with *C. brevicaudata*, which is generally a more northerly species with hairy achenes and with the sepals clearly pubescent on both surfaces, although rather sparsely so on the inner.

var. *subsericea* (Rehd. & Wils.) C. T. Ting (syn. *C. brevicaudata* var. *subsericea* Rehd. & Wils.) has the leaflets densely silky-hairy beneath, while the achenes are glabrous. Confined to shrubby slopes at 1200–1300 m (3950–4250 ft) in W Sichuan.

var. *tenuisepala* (Maxim.) C. T. Ting (syn. *C. brevicaudata* var. *tenuisepala* Maxim.; *C. b.* var. *filipes* Rehd. & Wils.) differs from the other varieties in its appressed-hairy ovaries and achenes. The leaflets

2. Clematis brevicaudata, Qinghai Province, NW China.
Photo: Rosemary Steele

are finely hairy to almost glabrous beneath. Wooded and grassy slopes, streamsides, to 1000 m (3300 ft) in N Guangxi, S Henan, W Hubei, NE Jiangsu, S Shaanxi, Shandong, S Shanxi and N Zhejiang.

▼ ▼ **Leaves primarily pinnate to bipinnate (species 11–23)**
❖   **Leaflets margins entire, rarely slightly toothed (species 11–14)**

11. *Clematis heynei* M. Johnson
(syn. *C. triloba* sensu Heyne ex Roth, non Thunb.)

DESCRIPTION. A vigorous climbing or creeping vine with 6-ribbed stems, silky-hairy, especially when young. Leaves pinnate to ternate, generally with 5 leaflets. Leaflets oval to elliptical, often with a heart-shaped base, to 75 mm (3 in) long and 67 mm (2.6 in) wide, the margin entire or with 2–7 lobes, but not toothed. Inflorescence panicle-like, many-flowered, primarily in lateral cymes, the flowers starry, 30–50 mm (1.2–2 in) across, scented. Sepals usually 4, occasionally 6–8, white, oval, 15–25 mm (0.6–1 in) long, 4–10 mm (0.16–0.4 in) wide, spreading widely apart, finely downy on the outside. Stamens a third to half the length of the sepals. Achenes oval, 3–5 mm (0.12–0.2 in) long, silky-hairy, with a plumose tail to 45 mm (1.8 in) long.

DISTRIBUTION. C & S India; to c. 1000 m (3300 ft).

HABITAT. Woodland margins, bushy and grassy places; Sept–Dec.

A subtropical species not in cultivation.

12. *Clematis tsaii* W. T. Wang

DESCRIPTION. Very similar to *C. chingii*, which it may only be a form of, but it is distinguished by possessing entire leaf-margins. The leaflets are rather more sparsely bristly above.

DISTRIBUTION. SW China (SE Tibet, C & NW Yunnan); 1500–200 m (4950–6550 ft).

HABITAT. Bushy slopes and open forests; Sept–Oct.

13. *Clematis peterae* Hand.-Mazz.*
(syn. *C. gouriana* Roxb. var. *finetii* sensu Rehd. & Wils., non Lévl. & Vant., *C. peterae* var. *mollis* W. T. Wang, *C. vitalba* var. *gouriana* sensu Finet & Gagn., non (Roxb.) Kuntze and var. *microcarpa* Franch.)

DESCRIPTION. A stout deciduous climber to 5 m (16.5 ft), with 5-ridged stems that are glabrous or finely pubescent when young, and often flushed with purple. Leaves pinnate, occasionally ternate, often densely downy beneath, sparsely so or glabrous above; leaflets ovate to elliptic-ovate, to 95 mm (3.7 in) long and 45 mm (1.8 in) wide, occasionally 2–3-lobed, rather thin and papery, with a rounded to slightly heart-shaped base and acuminate apex, the margin entire or with 1–2 teeth on each side. Flowers borne in few- to many-flowered lateral or terminal cymes, 10–15 mm (0.4–0.6 in) across. Sepals 4, white or creamy-white, spreading, oblong to obovate, 6–8 mm (0.24–0.32 in) long, 2–4 mm (0.08–0.16 in) wide, finely downy on both surfaces. Stamens two-thirds the length of the sepals. Achenes elliptic, 2–4 mm (0.08–0.16 in) long, glabrous, with a white plumose style to 20 mm (0.8 in) long.

DISTRIBUTION. C, W & S China (from SW Hebei, S Shaanxi and Sichuan southwards to N & C Yunnan, Guizhou & Hunan); 600–3400 m (2000–11,150 ft).

HABITAT. Mixed forest, especially close to streams; May–July.

Clematis peterae has a certain charm but to the gardener is scarcely distinguished from a host of other small white-flowered clematis. For this reason it is generally dismissed as of little garden value, or only for the 'specialist collection'.

var. *trichocarpa* W. T. Wang is distinguished from the typical plant (var. *peterae*) by having pubescent achenes. Although the two varieties overlap in distribution in Gansu, Hubei, S Shaanxi and Sichuan, var. *trichocarpa* has a generally more easterly distribution in S Anhui, Henan, Jiangsu, N Jiangxi and W Zhejiang, where it grows in similar habitats at 600–1900 m (2000–6200 ft).

subsp. *lishanensis* (T. Y. Yang & T. C. Huang) Grey-Wilson, stat. nov. (syn. *C. gouriana* subsp. *lishanensis* T. Y. Yang & T. C. Huang, *C. peterae* var. *lishanensis* (T. Y. Yang & T. C. Huang) W. T. Wang) is distinguished by having bipinnate leaves with up to 15 narrower, narrow-ovate to lanceolate, leaflets, sepals glabrous above and achenes with a yellowish plumose tail. This variety is restricted to C Taiwan at 1200–2600 m (3900–8500 ft), where it grows on open slopes close to forest margins.

H7: P2

14. *Clematis tamurae* T. Y. Yang & T. C. Huang
(syn. *C. austro-taiwanensis* Tamura ex T. Y. Yang & T. C. Huang)

DESCRIPTION. Similar to *C. peterae* but the lanceolate leaflets are generally smaller, not more than 60 mm (2.4 in) long and 18 mm (0.7 in) wide, the margin always untoothed, and the flowers are larger, 13–25 mm (0.5–1 in) across; sepals 10–15 mm (0.4–0.6 in) long and hairy on both surfaces, more densely so beneath. Achenes pubescent, with a yellowish or brownish plumose tail 25–40 mm (1–1.6 in) long.

DISTRIBUTION. Taiwan, especially in the south; to 1500 m (4950 ft).

HABITAT. Open forests and forest margins; Aug–Oct.

❖ ❖ **Leaflet margins toothed, often coarsely so (species 15–23)**

✴ **Flowers cream, greenish or greenish-white (species 15–21)**

✴ **Sepals hairy inside (species 15 & 16)**

15. *Clematis gouriana* Roxb.*
(syn. *Atragene indica* Heyne ex Wall., A. *japonica* Wight ex Wall.; *Clematis cana* Wall., *C. floribunda* sensu Kurz, non Planch. & Triana, *C. martinii* Lévl.,

C. substipulata Kuntze, *C. vitalba* β. *gouriana* (Roxb.) Kuntze, *C. v.* var. *gouriana* (Roxb.) Finet & Gagn., *C. v.* var. *micrantha* Lévl. & Vant.)

DESCRIPTION. A very variable deciduous climber with 5-ridged stems, which are rough-hairy or glabrous when young, becoming very woody below with age. Leaves pinnate (with 5–7 leaflets), occasionally ternate or biternate, glabrous, or sparsely puberulous along the veins; leaflets ovate to narrow-ovate or lanceolate, to 105 mm (4.1 in) long and 55 mm (2.2 in) wide, sometimes 3-lobed, the base rounded to almost heart-shaped, the apex acute to acuminate, the margin with a few coarse dentate teeth; lamina with 3–7 main veins, deep green and often shiny above. Flowers numerous in lateral and terminal cymes that make up large panicle-like inflorescences, rather small, 7–18 mm (0.28–0.7 in) across. Sepals 4, creamy-white, sometimes flushed with greenish-yellow, spreading, narrow-obovate to more or less oblong, 4–9 mm (0.16–0.35 in) long, 1.8–3.5 mm (0.07–0.14 in) wide, spreading widely apart to somewhat recurved towards the tip, puberulous on both surfaces but far more densely so beneath. Stamens about two-thirds the length of, or almost as long as, the sepals, the filament filiform but somewhat thickened towards the top. Achenes spindle-shaped, 3–5 mm (0.12–0.2 in) long, puberulous to hairy, with a white or yellowish plumose tail to 60 mm (2.4 in) long.

DISTRIBUTION. Himalayan foothills and lowlands (Nepal to Myanmar), N India, W & S China (Guangdong, Guangxi, Guizhou, W Hubei, Sichuan, C & S Yunnan), Philippines; to 2600 m (8500 ft).

HABITAT. Subtropical and warm broad-leaved forests and forest margins, thickets and shrubberies, streamsides; Sept–Oct.

Clematis gouriana is a vigorous plant in cultivation although it is not an invasive as its close relative *C. vitalba* in gardens. It has the advantage of having, in the best forms, rather larger flowers that can be borne in considerable numbers, these usually being followed by an impressive display of fluffy fruits.

H6; P2

subsp. *lishanensis* Yang & Huang* differs in having small palmate, coarsely toothed, stipule-like processes at the leaf-bases and slightly larger flowers, the sepals yellowish-green to pale yellow, to 10 mm (0.4 in) long and 5 mm (0.2 in) wide, are glabrous on the inside. Endemic to Taiwan (Chiayi, Haulien, Ilan, Kaohsiung,

Taichung) between 1200 and 2600 m (3900 and 8500 ft). This subspecies is in cultivation.

16. *Clematis subumbellata* Kurz
(syn. *C. kerriana* Drummond & Craib, *C. laxipaniculata* Pei, *C. vitalba* subsp. *subumbellata* (Kurz) Kuntze)

DESCRIPTION. Very similar to *C. gouriana* and sometimes treated as a form of that species, but leaves bipinnate or pinnate with up to 21 leaflets, the plant (especially the young stems, petioles and leaf undersurfaces) densely and finely pubescent.

DISTRIBUTION. SW China (S Yunnan), Laos, N Myanmar, N Thailand, N Vietnam; 400–1900 m (1300–6200 ft).

HABITAT. Forest margins, shrubberies and open bushy slopes; Dec–Feb.

✳ ✳ **Sepals glabrous inside (species 17–21)**

17. *Clematis grata* Wall.*
(syn. *C. cordata* Royle, *C. vitalba* subsp. *grata* (Wall.) Kuntze)

DESCRIPTION. A vigorous climber to 5 m (16.5 ft) with shallowly 4–5-ridged stems, densely downy when young. Leaves pinnate to bipinnate, with 5 primary divisions, occasionally 7, or ternate; leaflets rather thin, ovate to lanceolate, or more or less rhombic, generally 2–3-lobed, to 11.5 cm (4.5 in) long and 8 cm (3.2 in) wide, coarsely toothed, the base rounded to heart-shaped, the apex acuminate, hairy, more densely so beneath. Flowers fragrant, numerous in a panicle-like inflorescence, 15–25 mm (0.6–1 in) across. Sepals 4, rarely 5–6, greenish-white or cream, spreading, oval-lanceolate, 6–13 mm (0.24–0.5 in) long and 1–4 mm (0.04–0.16 in) wide. Stamens glabrous. Achenes elliptical, 2–3 mm (0.08–0.12 in) long, hairy, with a pale yellowish plumose tail to 35 mm (1.4 in) long.

DISTRIBUTION. E Hindu Kush and the Himalaya (E Afghanistan to Nepal), S Tibet, S China (Yunnan to Fujian) and Taiwan (including the islands of Kueishandao, Lanyu and Ludao); 600–2500 m (2000–8200 ft).

HABITAT. Forest margins, shrubberies, hedgerows, banks, occasionally amongst riverside boulders or on stream banks; July–Sept.

Introduced into cultivation as early as 1830, this vigorous species is still rare in cultivation. Although it

3. *Clematis grata* in cultivation.
Photo: Jack Elliott

4. *Clematis grata* in cultivation.
Photo: Raymond Evison

can look very attractive in the wild, as it does in many Himalayan valleys at fairly low altitudes, it rarely performs well in gardens. It can be large if allowed to scramble up trees and is usually disparagingly relegated to the 'wild garden'.

H5; P2

18. *Clematis grandidentata* (Rehd. & Wils.) W. T. Wang*
(syn. *C. argentilucida* var. *argentilucida* sensu M. Johnson, non (Lévl. & Vant.) W. T. Wang, *C. grata* var. *grandidentata* Rehd. & Wils.)

DESCRIPTION. Very similar in general appearance to *C. grata*, but leaflets somewhat larger, to 10 cm (4 in) long, the margin with a few coarse dentate teeth; flowers larger and borne in few-flowered (1–6-flowered) cymes, the sepals 4–5, 10–15 mm (0.4–0.6 in) long, 2.5–5 mm (1–2 in) wide. Achenes broader, 2–2.5 mm (1–2 in) (not 1.3–1.8 mm (0.5–0.7 in)) with a tail to 34 mm (1.3 in) long.

DISTRIBUTION. C & W China (E Qinghai, Shaanxi & SW Hebei southwards to NW Yunnan Guizhou, and east as far as W Anhui); 450–3200 m (1500–10,500 ft).

HABITAT. Open forest or forest margins and shrubberies; late May–Aug.

Occasionally cultivated, this species can be quite attractive when well-flowered. Some plants sold in cultivation under the name *C. grata* are in fact referable to this species. Unpruned plants tend to flower in May and June, pruned ones considerably later.

H5; P2

var. *lichiangensis* (Rehd.) W. T. Wang (syn. *C. argentilucida* var. *likiangensis* (Rehd.) W. T. Wang, *C. grata* var. *lichiangensis* Rehd.) is distinguished by having glabrous, not pubescent, achenes. It has a more limited distribution in Guizhou, SW Hebei, W Hubei, Sichuan, NW Yunnan and NW Zhejiang; generally above 2000 m (6500 ft).

19. *Clematis chingii* W. T. Wang

DESCRIPTION. Similar to *C. grata* but the leaflets relatively broader, ovate to broad-elliptic, 40–80 mm (1.6–3.1 in) long, 15–65 mm (0.6–2.6 in) wide, generally with 1–4 dentations on each side, with stiff bristle-like (strigose) hairs above. In addition, the stems tend to be 7–8-ridged, not 4–5.

DISTRIBUTION. S & SW China (N Guangdong, W Guangxi, SW Guizhou, W Hunan, E Yunnan); 200–1700 m (650–5600 ft).

HABITAT. Shrubberies and open bushy places; July–Sept.

20. *Clematis gratopsis* W. T. Wang
(syn. *C. grata* var. *lobulata* Rehd. & Wils.)

DESCRIPTION. Very similar to *C. grata*, but leaflets always 3-lobed to ternate and flowers generally in smaller cymes of up to 14 flowers, usually less, each 13–17 mm (0.5–0.67 in) across. In addition, the bracteoles are larger and leaf-like but simple, ovate to lanceolate (linear and rather inconspicuous in *C. grata*).

DISTRIBUTION. CW China (SE Gansu, W Hubei, NW Hunan, S Shaanxi, E Sichuan); 200–1700 m (650–5600 ft).

HABITAT. Shrubberies and other bushy places, particularly stream margins; Aug–Oct.

This species replaces *C. grata* in much of western central China, the latter being primarily a Himalayan and southern Tibetan plant.

21. *Clematis vitalba* L.* Traveller's Joy, Old Man's Beard
(syn. *C. dumosa* Salisb., *C. sepium* Lam., *C. scandens* Borkh., *C. taurica* Besser ex Nyman, *C. vitalba* var. *angustisecta* Gremli, var. *banatica* Schur, var. *bellojocoensis* Gand., var. *chrysostemon* Favrat ex Schinz & Keller, var. *crenata* Jord., var. *dumosa* Gand., var. *integrata* DC., var. *odontophylla* Gand., var. *prostrata* Kuntze, var. *radicans* Val de Lièvre, var. *simplicifolia* Godet, var. *transiens* Gand., var. *typica* Beck, var. *syriaca* Boiss.)

DESCRIPTION. A very vigorous rampant deciduous climber to 30 m (100 ft), although often 10–15 m 33–50 ft), with 6-ribbed and downy young stems, but old stems becoming very thick (to 10 cm (4 in) diameter, occasionally more), heavy and woody, pale brown. Leaves pinnate with 5 leaflets, these variable in shape from ovate to lanceolate or heart-shaped, occasionally 3-lobed, to 12 cm (4.7 in) long and 7.5 cm (3 in) wide, with a coarsely toothed to more or less entire margin, downy beneath, particularly along the main veins. Flowers borne in panicle-like cymes from the leaf-axils, 15–25 mm (0.6–1 in) across, with a faint almond scent. Sepals 4, greenish or creamish-white, narrow-oval, 8–12 mm (0.32–0.47 in) long, 3–5 mm (0.12–0.2 in) wide,

5. *Clematis vitalba* naturalized in Scotland, near Blairgowrie.
Photo: Christopher Grey-Wilson

6. *Clematis vitalba* in fruit, North Devon.
Photo: Christopher Grey-Wilson

7. Clematis vitalba on a wall in the Cevennes, France. Photo: Christopher Grey-Wilson

spreading widely apart to recurved, downy on both surfaces. Stamens as long as the sepals. Achenes scarcely compressed, hairy, with a silky plumose tails to 25 mm (1 in) long, which becomes greyish-white in time.

DISTRIBUTION. C & S & SE Europe (from C Britain and Germany southwards) eastwards to Turkey, Iran and the Caucasus Mountains, south to North Africa; naturalized farther north and in Ireland.

HABITAT. Deciduous and mixed woodlands, hedgerows, bushy places, riverbanks, railway and road embankments, old walls and buildings, often on calcareous soils; July–Oct.

This is a very familiar plant in southern Britain and much of central and southern Europe, especially prominent in the autumn and early winter when the plants are shrouded in their fluffy fruits, draped in festoons over trees and hedgerows. It is perhaps the most vigorous of all clematis and for this reason it is often overlooked in gardens. However, it is excellent in the wild garden or for covering perimeter fences. I have seen it used very effectively for covering fences around reservoirs and airports. With heavy annual pruning it

can be kept in bounds, but even then expect vigorous shoots at least 4 m (13 ft) long or more in a season on mature plants. In some woodlands this exceptional plant festoons the branches of lofty trees with thick strands like a tropical vine and can be most impressive; Tarzan would be delighted with it! The flowers are produced in masses in late summer in Britain, although in the south of France and elsewhere plants flower markedly earlier, often starting in June. The fluffy fruitheads last well into winter, long after the leaves on the trees have fallen and hedgerows and woodland shrouded in this clematis can be very beautiful on a cold winter's day. In gardens it can seed around profusely and annoyingly, often sowing into those places reserved for choicer and more inhibited plants. One of the joys of this plant is the way the seedheads remain intact well into winter, looking at their best on those bright, slightly misty, early winter days when the last leaves have fallen from the trees and hedgerows and the sun is low on the horizon.

The common name 'Traveller's Joy' is credited to Gerard who says that it is 'esteemed for pleasure by reason of the goodly shadow and the pleasant sent or savour of its flowers. And because of its decking and adorning waies and hedges where people travel, thereupon have I named it Traveller's Joy.'

Although it does not extend its native haunts north of central Britain it has been assumed in the past that this was because it was not hardy to the north. Evidence does not bear this out and it grows perfectly well and is fully hardy in gardens in Scotland and elsewhere. The reason for its northerly limit is probably due to the fact that it comes into flower too late to set viable seed.

H4; P2

✳ ✳ **Flowers pure white (species 22 & 23)**

22. *Clematis multistriata* H. Eichler

(syn. *C. leschenaultianus* sensu Koorders, non DC., *C. vitalba* subsp. *javana* sensu Kuntze, non DC., *C. v.* var. *grata* Koorders, non Wall. and var. *jarvana* sensu Koorders, non DC.)

DESCRIPTION. Very similar in most respects to *C. javana* (p.35), but stems 10–12-ribbed and leaves pinnate with 2–3 pairs of primary ternate segments (15–21 leaflets in all, instead of 9). A climber to 4 m (13 ft).

DISTRIBUTION. Malaysia (Bali, E Java, Lombok); 1400–2800 m (4600–9200 ft).

HABITAT. Open forests and scrub.

23. *Clematis taiwaniana* Hayata

(syn. *C. gouriana* sensu Hsieh, non Roxb., *C. grata* var. *ryukiuensis* Tamura).

DESCRIPTION. Similar to *C. grata* (p.39) in general appearance but distinguished primarily by its leaves which can be pinnate or biternate, the leaflets with a more coarsely dentate margin. In addition, the flowers are rather larger, 15–25 mm (0.6–1 in) across, the sepals 8–15 mm (0.32–0.6 in) long and 3–5 mm (0.12–0.2 in) wide, puberulous on both surfaces. The achenes are rather narrower and bear a yellowish plumose tail to 30 mm (1.2 in) long.

DISTRIBUTION. S Japan (Ryukyu Islands; Amami-oshima, Ishigaki, Okinawa) and Taiwan; to 2500 m (8200 ft).

HABITAT. Open forests, and forest margins, often close to streams; Apr–Sept.

Clematis taiwaniana has had a rather chequered history. Tamura considered it to be a variety of *C. grata* and this is followed by Magnus Johnson in 'Släktet Klematis' but, although clearly closely related, they have a very distinctive geographical range and can be further

distinguished by the details given in the description above. The 'Flora of Taiwan' includes the species as a synonym of *C. gouriana* without qualification. However, the entire leaf-margins of the latter, together with its considerably smaller flowers are quite distinctive and the two are unlikely to be confused. As defined here *C. taiwaniana* has a limited distribution in Taiwan and the Ryukyu Islands to the north.

SUBSECTION PIEROTIANAE
(THE PIEROTII GROUP)

A little-known group in gardens closely related to the previous one, but with rather larger flowers borne in few-flowered inflorescences, with the stamen filaments glabrous but clearly dilated towards the base. The flowers are generally white or cream, occasionally yellowish. The eight species are restricted to the eastern Himalaya, China and Japan and, one has to admit, the majority are not particularly garden-worthy.

▼ **Leaflet margins entire, or almost so (species 24–27)**
◆ **Leaves ternate or simple (species 24–25)**

24. *Clematis mashanensis* W. T. Wang

DESCRIPTION. A climber with shallowly 4–6-ribbed stems which are sparsely puberulous when young. Leaves ternate, leathery, somewhat puberulous on the midrib beneath; leaflets ovate, to 70 mm (2.8 in) long and 43 mm (1.7 in) wide, with a rounded base, acute apex and entire margin. Flowers solitary, lateral, flat, 45–50 mm (1.8–2 in) across, borne on a short 35–50 mm (1.4–2 in) long peduncle bearing a pair of ternate, leaf-like bracts. Sepals 4, lanceolate to almost oblong, 22–26 mm (0.87–1 in) long, 9–10 mm (0.35–0.39 in) wide, spreading, silky-hairy beneath but glabrous above. Stamens one-third to half the length of the sepals, with relatively large anthers 2.5–3 mm (0.1–0.12 in) long. Achenes hairy.

DISTRIBUTION. S China (Guangxi; Mashan Xian); c. 400 m (1300 ft).

HABITAT. Summit of a limestone hill; Apr.

25. *Clematis tinghuensis* C. T. Ting

DESCRIPTION. Very similar in general appearance to *C. formosana* but the leaves simple or ternate, the leaflets are broader, ovate to broad-ovate, to 80 mm (3.2 in) long and 50 mm (2 in) wide, with a rounded to somewhat heart-shaped base. The achenes are very different, narrow-ovate and 8–9 mm (0.32–0.35 in) long, with a short tail c. 6 mm (0.24 in) long, which is only plumose near the base.

DISTRIBUTION. SE China (S Guangdong; Mt Dinghushan); 250–400 m (800–1300 ft).

HABITAT. Open forest or forest margins; June–July.

◆ ◆ Leaves pinnate (species 26–27)

26. *Clematis parviloba* Gardn. & Champ.

DESCRIPTION. Deciduous climber with 6-ribbed stems, hairy when young. Leaves thinly leathery, pinnate, with 5 prime divisions that are often ternate, or alternatively leaves biternate; leaflets oval to lanceolate, sometimes 2–3-lobed, to 70 mm (2.8 in) long and 40 mm (1.6 in) wide, with an entire margin, or with a single tooth on each side, and 3 main veins. Flowers borne in lateral cymes with 5 or more flowers, each 20–35 mm (0.8–1.4 in) across. Sepals 4, white, generally tinged with green, elliptical, 9–17 mm (0.35–0.67 in) long, acute, spreading, downy beneath. Stamens just over half the length of the sepals. Achenes oval, 2.5–3 mm (0.1–0.12 in) long, densely hairy, with a tawny plumose tail to 30 mm (1.2 in) long.

DISTRIBUTION. W & S China (Fujian, Guangdong, Guangxi, Guizhou, Hong Kong, S Jiangxi, W Sichuan, Yunnan, S Zhejiang); 500–3200 m (1650–10,500 ft).

HABITAT. Forests and wooded ravines, shrubberies, streamsides; Apr–July, occasionally later.

var. *bartlettii* (Yamamoto) T. Y. Yang & T. C. Huang (syn. *C. bartlettii* Yamamoto, *C. matsudai* Hayata ex T. Y. Yang & T. C. Huang, *C. parviloba* subsp. *bartlettii* (Yamamoto) T. Y. Yang & T. C. Huang) is similar but a more densely downy plant (especially on the young stems and leaf undersurfaces), with flowers in 5–many-flowered cymes, larger 28–45 mm (1.1–1.8 in) across. In addition, the leaflets are clearly more toothed and are said to be soft and slightly fleshy to the touch rather than papery. Confined to N Taiwan at mid-altitudes, 1100–2500 m (3600–8200 ft), where it inhabits forests and wooded slopes; July–Nov.

var. *ianthera* W. T. Wang has entire leaflet margins and solitary flowers c. 46 mm (1.8 in) across; stamens longer than in var. *parviloba*, 12–14 mm (0.47–0.55 in) long (not 5–10 mm (0.2–0.39 in)). This interesting variety is restricted to shrubberies in W Sichuan (Mt Omei) at c. 800 m (2600 ft).

var. *tenuipes* (W. T. Wang) C. T. Ting (syn. *C. tenuipes* W. T. Wang) is distinguished by possessing more leathery ternate leaves and generally 1-flowered inflorescences with rather smaller flowers 25–30 mm (1–1.2 in) across. It is restricted to SE Yunnan (Funning Xian) at 700–1000 m (2300–3300 ft), where it flowers in Apr–May. Treated in the 'Flora of China' as a distinct species.

27. *Clematis wissmanniana* Hand.-Mazz.
(syn. *C. gratopsis* W. T. Wang var. *integriloba* W. T. Wang)

DESCRIPTION. Very similar to *C. parviloba*, differing in the thicker more papery, rather than membranous, blunt (obtuse) sepals. The white flowers are 20–32 mm (0.8–1.3 in) across.

DISTRIBUTION. SW China (Yunnan); 1220–1800 m (4000–5900 ft).

HABITAT. Open woodland and shrubberies; Sept–Oct.

▼ ▼ Leaflets clearly toothed, often coarsely so (species 28–31)
✳ Flowers yellowish-white; sepals 4–6 (species 28)

28. *Clematis zemuensis* W. W. Sm.

DESCRIPTION. Similar to *C. gouriana* but leaves biternate to bipinnate, the leaflets smaller, ovate, 15–35 mm (0.6–1.4 in) long and 10–25 mm (0.4–1 in) wide, with a coarsely toothed or somewhat lobed margin, sparsely hairy on both surfaces. Cymes 3–7-flowered, the flowers 20–30 mm (0.8–1.2 in) across, white tinged with yellow; sepals 4–6.

DISTRIBUTION. CE Himalaya (Sikkim, C Bhutan); 2745–3800 m (9000–12,500 ft).

HABITAT. Shrubberies, particularly of juniper and rhododendron; July–Sept.

This is an attractive species that would be well worth bringing into cultivation. It was described from the Zemu Valley in northern Sikkim and appears to have a rather restricted distribution in the wild.

✳ ✳ Flowers white; sepals always 4 (species 29–31)
❀ Leaves ternate or biternate (species 29 & 30)

29. *Clematis pierotii* Miq.*
(syn. *C. parviloba* Gard. & Champ.)

DESCRIPTION. A perennial with thin and rather weak scrambling or climbing, glabrous, stems to 3 m (10 ft), though generally less; stems flushed with violet-purple, short-hairy. Leaves usually biternate or occasionally ternate (the leaflets then 3-lobed), membranous; leaflets ovate to oblong or lanceolate, 15–50 mm (0.6–2 in) long, 8–20 mm (0.32–0.8 in) wide, usually 3-lobed, with a few uneven dentate teeth, the terminal leaflets usually more elongate and acuminate than the lateral. Flowers 1–3 in lateral cymes, 25–35 mm (1–1.4 in) across. Sepals white, spreading, lanceolate, 8–13 mm (0.3–0.5 in) long, acute, with dense white hairs outside, especially along the margins. Stamens slightly shorter than the sepals. Achenes lanceolate, 4–5 mm (0.16–0.2 in) long, with a white plumose tail to 20 mm (0.8 in) long (forms in which the tails are yellowish have been distinguished in the past as var. *ochraceoplumosa* Kuntze, but are scarcely worth distinguishing).

DISTRIBUTION. Japan (Kyushu, Honshu, Ryukyu Is., Shikoku).

HABITAT. Woods and shrubberies; Aug–Oct.

H6; P2

30. Clematis puberula Hook. f. & Th.
(syn. *C. parviloba* Gard. & Champ. subsp. *puberula* (Hook. f. & Th.) Kuntze)

DESCRIPTION. Similar to *C. parviloba* but the leaves often biternate, with the leaflets toothed or 3-lobed, hairy on both surfaces; flowers few to a cyme (often 3–7), these making up large leafy panicles, each flower 18–28 mm (0.7–1.1 in) across, white, the sepals softly hairy on the outside.

DISTRIBUTION. E Himalaya (Bhutan eastwards), Assam, Burma; 1219–2240 m (4000–7350 ft).

HABITAT. Woodland margins and shrubberies, often in rather dry habitats; Aug–Oct.

❀ ❀ **Leaves pinnate (species 31)**

31. Clematis pinnata Maxim.
(syn. *C. grata* sensu Ulbrich, non Wall.)
DESCRIPTION. A deciduous climber with 4–6-ridged stems which are usually finely pubescent when young. Leaves pinnate; leaflets 5, ovate, 50–120 mm (2–4.7 in) long, 30–75 mm (1.2–3 in) wide, rather papery, often 2–3-lobed, sparsely and finely hairy on both surfaces, more especially on the veins, the margin dentate. Inflorescences lateral or terminal, many-flowered, generally panicle-like,

the flowers 33–40 mm (1.3–1.6 in) across. Sepals white, 4, ascending, oblong to obovate, 16–20 mm (0.63–0.8 in) long, 2–5 mm (0.08–0.2 in) wide, downy beneath. Stamens about half the length of the sepals.

DISTRIBUTION. China (Beijing, W Hebei); 700–1200 m (2300–3900 ft).

HABITAT. Bushy slopes and shrubberies; July–Aug.

SUBSECTION POTANINIANAE (THE POTANIN GROUP)

A small group containing two delightful and vigorous species with relatively large 6-sepalled flowers with slender hairless filaments and hairless achenes. *C. potaninii* is long-established in cultivation and a well-flowered specimen is a real feature in the garden with its rounded, pristine, white blooms. However, it is not as well known in gardens, as it deserves.

32. Clematis potaninii Maxim.*
(syn. *C. fargesii* sensu Krüssmann, non Franch., *C. fargesii* var. *souliei* Finet & Gagn., *C. montana* var. *potaninii* (Maxim.) Finet & Gagn., *C. souliei* Franch. ex Finet & Gagn.)

DESCRIPTION. A vigorous deciduous climber to 7 m (23 ft), with green, strongly ribbed, downy, young stems, sometimes flushed with purple or violet. Leaves large, to 30 cm (12 in) long and almost as broad, pinnate to bipinnate, with 2–4 pairs (5–9 main divisions) of lateral segments which are generally ternate; leaflets ovate, to 70 mm (2.8 in) long and 52 mm (2 in) wide, but the lateral leaflets smaller than the end leaflets, all acute and with an incise-dentate margin, and a rounded to heart-shaped base. Flowers rather flat, 45–70 mm (1.8–2.8 in) across, borne in lateral cymes mostly of 1–3 flowers, in the middle of the current year's shoots on pedicels 37–62 mm (1.5–2.4 in) long. Sepals white or creamy white, normally 6 (occasionally 5 or 7), oval to lanceolate, to 23–36 mm (0.9–1.4 in) long, and 14–26 mm (0.6–1 in) wide, with a slightly undulate margin and 3–5 veins. Stamens with pale yellow anthers. Achenes glabrous, with a plumose tail to 30 mm (1.2 in) long, which is hairless at the base.

DISTRIBUTION. W & SW China (W & SW Sichuan, E Tibet, NW Yunnan); 1400–3658 m (4600–12,000 ft).

HABITAT. Shrubberies and woodland margins, ravines,

8. *Clematis potaninii* subsp. *potaninii*, NW Yunnan, Hei-shui. Photo: Phillip Cribb

often growing along stream and riversides; June–July, occasionally later.

subsp. *fargesii* **(Franch.) Grey-Wilson, stat. nov.***
(syn. *C. fargesii* Franch., *C. potaninii* var. *fargesii* (Franch.) Hand.-Mazz.) is similar to the typical plant (subsp. *potaninii*) but a less vigorous plant not more than 5 m (16 ft), often 2–3 m (6.6–10 ft), and similar leaves with just 2–3 pairs of primary lateral segments;

9. *Clematis potaninii* subsp. *potaninii*, NW Yunnan, Da-xue-shan.
Photo: Christopher Grey-Wilson

leaflets with a more rounded or somewhat heart-shaped base and more acutely toothed. Flowers smaller, 25–40 mm (1–1.6 in) across, but borne in larger lateral cymes of 3–7 flowers. Anthers smaller 1.5–2 mm (0.06–0.08 in) long (not 3–3.5 mm (0.12–0.14 in)). Similar habitats but a more northerly distribution in western China (N Sichuan and the neighbouring region of Gansu and S Shaanxi); July–Sept.

A vigorous and attractive species which can make an arresting sight in full flower. Unfortunately, it seldom performs as well in gardens as it does in the wild. I have been seen it in north-western Yunnan on several occasions. It is typically a plant of deep wooded river valleys and ravines, where in June the plants wreaths itself in glistening virginal anemone-like blooms and generally at its best after *C. montana* and its allies have ceased flowering. A bush draped in this clematis is an exciting find and this is the way the plant is best cultivated in gardens. As it flowers on the current season's shoots hard pruning in the early spring will help keep this vigorous species in check. The flowers start in July normally and continue intermittently until the autumn. If space is available, it can be left to roam unpruned when, in my experience at least, it will put on a greater display of bloom and start earlier, in June. The generally 6-sepalled flower are quite distinctive and especially fine in subsp. *potaninii*. Both subsp. *potaninii* and subsp. *fargesii* are in cultivation. They are very vigorous in the garden and look at their best when they are allowed to clamber up shrubs or small trees, especially dark-leaved evergreen shrubs.

Clematis potaninii is still far too often found under the synonym *C. fargesii* var. *souliei* and this has led to much confusion in the past. Ernest Henry Wilson first introduced it into cultivation from western China in 1911. It is a pity it does not have greater flower power in the garden, although granted the individual blooms are quite large and attractive. In the wild it is a very different 'creature' and plants can be very fine indeed when smothered with bloom. Of the two subspecies, subsp. *potaninii* is certainly the finest in gardens.

H7; P2

Hybrids between *C. potaninii* subsp. *fargesii* and *C. vitalba* quite frequently seen in gardens are found in nurseries and catalogues under the name Fargesioides', although the correct name is 'Paul Farges'* AGM (syn. *C.* × *fargesioides* 'Paul Farges' or 'Summer Snow'). The plant is vigorous (to 6–7 m (20–23 ft)) and bears scented creamy-white flowers throughout the summer and autumn months, each flower is about 40 mm (1.6 in) across. and with 4–6 sepals.

33. *Clematis trichotoma* Nakai
(syn. *C. apiifolia* Lévl., *C. vitalba* sensu Lévl., non L.)

DESCRIPTION. Similar to *C. potaninii* var. *fargesii* in general dimensions, but leaves normally pinnate with 2 pairs of lateral segments, rarely bipinnate, and the 3-flowered inflorescences are borne low down on the stems of the current year, each normally with 6 sepals but 4–7 is possible; flowers up to 12 mm (0.47 in) long and 5 mm (0.2 in) wide. The anthers are just 1–2 mm (0.04–0.08 in) long.

DISTRIBUTION. South Korea; to c. 850 m (2800 ft).

HABITAT. Open woodland and shrubberies, generally of deciduous and evergreen genera such as *Rhododendron*, *Acer*, *Betula*, *Quercus* and *Deutzia*; June–July.

An attractive species but without the impact in flower of the better forms of *C. potaninii*. The flowers of *C. trichotoma* are, however, scented, which is a real bonus in its favour; the scent is said to be similar to that of a *Philadelphus*. In the wild it is sometimes seen in association with *C. mandshurica*.

10. *Clematis* x *fargesioides* 'Paul Farges'
Photo: Raymond Evison

MAP TWO
Subgenus *Clematis*
Section Clematis
    subsection Dioicae ········
Section Lasiantha − − − − − − − −

SUBSECTION DIOICAE (THE AMERICAN UNISEXUALS)

A large group of some 18 species restricted to the Americas and, in many respects, they can be considered the American equivalent of the Vitalba Group. However, the plants are primarily unisexual, bearing either male or female flowers, or occasionally with some male or hermaphrodite flowers on otherwise female plants. They tend to be vigorous plants with rather small, often white or greenish flowers borne in large panicle-like inflorescences. They have been little exploited in cultivation, although a number would make attractive screening plants for temperate and subtropical gardens. As in the Vitalba Group the stamen filaments are slender and glabrous and the achenes hairy.

▼   **Leaves ternate, very occasionally pinnate on the same plant (species 34–40)**
◆   **Leaflets toothed (species 34–36)**
❊   **Male and female flowers borne on the same plant (species 34 & 35)**

34. *Clematis haenkeana* Presl.
(syn. *C. dioica* subsp. *americana sensu* (Herrera) Kuntze, non Mill., *C. sericea* (H. B. K.) Kuntze and subsp. *sericea* (H. B. K. ex DC.) Benoist, *C. d.* var. *brasiliana sensu* Cortés, non Eichler, *C. floribunda* Triana & Planch., *C. goudotiana* Planch. ex Triana &

Planch., *C. grahami* sensu Rusby, non Benth., *C. medusae* Planch. & Linden, *C. populifolia* Turcz., *C. sericea* H. B. K. ex DC., *C. thalictroides* Steud., *C. virginiana* var. *brasiliana* (DC.))

DESCRIPTION. A vigorous monoecious climber to 5 m (16ft), with reddish or yellowish silky-hairy stems, becoming glabrescent eventually. Leaves ternate or pinnate; leaflets 3 or 5, oval, to 17 cm (6.7 in) long and 10 cm (4 in) wide, generally much smaller, with a few coarse serrate teeth, sometimes more or less 3-lobed or entire, with a heart-shaped base, silky-hairy beneath but more or less glabrous above. Flowers borne in lateral or terminal panicle-like cymes to 15 cm (6 in) long, each flower 13–20 mm (0.5–0.8 in) across. Sepals cream or greenish-white, 4, oblong to narrow-obovate, 6.5–9.5 mm (0.26–0.37 in) long, c. 3 mm (0.12 in) wide, wide-spreading to recurved, silky-hairy on both surfaces. Stamens two-thirds as long as, or equal to, the sepals, with glabrous, linear filaments. Achene almost rounded to oval or rhombic, 3–3.5 mm (0.12–0.14 in) long, hairy, with a whitish or yellowish plumose tail to 65 mm (2.6 in) long.

DISTRIBUTION. N Argentina, Bolivia, Brazil, Colombia, Ecuador, S Mexico, Peru, Venezuela; 1700–2800 m (5600–9200 ft).

HABITAT. Forests and forest remnants, bushy places; Feb–May.

35. *Clematis uruboensis* Lourteig

DESCRIPTION. Similar to *C. haenkeana*, but flowers few, often only 3 to a cyme, but larger, 32–40 mm (1.3–1.6 in) across; sepals 4 or 5, 16–20 mm (0.63–0.8 in) long and 4–5 mm (0.16–0.2 in) wide.

DISTRIBUTION. Bolivia; 450 m (1500 ft).

HABITAT. Forest margins and bushy places; Apr.

❉ ❉ **Male and female flowers borne on separate plants (species 36)**

36. *Clematis virginiana* L.*, American Virgin's Bower, Devil's Darning Needle, Woodbine
(syn. *C. bracteata* Moench, *C. cordata* Moench, *C. cordata* Pursh, *C. dioica* subsp. *virginiana* (L.) Kuntze, *C. dominica* Lam., *C. holosericea* Pursh, *C. pennsylvanica* Donn, *C. virginiana* Pursh, *C. virginiana* L. forma *paucidentata* Kuntze, *C. v.* var. *bracteata* Loudon and *cordata* (Pursh) Kuntze)

DESCRIPTION. A vigorous dioecious deciduous climber

to 7 m (23ft) with the young stems 6–12 ribbed and with scattered hairs. Leaves ternate, more rarely 3-lobed or with 5 leaflets, these ovate to heart-shaped, to 100 mm (4 in) long and 75 mm (3 in) wide, with coarse, rather uneven teeth, hairy, sometimes sericeous beneath. Flowers borne in lateral panicle-like cymes to 15 cm (6 in) long, 15–30 mm (0.6–1.2 in) across, star-like, male and female on separate plants. Sepals 4, rarely 5, dull white or cream, elliptical, 6–12 mm (0.24–0.47 in) long, 3–5 mm (0.12–0.2 in) wide, downy outside, spreading widely apart. Stamens about two-thirds the length of the sepals, white. Achenes hairy, with a silvery plumose tail to 50 mm (2 in) long.

DISTRIBUTION. Canada (Manitoba to Nova Scotia) and much of the USA except for the Rocky Mountains westwards; to 410 m (1350 ft).

HABITAT. Open woodland, shrubby places, rocky slopes and canyons, roadsides, riverbanks, generally on moist soils; Aug–Oct.

This is decidedly not a plant for small gardens, being extremely rampant. Even in larger gardens it is perhaps best confined to woodland areas or to the wild garden, although it does not always flower particularly well. However, a well-flowered plant can be most attractive, the numerous flower clusters giving the plant a foamy appearance at a distance. It requires plenty of sunshine if it is to perform at its best.

The leaves of this species are known to cause dermatitis in some susceptible individuals.

H4; P2

◆ ◆ **Leaflets entire; untoothed, although sometimes lobed (species 37–40)**
❀   **Flowers 20–40 mm (0.8–1.6 in) across (species 37)**

37. *Clematis bonariensis* Juss. ex DC.
(syn. *C. dioica* subsp. *normalis* var. *eichleriana* Kuntze, *C. maldonadensis* Larranaga)

DESCRIPTION. An evergreen climber to 5 m (16.5 ft) with slender, ribbed stems, hairy when young. Leaves leathery, ternate, dark green above, paler beneath; leaflets oval to elliptical, 5–11 cm (2–4.3 in) long, 30–55 mm (1.2–2.2 in) wide, the lateral somewhat asymmetrical, with a rounded to heart-shaped base and an acute to somewhat acuminate apex, entire margin, generally with 3–5 main veins from the base. Flowers in small lateral or terminal cymes of 3–7 usually, much shorter than the subtending leaves, unisexual or hermaphrodite, each flower 20–24 mm (0.8–0.95 in) across. Sepals 4, white, elliptic to oblong, 9–11 mm (0.35–0.43 in) long, 2.5–4 mm (0.1–0.16 in) wide, spreading widely apart or somewhat recurved, with an obtuse apex, downy outside but glabrous inside apart form the margin, with 3 veins from the base. Stamens about one-third to a half the length of the sepals. Achene elliptic, 3–3.5 mm (0.12–0.14 in) long, hairy, with a plumose tail to 20 mm (0.8 in) long.

DISTRIBUTION. E Argentina, Brazil, Paraguay, Uruguay; to 900 m (3000 ft).

HABITAT. Forests and forest margins, bushy places; Sept–Nov.

❀ ❀ **Flowers not more than 18 mm (0.7 in) across (species 38–40)**

38. *Clematis dioica* L.

(syn. *C. americana* Mill., *C. dioica* subsp. *normalis* Kuntze, *C. dominica* Lam., *C. glabra* DC., *C. guadeloupae* Pers., *C. havanensis* H. B. K. ex DC., *C. mociniana* G. Don, *C. pallida* A. Rich., *C. polygama* Jacq., *C. rhodocarpa* Rose, *C. rufa* Rose)

DESCRIPTION. A rather variable climber with 6-ribbed stems, usually hairy at first. Leaves generally ternate but occasionally pinnate, thick and leathery; leaflets ovate to elliptic, 20–90 mm (0.8–3.5 in) long, 10–60 mm (0.4–2.4 in) wide, with a heart-shaped base, entire margin and with 3–5 main veins from the base. Flowers male or female, occasional hermaphrodite, borne in lateral or terminal panicle-like cymes 10–40 cm (4–16 in) long, usually multi-flowered, each flower 12–15 mm (0.47–0.6 in) across. Sepals 4, cream to greenish-white, elliptic to oval, 7–8 mm (0.28–0.32 in) long, 2.5–3 mm (0.1–0.12 in) wide, wide-spreading to recurved, silky-hairy outside. Stamens slightly shorter than the sepals. Achene oval to elliptic, c. 4 mm (0.16 in) long, sparsely hairy, with a plumose tail to 45 mm (1.8 in) long.

DISTRIBUTION. Mexico (Guadeloupe) and many Caribbean islands (Greater and Lesser Antilles).

HABITAT. Bushy places and savannah; Aug–May.

A widespread and very variable species. In Mexico a traditional medicine is prepared from the leaves of this species and this is reported to be a cure for various skin disorders, and it is even used as a cosmetic.

var. *australis* **Eichler** (*C. affinis* St. Hil., *C. brasiliana* sensu Hauman, non DC., *C. fluminensis* Velloso, *C. perulata* Kuntze, *c. uruguayensis* Arechavaleta) has

pinnate leaves with usually 3 pairs of lateral leaflets, the lowermost 1–2 pairs generally ternate. Similar distribution to var. *brasiliana* and doubtfully distinct; recorded from N Argentine, S & SW Brazil and the neighbouring parts of Paraguay and Uruguay.

var. *brasiliana* **(DC.) Eichler** (*C. brasiliana* DC., *C. caracasana* Humboldt, *C. caripensis* H. B. K., *C. dioica* subsp. *brasiliana* (DC.) Kuntze, *C. discolor* Gardn., *C. integra* Velloso) has distinguishing pinnate leaves with 5 leaflets and achenes with a tail to 60 mm (2.4 in) long. Distributed in South America from E, C & S Brazil to the neighbouring parts of Paraguay, Argentina, as well as S Bolivia.

var. *acapulcensis* **(Hook. & Arn.) Grey-Wilson, stat. nov.** (syn. *Clematis acapulcensis* Hook. & Arn., *C. barranacae* Jones, *C. dioica* subsp. *acapulcensis* (Hook. & Arn.) Kuntze) has biternate glabrous leaves. Widespread in Central America (Guatemala, Honduras, Mexico, Nicaragua as well as Costa Rica). The relationship of the Central and South American dioecious species needs further detailed research.

39. *Clematis stipulata* **Kuntze**

DESCRIPTION. Similar to *C. dioica*, but leaves 2–3-ternate, the leaflets rather small, not more than 50 mm (2 in) long.

DISTRIBUTION. Costa Rica and Mexico.

40. *Clematis subtriloba* **Nees von Esenbeck ex G. Don**

(syn. *C. sericea* sensu H. B. K. ex Kuntze, non DC., nor Mich., *C. subtriflora* Walp.)

DESCRIPTION. Very similar to *C. dioica*, but stems silky-hairy and leaves always ternate, the leaflets often 3-lobed. In addition, the cymes are small and mostly 3-flowered, not multi-flowered.

DISTRIBUTION. Mexico.

▼ ▼ **Leaves pinnate to bipinnate, occasionally biternate on the same plant (species 41–51)**
❖ **Leaves divided into numerous lobes (species 41)**

41. *Clematis millefoliolata* **Eichler**
(syn. *C. cochabambensis* Rusby)

DESCRIPTION. A climber to 3–4 m (10–13 ft) with whitish or yellowish silky young, ribbed stems. Leaves finely dissected, 2–3-pinnate; leaflets oval, to 30 mm (1.2 in) long and 24 mm (0.95 in) wide, mainly 3-

lobed, silky beneath; lower bracts large and leaf-like but with a single, lobed leaflet 10–20 mm (0.4–0.8 in) long. Flowers borne in lateral cymes, 30–40 mm (1.2–1.6 in) across. Sepals 4–5, yellow or greenish, elliptic, 14–20 mm (0.55–0.8 in) long, 4–9 mm (0.16–0.35 in) wide, grey-woolly all over, especially on the outside. Stamens two-thirds the length of the sepals. Achenes glabrous, with a yellowish plumose tail to 30 mm (1.2 in) long.

DISTRIBUTION. Bolivia and Peru; 3500–4100 m (11,500–13,500 ft).

HABITAT. Low shrubs and grassy places; Dec–Apr.

Clematis cochabambensis Rusby is sometimes separated out as a distinct species; it is said to be a slighter plant in the wild with rather smaller flowers and small linear-lanceolate bracts only 3–4 mm (0.12–0.16 in) long. Intermediates are found in the wild and it is difficult to uphold both species; however, this requires further investigation.

❖ ❖ **Leaves not divided into numerous lobes (species 42–51)**

✳ **Leaflets entire, rarely with a few small marginal teeth (species 42–47)**

✳ **Flowers 40 mm (1.6 in) or more across, pale yellow (species 42)**

42. *Clematis peruviana* DC.
(syn. *C. peruviana* var. *andina* Ball)

DESCRIPTION. Climber with yellowish-green hairy, ribbed young stems. Leaves bipinnate, generally with 3 pairs of primary divisions; leaflets often 3-lobed, to 45 mm (1.8 in) long and 40 mm (1.6 in) wide, the apex pointed to mucronate. Flowers borne in small lateral cymes, often of 2–3, hermaphrodite or male, 40–50 mm (1.6–2 in) across. Sepals 4, pale yellow, elliptic, to 22 mm (0.87 in) long and 10 mm (0.4 in) wide, wide-spreading, downy beneath. Stamens two-thirds the length of the sepals. Achenes oval, glabrous, with a white plumose tail to 60 mm (2.4 in) long.

DISTRIBUTION. Peru; 3000–3500 m (9850–11,500 ft).

HABITAT. Trees and bushes, rocky places; Feb–June.

✳ ✳ **Flowers not more than 36 mm (1.4 in) across, generally smaller, white to greenish or pinkish (species 43–47)**

✪ **Sepals 4–6, white tinged with green or pink (species 43–45)**

43. *Clematis alborosea* Ulbr.

DESCRIPTION. A climber to 2 m (6.6 ft) with hairy, often purplish young stems. Leaves pinnate. Leaflets 5 or 7, oval but rather asymmetrical, to 58 mm (2.3 in) long and 60 mm (2.4 in) wide, usually 3-lobed and with an entire margin. Flowers 20–25 mm (0.8–1 in) across, borne in small lateral cymes. Sepals 4–6, elliptical to narrow-oval, 10–17 mm (0.4–0.67 in) long, 3–7 mm (0.12–0.28 in) wide, white tinged with green or pink, spreading widely apart. Stamens about half the length of the sepals. Achenes compressed-oval, c. 3 mm (0.12 in) long, glabrous, with a yellowish plumose tail to 50 mm (2 in) long.

DISTRIBUTION. Bolivia and Peru; c. 2000 m (6500 ft).

HABITAT. Forests and bushy places; Dec.

44. *Clematis denticulata* Velloso*
(syn. *C. bangii* Rusby, *C. bonariensis* Gillies ex Hook. & Arn., non Juss., *C. d.* subsp. *C.* var. *mendocina* (Phil.) Hauman, *C. d.* var. *brasiliana* Lorentz var. *reducta* Hassler, *C. hilarii* Spreng., *C. h.* var. *guaranitica* St. Hil. & Tul., var. *montevidensis* (Spreng.) Speg. and var. *triloba* (St. Hil.) Speg., *C. mendocina* Philipp, *C. montevidensis* Spreng., *C. m.* var. *denticulata* (Vell.) N. M. Bacigalupo, *C. stroebeliana* sensu Kuntze, non Cesati, *C. triloba* sensu St. Hil., non Heyne ex Roth)

DESCRIPTION. Similar in many respects to *C. dioica*, but leaves generally pinnate with 5 leaflets, or sometimes bipinnate, or with at least the leaflets 2–3-lobed; leaflets to 80 mm (3.2 in) long and 50 mm (2 in) wide, often somewhat asymmetric, rather eucalyptus-like. Flowers greenish-white, generally rather larger, the sepals broad-elliptic, 7–13 mm (0.28–0.51 in) long and 2.5–7 mm (0.1–0.28 in) wide. Achene elliptic, 5–7 mm (0.2–0.28 in) long, hairy, with a whitish or yellowish plumose tail to 10 cm (4 in) long.

DISTRIBUTION. Argentina, Bolivia, Brazil, Chile, Paraguay, Peru, Uruguay.

HABITAT. Forests and bushy places, rocky river and stream margins, hedgerows; Nov–June.

A very widespread South American species which is locally common, particularly in Argentina. Sometimes confused with the equally widespread *C. dioica*, it is readily distinguished by its broad-sepalled flowers and by the very long tails to the achenes. The flowers can be unisexual or hermaphrodite.

var. *ulbrichiana* (Pilger) Lourteig has bipinnate leaves with 3–4 pairs of leaflets. Described from the Itatiaia area of Brazil at c. 2100 m (6900 ft). H8–9; P2

45. *Clematis seemannii* Kuntze

(syn. *C. parvifrons* Ulbr., *C. pseudomicrophylla* Kuntze)

DESCRIPTION. A climber to 2–3 m (6.6–10 ft), with slightly hairy stems that are often flushed with violet-purple. Leaves pinnate or bipinnate, with 2–4 prime divisions, occasionally the uppermost leaves ternate; leaflets small, oval to rounded or lanceolate, 5–35 mm (0.2–1.4 in) long, 4–27 mm (0.16–1.06 in) wide, often with 3 rounded lobes, otherwise entire, slightly hairy to more or less glabrous. Flowers 1–3 borne in lateral cymes , 15–36 mm (0.6–1.4 in) across. Sepals 4–5, greenish-white, ovate, 7–18 mm (0.28–0.7 in) long, 4–10 mm (0.16–0.4 in) wide, wide-spreading, downy inside and along the margin outside. Stamens half to two-thirds the length of the sepals. Achene spindle-shaped, reddish and glabrous, with a yellowish plumose tail to 35 mm (1.4 in) long.

DISTRIBUTION. Peru; c. 2500–3600 m (8200–11,800 ft).

HABITAT. Woodland margins, shrubs and river margins, rocky slopes; Feb–Mar.

✪ ✪ **Sepals always 4, white or ivory (species 46 & 47)**

46. *Clematis campestris* St. Hil.

(syn. *C. dioica* subsp. *campestris* (St. Hil.) Kuntze, *C. d.* var. *brasiliana* Lorentz & var. *campestris* (St. Hil.) Kuntze)

DESCRIPTION. A slender climber to 5 m (16ft); stems generally hairy at first but becoming glabrescent. Leaves pinnate with 5 or 7 leaflets, the basal pair often ternate or 3-lobed; leaflets narrow-elliptic, 20–70 mm (0.8–2.8 in) long, 4–11 mm (0.16–0.43 in) wide, with an acute apex and entire margin. Flowers hermaphrodite, mostly lateral, occasionally terminal, solitary or in cymes of 2–3, much shorter than the subtending leaves, each flower 25–30 mm (1–1.2 in) across. Sepals white, 4–5, rarely 6, oblong to elliptic, 13–15 mm (0.51–0.59 in) long, 4–6 mm (0.16–0.24 in) wide, spreading widely apart to recurved, with an acute or subacute apex, silky-hairy, especially along the margin. Stamens about two-thirds the length of the sepals. Achenes obovate to elliptic, c. 4 mm (0.16 in) long, hairy, with a yellowish or whitish plumose tail.

DISTRIBUTION. E Argentina, Brazil, Paraguay.
HABITAT. Forest margins, bushy places and riversides; Jan–Mar.

47. *Clematis coahuilensis* Keil

DESCRIPTION. Closely related to *C. dioica* but leaves pinnate with 5 or 7 rather small leaflets 20–50 mm (0.8–2 in) long and 10–30 mm (0.4–1.2 in) wide, often 3-lobed, with an entire to toothed margin. The ivory-coloured flowers are somewhat larger, c. 20 mm (0.8 in) across, the sepals about 10 mm (0.4 in) long and 4 mm (0.16 in) wide.

DISTRIBUTION. N Mexico (Coahuila, Durango, Nuevo Leon); 1200–2400 m (3900–7900 ft).

HABITAT. Bushy and rocky places, especially in canyons; June–Sept.

✳ ✳ **Leaflets toothed, often coarsely so (species 48–51)**
✤ **Leaves bipinnate, occasionally biternate (species 48)**

48. *Clematis catesbyana* Pursh

(syn. *C. dioica* subsp. *catesbyana* (Pursh) Kuntze, *C. micrantha* Small, *C. plukenetii* DC., *C. virginiana* (Pursh) Britton)

DESCRIPTION. A climber with slightly and minutely hairy to glabrous young stems and biternate to bipinnate leaves. Leaflets membranous, oval with a heart-shaped base, 30–60 mm (1.2–2.4 in) long and 15–35 mm (0.6–1.4 in) wide, generally with a few coarse teeth or lobes on each side, with 3 veins from the leaf-base. Flowers numerous in lateral cymes, making up leafy panicles, 12–25 mm (0.47–1 in) across, hermaphrodite or male. Sepals 4, white, narrow-oval, 6–12 mm (0.24–0.47 in) long, spreading. Stamens about two-thirds the length of the sepals. Achenes oval, hairy, c. 4 mm (0.16 in) long, with a silky plumose tail.

DISTRIBUTION. C & S USA (Virginia and Georgia to Louisiana, South Carolina, Oklahoma, Kansas and Florida).

HABITAT. Open woodland and bushy places; July–Aug.

Occasionally cultivated but not a particularly distinguished clematis in gardens. *C. micrantha* Small, which is restricted to Florida, is sometimes separated out on account of its small flowers (only 5–6.5 mm (0.2–0.26 in) across) and small achenes (not more than 3.5 mm (0.14 in) long), but it is doubtfully distinct, although it may warrant varietal recognition.

H8

11. Clematis ligusticifolia in cultivation. Photo: Christopher Grey-Wilson

12. Clematis lasiantha, Tulare County, California. Photo: Phil Phillips

❖ ❖ Leaves once pinnate (species 49–51)
◇ Flowers small, not more than 15 mm (0.6 in) across, greenish-white (species 49)

49. *Clematis grossa* Benth.

DESCRIPTION. A vigorous climber with 6-ribbed stems, hairy when young. Leaves pinnate, or ternate at the base of the inflorescences. Leaflets 5, heart-shaped, 40–70 mm (1.6–2.8 in) long and 30–45 (–60) mm (1.2–1.8 (–2.4) in) wide, coarsely toothed and often slightly lobed, sparsely hairy above, but dense silky-hairy beneath, with the margin ciliate. Inflorescence many-flowered, lateral cymes or terminal panicles; flowers 10–15 mm (0.4–0.6 in) across, male and female on separate plants. Sepals 4, white flushed with green, narrow-oval with a blunt apex, 7–10 mm (0.28–0.4 in) long, 2–3 mm (0.08–0.12 in) wide, downy on both surfaces, particularly on the outside and in bud. Stamens about two-thirds the length of the sepals. Achenes broad-elliptical, compressed, hairy, c. 3 mm (0.12 in) long, with a silky plumose tail to 40 mm (1.6 in) long.

DISTRIBUTION. Mexico.

HABITAT. Forest margins, wooded ravines and riverbanks; Aug–Nov.

◇ ◇ Flowers at least 15 mm (0.6 in) across, white (species 50 & 51)

50. *Clematis drummondii* Torr. & Gray
(syn. *C. nervata* Benth.)

DESCRIPTION. A dioecious deciduous climber with ribbed, hairy stems and pinnate leaves. Leaflets 5 or 7, oval to almost rhombic, often 3-lobed, the margin generally toothed. Flowers 15–28 mm (0.6–0.87 in) across, borne in lateral cymes. Sepals 4, white, oval, 8–14 mm (0.32–0.55 in) long, 4–6 mm (0.16–0.24 in) wide, spreading widely apart. Stamens slightly shorter than the sepals, with linear filaments. Achenes elliptical, 3–4 mm (0.12–0.16 in) long, hairy, with a plumose tail to 10 cm (4 in) long.

DISTRIBUTION. S & SW USA (Arizona, California, New Mexico, Texas) and N Mexico (Coahuila).
HABITAT. Bushy and rocky places, canyons, sandy woodland; Apr–Sept.

51. *Clematis ligusticifolia* Nutt. ex Torr. & Gray*
(syn. *C. dioica* subsp. *cordata* sensu Kuntze, non Pursh, *C. ligusticifolia* var. *brevifolia* Torr. & Gray and var. *californica* Watson, *C. neomexicana* Wooton & Standley)

DESCRIPTION. A vigorous deciduous climber to 10 m (33 ft), with ribbed stems, often suffused with purple and downy when young. Leaves bright, rather shiny green, pinnate, with 5 or 7 oblong to lanceolate leaflets, to 50 mm (2 in) long and 30 mm (1.2 in) wide, often 3-lobed or sometimes ternate, hairy on the veins above and beneath (or even downy) or more or less glabrous beneath, with 3 or 5 veins from the base. Flowers borne in lax lateral cymes, with long slender pedicels, male and female on separate plants, 15–25 mm (0.6–1 in) across. Sepals 4, pure white, elliptical, to 13 mm (0.5 in) long and 5 mm (0.2 in) wide, spreading widely apart, downy on both surfaces. Stamens with white anthers, glabrous. Achenes hairy, with a plumose tail to 40 mm (1.6 in) long.

DISTRIBUTION. CW and S USA (Montana, Idaho and North Dakota south to California, New Mexico, Utah, Nevada), Canada (S British Colombia) and N Mexico; mainly 500–2600 m (1650–8500 ft).

HABITAT. Woodland, particularly of conifers (*Juniperus, Pinus*) and oak, or bushy places, stream banks and rocks; Aug–Oct.

This species is sometimes seen in cultivation but it is rather vigorous and seldom produces the impact of bloom of some of its allies, indeed in Britain at least, the flower display can generally be described as spartan. In overall appearance it has the look of *C. vitalba* but it is a poor relation in the garden, although it is moderately attractive as a woodland plant.

Clematis neomexicana described from New Mexico ('upper Sonoran zone' in canyons at 1300–2300 m (4300–7550 ft)) appears to be little more than an ecological variant, growing no more than 2 m (6.6 ft) in height. It may be worth of varietal recognition.

H5; P2

SECTION LASIANTHA

52. *Clematis lasiantha* Nutt. ex Torr. & Gray*

DESCRIPTION. Dioecious subshrub or deciduous climber to 5 m (16ft), occasionally more, with ribbed stems, silky-hairy when young. Leaves ternate, occasionally pinnate with 5 leaflets, and rather papery. Leaflets ovate, 25–40 mm (1–1.6 in) long, 15–35 mm (0.6–1.4 in) wide, often with a slightly heart-shaped base, coarsely toothed and often 3-lobed, glabrous above but silky-hairy beneath, especially along the veins. Flowers male or hermaphrodite, borne in lateral

13. *Clematis lasiantha* (male plant), Tulare County, California.
Photo: Phil Phillips

cymes of 2–5, or solitary, each flower long-stalked and 25–45 mm (1–1.8 in) across. Sepals white or cream, oval to ovate, 12–20 mm (0.47–0.8 in) long, 4–10 mm (0.16–0.4 in) wide, silky-hairy all over, more densely so beneath. Stamens about half the length of the sepals. Achene ovate, hairy, with a yellowish or whitish plumose tail to 40 mm (1.6 in) long.

DISTRIBUTION. SW USA (W & C California) and Baja California; 500–1500 m (1650–4950 ft).
HABITAT. Mixed chaparral and scrub; Mar–May.

Clematis lasiantha often grows in the wild with other typical chaparral plants such as *Ceanothus, Ceratocarpus, Salvia*. In the wild it has a long summer dormancy coming back into growth at the end of the hot Californian summer and the arrival of rain. The individual flowers are quite large and a plant in full flower can be very impressive; however, it rarely performs particularly well in temperate gardens. It should certainly be more often planted in subtropical and Mediterranean-type gardens.

H8; P1

53. *Clematis pauciflora* Nutt. ex Torr. & Gray*
(syn. *C. lasiantha* subsp. *pauciflora* (Nutt.) Kuntze,
C. nuttallii K. Koch)

DESCRIPTION. Like a scaled-down version of *C.
lasiantha*, not more than 3 m (10 ft) with pinnate or
ternate leaves, the leaflets generally smaller, not more
than 25 mm (1 in) long and wide, with a wedge-
shaped, rounded or heart-shaped base. Flowers white,
smaller, 10–27 mm (0.4–1.1 in) across, more or less
glabrous inside. Achene ovate, glabrous, with a
greyish or whitish plumose tail to 30 mm (1.2 in) long.

DISTRIBUTION. SW USA (S California) and N Baja
California; 450–2210 m (1500–7250 ft).

HABITAT. Chaparral and other bushy places; Jan–Apr.

This species requires similar conditions to *C.
lasiantha*, but is scarcely as good a garden plant.

H9; P1

SECTION NARAVELIOPSIS

This interesting section contains some 17 species that are
scattered through India, China, Japan and south-eastern
Asia. As a group they are little known in our gardens but,
if seed is available, they certainly should be considered
for warmer gardens, especially in Mediterranean and
subtropical regions. They are essentially similar in
general appearance to the Vitalbas, bearing plenty of
rather small, often white, hermaphrodite flowers, with the
sepals spreading widely apart. The prime difference is to
be seen in the stamens of Section Narveliopsis which
have a pronounced (although small) appendage on the tip
of the anther; this is formed by an extension of the
connective. In addition, some of the outer stamens are
often transferred into linear, sterile, staminodes.

▼   **Flowers small, the sepals 7–17 mm (0.28–0.67 in)
    long (species 54–61)**
◆   **Leaves simple (species 54)**

54. *Clematis metouensis* M. Y. Fang

DESCRIPTION. Like *C. smilacifolia* (p.56) but the flowers
are yellow and always 4-sepalled, borne on glabrous
pedicels. In addition, the outer stamens have been
transformed into linear staminodes; flowers 22–32 mm
(0.87–1.3 in) across, with the sepals wide-spreading.
The simple leathery leaves are ovate, to 14.5 cm (5.7 in)
long and 12.6 cm (5 in) wide, with a rounded to slightly

heart-shaped, somewhat peltate base.

DISTRIBUTION. W China (SE Tibet; Mêdog Xian);
800–860 m (2600–2800 ft).

HABITAT. Mixed forests and forest margins; Aug–Sept.

◆ ◆   **Leaves ternate to pinnate or bipinnate
    (species 55–61)**
✳   **Leaves ternate (species 55–58)**
❀   **Main veins arising from the base of the leaflet
    (species 55–57)**

55. *Clematis antonii* (Elmer) H. Eichler
(syn. *Naravelia antonii* Elmer, *N. philippinensis*
Merrill)

DESCRIPTION. A dioecious climber with 16–20-ribbed
stems and ternate leaves. Leaflets ovate with a rounded
or slightly heart-shaped base, 7–12 cm (2.8–4.7 in)
long and 4–7.5 cm (1.6–3 in) wide, leathery, with an
entire margin and 5 or 7 main veins from the base.
Flowers borne in large leafy panicle-like racemes,
composed of a number of lateral cymes, each flower
about 15 mm (0.6 in) across. Sepals 4, brownish-
downy outside but yellowish-downy inside, elliptical,
7–8 mm (0.28–0.32 in) long, 3.5 mm (0.14 in) wide,
pointed, wide-spreading. Stamens (male flowers) half
to two-thirds the length of the sepals, the connective
projecting by 0.75–2 mm (0.03–0.08 in). Achenes
elliptical, c. 5 mm (0.2 in) long, yellowish or reddish-
brown hairy like the plumose tail.

DISTRIBUTION. Philippines (Luzon, Mindanao);
800–1200 m (2600–3900 ft).

HABITAT. Forests and shrubberies; July–Sept.

56. *Clematis herrei* H. Eichler

DESCRIPTION. A vigorous climber to 6 m (20 ft), with 12-
ribbed stems and ternate leaves. Leaflets oval to elliptical,
50–85 mm (2–3.3 in) long and 25–45 mm (1–1.8 in) wide,
with a rounded base and entire margin, usually with 3 or 5
veins from the base. Flowers borne in small lateral cymes,
often 3-flowered, c. 25 mm (1 in) across. Sepals 4, oblong,
12–14 mm (0.47–0.55 in) long and 3–4 mm (0.12–0.16 in)
wide, brown-downy outside but violet-purple and glabrous
inside. Stamens about as long as the sepals, with the
connective projecting for c. 3 mm (0.12 in). Achenes with
a plumose tail at least 35 mm (1.4 in) long.

DISTRIBUTION. Philippines (Negros).

HABITAT. Forests and bushy places; probably May–June.

57. *Clematis macgregorii* Merrill

DESCRIPTION. Dioecious climber with 12- or 18-ribbed rather slender stems. Leaves ternate. Leaflets usually heart-shaped, sometimes with a rather truncated base, with an entire to toothed margin and 5 or 7 veins from the base. Flowers borne in lateral cymes of up to 7, either male or female, 15–36 mm (0.6–1.4 in) across, the female flowers rather fewer and larger than the male. Sepals oval, 7–18 mm (0.28–0.7 in) long (generally not more than 12 mm (0.47 in) long in male flowers) and 2.5–3 mm (0.1–0.12 in) wide, spreading, downy outside, finely hairy to almost glabrous inside. Stamens 25 or more, longer than the sepals; in female flowers replaced by up to 8 staminodes that are slightly shorter than the sepals.

DISTRIBUTION. Philippines (N Luzon); c. 2000 m (6500 ft).

HABITAT. Moss forests.

❀ ❀ **Main veins not arising from the base of the leaflet; main veins pinnately arranged (species 58)**

58. *Clematis petelotii* Gagn.

DESCRIPTION. Similar to *C. smilacifolia* but leaves always ternate, the leaflets oblong, to 13 cm (5 in) long and 7 cm (2.8 in) wide, with a narrowed base, the main veins pinnately arranged, not arising from the base of the leaf-blade. In addition, the flowers are rather smaller, the 4 sepals 14–15 mm (0.55–0.59 in) long and 7–8 mm (0.28–0.32 in) wide.

DISTRIBUTION. N Vietnam (Hao-binh).

❊ ❊ **Leaves pinnate to bipinnate; rarely biternate in *C. menglaensis* (species 59–61)**
❖ **Flowers white (species 59)**

59. *Clematis menglaensis* M. C. Chang

DESCRIPTION. A woody climber with 14-furrowed glabrous stems and pinnate, bipinnate or biternate leaves. Leaflets papery, ovate to almost oblong, 25–70 mm (1–2.8 in) long, 12–40 mm (0.47–1.6 in) wide, with an untoothed margin and acute apex. Inflorescence lateral and panicle-like, with normally 7–14 flowers, each 20–25 mm (0.8–1 in) across. Sepals 4, white, spreading widely apart, oblong, 9–12 mm (0.35–0.47 in) long, and c. 4 mm (0.16 in) wide, acute. Stamens about two-thirds the length of the sepals, the connectives with a short, c. 0.4 mm (0.016 in) long, extension.

DISTRIBUTION. SW China (S & SE Yunnan); 800–1100 m (2600–3600 ft).

HABITAT. Shrubberies and open forest; Oct–Nov.

A little-known and improperly understood species described from the Mengla Xian in southern Yunnan in 1980.

❖ ❖ **Flowers brownish or violet-purple (species 60–61)**

60. *Clematis bourdillonii* Dunn

DESCRIPTION. An evergreen climber with multi-ribbed, somewhat downy, stems. Leaves thinly-leathery, pinnate to bipinnate, the leaflets elliptical to oval, 60–90 mm (2.4–3.6 in) long and 28–45 mm (1.1–1.8 in) wide, with a wedge-shaped base, with 5 or 7 main veins, and an entire margin. Flowers borne in lateral or terminal clusters, c. 20 mm (0.8 in) across. Sepals 4, oblong to lanceolate, 10–12 mm (0.4–0.47 in) long and 1.5–4 mm (0.06–0.16 in) wide, downy outside and along the margin, but glabrous inside, spreading widely apart. Stamens half to two-thirds the length of the sepals, the connective projecting by 1–2 mm (0.04–0.08 in).

DISTRIBUTION. SW India (Kerala); at rather low altitudes.

HABITAT. Evergreen forests; Apr–May.

61. *Clematis papillosa* H. Eichler

DESCRIPTION. A vigorous ?evergreen climber with ridged stems and pinnate leaves. Leaflets 5 or 7, oval to lanceolate, 80–140 mm (3.2–5.5 in) long, 45–80 mm (1.8–3.2 in) wide, with an entire margin and usually 3 or 5 veins from the rounded base. Flowers 20–24 mm (0.8–0.95 in) across, in lax slender lateral cymes to 60 mm (2.4 in) long. Sepals 4, brownish outside, brown with a violet-purple tinge inside, oblong, 10–14 mm (0.4–0.55 in) long, 3–4 mm (0.12–0.16 in) wide, spreading, finely downy. Stamens numerous, almost the length of the sepals. Fruits not known.

DISTRIBUTION. S Malaya (Taiping southwards), Sumatra.

▼ ▼ **Flowers large, the sepals 18–40 mm (0.7–1.6 in)
long (species 62–71)**
✳ **Sepals white (species 62–64)**
✳ **Leaves simple, finely toothed; stamens hairy
(species 62)**

62. *Clematis liboensis* Z. R. Xu

DESCRIPTION. A woody climber to 5 m (16ft), with
glabrous stems. Leaves simple and glabrous, broad-
ovate, 45–100 mm (1.8–4 in) long and 35–60 mm
(1.4–2.4 in) wide, almost leathery, with a slightly
heart-shaped base and a finely toothed margin.
Flowers in rather raceme-like 5-flowered cymes, each
flower 50–70 mm (2–2.8 in) across. Sepals 6, white,
wide-spreading, narrow-oblong, 25–35 mm (1–1.4 in)
long and 3–5 mm (0.12–0.2 in) wide, with a velvety
reddish-brown down beneath. Stamens finely hairy,
about one-third the length of the sepals, but the outer
transformed into glabrous linear staminodes which are
slightly longer than the sepals, but only 1–2 mm
(0.04–0.08 in) wide, and often flushed with purple at
the tip. The achenes are hairy with a plumose tail.

DISTRIBUTION. CS China (SE Guizhou; Libo Xian); c.
800 m (2600 ft).
HABITAT. Forests over limestone; Apr.

This interesting, yet little-known species, was only
described in 1988. It has a number of unique
characters for a member of the Section Narveliopsis.
Foremost are the long narrow staminodes which
exceed the sepals in length, and the finely pubescent
stamens. No other member of the section possesses
hairy stamens and this has to be considered a derived
character.

✳ ✳ **Leaves ternate to pinnate, with entire margins;
stamens glabrous (species 63 & 64)**

63. *Clematis filamentosa* Dunn

DESCRIPTION. Similar to *C. crassipes* with ternate
leaves, but the leaflets are papery rather than leathery
and the flowers smaller and white, 20–40 mm (0.8–1.6
in) across. A prominent feature of the flowers are the
outer stamens which have been transformed into linear
staminodes, 10–15 mm (0.4–0.6 in) long, twice the
length of the fertile stamens within.

DISTRIBUTION. S China (Guangdong, Guangxi, Hainan,
including Hong Kong); to 1600 m (5250 ft).

HABITAT. Forest, shrubberies and streamsides; Nov–Dec.

64. *Clematis loureiriana* DC.
(syn. *C. dioica* sensu Lour., non L.)

DESCRIPTION. Similar to *C. menglaensis* but leaves 1-
ternate or 1-pinnate, the leaflets elliptical, often with a
heart-shaped base and with 5–7 main veins from the
base. The flowers are also white, but somewhat larger,
35–40 mm (1.4–1.6 in) across, with 4 spreading
sepals. In addition, the species appear to be dioecious,
with separate male and female plants.

DISTRIBUTION. SE China (Guangxi, possibly also on
Hainan) and N Vietnam.

HABITAT. Forests and shrubberies; Nov–Dec.

✳ ✳ **Sepals not white, often yellowish, brownish,
purplish or purple-violet (species 65–71)**
✪ **Leaves simple; ternate in *C. smilacifolia* subsp.
munroiana (species 65 & 66)**

65. *Clematis fulvicoma* Rehd. & Wils.

DESCRIPTION. Similar to *C. smilacifolia*, but the simple
leaves are conspicuously net-veined (reticulate) on both
surfaces and always have an entire margin. In addition,
the flowers look entirely different, being somewhat
larger 45–60 mm (1.8–2.4 in) across, with the 6 sepals
(24–37 mm (0.95–1.46 in) long and 4–5 mm (0.16–0.2
in) wide) which are conspicuous clothed in a dense
velvet of brown or reddish-brown hairs. Achenes
narrow-rhombic, 6–7 mm (0.24–0.28 in) long, with a
yellowish plumose tail 40–70 mm (1.6–2.8 in) long.

DISTRIBUTION. Burma, SW China (S Yunnan), N Laos
and N Thailand; 1000–3000 m (3300–9850 ft).

HABITAT. Open forest and forest margins, shrubberies;
Oct–Dec.

66. *Clematis smilacifolia* Wall.*
(syn. *C. everetti* Hemsl., *C. glandulosa* Bl.,
C. loureiriana sensu Merrill, non DC., *C. smilaccensis*
Bl., *C. smilacina* Bl., *C. zollingeri* Turcz.)

DESCRIPTION. A very vigorous evergreen climber to 10 m
(33 ft) with ribbed stems. Leaves simple, glabrous,
broad-ovate, 6–18 cm (2.4–7 in) long, 5–12 cm (2–4.7
in) wide, occasionally larger (especially on young
plants), the base rounded to somewhat heart-shaped, the
apex acute to somewhat acuminate, with an entire to
irregularly toothed margin, 5–7-veined from the base,
dark green, sometimes with paler green spots or stripes;
petiole 30–80 mm (1.2–3.2 in) long. Flowers few (3–7

usually) in lateral cymes or in many-flowered terminal panicles, upright. Sepals 4, rarely 5–8, dark violet or violet-purple, narrow-oblong to ovate, 18–25 mm (0.7–1 in) long, 4–5 mm (0.16–0.2 in) wide, brown-velvety outside, with parallel veins, the margin often somewhat revolute; pedicels rusty-downy. Stamens a quarter to half the length of the sepals, with dark brown or whitish filaments and yellow anthers. Achene elliptic to rhombic, 6.5–8 mm (0.26–0.32 in) long, with a whitish or golden plumose tail 50–70 mm (2–2.8 in) long.

DISTRIBUTION. S & SW China (S Guangdong, Guangxi, S Guizhou, Hainan, SE Tibet, S Yunnan), NE India (Assam), Myanmar, E Nepal, Thailand, Vietnam and much of Malaysia (especially Java and Sumatra, but apparently absent from Borneo); 1000–2300 m (3300–7550 ft).

HABITAT. Subtropical broad-leaved and evergreen oak forests, bamboo thickets and scrub: July–Nov (flowering towards the end of the year in the north of its distribution).

var. *subpeltata* (Wall.) Kuntze (*C. esquirolii* Lévl. & Vaniot, *C. loureiriana* DC. var. *peltata* W. T. Wang and var. *subpeltata* (Wall.) Hand.-Mazz., *C. subpeltata* Wall.) is similar to the typical plant (var. *smilacifolia*) but the leaves are subpeltate to peltate with the petiole inserted at the leaf-base up to 15 mm (0.6 in) from the margin. The flowers are slightly larger with sepals to 30 mm (1.2 in) long and 7 mm (0.28 in) wide) and nearly always 4 per flower. Widespread from S China (W Guangxi, Guizhou and Yunnan) to Myanmar, Thailand, Laos, Vietnam, Java, Sumatra and the Celebes, to 1600 m (5250 ft). A rather poorly defined variety.

subsp. *andamanica* (Kapoor) Grey-Wilson stat. nov. (*C. smilacifolia* var. *andamanica* Kapoor) has larger and broader leaves, 4–29 cm (1.6–11.4 in) long and 1.8–14 cm (0.7–5.5 in) wide and rather smaller flowers with 4 sepals 16–19 mm (0.63–0.75 in) long. In addition, the stamens are noticeably shorter with the filaments no more than 6 mm (0.24 in) long, but with larger anthers, 4–6.5 mm (0.16–0.26 in) long (only 2–3.5 mm (0.08–0.14 in) long in the others). Var. *andamanica* is, as the name implies, endemic to the Andaman islands where it can be found in flower from September to October.

subsp. *munroiana* (Wight) Kuntze* (syn. *C. andersonii* (Clarke ex Kuntze) H. Eichl., *C. munroiana* Wight, *C. smilacifolia* subsp. *andersonii* Clarke ex Kuntze) has primarily ternate leaves; leaflets ovate to lanceolate, 28–120 mm (1.1–4.7 in) long, 8–78 mm (0.3–3.1 in) wide, with an entire or toothed margin. Lower bracts in the inflorescence simple but large and leaf-like. Sepals

very variable in size, 18–28 mm (0.7–1.1 in) long, 2–10 mm (0.08–0.4 in) wide. Widespread on the Indian subcontinent from southern Sikkim in the north to Madras and the Nilghiri Hills in the south, east to Assam, where it inhabits warm broad-leaved forests and flowering from July to October. *C. andersonii* is sometimes separated out and differs only in having marginally larger leaflets that are often more markedly toothed, and flowers often with 5 or 6 sepals. However, there is considerable overlap between the two. Available in the trade as *C. smilacifolia* subsp. *andersonii*.

✿ ✿ **Leaves ternate to pinnate (species 67–71)**
❖   **Sepals 35 mm (1.4 in) long or more (species 67)**

67. *Clematis korthalsii* H. Eichler

(syn. *C. coriacea* sensu Korthals, non DC., *C. smilacifolia* subsp. *normalis* var. *coriacea* (Korth.) Kuntze, *C. s.* var. *stipulata* Miq.)

DESCRIPTION. A vigorous climber to 16 m (52.5 ft), with 18-ribbed stems. Leaves ternate or pinnate, with 3 or 5 leaflets, with the leaf-petioles broadened and winged at the base, each pair fused around the stem at the node; leaflets ovate, 40–90 mm (1.6–3.5 in) long, 25–50 mm (1–2 in) wide, with a rounded or heart-shaped base and acute apex, 3–5-veined from the base, the margin entire. Flowers lateral, solitary or 2–3 in a cyme. Sepals 4, dark violet-purple inside and glabrous, velvety-brown outside, narrow-oblong, 35–40 mm (1.4–1.6 in) long, 6–7 mm (0.24–0.28 in) wide. Stamens about half the length of the sepals. Achenes elliptic to ovate, c. 7.5 mm (0.3 in) long, brownish-hairy, with a plumose tail 70–90 mm (2.8–3 in) long.

DISTRIBUTION. W Java; 1300–1500 m (4300–4950 ft).

HABITAT. Rain forests and forest margins.

❖ ❖ **Sepals 18–35 mm (0.7–1.4 in) long (species 68–71)**
✧   **Flowers yellow (species 68)**

68. *Clematis pianmaensis* W. T. Wang

DESCRIPTION. Similar to *C. menglaensis* but with strictly pinnate leaves, each with 5 leaflets, and larger, yellow, 4-sepalled flowers, 50–70 mm (2–2.8 in) across. The sepals are lanceolate, 27–35 mm (1.1–1.4 in) long and 8–10 mm (0.32–0.39 in) wide, with a dense yellowish down beneath.

DISTRIBUTION. SW China (W Yunnan; Lushui Xian); c. 2000 m (6500 ft).

HABITAT. Forest margins and scrub; Sept.

◇ ◇ **Flowers violet-purple, purple or brownish-gold (species 69–71)**

69. *Clematis crassipes* **Chun & How**

DESCRIPTION. A woody climber with 8-ridged, glabrous stems. Leaves ternate, leathery and glabrous, the leaflets ovate, to 10 cm (4 in) long and 9 cm (3.5 in) wide, though often smaller, with an entire or slightly crenulate margin. Flowers in 3–10-flowered lateral cymes, each flower 55–65 mm (2.2–2.6 in) across, borne on glabrous pedicels. Sepals 6, purple, spreading widely apart, oblong to ovate, 28–32 mm (1.1–1.3 in) long, 13–15 mm (0.51–0.59 in) wide, obtuse, downy beneath. Stamens about half the length of the sepals, the anthers with a pronounced apiculum 1–5 mm (0.04–0.2 in) long. Achenes narrow-rhombic, 5–6 mm (0.2–0.24 in) long, with a plumose tail to 50 mm (2 in) long.
DISTRIBUTION. SE China (SW Guangxi, Hainan).

HABITAT. Scrub and grassy slopes; May–June.

var. *pubipes* **W. T. Wang** is distinguished by possessing densely appressed-hairy pedicels and 4-sepalled flowers. Restricted to the Shangsi Xian in S Guangxi.

70. *Clematis tashiroi* **Maxim.***
(syn. *C. longisepala* Hayata, *C. tozanensis* Hayata, *C. yingtzulinia* Ying)

DESCRIPTION. Similar to *C. crassipes* but leaves usually pinnate, occasionally ternate, the 3 or 5 leaflets papery, the petiole expanded at the base and fused with the opposing petiole of the leaf-pair. The flowers are 30–50 (–60) mm (1.2–2 (–2.4) in) across, with 4–6 dark purple spreading sepals; anthers with a short apiculum, not more than 1 mm (0.05 in) long.

DISTRIBUTION. Japan (Ryukyu Is; Amami-Oshima, Okinawa) and Taiwan; 700–2800 m (2300–9200 ft).

HABITAT. Forest and stream margins, banks and beaches; Aug–Oct.

H6; P2

71. *Clematis theobromina* **Dunn**

DESCRIPTION. A vigorous climber with multi-ribbed stems and usually ternate, rarely simple, rather leathery leaves. Leaflets elliptical to oblong with a rounded or heart-shaped base, 22–120 mm (0.9–4.7 in) long and 10–70 mm (0.4–2.8 in) wide, entire, with 5, 7 or 9 veins from the base. Flowers in small cymes, often of 3 flowers, either lateral or terminal to the shoot, 36–55 mm (1.42–2.2 in) across. Sepals dark brown downy outside, golden with reddish-brown hairs within, 4–6, oval to lanceolate, 16–26 mm (0.63–1.02 in) long, 3–8 mm (0.12–0.32 in) wide, spreading. Stamens about two-thirds the length of the sepals.

DISTRIBUTION. S India (Nilghiri Hills); 1829–2134 m (6000–7000 ft).

SECTION ASPIDANTHERA

This interesting section comprises all the clematis species in Australasia, New Guinea, the Celebes and surrounding islands. The species primarily have white or greenish flowers, with male and female flowers on separate plants (dioecious) although they may be andro-dioecious or polygamo-dioecious. In many respects they closely match the New Zealand species of Section Novae-Zeelandiae. However, there are two fundamental differences: in the latter the sepals are always imbricate in bud, whilst in Section Aspidanthera they are clearly valvate; in Aspidanthera the connective of the anthers projects out at the end as a long pointed appendage, whereas in the Novae-Zeelandiae the species have no apparent projection of the connectives.

SUBSECTION ASPIDANTHERA (THE AUSTRALIAN GROUP)

The eight species of this subsection, which are primarily restricted to Australia, have flowers with 4, rarely 5, sepals and leaves that are simple or trifoliate in the main. They include a number of very garden-worthy species, particularly some of the forms of *C. aristata*, which are widely grown in Australia, at least. None are particularly hardy in temperate gardens but revel in those that can boast a Mediterranean-type climate. To ensure seed set, both male and female plants need to be grown in close proximity but beware, they cross readily with other species in the subsection.

▼ **Plants herbaceous, with non-climbing stems; leaves simple (species 72)**

72. *Clematis gentianoides* **DC.***, Bushy Clematis
(syn. *C. aristata* subsp. *gentianoides* Kuntze)

DESCRIPTION. A herbaceous perennial or subshrub to 50 cm (20 in) tall and 1.5 m (5 ft) across but sometimes as low as 20 cm (8 in), with the slender stems arising as tufts from a branched underground rhizome. Leaves deep green, simple, oval to ovate-lanceolate, 20–80 mm (0.8–3.2 in) long, with an entire to toothed margin, 3-veined. Flowers in terminal cymes, usually of 3–5, each 30–50 mm (1.2–2 in) across, starry, the female flowers with spreading staminodes, faintly scented; bracts leaf-like. Sepals white, often flushed with purple in bud, usually 4 but occasionally up to 8, linear-oval to linear-lanceolate, pointed, 20–30 mm (0.8–1.2 in) long. Achenes with a plumose tail to 30 mm (1.2 in) long.

DISTRIBUTION. Tasmania.

HABITAT. Open forests and rocky slopes, widespread; Sept–Nov (Apr–May in cultivation, northern hemisphere). An interesting herbaceous species which is hardy in the mildest areas and will certainly put up with some frost (to –10°C (14°F)) provided that the plants are not too wet during the winter months. Elsewhere it responds well to pot culture: the pots can be placed outdoors in the summer, but kept in a frost-free environment over-winter. Plants are quite variable from seed, and the larger and better-flowered forms are best selected carefully from any batch. It flowers over an extended season that will often last three months or more. The most distinctive of the Australasian species and the only one with simple, undivided leaves.

var. *procumbens* (Kuntze) Domin* (syn. *C. aristata* subsp. *procumbens* Kuntze, *C. gentianoides* var.

scandens Gunn) has spreading procumbent to somewhat ascending stems and entire margined leaves. This is the usual form seen in cultivation.

var. *tasmanica* (Kuntze) Domin (syn. *C. aristata* subsp. *tasmanica* Kuntze) has ternately or biternately lobed leaves with entire margins and rather larger flowers with the sepals up to 40 mm (1.6 in) long.

H8; P2

▼ ▼ **Plants vigorous climbers; leaves ternately divided (species 73–78)**
◆ **Anthers without a terminal appendage (species 73)**

73. *Clematis fawcetii* F. Muell.
(syn. *C. hexapetala* subsp. *colensoi* var. *fawcetti* Kuntze, *C. microphylla* var. *fawcetti* F. M. Bailey)

DESCRIPTION. A vigorous climber to 15 m (50 ft), although generally only 5–10 m (16–33 ft), with biternate leaves. Leaflets ovate to lanceolate, 20–40 mm (0.8–1.6 in) long, with an irregular and deeply incised dentate margin. Flowers borne in small lateral cymes with up to 5 flowers, at the upper nodes, 20–25 mm (0.8–1 in) across. Sepals white, linear-lanceolate, 10–12 mm (0.4–0.47 in) long and 2.5 mm (0.1 in) wide. Anthers without an appendage.

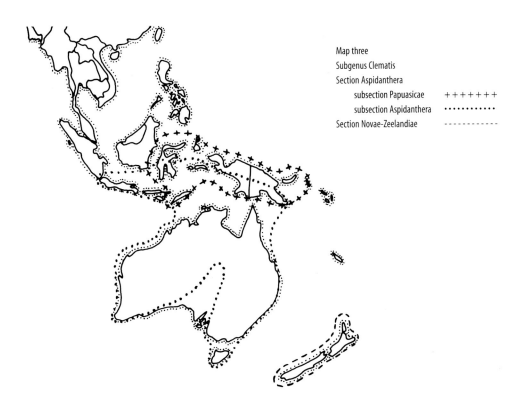

Map three
Subgenus Clematis
Section Aspidanthera
    subsection Papuasicae   +++++++
    subsection Aspidanthera   ··········
Section Novae-Zeelandiae   - - - - - - - - - - -

14. *Clematis gentianoides* (female plant) in cultivation.
Photo: Christopher Grey-Wilson

DISTRIBUTION. Australia (New South Wales, S Queensland).

HABITAT. Upland forests and scrub, rather uncommon; Sept–Oct.

Rather similar to *C. aristata* but far more limited in distribution, this species has rather spidery flowers with very slender sepals. It can be at once distinguished on close examination by the lack of anther appendages that are typical of Section Aspidanthera.

forma *colorata* (F. M. Bailey) Domin (syn. *C. microphylla* var. *colorata* F. M. Bailey) has flowers flushed with purple-red. S Queensland (Killarney).

◆ ◆ **Anthers with a terminal appendage (species 74–78)**
❊ **Stems and leaves hairy, often densely so (species 74)**

74. *Clematis gilbertiana* Turcz.*, Western Clematis (syn. *C. aristata* var. *occidentalis* Benth., *C. a.* var.

pubescens (Huegel ex Endl.) Domin., *C. a.* var. *pubescens* sensu F. v. Muell., *C. elliptica* mss!, *C. indivisa* sensu Steud., non Willd., *C. pubescens* sensu Huegel ex Endl., non Benth.)

DESCRIPTION. Similar to *C. aristata* but the young stems and leaves very hairy; leaves ternate, dull green, with narrow-ovate, toothed, leaflets up to 60 mm (2.4 in) long and 15 mm (0.6 in) wide. Flowers rather smaller, 20–40 mm (0.8–1.6 in) across. Achenes ovate, with a plumose tail 30–40 mm (1.2–1.6 in) long.

DISTRIBUTION. Western Australia.

HABITAT. Dry forests, especially Karri; Aug–Nov (Feb–early Apr in cultivation, northern hemisphere).

Often treated as a variety (var. *pubescens*) of *C. aristata* but the two are at least geographically distinct and are probably best treated as two closely allied species. Two formas (forma *oblongisepala* and forma *stenosepala*) were distinguished by Domin in 1925, based on details of the shape and size of the sepals, but it is difficult to maintain these in the light of the great deal of variation found within the species. Occasionally cultivated, especially in Australia and said to be hardier than most of the other Australian species.

H7; P1

❊ ❊ **Stems and leaves glabrous or only sparsely hairy (species 75–78)**
❀ **Leaflets usually toothed; flowers 30–60 mm (1.2–2.4 in) across (species 75)**

75. *Clematis aristata* R. Br.*, Goat's-beard (syn. *C. aristata* var. *normalis*)

DESCRIPTION. A moderately vigorous to extremely vigorous evergreen climber 5–12 m (16.5–40 ft) , but occasionally as much as 15 m (50 ft) tall, with glabrous or slightly hairy stems, often suckering. Leaves ternate or occasionally biternate; leaflets deep shiny green, ovate, to 80 mm (3.2 in) long and 35 mm (1.4 in) wide, though often less, entire or with a toothed margin, with 3–5 prime veins from the base. Inflorescence a short cyme often with 5 flowers (but 3–9 is possible), in the axils of the upper leaves, starry, 30–60 mm (1.2–2.4 in) across; bracteoles near the base of the pedicels. Sepals white, linear-lanceolate to lanceolate, 18–30 mm (0.7–1.2 in) long, 2–7 mm (0.08–0.28 in) wide, with an acute and somewhat recurved apex. Anthers with a pointed appendage 2.5–4 mm (0.1–0.16 in) long. Achenes hairy or glabrous, with a plumose tail 25–40 mm (1–1.6 in) long.

DISTRIBUTION. Australia (New South Wales).
HABITAT. Sclerophyll forests (trees with hard evergreen foliage) and dry scrub; Sept–Mar (Mar–May in cultivation, northern hemisphere).

This species is rather uncommon in cultivation; it would certainly be more widely grown if it were hardier but in most districts (except for the very mildest parts of Britain and the warmer states of the USA) it can only really be grown under glass, although it will withstand the occasional mild frost. Some forms in cultivation bear a silvery midrib on the upper surface of the leaflets and tend to have rather small flowers for the species.

    Clematis aristata is in fact an extremely variable species, especially as regards leaf and flower size and hairiness and a number of different taxa have been recognized in the past. The foliage of young plants and suckers can be an attractive purple beneath.

var. *blanda* (Hook.) Benth. (syn. *C. aristata* var. *blanda* Benth. & Muell., *C. blanda* Hook., *C. clitorioides* DC., *C. c.* var. *decipiens* Domin) from northern Tasmania and coastal Victoria , is a smaller plant with biternate leaves and smaller flowers; **var. *dennisae* W. R. Guilfoyle** (syn. *C. aristata* var. *sanderi* (W. Wats.) Domin, *C. sanderi* W. Wats.) from highland forests in Victoria (Healesville) has especially long leaflets which are coarsely toothed, while the filaments and staminodes are a conspicuous red; this plant was cultivated in England in the first decade of the twentieth century; **var. *longisecta* F. M. Bailey** (from SE Queensland) has ovate-lanceolate leaflets with bristle-like marginal teeth, and cream-coloured flowers; **var. *cocculifolia* (A. Cunn.) Grey-Wilson, stat. nov.** (syn. *C. aristata* subsp. *cocculifolia* (A. Cunn.) Kuntze, *C. cocculifolia* A. Cunn.) has leathery leaflets with entire margins, with a rounded to heart-shaped base.

    Other varieties have been described including var. *browniana* Domin, var. *coriacea* (DC.) Benth. (syn. *C. coriacea* DC.), var. *gunniana* Kuntze and var. *integrifolia* Domin, but the status of these requires further detailed investigation. It is doubtful whether most can be upheld in the light of the marked variation between individuals and populations of *C. aristata*.

H7; P1

15. *Clematis gilbertiana* (female plant) near Bridgetown, Western Australia. Photo: Phil Cribb

16. *Clematis aristata* (male plant), Tasmania. Photo: Sue Gluskie

❀ ❀ **Leaflets untoothed (entire); flowers 15–40 mm (0.6–1.6 in) across (species 76–78)**
❖   **Leaflets narrow, only 3–6 mm (0.12–0.24 in) wide (species 76)**

76. *Clematis microphylla* DC.*, Small-leaved Clematis (syn. *C. hexapetala* subsp. *microphylla* Kuntze)

DESCRIPTION. An evergreen climber 5–10 m (16–33 ft), with slender glabrous stems and ternate or biternate leaves. Leaflets matt green to greyish, narrow-oblong to oval, 10–30 mm (0.4–1.2 in) long, 4–8 (–10) mm (0.16–0.32 (–0.4) in) wide, obtuse-tipped and with an entire margin. Flowers in short cymes at the upper nodes, 25–40 mm (1–1.6 in) across. Sepals greenish-cream, narrow-oblong-lanceolate, 12–25 mm (0.47–1 in) long, somewhat twisted and spidery-looking. Achenes often rather warted, with a plumose tail up 40–60 mm (1.6–2.4 in) long, occasionally longer.

DISTRIBUTION. Australia and Tasmania.

HABITAT. Dry scrub, heathy places and coastal dune scrub; Aug–Nov (Mar–May in cultivation, northern hemisphere).

This species is by far the commonest and most widespread in Australia and Tasmania and it is perhaps rather surprisingly uniform over its range. However, some local variation has been noted although none of the varieties that have been described appear to stand up to close scrutiny.

var. *leptophylla* F. Muell. ex Benth. (syn. *C. hexapetala* subsp. *leptophylla* Kuntze) often has narrow 3-lobed leaflets which are not more than 10 mm (0.4 in) long (New South Wales and Victoria);

var. *linearifolia* (Steud.) Domin (syn. *C. linearifolia* Steud., *C. hexapetala* subsp. *linearifolia* (Steud.) Kuntze, *C. microphylla* var. *occidentalis* Benth.) has linear-lanceolate leaflets (W Australia). However, intermediates can be found and the leaf size and shape may well reflect habitat rather than genetically influenced variation.

Clematis microphylla is widely cultivated in Australia and has proved an adaptable plant on both light as well as heavy soils, where it is equally good as a climber as for ground cover. In more temperate regions it requires all the warmth and protection that can be found in the garden, although it makes a tolerably good conservatory plant, flowering in early spring. It has been recorded that the leaves have been used for treating skin irritations; however beware, it may also cause blistering if over-used.

H9; P1

❖ ❖ **Leaflets broad, at least 10 mm (0.4 in) and up to 50 mm (2 in) wide (species 77–78)**

77. *Clematis glycinoides* DC.* Forest Clematis (syn. *C. aristata* subsp. *glycinoides* Kuntze, *C. stenopetala* Brown ex DC., *C. stenosepala* DC.)

DESCRIPTION. A very vigorous evergreen climber 5–20 m (16.5–66 ft), with glabrous stems and simple to ternate leaves. Leaflets shiny green, ovate to lanceolate, 30–60 mm (1.2–2.4 in) long and to 20 mm (0.8 in) wide, glabrous and with entire margins. Flowers borne in lateral cymes towards the stem tips, 25–40 mm (1–1.6 in) across, starry. Sepals white or greenish, linear-elliptical, 12–18 mm (0.47–0.7 in) long, 3-veined. Anthers with a short blunt appendage. Achenes with a plumose tail 50–60 mm (2–2.4 in) long.

DISTRIBUTION. E Australia from Cape York Peninsula southwards (New South Wales, Queensland, E Victoria).

HABITAT. Moist forests and rainforests; Sept–Nov (Feb–Apr in cultivation, northern hemisphere).

This interesting species inhabits cooler and moister habitats than the other Australian species. It is very variable in the size of both the leaves and flowers. In cultivation it requires cooler moister conditions than *C. aristata* but, despite being very attractive, it is not much grown, even in Australia. In Queensland it is referred to as the Headache Vine, for its leaves when crushed are believed to alleviate headaches. The leaflets sometimes bear a narrow silvery stripe down the centre. In cultivation it flowers in early to mid-spring.
Several varieties have been described in the past but of these only **var. *submutica* Benth.** seems to have any validity. It is distinguished from the typical plant by possessing rather small leaves that are sparsely hairy beneath and anther appendages that are often gland-tipped. In is restricted to south-eastern Queensland.

H8; P1

78. *Clematis pickeringii* A. Gray*
(syn. *C. acuminata* sensu Malm, non DC., *C. aristata* sensu Backer, non R. Br. Ex Edw., *C. a.* subsp. *pickeringii* (A. Gray) Kuntze, *C. glycinoides* sensu Merrill & Perry, non DC.)

DESCRIPTION. Another very vigorous evergreen climber to 20 m (66 ft), though as little as 5 m (16.5 ft) in some habitats, with finely ribbed somewhat hairy stems and petioles. Leaves ternate, dark green; leaflets hairy, ovate to lanceolate, to 85 mm (3.3 in) long and 65 mm (2.6 in) wide, sometimes larger, with an entire margin. Flowers many borne in large, much-branched, terminal inflorescences, to 30 cm (12 in) long overall, each flower 15–30 mm (0.6–1.2 in) across. Sepals 4, white, lanceolate oblong, 7–14 mm (0.28–0.55 in) long and 1.5–3 mm (0.06–0.12 in) wide in female flowers but not larger than 0.7 mm (0.028 in) long and 2 mm (0.08 in) wide in the male, with a hairy margin and generally 3–5-veined. Anthers with a short blunt appendage. Achenes with a plumose tail up to 60 mm (2.4 in) long.

DISTRIBUTION. Java and the S Celebes eastwards to S New Guinea including Ceram, NE Australia (N Northern Territory and N Queensland), New Caledonia and Fiji; to c. 1300 m (4300 ft).

HABITAT. Rainforest, climbing high into the tree canopy; Dec–Feb (Apr–May in cultivation, northern hemisphere).

This large species has a native distribution that encompasses part of SE Asia as well as northern Australia. It is a species of monsoon rich rain forests, favouring subtropical areas. It is cultivated in tropical gardens in Australia and elsewhere where it can make a spectacular display in full flower. Grown in rather drier places than its native haunts it tends to become deciduous during the long dry winter period. It is seldom seen in the northern hemisphere. It is generally rare in cultivation.

H9; P1

SUBSECTION PAPUASICAE
(THE PAPUAN GROUP)

This is an interesting group of subtropical species centred on New Guinea. They are united within Section Aspidanthera along with the Australian Group and share with them the predominance of separate male and female plants (although androdioecious flowers are quite common in both groups) and anthers with a small appendage, a projection from the top of the connective. Unlike the Australian species, those of Subsection Papuasicae have no bracteoles in the inflorescence, which is rather raceme-like with the lateral or subsequent branches very much reduced. In

17. *Clematis glycinoides* (male plant), Mt Boss State Forest, New South Wales. Photo: Bill Baker

several (*C. phanerophlebia* and *C. papuasica*, in particular) the inflorescence is large with long branches. The leaves are primarily ternate, evergreen and rather leathery, with generally entire margins and with 3–7 main veins arising from close to the base of the leaf-blade. The flowers tend to be rather small and greenish and the species probably have little general horticultural appeal, although those who have seen it in the wild describe *C. phanerophlebia* as 'quite showy' in full flower.

Note: *Clematis crutwellii* Eichler, described from Papua New Guinea (Milne Bay District; 1720 m (5600 ft)) may be a distinct species, but I have very little information at hand. The leaflets are described as lanceolate to narrow-oval, and the flowers white with mauve at the base of the sepals.

▼   **Sepals very small, not more than 9 mm (0.35 in) long (species 79 & 80)**

79. *Clematis archboldiana* Merr. & Perry

An evergreen climber to 5 m (16.5 ft) with brownish-velvety stems, and ternate leaves. Leaflets oval to elliptic, to 60 mm (2.4 in) long and up to 35 mm (1.4 in) wide, usually with 3 or 5 main veins from near the base, the apex obtuse to subobtuse, brown-velvety pubescent beneath. Inflorescence raceme-like, as long as or rather shorter than the subtending leaves, the flowers small, only 12–14 mm (0.47–0.55 in) across, either male or female, borne on separate plants, although the female flowers generally have staminodes and often a few fertile stamens. Sepals 4, occasionally 5, elliptical, c. 6 mm (0.24 in) long and 2 mm (0.08 in) wide. Stamens almost as long as the sepals; anthers to 0.5 mm (0.02 in) long, with an appendage to 0.33 mm (0.013 in) long. Achenes elliptical, 2–3 mm (0.08–0.12 in) long, with a plumose tail 15–25 mm (0.6–tin) long.

DISTRIBUTION. W New Guinea (Irian Jaya).

HABITAT. Forests and forest margins.

80. *Clematis clemensiae* H. Eichler

DESCRIPTION. Similar to *C. archboldiana*, but the leaves are either simple or ternate, the leaflets generally larger, 65–90 mm (2.6–3.5 in) long and 37.5–55 mm (1.48–2.17 in) wide, with 3 or 5 main veins from near the base. In addition, the flowers are somewhat larger, the oval sepals c. 9 mm (0.35 in) long and 4.5 mm (0.18 in) wide, with the stamens about three-quarters the length of the sepals; anthers to 1mm (0.04 in) long with a short appendage, c. 0.2 mm (0.008 in) long.

DISTRIBUTION. Papua New Guinea.

HABITAT. Forests and forest margins.

This species was described from the Morobe District of Papua New Guinea in 1938.

▼ ▼ **Sepals longer, 10–15 mm (0.4–0.6 in) (species 81–84)**
◆ **Anther appendage not more than 0.75 mm (0.03 in) long; sepals 14–15 mm (0.55–0.59 in) long (species 81)**

81. *Clematis phanerophlebia* Merr. & Perry
(syn. *C. perspicuinervia* Merr. & Perry, *C. pickeringii* var. *novo-guineensis* Merr. & Perry)

DESCRIPTION. An evergreen climber with simple or ternate deep-green, shiny, leaves. Leaflets oval to elliptical, 50–140 mm (2–5.5 in) long and 15–60 mm (0.6–2.36 in) wide, with an acuminate to cuspidate apex and an entire or somewhat toothed margin, generally with 3 (occasionally 5) veins from the base, glabrous or with a few hairs on the veins. Inflorescence pendulous, to 50 cm (20 in) long, panicle-like, with a number of raceme-like branches; flowers 15–30 mm (0.6–1.2 in) across, the male and female borne on separate plants, the female flowers larger and with 4–6 staminodes. Sepals 4, white, those of male flowers oval, 6–7 mm (0.24–0.28 in) long and 2 mm (0.08 in) wide, those of the female flowers narrow-lanceolate, 14–15 mm (0.55–0.59 in) long and to 2.5 mm (0.1 in) wide. Stamens about two-thirds the length of the sepals; anthers 1.25–1.75 mm (0.05–0.07 in) long with an appendage 0.3–0.75 mm (0.012–0.03 in) long. Achenes elliptical, 1.5–2.5 mm (0.06–0.1 in) long, hairy, with a plumose tail 30–40 mm (1.2–1.6 in) long.

DISTRIBUTION. New Guinea; 600–2000 m (2000–6500 ft).

HABITAT. Forests and forest margins, secondary forest, bushy places; flowering almost throughout the year.

A handsome climber that would be well worth while introducing into tropical and subtropical gardens. Although the flowers are small they are borne in substantial inflorescences, perhaps the largest found in the genus overall.

◆ ◆ **Anther appendage 1–2.5 mm (0.04–0.05 in) long; sepals 10–13 mm (0.4–0.5 in) long (species 82–84)**
✳ **Anther appendage more than 2 mm (0.08 in) long; leaflets 50–90 mm (2–3.5 in) wide (species 82)**

82. *Clematis papuasica* Merr. & Perry
(syn. *C. aristata* sensu Holthuis & Lam., non R. Br., *C. a.* subsp. *glycinoides* sensu Hallier, non (DC.) Kuntze, *C. a.* subsp. *pickeringii* sensu Schum., non (A. Gray) Kuntze, *C. a.* var. *pickeringii* sensu Schum. & Hallier, non Kuntze, *C. papuasica* var. *pubescens* Merr. & Perry, *C. pickeringii* sensu Warb., non A. Gray)

DESCRIPTION. A vigorous evergreen climber to 10 m (33 ft) with pale brown or pale green stems, generally with crisped hairs when young. Leaves ternate; leaflets elliptical to oval or lanceolate, generally 10–17 cm (4–6.7 in) long and 5–9 cm (2–3.5 in) wide, occasionally larger, the base wedge-shaped to rounded or somewhat heart-shaped, the apex cuspidate to acuminate, generally with 5 main veins from the base. Inflorescences lateral, usually branched, each branch multi-flowered, with the lowermost flowers opening first; flowers 24–28 mm (0.95–1.1 in) across, the female ones with 6–8 staminodes. Sepals 4, oval to elliptical, 11–13 mm (0.43–0.51 in) long and 2.5–4 mm (0.1–0.16 in) wide. Stamens slightly shorter than the sepals in the male flowers; anthers 0.75–1 mm (0.03–0.04 in) long, the appendage 2–3 mm (0.08–0.12 in) long, clearly longer than the anthers.

Achenes oval, 5–6.5 mm (0.2–0.26 in) long, broad-rimmed, hairy, with a plumose tail generally 60–80 mm (2.4–3.2 in) long.

DISTRIBUTION. Taliabu Is, Amboina, Ceram, Kai Is and Missol, eastwards through New Guinea to the Solomon Is; to 2000 m (6500 ft).

HABITAT. Forests, forest margins, secondary forest and bushy places; Oct–Mar, perhaps at other times as well. The most widespread member of Subsection Papuasicae.

❋ ❋ **Anther appendage 1–1.75 mm (0.4–0.7 in) long; leaflets 30–65 mm (1.2–2.6 in) wide (species 83 and 84)**

83. *Clematis stenanthera* H. Eichler

(syn. *C. aristata* subsp. *glycinoides* sensu Hallier, non Kuntze).

DESCRIPTION. A very vigorous evergreen climber to 20 m (66 ft) with normally ternate leaves. Leaflets elliptical to oval, 7–12.5 cm (2.8–4.9 in) long and 4–6.5 cm (1.6–2.6 in) wide, with a wedge-shaped to rounded base, the apex acute to somewhat acuminate, slightly hairy above but glabrous beneath, with 5 main veins from the base. Flowers 20–22 mm (0.79–0.87 in) across, the female flowers with 12–14 staminodes; sepals lanceolate to narrow-oval, 10–11 mm (0.39–0.43 in) long and 2–3 mm (0.08–0.12 in) wide. Stamens a half to two-thirds the length of the sepals; anthers c 1.75 mm (0.07 in) long with an appendage of the same length. Fruits unknown.

DISTRIBUTION. N Sulawasi; c. 50 m (160 ft).

84. *Clematis tenuimarginata* H. Eichler

DESCRIPTION. Similar to *C. stenanthera*, but leaflets tending to be narrower, 30–45 mm (1.2–1.8 in) wide. The flowers are similar in size but the anthers are smaller, not more than 0.75 mm (0.03 in) long with an appendage c. 1 mm (0.04 in) long; the female flowers bear 6–8 staminodes. Achenes elliptical, 4–4.5 mm (0.16–0.18 in) long, hairy, with a plumose tail 50–60 mm (2–2.4 in) long.

DISTRIBUTION. Sulawasi eastwards to Ceram.

HABITAT. Forests and forest margins; Oct–Nov.

SECTION NOVAE-ZEELANDIAE (THE NEW ZEALAND GROUP)

An interesting and attractive group of 11 species which are all native to New Zealand. They are evergreen dioecious plants that are mostly climbers, although the high alpine *C. marmoraria* is a small suckering shrublet. As in other dioecious clematis the female flowers often have a number of vestigial stamens or staminodes outside the female parts, while in the male flowers vestigial female parts can often be observed within the bunch of fertile stamens. What distinguishes this section from other dioecious sections (e.g. Subgenus *Clematis*, which includes both Australian and New Guinea species and the American dioecious species) is the possession of imbricate rather than valvate sepals (the sepals overlap one another in bud rather than just meeting all along the margins). In this respect the New Zealand species match Subgenus *Pseudanemone* (formerly the genus *Clematopsis*). However, the species of *Pseudanemone* are fundamentally different in their herbaceous non-climbing habit, in their normally 4-sepalled nodding flowers and, more importantly, in having hermaphrodite flowers. The species of Subgenus *Pseudoanemone* are all native to Africa and Madagascar and the possession of imbricate sepals in both sections can only be viewed as a case of parallel evolution.

The members of Section Novae-Zeelandiae have white, greenish or greenish-yellow flowers borne early in the year on the shoots of the previous season. The majority of species are in cultivation and most are attractive and desirable. Of the sexes it is the male plants that generally have the larger and showier flowers and in cultivation the finer male plants can be selected from seedling matches once they reach flowering size. Be sure to retain just a few female plants for seed production: female plants may have smaller flowers but they are often produced in greater abundance. In temperate gardens most of the species are reasonably hardy provided they are given a warm sheltered wall, but are vulnerable to excessive winter wet. On the other hand, they make excellent subjects for the conservatory, although the vigorous growth of some will need to be kept in check.

▼ **Small alpine subshrubs (species 85)**

85. *Clematis marmoraria* Sneddon* AGM

DESCRIPTION. A small suckering evergreen shrublet not more than 10 cm (4 in) tall, the stems spreading to ascending, densely leafy. The stiff leathery leaves are

18. *Clematis marmoraria* (male plant), an award-winning specimen.
Photo: Robert Rolfe

deep green and shiny, basically ternate but the prime segments deeply incised once or twice into numerous very small, elliptical to oblong, segments. Flowers solitary in the leaf-axils with a bract pair just below the middle of the peduncle, 20–30 mm (0.8–1.2 in) across. Sepals white, though often flushed with green when young (especially in bud), usually 6, but 5–8 overall, obovate to elliptical, 10–14 mm (0.4–0.55 in) long, 4–6 mm (0.16–0.24 in) wide, occasionally larger, though somewhat smaller in female flowers. Achenes

19. *Clematis marmoraria* (male plant) in cultivation.
Photo: Christopher Grey-Wilson

hairy, with a tail to 30 mm (1.2 in) long, tawny plumose when ripe.

DISTRIBUTION. New Zealand: NE South Island. (NW Nelson; Arthur Range, on Mt Crusader and Hoary Head); c. 1400 m (4600 ft).

HABITAT. Marble rocks in the alpine herbfield; Nov–Jan (Apr–May in cultivation, northern hemisphere).

This is the smallest known species of *Clematis*. It is a true alpine and a great gem in cultivation, and could easily be mistaken for a *Ranunculus* or *Anemone* at first glance. *C. marmoraria* is endemic to a remote and restricted area in the Arthur Range, as far as it is known at present. It was only described in 1975 but is already well established in cultivation. It is at its best when given a deep pot in a gritty compost in an alpine house or well-ventilated unheated glasshouse. The species is readily raised from seed but plants are quite slow to build up to a decent size; plants may eventually reach 25 cm (10 in) across, but half that size is more normal. They should be kept moist at all times, although not over-watered during the winter dormant season. The seedheads, which will only be produced if both male and female plants are grown side by side, are attractive and eventually become an attractive golden-brown. *C. marmoraria* can also be grown outside with limited success in a raised bed or trough where some form of protection from winter wet is advisable. A plant in full flower is a very fine sight. Hybridized with *C. paniculata,* it has given rise to a beautiful and much-sought-after hybrid, C. × *cartmanii* 'Joe'*.

H7; no pruning generally required

▼ ▼Climbers or scramblers, never alpine
   (species 86–95)
◆   Stems practically leafless and rush-like (species 86)

86. Clematis afoliata J. Buchanan* Rush-stemmed Clematis

DESCRIPTION. An evergreen climber or a scandent shrub to 3 m (10 ft) with the stems becoming quite woody with age, often forming tangled shrub-like mounds. Stems leafless, the young ones dark green and glabrous, slender and rather rush-like, bearing pairs of twining petioles and petiolules to 60 mm (2.4 in) long, occasionally longer; however, in shaded and young plants leaf-blades are produced, these being small, ovate and entire. Flowers solitary or up to 5 in lateral clusters, nodding, bell-shaped, 30–40 mm (1.2–1.6 in) across, daphne-fragrant. Sepals generally 4 (occasionally 5–6), greenish-yellow, ovate-lanceolate, 15–25 mm (0.6–1 in) long, occasionally longer. Achenes hairy, with a tail to 20 mm (0.8 in) long.

Distribution. New Zealand: S North Island (Wellington) and N & C South Island (Canterbury, Marlborough & N Otago), more common and widespread on South Island; to c. 700 m (2300 ft).

Habitat. Rocky and open scrub, tussock grassland; Aug–Nov (Apr–May in cultivation; northern hemisphere).

This interesting species is unique in its reduced leafless state, or at least with leaves reduced to vestiges. The stems are green and remarkably rush-like, clambering rather than climbing. Although it will climb like many other species over bushes, it is also quite at home sprawling over rocks or banks, rather as *C. orientalis* and its allies often do in the wild. It was introduced into cultivation in 1908.

In cultivation it is rather hardier than is generally supposed: a plant has survived on a bank of the rock garden at Edinburgh Botanic Garden for many years. It is perhaps best suited for growing against a sheltered warm sunny wall where it will undoubtedly make an unusual feature, worth growing for its fragrance alone; however, a mature plant in full flower can look quite magnificent. In severe winters protecting the vulnerable base of the plant is desirable, if not essential. It is excellent in mild maritime regions and is generally more drought resistant than most clematis. Pruning, if desired, consists mainly of keeping the rather untidy entanglement in check; rigorous thinning of the stems may be necessary from time to time, a practice best carried out the moment the flowers have ceased. The best forms in cultivation have pale yellow rather than greenish-yellow flowers. The species received an Award of Merit (AM) when exhibited at the Royal Horticultural Society in May 1916.

H8; P1

◆ ◆ Stems leafy (species 87–95)

❊ Sepals 4, occasionally 5 (species 87 & 88)

87. *Clematis marata* Armstrong*
(syn. *C. hexapetala* L. f. subsp. *marata* (Armstrong) Kuntze)

Description. A low-growing evergreen climber with slender purplish stems and ternate leaves. Leaflets leathery and dull green, rather variable in shape but

20. *Clematis afoliata* (female plant) in cultivation. Photo: Christopher Grey-Wilson

generally with 3 or more lobes, or pinnately lobed, to 25 mm (1 in) long and 6 mm (0.24 in) wide, hairy on both surfaces. Flowers solitary or in clusters of 2–4 in the leaf-axils, nodding, 13–25 mm (0.5–1 in) across, cinnamon-scented. Sepals yellowish-green, occasionally blotched with brown, usually 4 but occasionally 5, ovate-oblong, 8–15 mm (0.32–0.6 in) long, somewhat smaller and greener in female flowers, silky-hairy beneath, often with a twisted margin. Achenes glabrous, with a plumose tail to 25 mm (1 in) long.

Distribution. New Zealand: South Island (Canterbury, Marlborough, Otago & Southland); to 1000 m (3300 ft).

Habitat. Rocky outcrops, hillsides, and scrub, sometimes on river terraces; Oct–Dec (Apr–May in cultivation, northern hemisphere).

Sometimes merged with *C. quadribracteolata* (a later name); however, J. Cartman (*Canterbury Bot. Soc. Journ.* vol. 20, 1975, pp. 36–37) has shown that they

21. *Clematis marata* (male plant) in cultivation. Photo: Christopher Grey-Wilson

22. *Clematis quadribracteolata* (female plant) in cultivation.
Photo: Raymond Evison

are quite distinct. The latter species has brown or purplish very narrow sepals and elliptic rather than spathulate bracts and the leaves are often a rather brownish-green colour overall. Both these species are readily distinguished from other New Zealand clematis by possessing only 4 sepals per flower.

Two clones have been named from cultivated material: 'Temple Prince' a male clone and 'Temple Queen' a female. Hybridization in cultivation between *C. marata* and *C. marmoraria* (see above) have resulted in two fine cultivars, 'Lunar Lass' and 'Moonman'.

H8; P1

88. *Clematis quadribracteolata* Colensoi*

DESCRIPTION. Similar to *C. marata* but leaves brownish-green and flowers purplish or brown with the sepals 5–15 mm (0.2–0.6 in) long but not more than 2 mm (0.08 in) wide, those of female flowers often darker. The achenes can be hairy or glabrous, with a tail up to 35 mm (1.4 in) long.

DISTRIBUTION. New Zealand: North Island (Bay of Plenty southwards); South Island, except for Tasman and much of the west coast and Southern Alps area.

HABITAT. Rocky scrub; Sept–Oct (Mar–Apr in cultivation, northern hemisphere).

Rather rare in cultivation but probably the first of the New Zealanders to come into flower. The small flowers are not particularly striking and the foliage is a strange greenish-brown. If this does not put most readers off then the tongue-twisting name almost certainly will.

H8; P1

❃ ❃   Sepals often 6, occasionally 7–8 (species 89–95)
❀   Flowers pure white to cream (species 89–91)
❖   Flowers not more than 40 mm (1.6 in) across (species 89 & 90)

89. *Clematis forsteri* Gmelin*
(syn. *C. colensoi* Hook. f., *C. hexapetala* L. f., non Pall., *C. hexapetala* Forster f., non Pall., *C. hexasepala* DC., non L. f.)

DESCRIPTION. Evergreen climber to 3 m (10 ft), occasionally more, with ternate leaves. Leaflets thinly leathery and bright rather pale green, lanceolate to oval, to 80 mm (3.2 in) long and 45 mm (1.8 in) wide, although as little as 10 mm (0.4 in) wide in some instances, the margin crenate or with shallow rounded lobes, glabrous. Inflorescence well-developed, in lateral cymes with up to 6 nodding to half-nodding flowers, each 25–40 mm (1–1.6 in) across, lemon-fragrant. Sepals white, sometimes flushed with green at the base when young, often 6 (but 5–8), narrow-oval to oblong, 15–30 mm (0.6–1.2 in) long in male flowers, but 10–25 mm (0.4–1 in) in female, half to widely spreading, silky hairy to subglabrous on the reverse; female flowers with few staminodes. Achenes hairy to glabrous, with a plumose tail up to 35 mm (1.4 in) long, often less.

DISTRIBUTION. New Zealand: North Island from c. 36° southwards and N South Island (Marlborough & Nelson).

HABITAT. Forest and scrub, particularly forest fringes, at low altitudes; Sept–Nov (Mar-May in cultivation, northern hemisphere).

Clematis forsteri represents a complex picture. It is treated in the strict sense above but some authors (e.g. Webb et al. in the 'Flora of New Zealand') treat it as part of a complex which contains three other elements: *C. australis, C. hookeriana* and *C. petriei*. Although

24. Clematis forsteri (male plant) in cultivation. Photo: Martyn Rix

23. Clematis forsteri (male plant) in cultivation. Photo: Jack Elliott

these can in essence be distinguished, many intermediates are known and there is also a strong suggestion that the variation may to some extent be caused by environmental factors as well as the usual genetic ones. I am inclined to the view that there are four very closely allied taxa that have scarcely yet established themselves as distinct species.

In cultivation *C. forsteri* makes a handsome climber for a sunny sheltered warm wall or fence and when well grown the stems are wreathed in numerous rather dainty flowers which appear in May. The scent has been likened to that of lemon verbena.

H8; P1

90. *Clematis australis* Kirk*

DESCRIPTION. Very like *C. forsteri* but leaflets more leathery, oblong to oval, to 35 mm (1.4 in) long, pinnate in the lower part but pinnately lobed above, dark green. Flowers solitary or 2–4 in a lateral cluster, starry, 20–30 mm (0.8–1.2 in) across, half-nodding, scented. Sepals whitish or very pale yellow-green, 5–8, narrow-ovate to narrow-oblong, 15–20 mm (0.6–0.8 in) long, silky-hairy beneath.

DISTRIBUTION. New Zealand: South Island (N Canterbury, Marlborough & Nelson); to c. 1200 m (3900 ft)

HABITAT. Montane thickets and forest margins to subalpine regions; Nov–Jan (Feb–early May in cultivation, northern hemisphere).

With its more dissected foliage, *C. australis* looks the most distinctive member of the *C. forsteri* complex. The flowers often have a rather spidery appearance. Plants with more finely lobed leaves have been distinguished in the past as var. *rutaefolia* (Hook. f.) Allan (syn. *C. colensoi* var. *rutaefolia* Hook. f., *C. hexasepala* var. *rutaefolia* Hook. f.), but intermediates do occur and it would be difficult to uphold this variety. The species flowers in early to mid-spring.

H8; P1

❖ ❖ **Flowers at least 50 mm (2 in) across (species 91)**

91. *Clematis paniculata* Gmelin*
(syn. *C. indivisa* Willd., *C. indivisa* var. *lobulata* Hook. f. , *C. integrifolia* Forster f.)

DESCRIPTION. A robust evergreen climber to 4 m (13 ft), sometimes more, with ternate leaves. Leaflets leathery,

deep green, ovate to oblong with a heart-shaped or truncated base, 5–10 cm (2–4 in) long, half as wide, the margin entire to crenate, or lobed towards the apex, more rarely deeply lobed. Flowers in compound lateral cymes, 50–90 mm (2–3.5 in) across, with the lower bracts often leaf-like, though smaller. Sepals white, usually 6 but occasionally 7–8, oblong to obovate, 25–35 (–40) mm (1–1.4 (–1.6) in) long and 8–15 mm (0.32–0.6 in) wide in male flowers, but generally not more than 25 mm (1 in) long and 10 mm (0.4 in) wide in the female. Achenes hairy, with a tail to 65 mm (2.6 in) long.

DISTRIBUTION. New Zealand: throughout the North and South Islands, including Three Kings Is. and Stewart Is.; to 650 m (2100 ft).

HABITAT. Lowland and lower montane forests, especially along the fringes; Aug–Nov (Feb–Mar in cultivation, northern hemisphere).

The largest-flowered and most beautiful of all the New Zealand clematis. It is rather variable in flower size and it pays to select cuttings from a good clone. In full flower it can be a shimmering mass of white bloom and quite exquisite. In the seedling stage the leaves are very variable; they can be linear and as much as 15 cm (6 in) long (or more), or ternate, with or without deep lobing. It has also been noted that plants may come into flower before they have attained their true adult foliage. The species was in fact introduced into cultivation as early as 1840. However, it was described almost 50 years previously by Gmelin based on specimens collected on the first of Captain Cook's voyages. Despite this, the species was long cultivated under the name *C. indivisa*, a synonym. In cultivation it is a very fine species in its best and largest-flowered forms. I fell for it just a few years ago when I came upon a magnificent specimen on a sheltered wall at the Royal Horticultural Society's garden at Rosemore in north Devon. It is only hardy in the mildest parts of Britain and does extremely well in sheltered gardens in Devon and Cornwall. Elsewhere it is best treated as a fine climber for a cool conservatory, although it is subject to attack from scale insects, and plants should be periodically examined for the first signs, as they can be badly damaged should the pest get a firm grip. *C. paniculata* is quite one of the most beautiful and floriferous species when well grown and guaranteed to attract attention. The best clones in cultivation are male ones and they often have attractive pinkish anthers.

Various varieties have been distinguished; **var. *decomposita*** has biternate leaves; **var. *linearis*** has linear, untoothed, leaves up to 17.5 cm (7 in) long; **var.**

lobata **Hook.**** (syn. var. *lobulata*, 'Lobata') has dentate to lobed leaf-margins and smaller 40 mm (1.6 in) across flowers. These, however, appear to represent the extremes of a variable species. In addition, one has to take into account the fact that the foliage may change shape considerably from seedling to mature plants, this being true of a number of the New Zealand species. In some forms of *C. paniculata* (especially those formerly grown under the name *C. indivisa*, the leaves may be simple and lanceolate for the first year or so, then the adult more typical trifoliate leaves will appear. This is the plant long-grown as *C. indivisa* var. *lobata*; however, the earlier name *C. paniculata* has precedence as of course it must if botanical nomenclature is to have any standing. At the same time it is unfortunate that this latter name was long used for the species we grow today under the name of *C. terniflora* (see p.103). Well, life is not meant to be easy! Whatever the name, this plant has received, and deservedly so, the highest acclaim from the Royal Horticultural Society in the form of an FCC (First Class Certificate) when it was shown by Lord Aberconway in May 1934.

25. Clematis paniculata (male plant) in cultivation. Photo: Jack Elliott

'Bodnant'* is an attractive and apparently rather hardier selection of *C. paniculata*, raised at the garden of that name in North Wales by Lord Aberconway. This cultivar has lusher and more lustrous bright green foliage and flowers 60 mm (2.4 in) across with a prominent boss of pink anthers. Given a sheltered sunny position and a warm wall it will eventually reach 4 m (13 ft) in height.

H7; P1

❀ ❀ **Flowers greenish or yellowish (species 92–95)**
 ✳ **Anthers not more than 1.5 mm (0.06 in) long (species 92 & 93)**

26. Clematis paniculata (female plant) in cultivation at Rosemore, North Devon. Photo: Christopher Grey Wilson

92. *Clematis cunninghamii* Turcz* Cunningham's Clematis
(syn. *C. hillii* Colenso, *C. parviflora* sensu A. Cunn., non A. DC.)

DESCRIPTION. An evergreen climber to 3 m (10 ft) or more, with ternate leaves. Leaflets rather thin, ovate, to 40 mm (1.6 in) long, with an entire to serrate margin, or deeply lobed or dissected, with tawny-coloured hairs beneath. Flowers borne in lateral cymes, 15–25 mm (0.6–1 in) across, faintly to moderately lemon-scented. Sepals usually 6 (occasionally 5–8), yellowish, narrow-oblong to almost elliptic, hairy beneath, those of male flowers 9–15 mm (0.35–0.6 in) long (rarely to 20 mm (0.8 in)), not more than 5 mm (0.2 in) wide, those of female flowers generally 8–13 mm (0.32–0.5 in) long,

27. *Clematis petriei* (female plant) in cultivation. Photo: Christopher Grey-Wilson

28. *Clematis petriei* (female plant) in cultivation. Photo: Christopher Grey-Wilson

and narrower. Achenes hairy, with a tail up to 25 mm (1 in) long.

DISTRIBUTION. New Zealand: North Island (Auckland, Gisborne), Three Kings Island.

HABITAT. Forests and forest fringes, at low altitudes; Sept–Nov (Mar–May in cultivation, northern hemisphere).

Sometimes confused with *C. foetida* which can be distinguished by having strongly scented flowers with the sepals densely pilose beneath.

Three varieties have been recognized. Besides var. *cunninghamii* (described above) there is var. *depauperata* Hook. which has very reduced leaflets and sepals with a fine apex and var. *trilobata* which has, as its name implies, 3-lobed leaflets. However, intermediates between all the types can be found in the wild.

This species is rather rare in cultivation and often sold under the name *C. parviflora*. This name had unfortunately been used by A. de Candolle in 1824; Cunningham's *C. parviflora* dates from 1837!

H8; P1

93. *Clematis foetida* Raoul*
(syn. *C. hexapetala* subsp. *foetida* Kuntze, *C. parkinsoninana* Colenso)

DESCRIPTION. Very similar in general appearance to *C. cunninghamii*, but with rather larger, scarcely hairy, leaflets which usually have an entire to sinuate margin, occasionally crenate or serrate. The flowers, which are

about 25 mm (1 in) across, are strongly scented, with yellow sepals which are densely pilose beneath. Achenes with tails up to 30 mm (1.2 in) long.

DISTRIBUTION. New Zealand: North Island (except for the central west; Taranaki), including Three Kings Island, and the South Island except for the NW the W coast and the extreme south.

HABITAT. Forests, particularly along the fringes; Sept–Nov (Apr–May in cultivation, northern hemisphere).

Occasionally seen in cultivation, it is a vigorous grower to 4 m (13 ft) or more given a warm sheltered nook in the garden. Despite its name, the flowers are quite sweetly scented. Juvenile plants look very similar to *C. marata* but change to the typical *C. foetida* after three or four years.

H8; P1

❀ ❀ **Anthers at least 2 mm (0.08 in) long (species 94 & 95)**

94. *Clematis hookeriana* Allan*
(syn. *C. colensoi* sensu Hook. f. 1864, *C. hexasepala* Hook.f., non L. f.)

DESCRIPTION. Very similar to *C. forsteri* but leaflets thicker and more leathery and with a more sharply toothed or lobed margin, not more than 30 mm (1.2 in) long and 15 mm (0.6 in) wide. Flowers solitary or a few in a lateral cluster, 25–30 mm (1–1.2 in) across. Sepals greenish to pale yellowish, 5–8, ovate, 15–18 mm (0.6–0.7 in) long, somewhat hairy beneath.

DISTRIBUTION. New Zealand: Cook Strait region (both islands), Kapiti Is., Stephens Is.; to 900 m (3000 ft). HABITAT. Rocky scrub; Nov–Jan (May–June in cultivation, northern hemisphere).

A form with more markedly lobed foliage (the leaflets often 2–3 lobed) is sometimes distinguished as var. *lobulata* Allan (syn. *C. colensoi* var. *rutaefolia* Hook. f.), and was described from the Port Nicholson area. It was introduced into cultivation (at least in Britain) by Collingwood Ingram in 1937 and received an Award of Merit (AM) from the Royal Horticultural Society when exhibited by him in May 1961.

H8; P1

95. *Clematis petriei* Allan*

DESCRIPTION. Similar to *C. forsteri* but the leaves less leathery with an entire margin or with 1–2 obtuse lateral lobes, but not toothed. Flowers solitary or in small lateral cymes, 25–35 mm (1–1.4 in) across. Sepals greenish-yellow, 5–8, ovate to oblong, 15–20 mm (0.6–0.8 in) long, hairy beneath, scented.

DISTRIBUTION. New Zealand: NW South Island (N Canterbury & Marlborough).

HABITAT. Bushy places and forest fringes; Nov–Dec (Feb–Apr in cultivation, northern hemisphere). This interesting small-flowered species is named after the Scottish botanist Donald Petrie, who made extensive studies of New Zealand plants. It is not one of the most exciting of the New Zealand species, but it does have a charm of its own, and a well-flowered specimens can bear hundreds of the small green flowers which are like little pixie hats. It has the advantage of being rather hardier than some of is New Zealand brethren. It is sometimes listed erroneously as *C. forsteri* subsp. *petriei*. As with most of these New Zealanders it is the male form that has the showier flowers, although it is of course the female that produces the fluffy seedheads; these can be quite attractive. Some nurseries sell male or female plants, but with most it is pot-luck what you get.

Two cultivars have been selected: 'Limelight' a male clone and 'Princess' a female clone.

H5; P1

HYBRIDS

C. 'Avalanche'* is a vigorous hybrid with stems of 3–4 m (10–13 ft) which was derived from *C. paniculata* (female plant) and *C.* x *cartmanii* 'Joe' which is a male clone. The leaves are deep glossy green and finely dissected and the rather flat white flowers 70–80 mm (2.8–3.2 in) across, are borne in panicle-like inflorescences, often in profusion. Another male clone, the flowers with 5–7 sepals. Like other cultivars in the New Zealand alliance, plants can be pruned back to keep them more compact; the stems are best pruned in late summer before the flowerbuds are initiated.

H7

29. *Clematis* x *cartmanii* 'Joe'. Photo: Jack Elliott

30. *Clematis* x *cartmanii* (male plant). Photo: Christopher Grey-Wilson

31. above left: *Clematis marmoraria* x *C. forsteri* (male plant).Photo: Mike Ireland
32. below left: *Clematis marmoraria* x *C. petriei* (male plant).Photo: Mike Ireland

33. *Clematis marmoraria* x *C. petriei* (male plant).Photo: Christopher Grey-Wilson

C. x *cartmanii* is the hybrid name given to all the crosses between *C. marmoraria* and *C. paniculata*. Of these by far the best known is the outstanding cultivar 'Joe'*, which is now widely available. It has non-clinging stems that will, in a good specimen reach almost 2 m (6.6 ft), although half that length is more normal. The deep green, shiny evergreen leaves are neatly dissected and are practically hidden by the mass of semi-nodding white blooms, each 30–40 mm (1.2–1.6 in) across, which first open in early spring; these are pure white, although with a flush of green in

bud, roughly saucer-shaped and usually with six broadly oval sepals. It is certainly hardy to –5°C (23°F) and can be trained to a warm west or south-west wall in the mildest regions. Elsewhere it is best grown in containers in a conservatory or alpine house. 'Joe' is a male clone. I had a wonderful specimen in an alpine house that had been planted in the top of an old chimney pot: the stems trailed down the pot and looked quite wonderful in full flower in the early spring. H9

Subgenus Two *Cheiropsis*

Horticulturally, this is one of the most important subgenera in the whole of *Clematis*, with a lot of species and forms, and derived cultivars, grown in our gardens. They are primarily climbers with ternate leaves and solitary or clustered flowers borne at the nodes, but not in formal inflorescences. The majority are showy in full flower.

SECTION MONTANAE
(THE MONTANA GROUP)

The nine species of Section Montanae are utterly delightful and can be counted among the most graceful and floriferous of clematis. *C. montana* and its forms, and a growing number of excellent cultivars, is too familiar in our gardens to warrant description. As a species it is widely available; one of the clematis even

the most humble of garden centres is likely to stock. The early-flowering habit of many of the montana types is a great delight in the garden and they burst into flower in the spring together with many other familiar plants. They are good in a variety of situations in the garden, and the more vigorous (they can be extremely vigorous!) are excellent for clambering up a lofty wall or old tree. The flowers are borne in clusters along the stems of the previous year and these can be wreathed in flowers for several metres. In addition, they are amongst the easiest clematis to cultivate, requiring little in the way of annual pruning, except to remove unwanted growth and to keep plants in check to some extent.

The species are exclusively Himalayan or Chinese in origin. The solitary flowers are usually 4-sepalled and the slender pedicels have no bracts at all (except for *C. brevipes*).

MAP FOUR
Subgenus *Cheiropsis*
Section Cheiropsis — — — — — — —
    subsection Williamsii _._._._._._.
Section Montanae ············
Section Fasciculiflora + + + + + + +

34. *Clematis chrysocoma*, Gang-ho-ba, N of Lijiang, NW Yunnan, China.
Photo: Christopher Grey-Wilson

35. *Clematis chrysocoma*, Bei-shui, N of Lijiang, NW Yunnan, China.
Photo: Christopher Grey-Wilson

▼   **Subshrubs, not more than 60 cm (24 in) tall (species 96 & 97)**

◆   **Leaves palmate (species 96)**

96. *Clematis acerifolia* Maxim.

DESCRIPTION. A subshrubby plant 20–60 cm (8–24 in) tall, with thin rounded, unfurrowed stems that become woody towards the base. Leaves papery, simple, palmate (maple-like), 36–75 mm (1.4–3 in) long, 38–80 mm (1.5–3.2 in) wide, generally with 5 main lobes, each lobe apiculate and with one or two small teeth, or margin entire, the base truncated to somewhat heart-shaped. Flowers solitary occasionally 2–4, rather flat or saucer-shaped, ascending to erect, 30–55 mm (1.3–2.2 in) across. Sepals 5–8, white or pinkish, spreading, elliptic, 17–27 mm (0.67–1.1 in) long, 7–15 mm (0.28–0.6 in) wide, usually 3-veined, glabrous. Stamens about one-quarter to one-third the length of the sepals. Achenes narrow-ovate, hairy, with a plumose style to 25 mm (1 in) long.

DISTRIBUTION. N China (Beijing, Hebei, E Shanxi); c. 200 m (650 ft).

HABITAT. Rocky or earthy slopes and cliffs; Apr–early June.

A delightful and unusual species which is inexplicably not in cultivation, despite the fact that it grows not far from Beijing. It is the only species of *Clematis* with palmate leaves. The flowers are borne with leaves from buds at the stem apex. *C. acerifolia* is generally placed in the Montanae, although its true allegiance is uncertain; the habit, leaf characteristics and the flowers, which consistently have more than 4 sepals, make it a very unusual species altogether.

◆ ◆   **Leaves ternate (species 97)**

97. *Clematis chrysocoma* Franch.*

DESCRIPTION. A subshrub to 2 m (6.6 ft), though generally only 20–50 cm (8–20 in) tall (in the wild at least), with the young stems, leaves and pedicels covered in a medium to dense golden or tawny down. Leaves ternate, with ovate to oval or more or less rhomboidal leaflets which are 3-lobed often and/or coarsely toothed, with the terminal leaflet larger than the lateral, densely tawny-pubescent beneath, less markedly so above. Flowers solitary mostly borne from the lower axils of the current year's shoots on long pedicels, 30–200 mm (1.2–8 in) long, occasionally longer, flat or somewhat cupped, 35–50 mm (1.4–2 in) across. Sepals 4, rarely 5–8, rose-pink to rose-purple, rarely pale pink or white, broad-oblong to oval, 17–25 mm (0.67–1 in) long and 8–18 mm (0.32–0.7 in) wide. Achenes ovate, 4–5 mm (0.16–0.2 in) long, densely pubescent, with a golden-brown plumose tail to 25 mm (1 in) long.

DISTRIBUTION. SW China (W Guizhou, N & W Yunnan, SW Sichuan); 1500–3200 m (4950–10,500 ft).

HABITAT. Open forests and shrubberies, often of evergreen oak (*Quercus*), *Rhododendron* or *Berberis*, grassy areas, occasionally in more exposed places, on banks, stony places or in coniferous forest clearings; May–July.

Clematis chrysocoma was first discovered in north-western Yunnan in 1884 by Abbé Delavay and introduced into cultivation (at the Royal Botanic Gardens, Kew) by Maurice de Vilmorin in 1910. There have been a number of introductions since and most of the plants at present in cultivation stem from seed collecting expeditions to the region in the past twenty years.

This interesting and much confused species has a limited distribution in the wild. It is closely related to *C. montana* but its growth habit and pubescence is very distinctive. In cultivation it behaves wholly differently to *C. montana*: the stems are often killed back partly or wholly to ground level during all but the mildest winters and subsequent shoots generally arise on the lower part of the previous year's stems or from below ground level. The flowers are generally borne on the current year's shoots and may not appear until mid-summer. In my garden, at least, the flowers are normally borne from August until October, well after the other Montana types have finished. However, plants which have survived intact over-winter without any die-back will produce their first flowers in June and July. The species is not a climber and is best planted amongst medium sized bushes where its shoots (which can reach 1.5 m (5 ft), although generally only 0.6–1 m (24–40 in) can scramble for support; this is what it often does in the wild. It sets seed readily in cultivation.

'Continuity'* was raised at Jackmans (Woking) by Albert Voneshan in the late 1950s. Like *C. chrysocoma* it is unfortunately not reliably winter hardy. However, it is well worth growing in mild regions in a sheltered part of the garden or in a conservatory. The leaves are less hairy and the leaf-stalks (petioles) and the pedicels are remarkably long, the latter up to 20 cm (8 in) which makes it a useful plant for cut flowers. The flowers are pale pink, about 50 mm (2 in) across and with 4–6 sepals. It flowers in the summer.

36. *Clematis chrysocoma*, a form with extra sepals, Hei-shui, N of Lijiang, NW Yunnan, China. Photo: Phillip Cribb

Confusion has been perpetuated in cultivation over the name *chrysocoma* for it is applied to a very vigorous plant with similar, although reduced, pubescence and flowers, which is commonly sold by nurseries and garden centres. Unfortunately, this confusion has been much perpetuated in the horticultural press. The plant in question is a true climber and can readily attain 9–10 m (30–33 ft). It was first described as *C. spooneri* by Rehder and Wilson in 1913 but subsequently (1917) placed under *C. chrysocoma* as var. *sericea*. To add to the confusion this plant had already been regarded as a variety of *C. montana* by Franchet (see var. *sericea* Franch. under *C. spooneri*). It is clearly nonsense to place this plant under *C. chrysocoma* or *C. montana* for it is quite distinctive in various details of its leaves, flowers and pubescence and I have opted to follow Rehder and Wilson in recognising it as a distinct, although closely allied, species, *C. spooneri*. In the wild *C. spooneri* has a limited distribution that coincides almost perfectly with that of *C. chrysocoma*. *C. montana*, which has a far greater distribution, is also common within the same general area. It cannot be ruled

37. *Clematis gracilifolia*, at Jui-zhai-gou, Sichuan, China.
Photo: Christopher Grey-Wilson

38. *Clematis gracilifolia*, form at Jui-zhai-gou, Sichuan, China.
Photo: Phillip Cribb

out that *C. spooneri* arose as a natural hybrid between *C. chrysocoma* and *C. montana*. Its general growth and flowering habit is that of *C. montana*, while the pubescence is more akin to that of *C. chrysocoma*, as is its habit of producing precocious flowers on the current year's shoots through the summer months, often long after the early display of flowers has finished.

If this is so then the '*Clematis chrysocoma* hybrid' introduced from the wilds of Yunnan in the 1980s by Roy Lancaster is of similar origin. It has attractive downy foliage that is bronze when young and bronze-tinted at maturity. The pink flowers appear in late spring and are saucer-shaped and about 50 mm (2 in) across. Probably H7.

In the wild *C. spooneri* is quite variable in leaf shape and the degree of pubescence, even from plant to plant in the same colony and this may add support to a theory of hybrid origin. Certainly hybrids between the supposed parent species can produce plants remarkably similar to *C. spooneri*. Indeed such a hybrid was raised by Messrs. Vilmorin at Verrières-le-Buisson, near Paris, early in the twentieth century and was named *C. × vedrariensis* Vilm. The exact cross was between *C. montana* var. *rubens* and *C. chrysocoma* and this hybrid is not very different from some forms of *C. spooneri* found in the wild apart from the fact that the wild plant has white flowers, not pale pink.

var. *laxistrigosa* W. T. Wang & M. C. Chang has the leaflets with whitish bristle-like hairs beneath, whilst sparsely hairy above. Similar habitats, but particularly streamsides, at 1100–2800 m (3600–9200 ft) in SW Sichuan (Ganluo Xian, Hanyuan Xian).

H7; P1

▼ ▼ **Climbers, often vigorous (species 98–104)**
❈   **Sepals normally 6 (species 98)**

98. *Clematis glabrifolia* K. Sun & M. S. Yan

DESCRIPTION. Very similar to *C. montana* but with ternate or pinnate leaves with glabrous, ovate to elliptic leaflets with entire margins, and flowers with 6 white sepals. The flowers are borne in groups of 2–7 at the nodes on the previous year's shoots as in *C. montana* and are 36–40 mm (1.4–1.6 in) across, the sepals 18–20 mm (0.71–0.79 in) long and 8–10 mm (0.32–0.4 in) wide, with a rounded or somewhat notched apex. Achenes pubescent.

DISTRIBUTION. N China (S Gansu; Wen Xian); c. 500 m (1650 ft).

HABITAT. Grassy slopes; Mar–Apr.

99. *Clematis brevipes* Rehder

DESCRIPTION. A deciduous climber closely related to
C. gracilifolia but distinct on account of the flowers
which arise in the axils of the current year's shoots,
not the previous. The leaves are pinnate; leaflets 5,
papery, ovate to elliptical, sometimes 3-lobed, 30–45
mm (1.2–1.8 in) long, only partly developed at
flowering time. Flowers solitary, flat or slightly
cupped, 30–38 mm (1.2–1.5 in) across, borne on
pedicels 10–25 mm (0.4–1 in) long with a small pair
of bracts about the middle or above. Sepals 4, creamy-
white or yellowish-white, spreading, oval to almost
rounded, 15–19 mm (0.6–0.75 in) long, 12–15 mm
(0.47–0.6 in) wide, downy only beneath. Ovaries and
achenes pubescent. The flower colour and hairy
achenes serve to distinguish this species easily from
C. gracilifolia.

DISTRIBUTION. N China (S Gansu; by Min Xian).

HABITAT. Shrubberies and open woodland; Apr–May.

This interesting member of the Montana Group is
readily recognized. It was discovered in southern Gansu
in 1925 by Joseph Rock during the Arnold Arboretum
expedition to north-western China and north-eastern
Tibet. Although it has rather small flowers this is an
interesting and pretty little species that would be very
nice to receive into cultivation, especially as some
forms have cream or yellowish flowers.

100. *Clematis gracilifolia* Rehd. & Wils.*
(syn. *C. gracilifolia* var. *pentaphylla* (Maxim.) W. T.
Wang, *C. montana* Buch.-Ham. var. *batangensis* Finet
and var. *pentaphylla* Maxim.)

DESCRIPTION. A deciduous climber 2–4 m (6.6–13 ft)
with rather delicate greyish ribbed stems, green and
somewhat downy when young. Leaves pinnate with 5
or 7 papery leaflets, occasionally ternate; leaflets ovate
to oblong or obovate, 15–75 mm (0.6–3 in) long, with
a few coarse teeth or 1–2 lobes towards the base,
occasionally 3-lobed. Flowers in clusters of 2–5,
occasionally solitary, with several leaves from the
nodes of the previous season's shoots, 20–35 mm
(1–1.4 in) across, occasionally larger, flat or slightly
cupped, borne on slender downy pedicels to 80 mm
(3.2 in) long. Sepals 4, rarely 5, white, oval to
obovate, 10–18 mm (0.4–0.7 in) long, 6–15 mm
(0.24–0.6 in) wide, with a rounded apex, downy

outside, glabrous inside. Stamens about one-third the
length of the sepals. Achenes broad-ovate, 4–5 mm
(0.16–0.2 in) long, glabrous, with a plumose tail to 25
mm (1 in) long.

DISTRIBUTION. China (S Gansu, W Sichuan, E & SE
Tibet, NW Yunnan); 2000–3800 m (6500–12,500 ft).

HABITAT. Open forests and shrubberies, streamsides,
generally of mixed deciduous and evergreen species,
particularly *Rhododendron, Rosa, Berberis* and *Acer*;
Apr–June.

This species was first discovered in the early 1900s by
Ernest Henry Wilson in Sichuan and it was introduced
into cultivation by him in 1910. Later collections were
made by William Purdom (in Gansu) and George
Forrest (from north-western Yunnan) and, more
recently, by several seed collecting expeditions in
south-western China. It is an altogether delightful and
graceful species much neglected in gardens in favour
of its more robust and larger-flowered cousin C.
montana. However, *C. gracilifolia* is certainly worth
obtaining for it can be very floriferous and being less
bulky is more suitable for draping over bushes and
smaller trees in the garden. It generally comes into
flower ahead of *C. montana*.

Several varieties have been described based primarily
on details of the leaves; however, in this species at
least, leaves can vary a great deal within a colony,
sometimes even on the same plant. I have observed the
species in several areas in the wild, most notably in
north-western Yunnan (Da-xue-shan) and in northern
Sichuan (Songpan region) where it is very frequent.
The degree of lobing or dissection of the leaflets is
remarkably variable in some populations as well as the
number of leaflets. It is quite common to see ternate
and pinnate leaves on the same stem, indeed
intermediate leaf forms in which the terminal leaflet of
a ternate leaf is deeply 3-lobed, are commonplace.
Flower size is equally variable, although those tending
to the smaller dimensions given above are certainly far
more common than those with larger flowers.
Hybridization in the wild in north-western Yunnan and
southern Sichuan between this species and forms of *C.
montana* cannot be ruled out and may perhaps account
for some of the variability seen in certain populations. I
cannot therefore uphold the varieties that have been
described, although they may be worthy of some status
horticulturally. For completeness I present them below:

var. *dissectifolia* W. T. Wang & M. C. Chang is
distinguished by having deeply cut 2–3-parted leaflets
and small flowers 15–23 mm (0.6–0.9 in) across, the

39. *Clematis gracilifolia* var. dissectifolia at Wolong, W. Sichuan, China.
Photo: Christopher Grey-Wilson

sepals only 7–11 mm (0.28–0.43 in) long. Known only from W Sichuan and the neighbouring regions of E Tibet and Qinghai at 2800–4000 m (9200–13,100 ft). May–June.

var. *macrantha* **W. T. Wang & M. C. Chang** (syn. *C. gracilifolia* var. *trifoliolata* M. Johns.) has ternate to pinnate rather larger leaves, the leaflets undivided to 3-lobed (to 50 mm (2 in) long and 25 mm (1 in) wide) and larger flowers 50–65 mm (2–2.6 in) across; sepals 25–32 mm (1–1.3 in) long. Described from W Sichuan (Baoxing) but also known from N Sichuan and further north in Gansu (Choni area); similar habitats and altitudes to var. *gracilifolia*.

H6; P1

❀ ❀ **Leaves generally ternate (species 101–104)**
❖   **Sepals long-acuminate (species 101)**

101. *Clematis tongluensis* **(Brühl) Kapoor***

(syn. *C. montana* sensu Hk. f. & Th., non Buch.-Ham., *C. m.* subsp. *sinchungica* (Kuntze) Gupta and subsp. *sinchungica* Kuntze, *C. m.* var. *tongluensis* Bruehl)

DESCRIPTION. A deciduous climber to 5 m (16.5 ft) with 12-ribbed stems and ternate leaves. Leaflets ovate to ovate-lanceolate, to 85 mm (3.3 in) long, and 50 mm (2 in) wide, sometimes 2–3-lobed, with 3 or 5 main veins and a rather unevenly serrate margin, somewhat hairy on the veins beneath. Flowers solitary or two, produced from lateral buds on the previous year's shoots, borne on slender pedicels 12–30 cm (4.7–12 in) long, 6–12 cm (2.4–4.7 in) across. Sepals 4, occasionally 5–6, white, oblong-elliptic, 30–60 mm (1.2–2.4 in) long, 8–20 mm (0.32–0.8 in) wide, acuminate, spreading widely apart. Stamens glabrous, with purple anthers. Achenes hairy, with a tail to 30 mm (1.2 in) long.

DISTRIBUTION. E Himalaya (E Nepal to N Sikkim & C & N Bhutan); 2300–3500 m (7550–11,500 ft).

HABITAT. In coniferous or mixed forests, growing on bushes and bamboo; June–July.

A very attractive species of the *C. montana* persuasion, which is readily distinguished on account of its markedly acuminate sepals. It is still very rare in cultivation, but the larger-flowered forms often seen in the wild in the eastern Himalaya would be well worth introducing.

H6; P1

var. *khasiana* (Brühl) Kapoor (syn. *C. montana* var. *khasiana* Brühl, *C. m.* subsp. *sinchungica* Kuntze var. *khasiana* (Brühl) A. L. Gupta) is distinguished by its rather larger flowers, the sepals to 35 mm (1.4 in) long and 18 mm (0.7 in) wide. Restricted to the Khasia Hills in Assam, south-east of the typical variety, and flowering rather earlier, Apr–May.

❖ ❖ **Sepals with a rounded, notched or subacute apex (species 102–104)**

✳ **Leaflets untoothed or almost so (species 102)**

102. *Clematis venusta* M. C. Chang*

DESCRIPTION. Very close to *C. montana*, but distinguished by having lanceolate leaflets which are entire or occasionally with 1–2 tiny teeth in the upper half on each side. The flowers are white, 50–80 mm (2–3.2 in) across, 1–3 arising at the nodes on the previous year's shoots; sepals elliptical, 25–40 mm (1–1.6 in) long, 20–25 mm (0.8–1 in) wide. Achenes glabrous to slightly hairy.

DISTRIBUTION. SW China (NW Yunnan; primarily in the Lijiang-Zhongdian region); 2300–2700 m (7550–8850 ft).

HABITAT. Open forest and forest margins, shrubberies; April–early June.

40. *Clematis tongluensis*, Kanchenjunga region, E. Nepal.
Photo: Christopher Grey-Wilson

41. Clematis venusta near San-dau-wan, N of Lijiang, NW Yunnan, China. Photo: Christopher Grey-Wilson

This interesting species, that does not appear to be cultivation is quite common in the Lijiang area. The sepals have a distinctive appearance, generally with a rather wavy and somewhat revolute margin, while the pointed apex is similarly recurved. The species may have been brought into cultivation in recent years under the *C. montana* 'umbrella', for unless closely examined it is difficult to distinguish it in the wild in the fruiting stage from that species.

H6; P1

※ ※ **Leaflets toothed to somewhat lobed (species 103 & 104)**

103. *Clematis montana* Buch.-Ham. ex DC.*

(syn. *C. insulari-aslpina* Hayata, *C. kuntziana* Lévl. & Vant., *C. montana* var. *angustifoliola* Kuntze, var. *brevifoliola* Kuntze, var. *brevipedunculata* Kuntze, var. *edentata* Kuntze, var. *flavida* Kuntze, var. *incisa* Kuntze, var. *nutantiflora* Kuntze, var. *obtusisepala* Kuntze, var. *pubescens* Kuntze and var. *rubens* sensu Kuntze ex Hook. f. & Th., non Wils., *C. punduana* Wall.)

DESCRIPTION. A moderately vigorous to very vigorous climber to 12 m (40 ft), although often 5–8 m (16.5–26 ft), with rounded 6–12-ribbed stems that are generally slightly hairy when young, often flushed with purple and brownish-violet. Leaves ternate, rather thin, mid to deep green above, paler and rather shiny beneath; leaflets variable from oval to elliptical or lanceolate, to 90 mm (3.6 in) long and 45 mm (1.8 in) wide, acute to subacute or acuminate, generally with a few coarse, rather uneven, teeth on each side or even slightly lobed, sometimes entire, with 3 main veins, usually sparsely hairy on both surfaces. Flowers solitary or borne in few-flowered clusters from the lateral buds of the previous year's shoots (occasionally a few later on the current year's shoots), fragrant or not, mainly 40–60 mm (1.6–2.4 in) across, on slender pedicels to 12 cm (4.7 in) long. Sepals white, occasionally with a flush of pink beneath, oval to elliptical, 18–30 mm (0.7–1.2 in) long, 0.5–25 mm (1 in) wide, spreading widely apart, hairy beneath, with an obtuse to acute or even somewhat emarginate apex. Stamens glabrous, with pale yellow anthers. Achenes compressed-rounded to elliptic, 3–5 mm (0.12–0.2 in) long, glabrous (like the ovaries), with a plumose tail 25–40 mm (1–1.6 in) long.

DISTRIBUTION. Himalaya (from NW Pakistan to Assam and Upper Burma) and most of mountainous China (from S Gansu, to S Shaanxi, Hubei and S Anhui southwards, including S & E Tibet), C Taiwan; 1200–4000 m (3900–13,100 ft).

HABITAT. Woodland, mixed or deciduous, shrubberies, or in more open places over bushes or rocks, favouring the upper forest belt, stream margins, often close to or slightly above the tree line; Apr–early July.

Few species command the gardener's attention more than *C. montana*. Extremely popular, easy, fully hardy and adaptable to a wide variety of conditions in the garden, *C. montana* has been popular for many years. It was introduced from the Himalaya in 1831 by Lady Amherst. Since then further introductions from the Himalaya and western China, as well as a selection and hybridization in cultivation has led to a plethora of exciting forms and colours. Today there are some excellent cultivars and an exciting choice for the gardener; many cultivars are freely available in the nursery trade and garden centres and the list of new cultivars grows as each year passes. Although the display of flowers is often quite startling in sheer 'flower power' it is generally rather short-lived and the whole event can be over in a fortnight, but this is certainly not to their disadvantage, for I would grow them if they lasted but a single day. Many forms of *C. montana* will seed around in the garden; however, seedlings are rarely as good as their parents, although you may always be lucky and quite unintentionally produce a plant of rare beauty. The ordinary forms of *C. montana*, particularly most of those grown from wild collected seed, have white flowers. If you want a pink form then check the list

42. Clematis montana above Napa-hai, Zhongdian, NW Yunnan, China. Photo: Christopher Grey-Wilson

of cultivars below for a suitable name. Many of the cultivars are scented, but not all, and this applies equally to plants in the wild.

The wild forms of *C. montana*, especially in the Himalaya and south-western China are nearly always white-flowered, occasionally with a hint of pink or mauve on the sepal reverse. Early in the twentieth century Ernest Henry Wilson, an indefatigable plant hunter, introduced a rose-red-flowered form (later described as var. *rubens*) from Hubei in western China and this opened up the possibilities of producing a greater range of colours, particularly pinks, into the montana range. Wilson also introduced the later, white-flowered form which was later given his name, var. *wilsonii*.

The species can be divided into two subspecies based primarily on the characters of the leaves: subsp. *montana* has ternate leaves, whilst subsp. *praecox* has basically pinnate leaves. The taxonomy of *C. montana* requires further detailed investigation and the author has to admit that the subdivisions presented below are far from perfect. The species is extremely variable from one region to another, sometimes within one

43. Clematis montana, Napa-hai, Zhongdian, NW Yunnan, China.
Photo: Phillip Cribb

44. *Clematis montana*, a Nepalese form photographed in the Gurka Himal. Photo: Christopher Grey-Wilson

locality. The shape and details of the leaves and the size of the flowers appear to be immensely variable and even the extent and variability of the typical manifestation of the species (*C. montana* subsp. *montana*), which has an enormous west-east range in the wild, is far from clear-cut. Of course, this wide variability has been greatly to the advantage of the gardener, with numerous forms to choose from.

45. *Clematis montana*, a form with pink-banded sepals found above Wolong in W Sichuan, China. Photo: Christopher Grey-Wilson

subsp. *montana* var. *grandiflora* Hook.* AGM
(syn. *C. anemoniflora* D. Don, *C. montana* var. *anemoniflora* (D. Don) P. Brühl, *C. m.* subsp. *normalis* Kuntze var. *anemoniflora* (D. Don) Kuntze, *C. m.* subsp. N. var. *grandiflora* Hook.) has leaflets up to 90 mm (3.5 in) long, and generally produces solitary or two flowers from each lateral bud, these large, 7–12 cm (2.8–4.7 in) across, but those up to 14 cm (5.5 in) across have been recorded, borne on pedicels 10–20 cm (4–8 in) long; sepals oval to more or less oblong, generally 35–68 mm (1.4–2.7 in) long and 13–26 mm (0.5–1 in) wide, with an obtuse to subacute apex. Stamens with anthers 3–4 mm (0.12–0.16 in) long (mainly 1.5–3 mm (0.06–0.12 in) long in the other varieties). Ovaries and achenes glabrous. Scattered localities in the Himalaya from northern India eastwards and in parts of W & C China (S Gansu, Guizhou, W Hubei, W Hunan, S Shaanxi, Sichuan, S Tibet, NW Yunnan) at 1100–3500 m (3600–11,500 ft). Most frequent in shrubberies, forest margins and along streamsides. This is a very fine but extremely variable plant. I have seen it on a number of occasions in north-western Yunnan, especially in the Lijiang region, where it commonly grows alongside more ordinary forms of *C. montana*. It has a distinctive look with exceptional flowers fully 10–12 cm (4–4.7 in) across. with broad, rather pointed, white sepals and a spreading boss of stamens that bear long anthers. Despite its flower size, var. *grandiflora* does not appear to be particularly vigorous and plants more than 4 m (13 ft) are exceptional. Strangely, large-flowered forms of *C. montana* appear here and there almost throughout the range of the species, but it has yet to be ascertained whether all these belong in fact to the same taxon as has been assumed by most authors. Var. *grandiflora* was described from the Himalaya, while all the plants cultivated under the name today appear to have originated in western China. Of recent collections those of CLD (Chungtien, Lijiang, Dali 1992) and the ACE (Alpine Garden Society 1994) expeditions stand out. Plants widely sold under the name var. *grandiflora* are, unless they have come from a *bone fide* expedition source, very doubtfully authentic; they are generally listed for some inexplicable reason as forma *grandiflora*. The true plant is quite magnificent. It was first described as a distinct species, *C. anemoniflora*, by D. Don in 1825, a name not taken up by Hooker when he made the same plant a variety of *C. montana* almost 20 years later. The epithet 'anemoniflora' is in fact extremely apt for the large flowers do bring to mind some exotic anemone. The Himalaya manifestations of this variety appear to have consistently yellow anthers, whereas those in western China have (at least all those that I have seen in the wild!) purplish anthers.

subsp. *montana* **var.** *manipurensis* **(Brühl) Kapoor**
(syn. *C. m.* subsp. *normalis* Kuntze var. *manipurensis*
Brühl) has leaflets that are often 2–3-lobed and with 3 or
5 main veins and rather smaller flowers, mainly 40–70
mm (1.6–2.8 in) across; sepals 25–40 mm (1–1.6 in)
long, 6–17 mm (0.24–0.67 in) wide. Restricted to NE
India (Manipur) and Burma (Nagaland) at 2134–3048 m
(7000–10,000 ft), where it flowers during April and May.

subsp. *montana* **var.** *rubens* **Wilson* AGM**
(syn. *C. m.* var. *grandiflora* sensu Wang, non Hook.)
has foliage flushed with purple when young but
bronzing later, deep purple stems, petioles and
pedicels and flowers of average size (50–60 mm
(1–1.4 in) across.) which are reddish-pink (originally
described as rosy-red), with a faint vanilla scent (now
sold as *C. montana* var. *rubens* "Odorata"). The
ovaries and achenes are glabrous.

This lovely variety was first noted by Augustine
Henry near Ichang in Hubei Province of China in 1886,
but it was not introduced into cultivation until about
1900 when it was collected by Ernest Henry Wilson for
the firm of Veitch & Sons; it was awarded a First Class
Certificate when shown at the Royal Horticultural
Society in 1905 from the garden at Coombe Wood. In
the wild its precise distribution is unknown, although it
is known from both Sichuan and Hubei. It is quite one
of the finest clematis seen in gardens and is reliable
and floriferous. Unfortunately, many plants sold under
the name are inferior with paler and pinker blooms and
foliage without such marked coloration. It has been
questioned whether or not the original clone is still in
cultivation and great care should be taken when
selecting plants under the name to ensure that, at least,
they are a good pink colour.

subsp. *montana* **var.** *sterilis* **Hand.-Mazz.** is a less
vigorous plant to 4–5 m with elliptical to lanceolate
entire leaflets not more than 30 mm (1.2 in) long
normally. Flowers white, borne in denser clusters, rather
small, generally 20–35 mm (0.8–1.4 in) across, the
sepals 10–17 mm (0.4–0.67 in) long and 3-9 mm
(0.12–0.35 in) wide; pedicels not more than 40 mm (1.6
in) long. Achenes glabrous as in the typical plant, var.
montana. Apparently restricted to SW Sichuan and NW
Yunnan in SW China at 2400–3000 m (7900–9850 ft),
but almost certainly also in SE Tibet.

subsp. *montana* **var.** *trichogyna* **M. C. Chang** is
distinguished by possessing elliptical sepals which are
clearly mucronate (mucron of 2–3 mm (0.08–0.12 in))
at the apex, and appressed-hairy achenes. The scented
flowers are 50–80 mm (2–3.2 in) across, borne on
pedicels 9–14 cm (3.5–5.5 in) long; sepals white,

46. *Clematis montana* subsp. *montana* var. *grandiflora*, Wang-hi, N of Lijiang,
NW Yunnan, China. Photo: Christopher Grey-Wilson

47. *Clematis montana* subsp. *montana* var. *sterilis*, Kangding, W Sichuan, China.
Photo: Phillip Cribb

48. *Clematis montana* subsp. *montana* var. *wilsonii* in cultivation. Photo: Christopher Grey-Wilson

49. *Clematis montana* subsp. *praecox*, W of Ugyenscholing, Bhutan. Photo: Christopher Grey-Wilson

25–40 mm (1–1.6 in) long and 14–32 mm (0.55–1.3 in) wide. Described from NW Yunnan at 2550–3200 m (8400–10,500 ft).

subsp. *montana* var. *wilsonii* Sprague* (syn. *C. montana* var. *wilsonii* forma *platysepala* Rehd. & Wils., *C. repens* Veitch) is similar to var. *montana* but the leaflets are somewhat smaller generally (not more than 60 mm (2.4 in) long and 30 mm (1.2 in) wide), while the flowers are white, often flushed with green beneath, 40–80 mm (1.6–3.1 in) across; sepals 25–40 mm (1–1.6 in) long, 12–25 mm (0.47–1 in) wide, often with a somewhat emarginate apex, borne on pedicels 8–20 cm (3.2–8 in) long. The ovaries and achenes are glabrous, the plumose tails 40–60 mm (1.6–2.4 in) long. The prime feature of this variety is that it flowers later than the others, generally in June and July (occasionally even in early August), and this makes it invaluable in the garden for extending the flowering period of the Montana Group. In the wild it is found in the mountains of W & SW China (N Yunnan, W Sichuan and W Hubei) at 2400–3600 m (7900–11,800 ft), growing in shrubberies and along forest margins. It was introduced into cultivation in 1907 from Hubei by Ernest Henry Wilson and has been a popular plant ever since and is now widely available. Wilson actually introduced several collections from various regions in western China and several clones are in circulation, although beware, they are not always correctly named. Wilson commented that it was the commonest form of the species seen in western Sichuan. The flowers are pleasantly scented (said to be reminiscent of hot chocolate) and appear, on average, about a month after the other montanas (early summer). At first they are green and the flowers look slightly drab as they begin to open from their nodding buds, but as they expand and become upright the whole plants becomes a shimmering mass of white flowers which is quite glorious. A few precocious flowers may appear later in the years, as they can with so many in the Montana Group, but this varies very much from season to season. A form with broad obovate sepals which apparently flowers at the 'normal time' was distinguished by Rehder and Wilson as forma *platysepala*. However, they did not indicate how this forma could be distinguished from ordinary white-flowered forms of *C. montana* subsp. *montana* and, in any case, forma *platysepala* no longer appears to be in cultivation.

In my garden var. *wilsonii* comes into flower in mid-June and always attracts attention. It is well worth growing and continues the montana tribe well into summer.

subsp. *praecox* Kuntze (syn. *C. montana* var. *praecox* (Kuntze) Brühl)

DESCRIPTION. Leaves to 11 cm (4.3 in) long, pinnate (or ternate with the terminal leaflet deeply 3-lobed), the lower leaflets often 3-lobed to ternate; leaflets oval to rhombic, with a cuneate to sub-rounded base, to 46 mm (1.8 in) long and 42 mm (1.7 in) wide. Flowers in small lateral clusters, generally appearing in advance of the leaves on the previous year's stems, rather small, 25–45 mm (1–1.8 in) across, borne on pedicels to 90 mm (3.5 in) long, though generally only 20–60 mm (0.8–2.4 in). Sepals narrow-oval to elliptical. 10–20 mm (0.4–0.8 in) long, 4–11 mm (0.16–0.43 in) wide. Achenes hairy, with a plumose tail to 30 mm (1.2 in) long.

DISTRIBUTION. Bhutan, E Nepal, Sikkim, Bhutan & S Tibet (Chumbi); 2743–4267 m (9000–14,000 ft).

HABITAT. Similar to subsp. *montana*; Apr–June (–Aug).

This subspecies is little known and much confused in the wild with other forms of *C. montana*. The leaf characters are useful for determining plants out of flower. In flower the blooms generally appear in advance of the leaves so that the bare stems are adorned with bunches of small flowers at the nodes.

subsp. *praecox* var. *chumbica* Brühl has leaflets that are 3-lobed and oblong sepals, 15–25 mm (0.6–1 in) long. Doubtfully distinct. Recorded from Sikkim and the Chumbi region of S Tibet.

Subsp. *praecox* var. *intermedia* Brühl (syn. *C. montana* subsp. *montana* var. *intermedia* (Brühl) S. L. Kapoor) described from Sikkim (Tonglu) appears to be intermediate between *C. montana* subsp. *praecox* and the closely related *C. tongluensis*.

Cultivars of *C. montana*: as a point of interest, those plants with the deeper-flushed stems and pink or purplish leaf pigmentation are those with the deepest-coloured flowers. Young plants reared from cuttings do not always flower well during their first few years but once they start the display of bloom can be wholly reliable; hard pruning will only exasperate the situation. The more vigorous cultivars are excellent for scrambling up into old trees but beware of putting them in trees such as apples which flower at the same time, for the display will be lost amongst the mass of apple bloom, especially if both are pink. 'Alexander'* (large and luxuriant foliage with 50–60 mm (2–2.4 in) creamy-white scented flowers with creamy anthers, a wild form introduced from India by Colonel R. D. Alexander which requires a sunny position); 'Boughton Star'* (dark green, well-serrated foliage which is flushed with bronze at first, and semi-double

50. *Clematis montana* 'Elizabeth'. Photo: Christopher Grey-Wilson

51. *Clematis montana* 'Gurkha Star'. Photo: Christopher Grey-Wilson

52. *Clematis montana* 'Tetrarose'. Photo: Christopher Grey-Wilson

cup-shaped flowers of dusky rose); 'Elizabeth'* (charming pale pink flowers scented strongly of vanilla, with bronzed young foliage; plant in a sunny position, otherwise the flowers will be practically white); 'Freda'* (deep pink, slightly scented, flowers with reddish margins contrasts with the boss of yellow anthers and well-bronzed young foliage); 'Gothenburg'* (cream flowers flushed with pink contrast with the bronzed foliage in which each leaflet has a silvery midrib); 'Mrs Margaret Jones'* (creamy-white flowers flushed with green are semi-double and

53. *Clematis spooneri* in cultivation. Photo: Christopher Grey-Wilson

starry but without anthers; requires a sunny position); 'Marjorie'* (the first semi-double cultivar introduced; creamy-pink flowers open from green buds flushed with pink); 'Mayleen'* (a relatively recent introduction, this cultivar has satiny rose-pink flowers with a powerful vanilla fragrance, contrasting with well bronzed young foliage); 'Peveril'* (large white flowers, 70–80 mm (2.8–3.2 in) across. contrast with the green foliage; late-flowering); 'Pink Perfection'* (pink, vanilla-scented, flowers and bronzed young foliage); 'Picton's Variety'* (less vigorous than most with deep mauve flowers with a hint of lilac, often with 5–6 sepals; plant in a bright sunny position to get the best flower colour); 'Pleniflora'* (an invalid cultivar name but an attractive plant with semi-double white flowers with rather narrow sepals and staminodal petals, contrasting with the neat green foliage); 'Tetrarose'* AGM (an artificial Dutch cultivar with luxuriant foliage which is bronze at first but matures to a deep bronzy purple; flowers lilac-rose, the sepals thick and satiny; prone to winter die-back and not always as floriferous as some of its cousins); 'Vera'* (deep pink flowers with a vanilla scent contrast with the slightly bronzed young foliage). Mostly flowering in May and June, unless otherwise indicated.

H6; P1

104. *Clematis spooneri* Rehd. & Wils.* AGM
(syn. *C. chrysocoma* Hort. p.p., *C. chrysocoma* var. *glabrescens* Comber and var. *sericea* Schneid., *C. chrysocoma* var. Hand.-Mazz., *C. montana* var. *glabrescens* (H. F. Comber) W. T. Wang & M. C. Chang and var. *sericea* Franch.)
A vigorous deciduous climber 6–9 m (20–30 ft). Leaflets 4.5–14 cm (1.6–5.5 in) long. Flowers 7–9 cm (2.8–3.5 in) across, borne on pedicels 9–14 (–19) cm (3–5.5 (–7.5) in) long, not scented; stems and buds covered in a sparse golden down when young. Sepals white, 28–40 mm (1.1–1.6 in) long, 14–32 mm (0.55–1.3 in) wide, obtuse. Ovaries finely pubescent (puberulous). Achenes appressed puberulous, with a plumose style 45–70 mm (1.8–2.8 in) long.

DISTRIBUTION. SW China (NW Yunnan & S Sichuan and the neighbouring parts of Tibet); 2100–3500 m (6800–11,500 ft).

HABITAT. Forest margins and shrubberies; May–June. This species has had an extremely confused history. First described as a variety of *C. chrysocoma* and later a variety of *C. montana,* it is not surprising that it has perplexed both botanists and gardeners. There is no doubt that the plant in question is to be found in the wild, indeed it appears to be quite common in north-western Yunnan, especially in the Lijiang region. It is both a vigorous climbing species, very different to the shrubby *C. chrysocoma*, while at the same time having hairier buds and leaves than those of *C. montana*. Sometimes the sepals have a slight pink flush along the centre. To my mind it certainly seems in some respects to be intermediate and it is possible to postulate a hybrid origin between these two species, although this cannot be substantiated at present. What is quite clear is that *C. spooneri* is emphatically not the same as *C. chrysocoma*, nor a variety of that species, despite many erroneous references to it being so in the horticultural press, often by extremely informed gardeners. This is as it may be, but *C. spooneri* is distinctive in the wild and appears to come true from seed and for this reason alone it would seem best to recognize it as a separate species. Its precise wild distribution is uncertain due to confusion with these other species in the past. Interestingly, the artificial hybrid *C.* × *vedrariensis*, produced by Vilmorin in France earlier in the twentieth century looks very similar to some of the wild forms of *C. spooneri* except for the fact that the flowers are pink. This is hardly surprising as it was a cross between *C. spooneri* and the lovely pink form of *C. montana*, var. *rubens*. In fact it is clear that all crosses between *C. montana* and *C. spooneri* should bear the name C. × *vedrariensis*.

It was introduced from China in the 1890s. The Award of Garden Merit was given to the species under the name *C. montana* var. *sericea*, a synonym. Although the main flowering period is in late spring and early summer, some bloom is generally produced later in the summer on the current year's growths.

C. × *vedrariensis* Vilm. (syn. *C. verrierensis* Hort.). A vigorous deciduous climber to 6 m (20 ft) with ribbed and downy young stems and ternate leaves; leaflets ovate with a wedge-shaped base and pointed apex, often 3-lobed, dull purplish green and with pale yellowish hairs above, paler and more densely hairy beneath. Flowers solitary from the leaf-axils, borne primarily on last year's shoots, but sometimes also on the present years, 50–65 mm (2–2.6 in) across. Sepals 4, occasionally 5–6, clear pale rose-pink, broad-oval. Stamens yellow in quite a dense boss.

This very interesting hybrid was raised by Messrs Vilmorin, the famous Versailles nursery, and first exhibited at the May meeting of the National Horticultural Society of France in 1914. It inherits the general hairiness of *C. chrysocoma* with the vigour and floriferousness of *C. montana* var. *rubens*, the

54. *Clematis* x *vedrariensis* 'Highdown'. Photo: Raymond Evison

parent species. It has, unfortunately, been much confused in horticulture with *C. spooneri*. Part of this has arisen from the fact that Vilmorin crossed the recently introduced *C. spooneri* (*C. chrysocoma* var. *sericea*) with both *C. montana* var. *rubens* and his own hybrid *C.* × *vedrariensis*, using the former as the male parent. The result of these crosses were very similar and the plants were assumed under the general name of '*C. spooneri rosea*'. As *C. spooneri* is now recognized as a distinct species then this cannot be correct. Furthermore, this hybrid cannot be considered to be another manifestation of *C.* × *vedrariensis* as the two have a somewhat different parentage. The plant generally sold as *C. spooneri* 'Rosea' (or 'Spooneri Rosea') today is generally assumed to be *C.* × *vedrariensis* 'Rosea'* and has delightful flowers of mid rose-pink, often produced in abundance and rather later than most of the earlier forms of *C. montana*. 'Highdown'* is very similar. 'Hidcote'* is another manifestation of the same hybrid, a fine selection with deeper-rose-pink flowers which come perilously close to *C. montana* var. *rubens*.

H6; P1

SECTION CHEIROPSIS

This section includes the popular Mediterranean *C. cirrhosa* and two lesser known Asian species. They are unique in Subgenus *Montanae* is possessing nodding flowers. Although none are spectacular, they do have a quiet charm that attracts many gardeners. The three species of this section both bear a pair of small bracts on the 'pedicels', either near the middle or towards the top.

SUBSECTION CHEIROPSIS
(THE CIRRHOSA GROUP)

▼ **Sepals 25 mm (1 in) long or more (species 105)**

105. *Clematis cirrhosa* L.*
(syn. *Atragene cirrhosa* Pers.; *Cheiropsis calyculata* Hort. ex C. K. Schneid., *C. elegans* Spach; *C. cirrhosa* var. *pedicellata* DC., *C. c.* forma *obtusifolia* Kuntze, forma *scandens* Kuntze and forma *suberecta* Kuntze, *C. c.* var. *normalis* Kuntze and var. *typica* Maire, *C. pedicellata* R. Sweet)

DESCRIPTION. An evergreen climber to 8 m (26 ft), occasionally more, with slender, finely silky, 6-ribbed, young stems. Leaves glossy deep green, sometimes flushed with bronze, entire to 3-lobed or ternate, 18–50 mm (0.7–2 in) long, 12–38 mm (0.47–1.5 in) wide, generally with a heart-shaped base and coarsely toothed margin, glabrous. Flowers solitary or paired, broad-campanulate and nodding, generally several (2–5) produced on very short lateral shoots

55. Clematis cirrhosa var. cirrhosa in cultivation. Photo: Jack Elliott

(brachyblasts), generally honey-scented, downy outside, 40–70 mm (1.6–2.8 in) across; peduncles with a small, partly fused, pair of bracts cupped immediately below each flower or flower pair. Sepals 4, rarely 5, white to cream or greenish white, sometimes flecked with red or purple within, occasionally with a suffusion of reddish-purple, especially towards the base, oval to elliptic, 25–35 mm (1–1.4 in) long, 3-veined. Achenes pubescent, with a silky-white plumose tail to 50 mm (2 in) long.

DISTRIBUTION. Throughout the Mediterranean region as well as Portugal.

HABITAT. Woodland, scrub and hedgerows, often in maquis, occasionally in more open rocky places; Dec–Mar, but occasionally some flower through the summer months.

A very beautiful and valuable species for the winter garden, especially in a sheltered sunny site close to the house where its beauty can be more easily admired. Few plants put on such a fine show of bloom in the depths of winter and, although the individual flowers are rather small, they are produced in enough quantity to compensate. During severe winter weather the foliage and flowerbuds may be severely scorched and a warm sheltered corner of the garden and excellent drainage are to be recommended. In the mildest regions it can be grown with great success on arches and pergolas and will even succeed well against uninviting north-facing walls and fences. It pays to buy good or named forms from nurseries and garden centres, as some seedlings can be very poor.

It is well documented that the ancient Greeks twined the long stems of this species into wreaths and garlands that were used during festive occasions as well as for processions. It was also one of the sacred plants of Dionysus, together with other plants such as ivy, the grape vine and sarsaparilla.

Clematis cirrhosa is a common constituent of the flora of the Mediterranean region where it is often overlooked as it has generally finished flowering when most travellers venture to the region. However, the silky tassels of fruits festooning bushes and trees can be equally enticing and delightful and appear early in the year. The species was introduced into cultivation as long ago as the 1590s. As might be expected from its wide distribution (it creeps southwards into the mountains of North Africa and western Asia) the species is very variable and a number of separate taxa have been distinguished over the years. Undoubtedly some splendid forms exist in the wild that have yet to be introduced to our gardens; some will undoubtedly prove less hardy than others, but this is only to be expected from such a widely distributed species, which also has a wide altitudinal range in its native haunts. Although the variations found in the wild are not always clear-cut, and intermediates abound, some form of division seems appropriate and I follow the splits recommended by previous botanists, notably, in this instance, Otto Kuntze (1885):

var. *cirrhosa*. The type variety has oval to heart-shaped, generally coarsely toothed leaves which are sometime faintly trilobed and creamy-white flowers which are plain or only faintly spotted with purple inside, sometimes stained with green on the outside. It is found more or less throughout the range of the species but is often absent, or limited, in areas occupied by some of the other varieties. 'Wisley'* (='Wisley Cream') has good sized plain cream flowers, with a hint of green, set against rather paler foliage that bronzes well during the winter months. It was raised by the late Ken Aslet at the Royal Horticultural Society's garden at Wisley in the 1970s. 'Ourika Valley'* was named after the valley in the High Atlas Mountains of Morocco where seed was collected by Captain Peter Erskine in 1986. It is one of the hardiest and most free-flowering cultivars with plain, pale yellow flowers which at 40–50 mm (1.6–2 in) long, are rather larger than those of the typical plant. They are borne mainly in late winter and early spring.

var. *balearica* (Rich. & Juss.) Willk. & Lange* (syn. *Atragene balearica* Pers.; *Cheiropsis balearica* Spach; *Clematis balearica* (Rich.) Juss., *C. cirrhosa* sensu Batise, non L., *C. cirrhosa* forma *balearica* (Rich. & Juss.) Maire, *C. c.* var. *angustifolia* Loudon, *C. c.* var. *semitriloba* Rouy & Fouc., *C. calycina* Aiton). Like var. *cirrhosa* but leaves small, generally ternate, with incised lobing or teeth, the end leaflets often itself 3-lobed, generally flushed with bronze-purple, especially during the winter months. Flowers rather smaller, the sepals not more than 25 mm (1 in) long, creamy white with reddish-brown speckling within, rather narrower and somewhat twisted. This variety, which is the finest for average garden conditions, is restricted in the wild to the islands of the western Mediterranean, primarily the Balearics, Corsica and Sardinia. It is rather less vigorous and dense than the typical plant in gardens. The flowers tend to turn rather pink on ageing.

Var. *balearica*, often called the 'Fern-leaved Clematis', is undoubtedly the most popular manifestation of the species in gardens and is generally considered to be rather hardier than the typical plant. It was introduced into cultivation in 1783. The citrus-scented flowers are altogether charming and deserve close inspection; the little pale green bells generously

56. *Clematis cirrhosa* var. *cirrhosa* in cultivation. Photo: Raymond Evison

57. *Clematis cirrhosa* var. *cirrhosa* in fruit; S Spain, near Ronda. Photo: Martyn Rix

58. *Clematis cirrhosa* var. *balearica* in cultivation. Photo: Jack Elliott

flecked with reddish-brown within remind one of a hellebore; in fact the two are distantly related. The strongly toothed foliage is attractively bronzed during the winter months, while after flowering, the silken seed tassels are an added attraction that should not be overlooked. The plant received an Award of Merit (AM) when shown at the Royal Horticultural Society in 1974.

In colder districts, or where no suitable sheltered wall exists, then this lovely plant should be considered for the conservatory, where its charms can be enjoyed protected from the harsh winter weather. Conservatory plants will

59. *Clematis cirrhosa* var. *purpurascens* 'Freckles'. Photo: Christopher Grey-Wilson

bloom continuously from about late October right through the winter months. A rigorous pruning (to within a metre (3 ft) of the ground, if necessary) immediately after flowering will help to keep it in check.

var. *barnadesii* Pau. is similar to var. *purpurascens* This variety is restricted to southern Spain in the vicinity of Alicante southwards to Cartagena. It may well be little more than a form of var. *purpurascens*.

var. *gigantiflora* Kuntze (syn. *C. cirrhosa* var. *grandiflora* Choulette, *nomen nudum*) has unlobed but coarsely toothed leaves similar to var. *cirrhosa*, but extra large plain cream flowers 60–100 mm (2.4–4 in) across, with sepals up to 50 mm (2 in) long and 30 mm (1.2 in) wide. It is found in northern Algeria in the Constantine region.

var. *micrantha* Maire is distinguished from var. *cirrhosa*, which it closely resembles in leaf, by it smaller flowers which are not more than 30 mm (1.2 in) across. Described from the Bousarea region of northern Algeria.

var. *purpurascens* Kuntze* (syn. *C. cirrhosa* var. *dautezi* Debeaux) is distinguished by its 3-lobed, rather shallowly toothed, leaves and creamy flowers which are blotched inside with maroon-purple or carmine, this colour sometimes staining the whole of the inside of the flower. It is restricted to Mallorca, Gibralta and several places in northern Algeria. 'Freckles'* AGM is a particularly fine selection raised by the Raymond Evison in 1987, with the inside of the flowers generously blotched with maroon-purple. It was named by Raymond Evison, Director of the Guernsey Clematis Nursery and has become a deservedly popular plant. 'Freckles' tends to put on its main display of flowers in the late autumn, before the winter frosts arrive. Like the other manifestations of *C. cirrhosa*, it is an excellent climber for Mediterranean-type gardens and conservatories.

var. *semitriloba* (Lag.) Kuntze* (syn. *C. × candargii* Camus, *C. cirrhosa* forma *semitriloba* (Lag.) Baill., *C. c.* var. *atava* Kuntze, *C. polymorpha* Viv., *C. semitriloba* Lag.) is distinguished primarily by its ternate or 3-lobed leaves, with the leaflets often 3-, sometimes 5-, lobed and toothed, the teeth not incised as in var. *balearica*. The flowers are average sized, 40–50 mm (1.6–2 in) across, cream with some faint purple spotting or flecking inside. Known form widely scattered localities through much of the range of the species; particularly S Spain, Corsica, Crete, parts of Greece and Palestine.

var. *subedentata* **Kuntze** Leaves lanceolate, unlobed but usually shallowly toothed, sometimes entire. This variety is known from the eastern Mediterranean (from Izmir in western Turkey to the Lebanon) and parts of North Africa.

H7; P1

▼ ▼ **Sepals not more than 25 mm (1 in) long (species 106)**

106. *Clematis napaulensis* DC.*
(syn. *C. cirrhosa* subsp. *nepalensis* (DC.) Kuntze, *C. forrestii* W. W. Sm., *C. montana* sensu D. Don, non Buch.-Ham., *C. nepalensis* sensu B. Fretwell)

DESCRIPTION. An evergreen climber to 10 m (33 ft) (less in cultivation) with furrowed, greyish young shoots that become very woody with age. Leaves glabrous, ternate or pinnate, with 3–5 prime divisions, the lowermost often further 3-lobed; leaflets rather thin, ovate-lanceolate, 38–100 mm (1.5–4 in) long, 12–33 mm (0.47–1.3 in) wide, acuminate, entire or with a few large teeth or lobes, glabrous. Flowers solitary, nodding, bell-shaped, 16–18 mm (0.63–0.7 in) across, but up to 10 produced at each node pair, nodding on downy stalks, with a small fused pairs of downy, 5–9 mm (0.2–0.35 in) long, greenish bracts, cupped midway along the stalks, borne from nodes of previous year's shoots, unscented. Sepals 4, creamy-yellow to greenish-white, erect, ovate to elliptical, 15–25 mm (0.6–1 in) long and 4–11 mm (0.16–0.43 in) wide, silky outside, with the tips rolled or recurved. Stamens with prominent purple filaments, as long as the sepals and often appearing to protrude from the flower because of the recurved tips and margins of the sepals. Achenes obovate, 3–4 mm (0.12–0.16 in) long, hairy, rimmed, with a silky tail 35–50 mm (1.4–2 in) long.

DISTRIBUTION. Himalaya from E Nepal and N India (Sikkim) to C & S Bhutan, as well as SW China (S Guizhou, SE Tibet, Yunnan); 1220–2440 m (4000–8000 ft).

HABITAT. Subtropical and warm temperate forests, clambering over bushes and small trees, sometimes along streams; Nov–Mar.

This interesting and rather unusual species was first described from the Himalayan foothills. However, it was introduced from Yunnan in China by George Forrest in 1912. At the time the Chinese plant was thought to be a distinct new species and it therefore

60. *Clematis napaulensis* in cultivation in Ireland. Photo: Susyn Andrews

named after George Forrest, the name being subsequently absorbed into synonymy. *C. napaulensis* produces its flowers in the depths of winter and its chief attraction is in the prominent purple anthers. It is only hardy outside in the warmest gardens where frost is the exception. There are good specimens at Malahide Castle in the Republic of Ireland and Caerhays Castle in Cornwall, but there are other specimens outdoors elsewhere in southern Ireland and south-western Britain. Elsewhere it is best grown in a cool glasshouse or conservatory where it can be readily protected from the worst winter weather.

It is clearly closely related to the Mediterranean *C. cirrhosa* but could never be mistaken for that species. The small clustered bell-shaped flowers with their distinctive cupped bracts are good clues to this pair of species. Although the flowers are solitary they appear to be crowded as a cluster are normally produced at each node. The foliage is scarcely as attractive as its close cousin *C. cirrhosa*, and the flowers lack any hint of a scent.

Specimens of this species from the north-western Himalaya tend to have consistently smaller and fewer flowers (1–2 per axil), the sepals not more than 18 mm (0.7 in) long and 5 mm (0.2 in) wide. These may require varietal recognition. A specimen exhibited at the Royal Horticultural Society by the Director of the Royal Botanic Gardens Kew, in 1957, received an Award of Merit (AM). This species is often misspelled nepalensis or nepaulensis.

H8; P1 (after frost has ceased)

61. *Clematis williamsii* in cultivation. Photo: Raymond Evison

SUBSECTION WILLIAMSIANAE

107. *Clematis williamsii* **A. Gray***
(syn. *C. montana* var. *bissetii* Kuntze and var.
williamsii (A. Gray) Kuntze; *Clematopsis williamsii*
(A. Gray) Tobe)

DESCRIPTION. A moderately vigorous deciduous climber
to 3 m (10 ft) with downy green stems flushed with
brown. Leaves ternate, the leaflets oblong to oval, to 80
mm (3.2 in) long and 35 mm (1.4 in) wide, with a few
coarse teeth, or sometimes 3-lobed. Flowers solitary,
nodding, broad-campanulate, 35–45 mm (1.4–1.8 in)
across, on slender peduncles with a small pair of partly
fused bracts near the centre, from short lateral shoots
borne on the previous year's stems. Sepals white flushed
with green, oval to elliptical, 12–20 mm (0.47–0.8 in)
long, 8–14 mm (0.32–0.55 in) wide, downy outside.
Stamens glabrous, almost as long as the sepals, cream.
Achenes hairy, with a plumose tail to 25 mm (1 in) long.
DISTRIBUTION. Japan (Honshu, Kyushu, Shikoku).

HABITAT. Shrubberies and open forests; May–June,
occasionally earlier.

This is a dainty, yet attractive species that has only
recently come into cultivation. It is unique in Asia in
being the only species with imbricate (overlapping)
rather than valvate sepals. At present its hardiness is
untested in our gardens.

Probably H7 or 8; P1

SECTION FASCICULIFLORAE

This section is often placed in Section Flammula
(Magnus Johnson gave its own subsection,
Fasciculiflorae) but it seems to me that it is better
placed in Subgenus Cheiropsis. The clustered, nodding,
bell-shaped flowers and ternate leaves seem more akin
here rather than in Subgenus *Flammula*, whose
numerous species bear rather flat flowers (with wide-
spreading sepals) borne in distinctive inflorescences.

108. *Clematis fasciculiflora* **Franch.***
(syn. *C. montana* var. *fasciculiflora* (Franch.) Brühl)

DESCRIPTION. An evergreen climber, often rather shrubby,
with ribbed stems to 6 m (20 ft) and leathery ternate
leaves. Leaflets elliptical to narrow-ovate or lanceolate,
50–85 mm (2–3.3 in) long, 8–35 mm (0.32–1.4 in) wide,
occasionally wider, with an acuminate apex and an entire
margin. Flowers nodding-campanulate, 14–17 mm
(0.55–0.67 in) across, borne in clusters of 3–7 in the leaf-
axils of the current year's shoots, downy outside, each on
slender, equally downy stalks to 12 mm (0.47 in) long,
fragrant. Sepals 4, erect, creamy-yellow to whitish, oval
to elliptic, 12–20 mm (0.47–0.8 in) long, 5–12 mm
(0.2–0.47 in) wide. Stamens about two-thirds the length
of the sepals. Achenes lanceolate to oval, 5.5–8 mm
(0.22–0.32 in) long, glabrous, with a short plumose tail to
15 mm (0.6 in) long.

DISTRIBUTION. SW China (W Guangxi, SW Guizhou,
SW Sichuan, Yunnan), N Myanmar, N Vietnam;
1100–2500 m (3600–8200 ft).

HABITAT. Open forests, particularly of pine, shrubberies
and thickets, streamsides; late Nov–early Apr.

The interesting species was discovered in Yunnan in 1885
by Abbé Delavay and introduced into cultivation in 1910
by George Forrest, where it was grown at the Royal
Botanic Garden, Edinburgh. The small bell-flowers
appear to be in whorls at the nodes and although not
showy, they have a certain fascination, but the species is
generally regarded as having only a limited horticultural
appeal. In the finest forms the leaves have a purplish tint
and a silver band down the midrib of each leaflet.
  A George Forrest collection (10573) gathered form the
mountains NE of the Yangtse bend in NW Yunnan has
very narrow leaflets, only 4–6 mm (0.16–0.24 in) wide and
was distinguished as var. *angustifolia* Comber, although it
fits well within the circumscription of the species.

H8; P1

Subgenus Three *Flammula*

An extensive subgenus containing some 53 species, many of which are in cultivation. They bear rather flat, often starry flowers, that are predominantly white or cream and are often confused with the members of the somewhat larger Subgenus *Clematis*, which have rather similar flowers with glabrous stamens. The prime difference is seen in the seedlings; in Subgenus *Clematis* the leaves are alternate in seedlings, while in Subgenus *Flammula* they are opposite. This might seem a trifling difference to the gardener, although it can be easily observed in batches of young plants. However, evolutionary the early development of the plant from seedling to maturity is seen as quite significant.

SECTION FLAMMULA

SUBSECTION FLAMMULA
(THE FLAMMULA GROUP)

Twelve species distributed from Europe to eastern Asia, primarily in the Temperate Zone. The species include the familiar European *C. flammula*, which is eagerly sought by gardeners, as well as the handsome herbaceous *C. recta*. The flowers, which are relatively small and usually white, are borne in large clusters during the summer on the current season's shoots.

MAP FIVE
Subgenus F*lammula*
   Subsection Flammula   – – – – – – – –

62. Clematis mandshurica in cultivation. Photo: Daan Smit

63. Clematis recta in cultivation. Photo: Christopher Grey-Wilson

▼   **Plants perennial, without climbing stems (species 109–113)**

◆   **Leaves pinnate (species 109–111)**

❉   **Stems glabrous or hairy only at the nodes;sepals downy outside; achene tails 30–35 mm (1.2–1.4 in) long (species 109 & 110)**

109. *Clematis mandshurica* Rupr.*

(syn. *C. liaotungensis* Kitagawa, *C. recta* auct., non L., *C. r. subsp. mandshurica* (Rupr.) Kuntze, *C. terniflora* auct., non DC., *C. t.* var. *mandshurica* (Rupr.) Ohwi)

DESCRIPTION. Very similar to *C. terniflora* and included within that species as a variety by some authors. However, the plant is a spreading to scandent perennial to 1.2 m (4 ft). The prime differences are seen in the near glabrous stems (finely pubescent only at the nodes) and pedicels, in the slightly apiculate (rather than obtuse) apex to the anthers, and in the smaller achenes, just 4–6 mm (0.16–0.24 in) long. The flowers are 20–30 mm (0.8–1.2 in) across and pure white, the sepals 4, occasionally 5, 11–17 mm (0.43–0.67 in) long and 4–6 mm (0.16–0.24 in) wide.

DISTRIBUTION. NE China (Hebei, Heilongjiang, Jilin, Liaoning, E Inner Mongolia) Korea, Mongolia and SE Russia (Amur and Ussuriland); to 800 m (2600 ft).

HABITAT. Shrubberies and open wooded slopes; June–Aug.

Treated in the 'Flora of China' as a variety of *C. terniflora*. *C. mandshurica* has a more northerly distribution than *C. terniflora* and the two species do not appear to overlap, except perhaps in North Korea.

H7; P2

110. *Clematis sichotealinensis* Ulanova

DESCRIPTION. Closely related to *C. mandschurica*, differing in having smaller leaflets, not more than 20 mm (0.8 in) long and 12 mm (0.47 in) wide, with the sepals hairy only on the margins and the achenes with shorter tails, not more than 25 mm (1 in) long. Plants generally not more than 90 cm (3 ft) in height, often only 30–60 cm (12–24 in).

DISTRIBUTION. SE Russia (Ussuriland; Primorsk).

HABITAT. Similar habitats to *C. mandschurica*; June–July.

A little-known species that would make an interesting addition to the flower border. It is likely to be fully hardy.

❀ ❀ **Stems hairy, sometimes sparsely so; sepals glabrous outside or very slightly hairy; achene tails to only 25 mm (1 in) long, often less (species 111)**

111. *Clematis recta* **L.***
(syn. *C. erecta* Allioni, *C. recta* subsp. *normalis* Kuntze, *C. r.* var. *magnusiana* Kuntze, var. *saxatilis* Wierzb. ex Reichenb., var. *stricta* Wend. and var. *umbellata* Reichenb.)

DESCRIPTION. A clump-forming herbaceous perennial to 2 m (6.6 ft), but often only 1 m (39 in), sometimes less. Stems normally upright bearing pairs of pinnate deep green or blue-green leaves. Leaflets usually 5 or 7 oval to lanceolate, 30–60 mm (1.2–2.4 in) long, with an entire margin. Flowers borne in large terminal panicles, often enveloping the upper half of the plant, each 20–30 mm (0.8–1.2 in) across and star-like, often hawthorn-scented. Sepals 4, rarely 5–6, narrow-oval, 8–15 mm (0.32–0.6 in) long, 3–7 mm (0.12–0.28 in) wide. The stamens are about two-thirds the length of the sepals and bear creamy-white anthers. Achenes oval, 4–6 mm (0.16–0.24 in) long, glabrous, with a silky plumose tail to 30 mm (1.2 in) long, often less.

DISTRIBUTION. C, S & E Europe (from N Spain and France eastwards, northwards to Germany and Poland), W & C Russia.

HABITAT. Open woodland, bushy places and dry hill-slopes; June–Aug.

This fine herbaceous species is widely seen as a tall specimen plant at the back of the flower border. It was introduced into Britain as long ago as 1597. The best forms seen in gardens today are fairly compact, 1–1.2 m (3.3–4 ft) tall, with dense growth and numerous flowers; however, there are poorer less floriferous forms around, especially from seed-raised stocks. The growths are rarely self-supporting and require some canes or pea sticks to keep them upright; this is a character it has unfortunately acquired in cultivation for in the wild most plants seem to be dwarfer and more self-supporting, as its specific name indicates, but perhaps it finds the richer fare of the garden environment too much for its fragile constitution. Alternatively, plants can be allowed to flop on the ground and can be quite effective grown in this manner. Plants thrive best in a moist not too light soil in full sun. Some forms have extremely strongly scented flowers, an attractive fragrance that can fill the garden on a warm sunny day. The dwarfer forms of the typical plant, which often only grow a metre tall, are worth seeking out. Several named clones are available: 'Grandiflora'* has larger flowers than the normal, 'Plena' (syn. *C. recta* var.

64. Clematis recta 'Purpurea' in flower. Photo: Jack Elliott

65. Clematis recta 'Purpurea' before flowering. Photo: Jack Elliott

66. Clematis kirilowii, photographed near Beijing, China.
Photo: Christopher Grey-Wilson

pleniflora Hort. ex Kuntze, *C. recta* 'Flore Pleno') has double flowers (this clone may be extinct, although various semi-double forms are certainly still grown); 'Purpurea'* is very fine with purple leaves, which are particularly dark and rich when young, and contrast wonderfully well with the white flowers in mid-summer. The latter clone can be grown from seed, although only a small percentage of seedlings usually reveal the purple foliage colours. Trimming back the growths during the summer months encourages further purple foliage to develop, otherwise the plant gradually turns green as the seasons advance. Exceptionally good clones can be readily propagated by dividing the parent plant, which is a more sure way of maintaining it in cultivation rather than hoping that seedlings may be just as good.

H3; P2 (late winter)

◆ ◆ Leaves bipinnate (species 112 & 113)
❀　　Flowers 20–30 mm (0.8–1.2 in) across; plant
　　　2–70 cm (0.8–28 in) tall (species 112)

112. *Clematis pseudoflammula* Schmalh. ex Lipsky*

DESCRIPTION. Very similar to *C. recta*, but plant not more than 70 cm (28 in) tall, with bipinnate leaves and smaller leaflets only 30–50 mm (1.2–2 in) long.

DISTRIBUTION. S & E Ukraine and S Russia and the Caucasian states; c. 700 m (2300 ft).

H5; P2

❀ ❀ Flowers 30–35 mm (1.2–1.4 in) across; plant
　　　1–1.5 m (3.3–5 ft) (species 113)

113. *Clematis taeguensis* Y. Lee

DESCRIPTION. Very similar to *C. mandschurica* but leaves bipinnate, the leaflets lanceolate to narrow-oval, not more than 50 mm (2 in) long and 14 mm (0.55 in) wide, and flowers rather larger, 30–35 mm (1.2–1.4 in) across. The plant forms an open bush with ascending stems to 1.5 m (5 ft).

DISTRIBUTION. S Korea (Taegu region).

HABITAT. Riverside cliffs; probably July–Aug.

▼ ▼ Plants climbers with twining petioles (species 114–120)
❖　　Leaflets distinctly net-veined (species 114 & 115)
✳　　Petiole not noticeably expanded at the base; sepals
　　　usually 4, occasionally 5–6 (species 114)

114. *Clematis kirilowii* Maxim.*
(syn. *C. matsumurana* Yabe, *C. recta* subsp. *kirilowii* (Maxim.) Kuntze)

DESCRIPTION. A deciduous climber to 2 m (6.6 ft), rarely more, with slightly hairy 4–8-furrowed stems. Leaves pinnate to bipinnate; leaflets narrow-ovate to oblong, occasionally, to 60 mm (2.4 in) long and 28 mm (1.1 in) wide, occasionally larger, leathery, with an entire margin, occasionally 3-lobed and rounded, truncated or somewhat cuneate at the base, glabrous to slightly hairy on the veins above and beneath, or more densely so beneath, prominently net-veined. Inflorescences lateral or terminal, 3-many-flowered cymes, the flowers 14–30 mm (0.55–1.2 in) across. Sepals white, usually 4 but occasionally 5–6, spreading, oblong, 7–15 mm (0.28–0.6 in) long and 3–6 mm (0.12–0.24 in) wide, finely pubescent on the outside. Stamens about half the length of the sepals. Achenes elliptic, 4–5 mm (0.16–0.2 in) long, with plumose tails to 20 mm (0.8 in) long.

DISTRIBUTION. C & E China (N Anhui, W Hebei, Henan, Jiangsu, Shandong, SE Shanxi); 150–1700 m (490–5600 ft).

HABITAT. Thickets, grassy slopes and streamsides; June–Aug.

A very variable species within which a number of more or less clear-cut varieties can be recognized:

var. *bashanensis* M. C. Chang has strictly pinnate leaves, the leaflets narrow-ovate to triangular-ovate or lanceolate, to 45 mm (1.8 in) wide, generally glabrous; sepals 7–12 mm (0.28–0.47 in) long. Similar habitats to 100 m in Anhui, S Henan, W Hubei, S. Jiangsu, S Shaanxi and E Sichuan; May–Aug (var. *pashanensis* of M. Johns.)

var. *chanetii* (H. Lévl.) Hand.-Mazz. (syn. *C. chanetii* H. Lévl.) is very similar to the typical plant, but with narrower, linear to lanceolate, leaflets, not more than 10 mm (0.4 in) wide. Similar habitats to 900 m (3000 ft); restricted to W Hubei, Shandong and SE Shanxi; June–Aug.

var. *latisepala* (M. C. Chang) W. T. Wang (syn. *C. terniflora* DC. var. *latisepala* M. C. Chang) is distinguished primarily on its apiculate rather than obtuse anthers (possessed by the other varieties). In addition, the leaves are strictly pinnate and similar in size and shape to those of var. *bashanensis*. Similar habitats, to 2000 m (6500 ft), being restricted to S & W Henan, W Hubei, SE Shaanxi and S Shanxi; Apr–Aug.

H4; P2

✳ ✳ **Petiole base expanded and fused across stem to opposing petiole; sepals usually 5–7 (species 115)**

115. *Clematis dilatata* Pei

DESCRIPTION. Very closely related to *C. kirilowii*, especially in its net-veined (reticulate) leaves, but distinguished primarily on account of its larger 5–7-sepalled flowers which are white flushed with pink; sepals lanceolate to oblong, 18–35 mm (0.7–1.4 in) long, 5–10 mm (0.2–0.4 in) wide, acute, which are downy on both sides, especially beneath. In addition, the petioles are characteristically expanded at the base and fused to the opposite petiole of the pair.

DISTRIBUTION. E China (C & S Zhejiang); 300–800 m (1000–2600 ft).

HABITAT. Forests, forested ravines, streamsides; May–June.

❖ ❖ **Leaflets not distinctly net-veined (species 116–120)**
✳ **Flowers pale pink, 35–75 mm (1.4–3 in) across; leaflets often finely toothed (species 116)**

116. *Clematis akoensis* Hayata
(syn. *C. dolichosepala* Hayata, *C. owatarii* Hayata)

DESCRIPTION. A climbing plant to 4 m (13 ft) with reddish, ridged stems that are hairy at first. Leaves pinnate or sometimes ternate, glabrous; leaflets 3 or 5, broad-elliptic to almost triangular, to 74 mm (3 in) long and 54 mm (2.1 in) wide, with a truncated or slightly heart-shaped base, 3 or 5 main veins from the base and a slightly serrated margin. Flowers in lax lateral cymes of normally 1–5, each flower 35–75 mm (1.4–3 in) across. Sepals 5–6, pale pink, elliptic, 20–35 mm (0.8–1.4 in) long, 5–13 mm (0.2–0.5 in) wide, wide-spreading, glabrous inside but downy outside. Stamens almost half the length of the sepals. Achene ovate to elliptic, 5–8 mm (0.2–0.32 in) long, yellowish-brown or reddish-brown hairy, with a pale yellow plumose tail to 45 mm (1.8 in) long.

DISTRIBUTION. S Taiwan (Pingtung & Taitung); at low altitudes to 800 m (2600 ft).

HABITAT. Forest margins, shrubberies and hedgerows; Nov–Feb.

An attractive species that would be well worth while bringing into cultivation. The relatively large pale pink flowers makes *C. akoensis* one of the most desirable members of the *C. flammula* persuasion. It would be highly advantageous to seek out the larger-flowered and better-coloured forms in the wild.

✳ ✳ **Flowers white, smaller, 8–35 mm (0.32–1.4 in) across; leaflets untoothed (species 117–120)**
✪ **Leaves usually bipinnate (species 117)**

117. *Clematis flammula* L.* Fragrant Clematis
(syn. *C. recta* subsp. *flammula* (L.) Kuntze)

DESCRIPTION. A vigorous deciduous climber to 5 m (16ft), occasionally more, forming a dense entanglement, which is generally rather bare below in the wild; stems glabrous, green and ribbed. Leaves deep green usually bipinnate, the leaflets very variable in size and shape from narrow-elliptic or lanceolate to oval, oblong or almost round, unlobed or, more often, 2–3 lobed, but untoothed, to 40 mm (1.6 in) long, with 3 or 5 main veins, glabrous. Flowers borne in large leafy panicles (composed of lateral and terminal raceme-like cymes, often with more than 15 flowers), 15–25 mm (0.6–1 in) across, strongly fragrant. Sepals 4, elliptical, 8–20 mm (0.32–0.8 in) long, 2–5 mm (0.08–0.2 in) wide, white, downy only beneath. Stamens about two-thirds the length of the sepals, with creamy-white anthers. Achenes glabrous with a white plumose tail 20–50 mm (0.8–2 in) long.

DISTRIBUTION. Mediterranean region (including north Africa) eastwards to N Iran and the Caucasus; in

67. Clematis flammula, slopes of Mt Olympus, N Greece.
Photo: Christopher Grey-Wilson

Europe north as far as the Alps and CS France, however, naturalized further north, especially in the Czech Republic, Slovakia and Romania. According to the 'Flora URSS' (vol 7, 1937, p. 319) this species is also recorded from Afghanistan, but I have not seen authenticated specimens from that country.

HABITAT. Bushy places, hedgerows, rock hill-slopes, sometimes sprawling down banks or rocks or growing on old walls; July–Sept.

68. Clematis flammula in cultivation. Photo: Christopher Grey-Wilson

This is one of the most delightful and exuberant of late summer-flowering clematis in gardens, producing a billowing mass of foaming bloom sweetly scented of Meadowsweet, or is it Hawthorn? The smell invades every corner of the garden on a warm late summer's evening, both enticing and intoxicating. It thrives is warm sunny niches in the garden and looks especially fine when allowed to tumble over a wall or bank. It is extremely variable in the wild, especially as regards leaflet size and shape and flower size and the forms normally seen in gardens tend to have been selected for flower size. Strangely enough, it is often confused in gardens with the widespread European *C. vitalba,* which scientifically is placed in a different section of the genus by most authorities. The two are, though, very different. *C. vitalba* has pinnate leaves with usually toothed leaflets and the flowers are greenish-white rather than pure white and unscented, the sepals downy on both surfaces. In addition, the achenes of both are significantly different, those of *C. flammula* quite large, flattened and glabrous, those of *C. vitalba* narrow, unflattened and hairy.

Clematis flammula has a long history in cultivation that stretches back until at least 1590. This is an easy species to grow and freely available; its chief requirements being a warm sheltered sight and excellent drainage. Unfortunately, it is not a particularly easy plant to propagate from cuttings, so that many plants are seed-raised and as a result rather variable in flower size and scent. In the worst the flowers are small and a rather dingy greenish-white, while in the best they are broad-sepalled, glistening white and powerfully scented. It pays to seek plants from a reputable source or, alternatively, to raise plants from seed from a good mother plant and select only the best seedlings when they come into flower; they are at their peak in August. 'Ithaca'* has small flowers but with wide sepals and is primarily distinguished by its leaves which bear an irregular silvery variegation down the middle. It is, to my knowledge, the one of very few variegated clematis in cultivation and well worth seeking out.

The species is sometimes erroneously referred to as Virgin's Bower, a common name frequently applied to species of clematis which should, in Europe at least, be more strictly applied to *C. cirrhosa.*

I grow it against a black weather-boarded shed in my garden where it is normally in full flower with the large-flowered blue-purple *C.* 'Jackmanii'. The two intermingle quite wonderfully, a chance combination which was certainly not deliberate but which I shall certainly recreate again at some stage. *C. flammula* would also mix well with many of the *C. viticella* cultivars.

Although *C. flammula* is really a much better garden plant than *C. vitalba* (being less vigorous, with neater leaves and white, better-perfumed, flowers) it does have one drawback in that the fruits are of little consequence and can in no way rival those of the latter species; good viable seed is generally only set after a good hot summer. Seed sown in the late autumn or winter will often produce some seedlings the following spring but most, for some reason, will appear the following spring. Plants build up a sizeable trunk in time which can eventually become hollow. At this stage plants may be ten years old or more and are prone to suddenly die, especially if they are consistently hard pruned. This is not too serious as plants are readily replaced.

Maire in 'Flore de l'Afrique du Nord' (1964) attempted to subdivide *C. flammula* into a number of varieties and lesser categories. This looks good at face value but taken outside the context of North Africa most of the criteria separating the taxa fail and numerous intermediates can be found. Much of the variation could perhaps be explained by habitat differences and climate; for instance plants growing in more exposed hotter places may have smaller narrower leaves and smaller flowers, especially those found growing in coastal habitats. Maire's prime divisions are as follows:

var. *flammula* (syn. var. *genuina* Battand., var. *typica* Posp., var. *vulgaris*) has bipinnate leaves (leaflets oval to lanceolate, generally unlobed) and flowers medium sized, 10–25 mm (0.4–1 in) across, the sepals not more than 12 mm (0.47 in) long.

var. *fragrans* Ten, non Salisb. (syn. var. *latifolia* Koch, var. *rotundifolia* DC.) is similar to var. *flammula* but with rounded to ovate leaflets.

var. *grandiflora* Pomel has mainly pinnate leaves (leaflets with a rounded base, usually unlobed) and large flowers, 25–35 mm (1–1.4 in) across, the sepals 12–20 mm (0.47–0.8 in) long.

var. *heterophylla* Viz. is similar to var. *flammula* but leaves variable, some pinnate with heart-shaped leaflets, others bipinnate with narrow-lanceolate leaflets.

var. *maritima* (L.) DC. (syn. *C. flammula maritima repens* Bauhin, *C. maritima* L., *C. maritimus* Lam.) has flowers the size of var. *flammula* but the leaves are bi- or tri-pinnate with linear to linear-lanceolate leaflets.

var. *parviflora* Pomel (syn. var. *saint-marini* Pamp.) is similar to var. *flammula* but with lanceolate to ovate leaflets that are often lobed, and smaller flowers, 8–16 mm (0.32–0.63 in) across, the sepals only 4–8 mm (0.16–0.32 in) long.

69. *Clematis flammula* in cultivation, with *C.* 'Jackmanii'.
Photo: Christopher Grey-Wilson

70. *Clematis flammula* var. *maritima*, S Spain. Photo: Martyn Rix

71. Clematis x triternata 'Rubromarginata'. Photo: Jack Elliott

Clematis x **triternata** DC. (syn. *Atragene triternata* Desf. ex DC.) includes all hybrids between *C. flammula* and *C. viticella*. Of these the best and most widely grown is the putative hybrid 'Rubromarginata'* (syn. *C. flammula* var. *rubromarginata* various authors, *C. triternata* forma *rubromarginata* (Jouin) Rehder) which has *C. flammula* as its seed parent. It was first produced at the Jackman's nursery in the mid-nineteenth century and is still widely grown today. Like its seed parent it is a vigorous and free-flowering plant, the flowers appearing in late summer and autumn. These are like those of *C. flammula* but larger, 30–45 mm (1.2–1.8 in) across, white with the margins suffused with reddish-purple, the flowers sometimes with up to 6 sepals. They are borne in large panicle-like trusses and are powerfully hawthorn-scented. This plant can look exceeding dingy and unexciting if wrongly placed in the garden; it needs an open airy well-lit position to look at its best, and its best can be very effective. 'Roseopurpureo' is often said to be the same as the foregoing but the original description indicates a plant with rather larger flowers 40–54 mm (1.6–2.1 in) across and more rose than purple. It was produced at the Jackman nursery round about 1874. 'Violacea' (syn. *C. violacea* A. DC.) which may no longer be in cultivation, was a Swiss plant but of similar parentage. The flowers, which have 4–8 sepals, are similar in size to the foregoing, but are violet in colour.

Clematis x **aromatica** Lennée & Koch (syn. *C. aromatica* Levalée, *C.* 'Aromatica', *C. caerulea* var. *odorata* Bertin ex Carrière, *C. odorata* Hort. ex Levalée, *C. poizati* Hort. ex Levalée) is a hybrid

between *C. flammula* and *C. integrifolia*, which seems at first glance to be a rather unlikely combination. It was first described as long ago as 1855 (in Berlin), although the first important reference was in the *Revue Horticole* in 1877. It is a vigorous semi-herbaceous plant to 1.5 m (5 ft), occasionally more, with the stems dying back to a woody base in the winter. The coarse ternate to pinnate leaves are deep green and are hidden in July until the autumn by swathes of violet flowers with white stamens and a powerful hawthorn scent, derived from *C. flammula*. The individual flowers are 30–40 mm (1.2–1.6 in) across and look rather spidery because the sepal margins tend to roll back; however, their poor quality is more than compensated for by their profusion. Although this can be a pleasing plant in the garden, many find it not vigorous enough (as the above description implies) nor indeed flowery enough to warrant the space and time.

H6; P2

❂ ❂ **Leaves ternate to pinnate (species 118–120)**
❖ **Stems to 2 m (6.6 ft); leaves grey-green (species 118)**

118. *Clematis elisabethae-carolae* W. Greut.

DESCRIPTION. A bushy plant with stems to 2 m (6.6 ft), often less; stems wiry greenish, ribbed. Leaves grey-green, pinnate to ternate with 3–5 lanceolate to narrow-ovate leaflets, 30–60 mm (1.2–2.4 in) long and 10–25 mm (0.4–1 in) wide, with an entire margin and generally 3 veins from the base. Flowers in terminal panicle-like cymes, each flower 25–30 mm (1–1.2 in) across, scented of orange blossom. Sepals white, 4–6, oval-lanceolate, wide-spreading. Stamens about half the length of the sepals. Achenes glabrous with a plumose tail to 25 mm (1 in) long.

DISTRIBUTION. W Crete (Lefka Ori); 1250–1850 m (4100–6050 ft).

HABITAT. Craggy limestone rocks, in hollows and crevices; June–July.

An interesting species only described in 1965 and endemic to a rather limited area in the White Mountains of western Crete. It would make an interesting introduction to cultivation. It finds its closest ally in *C. flammula* which is a far more robust plant with long climbing or clambering stems and generally bipinnate leaves. Interestingly, *C. flammula*, which is widespread in the Mediterranean region is not known from Crete.

❖ ❖ **Stems 3 m (10 ft) or more; leaves deep green
(species 119 & 120)**

119. *Clematis terniflora* DC.*

(syn. *C. dioscoreifolia* Lévl. & Vant., *C. d.* var. *robusta*
(Carr.) Rehder, *C. flammula* var. *robusta* Carr.,
C. maximowicziana Franch. & Savat., *C. m.* var.
robusta (Carr.) Nakai *C. paniculata* sensu Thunb., non
Gmelin, *C. recta* subsp. *paniculata* (Thunb.) Kuntze
pro parte and subsp. *terniflora* (DC.) Kuntze, *C. r.* var.
mandshurica sensu Maxim., non Rupr. and var.
paniculata (Thunb.) Pavol., *C. terniflora* var. *robusta*
(Carrière) Tamura)

72. *Clematis terniflora* in cultivation. Photo: Raymond Evison

DESCRIPTION. A very vigorous and robust deciduous
climber to 10 m (33 ft), occasionally more, the stems
forming a thick entanglement, downy when young,
generally 6–12 ribbed. Leaves dark green on both
sides, pinnate with 5 or 7 leaflets, occasionally ternate,
long-petioled (to 9 cm (3.5 in) long); leaflets ovate to
heart-shaped, 30–95 mm (1.2–3.7 in) long, 28–64 mm
(1.1–2.5 in) wide, occasionally 2–3-lobed, but with an
entire margin, glabrous or almost so, usually 3-veined.
Branches and pedicels finely hairy. Flowers hawthorn-
scented, borne in lateral cymes on the current year's
shoot, each with 3 to many flowers, 14–30 mm
(0.55–1.2 in) across, star-like. Sepals 4, white, oblong,
10–17 mm (0.4–0.67 in) long, 2–6 mm (0.08–0.24 in)
wide, spreading widely apart, downy outside. Stamens
half the length of the sepals. Achenes orange-yellow,
pear-shaped, compressed, 6–9 mm (0.24–0.35 in)
long, hairy, with greyish-or reddish-brown plumose
tails to 40 mm (1.6 in) long.

DISTRIBUTION. C & E China (S Anhui, S Henan,
C Hubei, Jiangsu, Jiangxi, SE Shaanxi, Zhejiang),
Japan and Korea; to 400 m (1300 ft).

HABITAT. Shrubberies and open woodland, woodland
margins, grassy places, roadsides, hedgerows and old
walls; late June–Sept.

This species can be likened to an eastern equivalent of
C. flammula. Although it can look splendid in its Asiatic
homelands it has never been particularly popular in
western gardens. This is in part because it is an
extremely vigorous and invasive species, but perhaps
more because it generally fails to flower profusely and
the results are usually disappointing. However, in
gardens in the eastern United States it responds far better
and is considered well worth growing and produces a
mass of flowers; the flower clusters are borne quite
densely along the leafy stems so that they appear to be
large panicles. This is almost certainly due to the higher
summer temperatures more reliable ripening of the wood
in those favoured eastern American gardens where its
billowing columns of white are quite a feature, even
spectacular, during the autumn. In Britain a warm sunny
site such as a south- or west-facing wall are probably the
best chance of success, but beware, it is far more
vigorous even than *C. flammula*. Although generally
regarded as a deciduous species, plants can be semi-
evergreen in mild gardens. After a hot summer it will
even flower well in the British Isles; it certainly creates a
better spectacle in France where the summers are more
reliably hot and sunny, being at its best from August to
early October. Given the right conditions it makes a fine
plant for covering large old walls or fences, or simply
allowed to scramble into trees.

The species was first introduced by von Siebold
who sent seed to the Botanic Garden in Gent, Belgium,
in 1830 from Japan. However, its introduction is often
credited to Thunberg who lived in Japan during the late
eighteenth century, because of a confusion in the
naming, the date of introduction is therefore probably
around 1796. Thunberg described it as *C. paniculata*,
the name by which it has been long known in gardens.
Unfortunately, his name was preceded three years
earlier by Gmelin's *C. paniculata*, a New Zealand
species, see p.70. It was subsequently known as *C.
maximowicziana* Franch. & Savat. (1879), only to be
replaced by an earlier name, *C. terniflora* DC. of 1818,
bringing us neatly back to the name under which von
Siebold's plant was first cultivated. Such are sometimes
the contortions of taxonomic nomenclature, especially
when several supposed species are later found to one
and the same entity.

var. *garanbiensis* (Hayata) M. C. Chang (syn. *C. garanbiensis* Hayata, *C. terniflora* sensu *Tamura*, non DC., *C. terniflora* var. *robusta* sensu Hsieh, non (Carr.) Tamura) has ternate or pinnate leaves and smaller leaflets not more than 40 mm (1.6 in) long, stems finely hairy only at the nodes, glabrous pedicels and rather smaller flowers, the sepals to 13 mm (0.5 in) long. Restricted to Taiwan where it grows amongst coastal rocks.

Var. *robusta* (Carr.) Tamura* is sometimes distinguished; it is an even more robust form (said to be a hexaploid plant) than the typical plant, with stems 18-ribbed and with larger leaves to 35 cm (14 in) long, the leaflets often with a silvery stripe down the centre. The flowers are also larger and fuller-petalled, generally about 50 mm (2 in) across. It is sometimes seen in cultivation but in the wild at least it cannot be satisfactorily separated from var. *terniflora*. Like the typical plant it is only suitable for dry sunny, warm or even hot sites; it does marvellously well in the eastern USA.

H5; P2

120. Clematis papuligera Ohwi

DESCRIPTION. Very similar to *C. terniflora* but leaves ternate or pinnate, rather shiny beneath and with tiny glands on the veins.

DISTRIBUTION. Korea (Mt Chiisan & Mt Chojusan, Chinampo, Kan-ouen-to).

HABITAT. Shrubberies and other bushy places.

SUBSECTION MEYENIANAE
(THE ARMANDII GROUP)

A group of 12 handsome evergreen climbers, with large often lustrous leaves and flowers primarily borne from large over-wintering buds on the previous year's shoots. Of the species *C. armandii* is by far the most familiar to gardeners, although several of the others offer considerable potential.

▼   Flowers small, the sepals not more than 9 mm (0.35 in) long (species 121 & 122)
◆   Leaves generally simple, occasionally ternate; flowers white (species 121)

121. Clematis chekiangensis Pei

DESCRIPTION. Rather similar to *C. finetiana* but readily distinguished by its usually simple, rarely ternate,

leaves and small white flowers, c. 15–17 mm (0.6–0.67 in) across, which are borne in cymes of up to 10; the small oblong sepals are 7–9 mm (0.28–0.35 in) long. DISTRIBUTION. E China (Zhejiang; Qingyuan Xian).

HABITAT. Shrubberies; June.

◆ ◆   Leaves always ternate; flowers pale yellow (species 122)

122. Clematis lingyunensis W. T. Wang

DESCRIPTION. Closely related to *C. armandii* but with rather smaller net-veined leaflets (not more than 92 mm (3.6 in) long and 58 mm (2.3 in) wide), smaller pale yellow flowers (9–12 mm (0.35–0.47 in)), the sepals linear-lanceolate, 5–6 mm (0.2–0.24 in) long and 2–3 mm (0.08–0.12 in) wide, glabrous apart from the margin. As with *C. armandii* the inflorescences are borne from large lateral buds on the previous year's shoots.

DISTRIBUTION. S China (NW Guangxi; Lingyun Xian); altitude not recorded.

HABITAT. Open forest and streamsides; Apr–May.

With its yellow flowers *C. lingyunensis* holds a unique place in the *C. armandii* group. Despite the fact that the flowers are not large it would be a most worthwhile introduction to gardens, besides being of great potential benefit in a breeding programme. It apparently has a very limited distribution in the wild.

▼ ▼   Flowers larger, the sepals (9–) 10–30 mm ((0.35–) 0.4–1.2 in) long (species 123–132)
✲   Plants autumn or winter-flowering, July to December (species 123 & 124)
✺   Leaves ternate; flowers 20–28 mm (0.8–1.1 in) across (species 123)

123. Clematis hedysarifolia DC.
(syn. *C. naravelioides* Kuntze)

DESCRIPTION. A vigorous evergreen climber with deep green ternate leaves. Leaflets oval to lanceolate, sometimes 2–3 lobed, very variable in size from 20–150 mm (0.8–6 in) long and 5–92 mm (0.2–3.6 in) wide. Flowers in lateral cymes, rather small, each 20–28 mm (0.8–1.1 in) across. Sepals 4–5, greenish-yellow, narrow-oblong, 6–10 mm (0.24–0.4 in) long, 1–4 mm (0.04–0.16 in) wide. Achenes hairy, with a plumose tail to 50 mm (2 in) long.

DISTRIBUTION. India (except the N & NW), Burma;

also apparently recorded from SE China (Guangdong); to 1000 m (3300 ft).

HABITAT. Forests and forest fringes; Sept–Jan.

The only species in Subsection Meyenianae to be found on the Indian Subcontinent.

❀ ❀ **Leaves pinnate, with 5 leaflets; flowers 30–50 mm (1.2–2 in) across (species 124)**

124. *Clematis quinquefoliolata* Hutch.*
(syn. *C. meyeniana* var. *heterophylla* Gagn.)

DESCRIPTION. A vigorous evergreen climber 3–5 m (10–16.5 ft), with ribbed stem,s downy when young, and pinnate leaves. Leaflets 5, lanceolate to narrow-ovate, to 10 cm (4 in) long and 35 mm (1.4 in) wide, sometimes 3-lobed, with an entire margin and obtuse to short-acuminate apex, rounded to somewhat heart-shaped at the base. Flowers in lateral cymes with 3–7 flowers, each 30–50 mm (1.2–2 in) across, starry. Sepals 4–6, milky-white, narrow-oblong, to 14–26 mm (0.55–1 in) long, 3–7 mm (0.12–0.28 in) wide. Stamens with white filaments and yellow anthers, about half the length of the sepals. Achenes silky, with a tawny, plumose tail to 75 mm (3 in) long, generally 40–55 mm (2.6–2.2 in).

DISTRIBUTION. C & SW China (NE Guizhou, Hubei, NW Hunan, E Sichuan, N Yunnan); 1000–1800 m (3300–5900 ft).

HABITAT. Wooded slopes, shrubberies and streamsides; July–Sept.

An interesting species of the *C. armandii* persuasion but it is readily distinguished by its pinnate rather than ternate leaves, as well as autumn-flowering habit. It was discovered in the mountains of central China by Augustine Henry and introduced into cultivation in 1900 by E. H. Wilson. The 5-foliolate leaves readily separated it from its closest allies, *C. armandii* and *C. meyeniana*. Although an attractive plant, it has not gained in popularity in gardens; Ernest Henry Wilson was particularly struck by its yellowish-brown (fulvous) fruit clusters. Perhaps not in cultivation at the present time.

H8; P2

Map six

Subgenus Flammula

Section Flammula

subsection Meyenianae ————

subsection Chinenses – – – – – –

subsection Angustifoliae + + + + + + +

subsection Crassifoliae · · · · · · · · · ·

73. *Clematis armandii* in cultivation. Photo: Christopher Grey-Wilson

❊ ❊ **Plants spring-flowering, March to early June (species 125–132)**
❖ **Leaves usually pinnate, occasionally ternate on the same plant (species 125–127)**
✖ **Leaflets always 7 per leaf (species 125)**

125. *Clematis hastata* Finet & Gagn.

DESCRIPTION. Similar to *C. quinquefoliolata* but the pinnate leaves with 7 leaflets usually, each lanceolate to oval, often ternate or 3-lobed (especially the lowest pair of leaflets), to 55 mm (2.2 in) long and 45 mm (1.8 in) wide, more or less heart-shaped at the base. Flowers white, 25–45 mm (1–1.8 in) across, with the sepals 13–22 mm (0.5–0.87 in) long and 4–10 mm (0.16–0.4 in) wide, with 3–5 veins. A major difference can be observed in flowering time with the flowers of *C. quinquefoliolata* borne on the current year's shoots in summer, whereas those of *C. hastata*, *C. armandii* and *C. meyeniana* and their close allies are borne from buds on the previous years shoots in the early spring.

DISTRIBUTION. W China (N & NE Sichuan); altitude not recorded.

HABITAT. Shrubberies and bushy valley slopes; April.

✖ ✖ **Leaflets usually 5, sometimes 3, per leaf (species 126 & 127)**

126. *Clematis vanioti* Lévl. & Port.
(syn. *C. armandii* Franch. var. *pinfaensis* Finet & Gagn., *C. phaseolifolia* W. T. Wang)

DESCRIPTION. Similar to *C. finetiana* but young stems often finely downy, and leaves with 3 or 5 leaflets (ternate or pinnate), the leaflets more papery and without three main veins. The flowers are slightly smaller, 20–34 mm (0.8–1.3 in) across, the sepals cream and oblong, densely downy beneath.

DISTRIBUTION. SW China (S Guizhou & SE Yunnan); 600–1550 m (2000–5100 ft).

HABITAT. Forests and forest margins; Mar–Apr.

127. *Clematis zygophylla* Hand.-Mazz.

DESCRIPTION. Closely related to *C. armandii* and *C. lingyunensis*, but leaves ternate or pinnate and the 3 or 5 leaflets always narrow-lanceolate, to 14 cm (5.5 in) long and 20 mm (0.8 in) wide, with a somewhat curved acuminate apex. The white flowers are 30–35 mm (1.2–1.4 in) across, with 4 sepals, 15–18 mm (0.6–0.7 in) long and 205 mm wide, the stamens about one-third the length of the sepals.

DISTRIBUTION. CS China (Guizhou; Anshun Shi); altitude not recorded.

HABITAT. Probably forest margins and shrubberies; Apr–May.

❖ ❖ **Leaves always ternate (species 128–132)**
✳ **Flowers solitary, c. 60 mm (2.4 in) across (species 128)**

128. *Clematis baominiana* W. T. Wang
(syn. *C. villosa* sensu B. M. Yang, non DC.)

DESCRIPTION. A vigorous evergreen climber to 10 m (33 ft) with ternate leaves. Leaflets papery, rhombic to obovate, to 70 mm (2.8 in) long and 40 mm (1.6 in) wide, generally unlobed but the margin usually with 1–2 small teeth in the upper half, hairy on both surfaces. Flowers solitary, in 1-flowered lateral cymes, c. 60 mm (2.4 in) across. Sepals white, 6, spreading, linear-lanceolate, about 30 mm (1.2 in) long and 3 mm (0.12 in) wide, densely downy beneath, otherwise glabrous. Stamens about half the length of the sepals. Achenes ovate, c. 5 mm (0.2 in) long, pubescent, with a plumose style to 30 mm (1.2 in) long.

DISTRIBUTION. C China (Hunan; Taojiang Xian).
HABITAT. Hill-slopes, shrubberies; Apr–May.

A recently described and little-known species. The relatively large flowers make it an appealing possibility for cultivation.

⁕ ⁕ Flowers in lateral clusters, often many per cyme, 20–50 mm (0.8–2 in) across (species 129–132)

✪ Flowers borne on the previous year's shoots, with a basal cluster of bud-scales (species 129)

129. *Clematis armandii* Franch.*

(syn. *C. a.* var. *biondiana* (Pavol.) Rehd. and var. *kiangnanensis* Court., *C. biondiana* Pavol., *C. hedysarifolia* subsp. *armandii* Kuntze, *C. meyeniana* sensu Hook. f., non Walp., *C. ornithopus* Ulbr.)

DESCRIPTION. A vigorous evergreen climber to 10 m (33 ft) bearing tough, hard, leathery, ternate leaves; young stems minutely hairy. Leaflets deep glossy green, sometimes flushed with bronze when young, oblong-lanceolate to narrow-ovate, to 16 cm (6.3 in) long and 6.5 cm (2.6 in) wide, with an entire margin and 3 (–5) main veins from the base, which can be rounded to somewhat truncated or heart-shaped. Flowers borne in lateral clusters of 7 or more (often many) normally and appearing before the new leaves emerge, panicle-like, 30–50 mm (1.2–2 in) across (occasionally larger in some cultivated forms), cupped or starry, hawthorn-fragrant. Sepals 4, occasionally 5, pure white to cream, occasionally with a pink flush, especially in bud, narrow-oblong to elliptical, 12–24 mm (0.47–0.95 in) long and 2-7 mm (0.08–0.28 in) wide. Achenes hairy, with a plumose tail to 30 mm (1.2 in) long.

DISTRIBUTION. W & C China (Hubei, S Shaanxi, Sichuan and E Tibet southwards to Yunnan and Guangdong, and eastwards to Zhejiang), N Myanmar and N Vietnam.

HABITAT. Wooded places and shrubberies, streamsides in hills and mountains, particularly in subtropical and warm-temperate areas; Mar–May.

A popular and widely cultivated species which is extremely beautiful in its finest forms and remarkably floriferous. The species was named in honour of the French Missionary and plant collector Armand David, whose name is perhaps best celebrated in an animal rather than a plant, in Père David's Deer. This clematis was introduced into Britain in 1900 by Ernest Henry (Chinese) Wilson. In cultivation it is not fully hardy but will succeed in many southerly and westerly regions on a sunny, sheltered south or south-west facing wall, although it is certainly one of the hardiest of the evergreen species. It greatly dislikes cold winter winds, which can shrivel the foliage and scorch the

74. *Clematis armandii*, narrow-sepalled form in cultivation.
Photo: Christopher Grey-Wilson

flowerbuds, or even prevent blooming altogether. However, given a sheltered position, *C. armandii* can be a luxuriant climber, dare one say too vigorous at times. Regular pruning is essential to keep plants in order, for left alone it will form a dense and heavy entanglement with many dead stems and leaves trapped within. It was thought at one time that *C. armandii* would not tolerate drastic pruning; however, mature plants cut to the ground by severe winter weather will often sprout again from the base once warmer weather arrives. Annual pruning immediately after flowering will not only keep the plant in order, but help to remove any unsightly damaged or bruised foliage. To my eyes, at least, the foliage is extremely handsome, although a number of writers in the past have been singularly unimpressed by it. Unnamed clones vary a good deal in flower quality and floriferousness and it pays to select a good form in flower at nurseries and garden centres. Even named clones need to be chosen with care, as plants found under names such as 'Apple Blossom' or 'Snowdrift' are not always correct. Why some nurserymen sell inferior clones I have no idea, although clearly it is easier to raise plants from seed than from cuttings, and there is always a strong demand for *C. armandii*. These remarks are not intended to put the reader off acquiring this outstanding species but to be careful in selecting a good and floriferous clone.

Although it is most often seen as a wall climber, it can look very attractive when allowed to ramble over wall shrubs, such as a ceanothus. It can also be an

75. *Clematis armandii* 'Apple Blossom'. Photo: Christopher Grey-Wilson

extremely imposing cool conservatory climber flowering in the later winter; under glass it tends to produce rather more open flower clusters and this certainly adds to its elegance. In a confined space the scent of the blooms can be very powerful if not overwhelming; to me the scent is decidedly hawthorn, although some describe it as vanilla-scented, but that depends much upon the individual nose! Under glass the stems need careful thinning and training if the plant is not to look a mess.

Although it is generally the large-flowered cultivars that are afflicted by clematis wilt, the disease can also attack this species. Although it rarely kills an entire plant, whole shoots, or sections of the plant, may die back causing unsightly areas of dead stem and foliage. Like some of the other evergreen clematis, the foliage can be infested by nasty scale insects.

'Apple Blossom'* has cupped vanilla-scented flowers which are ruddy pink in bud, but which gradually fade to white, and contrast with the bronze-tinted young foliage, the flowers pinking nicely as they age; it received a First Class Certificate (FCC) in 1914 and an Award of Garden Merit (AGM), from the Royal Horticultural Society in 1938; 'Jefferies'* has pure white flowers and narrow leaflets with long slender points, occasionally repeat flowers in the summer (discovered by Raymond Evison at the nursery of Jeffries near Cirencester in Gloucestershire); 'Rubra' (='Hendersonii Rubra') has deep pink flowers, fading with age; 'Snowdrift'* has large waxy white flowers, 50–60 mm (2–2.4 in) across,

borne on drooping stalks and copper-flushed young growth (many plants sold under this name are not the true cultivar). It received an AGM in 1969. All early to mid-spring.

The botanical varieties are distinguished primarily on the details of the inflorescence and flower size:

var. *farquhariana* (Rehd. & Wils.) W. T. Wang (syn. *C. armandii* forma *farquhariana* Rehd. & Wils.) is similar to var. *hefengensis* but with small 4–5-sepalled flowers, the sepals 25–40 mm (1–1.6 in) long and 6–12 mm (0.24–0.47 in) wide. The cymes are nearly always 3-flowered. Similar habitats, 500–1500 m (1650–4950 ft), in W Hubei, W Hunan and E Sichuan.

var. *hefengensis* (G. F. Tao) W. T. Wang (syn. *C. hefengensis* G. F. Tao) is very similar to the typical plant but with broader more oval leaves which are decidedly heart-shaped at the base, and larger flowers (mostly 60–80 mm (2.4–3.2 in) across.), in cymes of only 1–3, although with 5–6 rather broader sepals, each 37–47 mm (1.5–1.9 in) long and 10–20 mm (0.4–0.8 in) wide. Confined to SW Hubei province (Hefeng) at c. 1400 m (4600 ft).

H6; P1

✪ ✪ **Flowers borne on the current year's shoots, the cymes without a basal cluster of bud-scales (species 130–132)**
❖ **Leaflets thinly leathery, net-veined on both surfaces (species 130)**

130. *Clematis jialasaensis* W. T. Wang

DESCRIPTION. Similar to *C. meyeniana* but the leaflets glabrous and finely reticulate on both surfaces, and stamens only half the length of the sepals. The white flowers are 20–26 mm (0.8–1 in) across; sepals 10–13 mm (0.4–0.5 in) long and 2.5–4 mm (0.1–0.16 in) wide.

DISTRIBUTION. SE Tibet (Mêdog Xian); c. 2100 m (6900 ft).

HABITAT. Valleys in broad-leaved evergreen forests and forest margins; Apr.

A recently described and little-known species apparently restricted to south-eastern Tibet. The flowers are borne in large panicle-like inflorescences that would make this attractive species well worth while introducing into cultivation.

✢ ✢ Leaflets leathery, not net-veined (species 131 & 132)

131. *Clematis finetiana* Lévl. & Vant.*
(syn. *C. meyeniana* var. *pavoliniana* (Pamp.) Sprague,
C. pavoliniana Pamp.)
DESCRIPTION. A semi-evergreen climber to 4–5 m (13–16.5
ft) with glabrous stems (often flushed with reddish-brown)
and ternate, bright dark green leaves. Leaflets thinly-
leathery, narrow-ovate to oval-lanceolate, 50–100 mm (2–4
in) long, 35–50 mm (1.4–2 in) wide, with 3 main veins
from the base, an entire margin and a rounded or
somewhat heart-shaped base, glabrous. Flowers strongly
fragrant, in lateral clusters of 3–7, 20–40 mm (0.8–1.6 in)
across, starry. Sepals 4 white, often greenish on the
outside, lanceolate, 10–20 mm (0.4–0.8 in) long and 2–5
mm (0.08–0.2 in) wide, with an acute tip; stamens almost
as long as the sepals, yellow. Achenes pubescent, with a
reddish-brown plumose style to 25 mm (1 in) long.

DISTRIBUTION. C, E & S China (Sichuan to Hubei,
Anhui and S Zhejiang southwards, but not Yunnan); to
1200 m (3900 ft).

HABITAT. Open woodland and shrubberies, particularly
along riverbanks and in ravines; late Apr–June.

Clematis finetiana is closely allied to *C. armandii* but
scarcely has the impact of that species in cultivation,
indeed it is considered to be rather less hardy. Ernest
Henry Wilson introduced the species into cultivation in
1908 from the Ichang area of Sichuan. In gardens it
requires a very sheltered warm site if it is to grow and
flower well.
    Clematis 'Jeuneiana', a reputed hybrid between *C.
armandii* and *C. finetiana*, was raised by B. H. B.
Symons-Jeune round about 1920. It has clusters of up
to 30 flowers at each node; the flowers, c. 25 mm (1
in) across, are described as white flushed with silvery-
rose beneath. It is an exceptional plant but nexplicably
rare in cultivation.

var. *pedata* W. T. Wang is distinguished by having
pedate leaves with 5 leaflets. It was described from the
vicinity of Dayong Xian in NW Hunan Province, close
to the Sichuan and Hubei borders at c. 600 m (2000 ft).

H8; P1

132. *Clematis meyeniana* Walp.*
(syn. *C. craibiana* Lace, *C. hedysarifolia* DC. subsp.
meyeniana Walp. and subsp. *oreophila* Hance, *C.
hothae* Kurz, *C. meyeniana* forma *major* Sprague and
forma *retusa* Sprague, *C. oreophila* Hance, *C.
virginiana* sensu Lour., non L.)

76. Clematis finetiana in the wild; Shizong-Xingyi, China. Photo: Phillip Cribb

DESCRIPTION. A vigorous evergreen climber to 7 m
(23ft), sometimes more, with hairy purplish-brown
ridged stems and deep green, leathery, ternate, rather
waxy leaves with hairy petioles. Leaflets ovate to
lanceolate or elliptical, to 12.5 cm (5 in) long and 7.5
cm (3 in) wide, with a short to long-acuminate apex,
entire margin and with 3 main veins arising from the
rounded to heart-shaped base, smooth above. Flowers in
lateral clusters (of 3–5 flowers in a cyme), which make

77. Clematis meyeniana in the wild in Hong Kong. Photo: Raymond Evison

up large lax 'panicles', each flower 18–26 mm (0.7–1 in) across, occasionally larger, starry, with a central boss of bright yellow stamens. Sepals 4, white, sometimes with a pink flush, narrow-elliptical, 9–13 mm (0.35–0.5 in) long and 2–4 mm (0.08–0.16 in) wide, 3-veined, with a slightly notched apex and downy margin, wide-spreading to somewhat reflexed. Stamens about two-thirds the length of the sepals. Achenes elliptic, 5–7 mm (0.2–0.28 in) long, yellowish-pubescent, with golden plumose styles up to 40 mm (1.6 in) long.

DISTRIBUTION. S & SE China (Yunnan to Guizhou and S Zhejiang southwards, including Hainan and Hong Kong), S Japan, Taiwan, Laos and N & C Vietnam; to 2000 m (6500 ft).

HABITAT. Shrubberies and ravines, open woodland, woodland margins, streamsides; Apr–July.

A fine species distributed primarily in subtropical regions and for that reason not particularly hardy in temperate western gardens and rarely seen. The best specimens are generally seen in large conservatories (it thrives in the Temperate House at the Royal Botanic Gardens, Kew!), where it tends to flower during February and March. Although smaller-flowered than *C. armandii*, it is just as fine in full bloom in the early spring, the airiness of its inflorescences a most striking feature. It may be that hardier forms can be found in the wild that will succeed better in the open garden. In any case, this fine species should be tried more often in subtropical and warm-temperate gardens, where dangers from winter frosts are not a problem.

var. *granulata* Finet & Gagn. (syn. *C. granulata* (Finet & Gagn.) Ohwi)

DESCRIPTION. Similar to typical plant (var. *meyeniana*) but leaflets finely rugose (granular) above; cymes many-flowered. Similar habitats to 1300 m (4300 ft), in S China (Guangdong, Guangxi, Hainan & SE Yunnan), Laos and N Vietnam.

DISTRIBUTION. SE China (Hainan), N Laos, N & C Vietnam.

var. *insularis* Sprague (syn. *C. lutchuensis* Koidz., *C. meyeniana* sensu Walp., Merrill & Rolfe)

DESCRIPTION. Leaves generally smaller and broad-ovate to heart-shaped, not more than 6 cm (2.4 in) long, but up to 11.5 cm (4.4 in) wide with 3–5 main veins. In addition, the petals are narrower.
DISTRIBUTION. S Japan (S Kyushu) southwards to the

N Philippines (Luzon), including Taiwan and the Ryukyu Islands, at rather low altitudes.

var. *uniflora* W. T. Wang has smooth leaflets like the typical plant but the cymes are 1-flowered. Similar habitats, but primarily a forest variety.

DISTRIBUTION. Restricted to SE China (Fujian) at 1300–1500 m (4300–4950 ft).

H9; P1

SUBSECTION CHINENSES (THE CHINENSIS GROUP)

A group of just six species, native to China and Japan with untoothed leaves that turn curiously black when dried. The flowers are borne in the summer and early autumn on the current season's shoots. Only *C. chinensis* and *C. obscura* are cultivated, although the latter is extremely rare in gardens.

▼ **Leaflets densely and finely hairy above (species 133)**

133. *Clematis shensiensis* W. T. Wang (syn. *C. wutangensis* W. T. Wang)

DESCRIPTION. Closely related to *C. chinensis*, but leaflets densely and finely pubescent (with curled hairs) above and flowers distinctly larger, 25–46 mm (1–1.8 in) across, with usually 4, occasionally 6, sepals which are 13–20 mm (0.5–0.8 in) long.

DISTRIBUTION. NC China (S Henan, W Hubei, S Shaanxi, S Shanxi); 700–1300 m (2300–4300 ft).

HABITAT. Shrubberies and cliffs, streamsides; May–June

▼ ▼ **Leaflets sparsely hairy to glabrous above (species 134–138)**
◆ **Flowers with 5–6 sepals (species 134)**

134. *Clematis obscura* Maxim.*

DESCRIPTION. Very similar to *C. anhweiensis* and *C. chinensis*, but clearly distinguished by the flowers which normally have 5–6 instead of 4 sepals; flowers relatively large, 25–48 mm (1–1.9 in) across, the sepals 12–24 mm (0.5–1 in) long and 4–8 mm (0.16–0.32 in) wide with the stamens about one-third the length of the sepals. The leaves can be pinnate or bipinnate. Like *C.*

anhweiensis this is an earlier-flowering species than *C. chinensis* and for this reason it would probably make a better garden plant, at least in temperate gardens.

DISTRIBUTION. CN & W China (Gansu, W Henan, Hubei, S Shaanxi, S Shanxi, NW Sichuan); 400–2600 m (1300–8500 ft).

HABITAT. Wooded slopes and shrubberies; Apr–June.

H7; P2

◆ ◆ **Flowers with 4, rarely 5, sepals (sepals 135–138)**
❋ **Leaves bipinnate (species 135)**

135. *Clematis kyushuensis* **Tamura**
(syn. *C. chinensis* sensu Koidz., non Osbeck)

DESCRIPTION. Similar to *C. chinensis* but readily distinguished on account of its mostly bipinnate leaves with the leaflets truncated at the base. Flowers larger, the sepals 10–15 mm (0.4–0.6 in) long and 2–3 mm (0.08–0.12 in) wide. In addition, the achenes are larger, 5–6 mm (0.2–0.24 in) long, with a short plumose tail to 20 mm (0.8 in) long only.

Clematis kyushuensis also comes close to *C. fujisanensis* in general appearance, especially in the size of the leaves and flowers. However, the leaflets are acute-tipped rather than obtuse in the former, while the sepals are more pointed and narrower in the latter.

DISTRIBUTION. Japan (Kyushu).

var. *bipinnata* **Tamura** has bipinnate leaves in which most of the lower leaflets are ternate, while the others are generally bilobed. Recorded only from Kyushu (Hiuga and Satsuma provinces), where it apparently overlaps with the ordinary form, var. *kyushuensis*.

❋ ❋ **Leaves pinnate or ternate (species 136–138)**
❀ **Flowers cream; leaves with 3 or 5 leaflets (species 136)**

136. *Clematis anhweiensis* **M. C. Chang**

DESCRIPTION. Similar to *C. chinensis*, but flowers in small cymes (1–5-flowered normally); flowers larger, 20–40 mm (0.8–1.6 in) across, the sepals 10–20 mm (0.4–0.8 in) long and c. 4 mm (0.16 in) wide. Flowering much earlier in the year.

DISTRIBUTION. E China (S Anhui and neighbouring areas of Zhejiang); to 300 m (1000 ft).

HABITAT. Open wooded slopes, shrubberies and streamsides; May–June.

❀ ❀ **Flowers white; leaflets 5 (species 137 & 138)**

137. *Clematis chinensis* **Osbeck***
(syn. *C. cavalerieri* Lévl. & Porter, *C. chinensis* Lour., *C. chinensis* Retz., *C. funebris* Lévl. & Vant., *C. liukiuensis* Warb., *C. longiloba* DC., *C. minor* Lour., *C. oligocarpa* Lévl. & Vant., *C. recta* subsp. *chinensis* (Retz.) Kuntze, *C. sinensis* Lour., *C. terniflora* sensu Maxim., non DC.)

DESCRIPTION. A moderately vigorous semi-evergreen to deciduous climber to 3 m (10 ft) with slender 6-ribbed stems that are downy only at the nodes, and with pinnate leaves. Leaflets generally 5 but the lower pair sometime ternate, ovate to heart-shaped, 20–95 mm (0.8–3.7 in) long and 10–64 mm (0.4–2.5 in) wide, generally smaller, somewhat downy on the veins beneath at first, with an entire margin, 3–5-veined. Flowers borne in many-flowered cymes from the leaf-axils and making up large cymose panicles, each flower 12–22 mm (0.47–0.87 in) across, starry, fragrant. Sepals 4 white, narrow-lanceolate, 6–10 mm (0.24–0.4 in) long, not more than 3 mm (0.12 in) wide, spreading widely apart to somewhat reflexed, velvety on the margins and outside. Stamens half the length of the sepals. Achenes ovate, 3 mm (0.12 in) long, hairy, with a white or yellowish plumose tail to 35 mm (1.4 in) long.

DISTRIBUTION. C, S & E China (S Shaanxi and S Anhui southwards to Yunnan, Fujian, Guangdong and Hainan),

78. Clematis chinensis in cultivation. Photo: Raymond Evison

79. *Clematis uncinata* near Jui-zhai-gou, NW Sichuan, China.
Photo: Christopher Grey-Wilson

Japan (Ryukyu Is.), SE Taiwan, N Vietnam; to 1500 m (4950 ft).

HABITAT. Forest margins, shrubberies, streamsides and hedgerows; Aug–Oct.

This species has been known since the late eighteenth century, but Ernest Henry Wilson only introduced it into cultivation round about 1900 from western China. It is a strong-growing and pleasant species which, when it flowers well, produces a charming display of delightfully scented blossom. Unfortunately, however, the flowers come late in the year and a full display can be easily ruined by an early frost. A warm sunny position in the garden is advisable, although the plant should never be allowed to become too dry.

var. *vestita* (Rehd. & Wils.) W. T. Wang (syn. *C. chinensis* forma *vestita* Rehd. & Wils.) is readily distinguished by the generally smaller (to 35 mm (1.4 in) long and 20 mm (0.8 in) wide) leaflets which are densely and finely hairy beneath. Restricted to grassy slopes in E China (Anhui, Hubei, Jiangsu and Zhejiang).

H7; P2

138. *Clematis fujisanensis* Hisauti & Hara
(syn. *C. chinensis* sensu Hisauti, non Osbeck)

DESCRIPTION. Similar to *C. chinensis*, but plants either hermaphrodite or male, with violet-purple-flushed stems. Leaves pinnate or ternate, with 3 or 5 leaflets. In addition,

the flowers are creamy-white and rather larger, 15–30 mm (0.6–1.2 in) across, with 4 or 5 sepals, and the achenes are somewhat larger with a tail to 50 mm (2 in) in length.

DISTRIBUTION. Japan (Hondo).

HABITAT. Similar places; Aug–Oct.

SUBSECTION UNCINATAE
(THE ARTICULATE GROUP)

139. *Clematis uncinata* Champ. ex Benth.*
(syn. *C. alsomitrifolia* Hayata, *C. chinensis* Retz. var. *uncinata* (Champ. ex Benth.) Kuntze, *C. drakeana* Lévl. & Vant., *C. floribunda* (Hayata) Yamamoto, *C. gagnepainiana* Lévl. & Vant., *C. longiloba* sensu Miq., non DC., *C. ovatifolia* Ito, *C. uncinata* forma *retusa* Sprague, *C. u.* var. *biternata* W. T. Wang, var. *floribunda* Hayata and var. *ovatifolia* (Ito) Ohwi)

DESCRIPTION. An evergreen climber to 12 m (40 ft), but generally 4–8 m (13–26 ft), with ridged, glabrous, rather slender stems. Leaves pinnate, thinly leathery to papery, pinnate, deep blue-green above, paler and rather glaucous beneath; leaflets 5, ovate to ovate-lanceolate, 32–100 mm (1.3–4 in) long, 14–38 mm (0.55–1.5 in) wide, pointed or somewhat notched at the apex and rounded base, glabrous, 3-veined, the margin entire, glaucous and somewhat reticulate beneath; petioles and petiolules articulate. Flowers fragrant, numerous borne in lateral or terminal panicles to 30 cm (12 in) long, each flower 20–30 mm (0.8–1.2 in) across, star-like. Sepals 4, creamy-white, narrow-oblong to lanceolate, 10–15 mm (0.4–0.6 in) long, 2–4 mm (0.08–0.16 in) wide. Stamens two-thirds the length of the sepals, with yellow anthers. Achenes spindle-shaped, glabrous, with a plumose tail to 20 mm (0.8 in) long.

DISTRIBUTION. C & S China (S Gansu, Anhui and S Jiangsu southwards to SE Yunnan, Guangxi, and Guangdong), S Japan (Honshu and Kyushu, Ryukyu Is.), Taiwan and N Vietnam; to 2500 m (8200 ft).

HABITAT. Bushy places and shrubberies in ravines and other rocky places, streamsides; late May–July. Champion discovered this widespread species in a ravine behind Mt Parker in Hong Kong in 1848, although its discovery is sometimes credited erroneously to Augustine Henry in 1884. It is a pleasing plant in cultivation but, unfortunately, somewhat tender. However, it will succeed in warm sheltered gardens and seems to be tolerant of quite dry soils. It is at its best when allowed to scramble over bushes and small trees, especially close to protecting walls or fences. It rarely reaches more than 4 m (13 ft) in cultivation. This is a rather beautiful species and it certainly deserves to be more widely known in gardens. It received an Award of Merit (AM) from the Royal Horticultural Society in 1922.

var. *coriacea* Pamp. (syn. *C. leiocarpa* Oliver) is distinguished primarily by its more leathery, often bipinnate leaves with the leaflets not more than 60 mm (2.4 in) long, markedly glaucous beneath but not reticulate, and similar sized flowers. Restricted to WC China (S Gansu, W Hubei, NW Hunan, S Shaanxi & NE Sichuan) in similar habitats at 500–2000 m (1650–6500 ft).

var. *okinawensis* (Ohwi) Ohwi (syn. *C. alsomitrifolia* sensu Tamura, non Hayata, and sensu Chang-fu Hsieh (in 'Fl. Taiwan'), non Hayata, *C. okinawensis* Ohwi, *C. o.* var. *trichocarpa* (Tamura) Tamura, *C. trichocarpa* Tamura) is very similar to the typical plant, but leaves bipinnate (with usually 7, 9 or 11 leaflets), the leaflets leathery, narrow-oval, mostly 30–50 mm (1.2–2 in) long and 20–30 mm (0.8–1.2 in) wide, and with smaller flowers, 15–20 mm (0.6–0.8 in) across, the sepals not more than 9 mm (0.35 in) long and 3–7 mm (0.12–0.28 in) wide. In addition, the stamens are not more than 7 mm (0.28 in) long (8–10 mm (0.31–0.4 in) in *C. uncinata*) and the achenes are hairy. Restricted to Taiwan and S Japan (Ryukyu Is., Okinawa), to 600 m (2000 ft); similar habitats, Apr–July. Doubtfully recorded from SE mainland China.

H8; P2

Subsection Angustifoliae

140. *Clematis hexapetala* Jacq.*
(syn. *C. angustifolia* Jacq., *C. a.* forma *dissecta* (Yabe) Kitag., *C. a.* var. *breviloba* Freyn, var. *dissecta* Yabe and var. *longiloba* Freyn, *C. hexapetala* sensu Pall., non L. f., *C. hexapetala* forma *breviloba* (Freyn) Nakai, forma *dissecta* (Yabe) Kitagawa and forma *longiloba* (Freyn) S. H. Li & Y. H. Huang, *C. hexapetala* var. *longiloba* (Freyn) S. Y. Hu and var. *smithiana* S. Y. Hu, *C. lasiantha* Fischer, *C. pallasii* Gmelin, *C. recta* subsp. *breviloba* Freyn, *C. sibirica* Lam.)

DESCRIPTION. A perennial herb with erect stems to 1 m (40 in) tall, but often 30–50 cm (12–20 in), with 8–12-furrowed simple or branched stems, which are slightly pubescent at first. Leaves leathery, 1–2-pinnately lobed, the lobes elliptic to linear-lanceolate or linear, the end lobe the largest, to 10 cm (4 in) long and 20 mm (0.8

in) wide, the margin entire, sparsely pubescent on both surfaces. Inflorescences lateral or terminal, 3–many-flowered cymes with leaf-like bracts; flowers 25–40 mm (1–1.6 in) across. Sepals white, normally 5 or 6, occasionally 4, 7–8, spreading, narrow-oblong, 10–25 mm (0.4–1 in) long, 3–10 mm (0.12–0.4 in) wide, velvety-pubescent on the outside, glabrous inside. Stamens one-third to a half the length of the sepals. Achenes obovate, 2.5–3.5 mm (0.1–0.18 in) long, hairy, with a plumose tail 15–30 mm (0.6–1.2 in) long.

DISTRIBUTION. NE China (Inner Mongolia, C & N Gansu, Ningxia and Shaanxi, north-eastwards to Jilin, Liaoning and Heilongjiang), Korea, Japan (Honshu, Hokkaido), C & E Mongolia, SE Russia (SE Siberia); to 1300 m (4300 ft).

HABITAT. Dry places, particularly rocky and grassy slopes and sand dunes; June–Aug.

var. *tchefouensis* (Debeaux) S. Y. Hu (syn. *C. angustifolia* var. *tchefouensis* Debeaux, *C. hexapetala* var. *elliptica* S. Y. Hu and var. *insularis* S. Y. Yu) is distinguished by its sepals that are velvety only along the margin on the outside, otherwise glabrous. Restricted to grassy slopes in E China (N Jiangsu and E Shandong), to 500 m (1650 ft); not overlapping in distribution with the typical plant.

H7; P2

80. Clematis hexapetala in cultivation. Photo: Daan Smit

81. *Clematis campaniflora* in cultivation. Photo: Daan Smit

SUBSECTION CRASSIFOLIAE

141. *Clematis crassifolia* Benth.

DESCRIPTION. A more or less glabrous climber to 3.5 m (11.5 ft). Leaves leathery, ternate; leaflets petioluled, ovate to elliptic, 80–120 mm (3.2–4.7 in) long and 35–65 mm (1.4–2.6 in) wide, sometimes smaller, with a broad wedge-shaped to rounded base and entire margin, with 3 main veins from the base. Flowers numerous in lateral cymes or terminal panicles with rather small bracts, 25–40 mm (1–1.6 in) across. Sepals 4, white, sometimes flushed with pink on ageing, linear-lanceolate to narrow-oblong or elliptic, 12–21 mm (0.47–0.83 in) long, 2–5 mm (0.08–0.2 in) wide, velvety-pubescent all over, more densely so outside, sometimes almost glabrous inside. Stamens about half the length of the sepals with wavy filaments and very short (1.5 mm (0.1 in) long) anthers. Achenes ovate to elliptic, 4–6 mm (0.16–0.24 in) long, hairy, with a yellowish or white plumose tail 25–40 mm (1–1.6 in) long.

DISTRIBUTION. SE China (C & S Fujian, Guangdong, Guangxi, Hong Kong, S Hunan), N & C Taiwan (Nantou, Taipei, Taoyuan), S Japan; 300–2300 m (1000–7550 ft).

HABITAT. Forest margins, shrubberies, streamsides and ravines; Nov–Jan.

SECTION VITICELLA

No section in the genus *Clematis* is more important to horticulturists and gardeners than Viticella, for it contains all the very largest-flowered species and through them, directly or indirectly, all the large-flowered cultivars that adorn our gardens. Its significance cannot be under-estimated, for today the large-flowered clematis cultivars are of great importance and extremely popular; it would be difficult to find a garden centre in the country that did not stock at least half a dozen cultivars. Many of the species have large and colourful blooms, often in shades of blue, purple, lavender or mauve, or white, with coloured stamens. The section includes *C. viticella* itself, an important species in modern clematis breeding programmes, *C. florida*, one of the great treasures in the genus, and the important *C. lanuginosa* and *C. patens*, two Chinese species that laid the foundation for the development of the large-flowered cultivars of today's gardens.

SUBSECTION VITICELLA
(THE VITICELLA GROUP)

Five species of European and Asia origin of which *C. viticella* itself is by far the best known. All have nodding or half-nodding, usually 4-sepalled, flowers borne on the current season's shoots.

▼ **Flowers erect to ascending, with 5–6 sepals (species 142)**

142. *Clematis cadmia* Buch.-Ham. ex Wall.
(syn. *C. bracteata* sensu (Roxb.) Kurz, non DC., *C. b.* subsp. *stronachii* (Hance) Kuntze, *C. stronachii* Hance; *Thalictrum bracteatum* Roxb.)

DESCRIPTION. A slender climber 3–5 m (10–16.5 ft) with 6-ribbed hairy stems, often flushed with reddish-brown. Leaves pinnate with 5 or 7 leaflets, the lowermost pair or pairs often ternate, rather papery; leaflets ovate to lanceolate, 15–78 mm (0.6–3.1 in) long, 8–38 mm (0.32–1.5 in) wide, with an acute or subacute apex and entire margin, with 3–7 primary veins, sparsely hairy beneath. Flowers solitary or 2–3, lateral or sometimes terminal, 35–85 mm (1.4–3.3 in) across. Sepals 5–6, sometimes 4, pale blue or violet-blue, occasionally almost white, elliptic to oblanceolate, 16–42 mm (0.63–1.7 in) long, 3–14 mm (0.12–0.55 in) sparsely downy outside but glabrous inside. Stamens a quarter the length of the sepals or less. Achenes ovate, compressed, 5–7 mm (0.2–0.28 in) long, slightly hairy or glabrous, attenuated into a short finely hairy but non-plumose tail only 1–4 mm (0.04–0.16 in) long.

DISTRIBUTION. Bhutan?, S & SE China (S Anhui, Guangdong, Guangxi, Hunan, S. Jiangsu, N Jiangxi, N Zhejiang), NE India (Manipur and Sylhet), N Myanmar, and N Vietnam; at generally low altitudes.

HABITAT. Open broad-leaved forests, shrubberies, grassy banks and streamsides; Apr–July, occasionally later.

A double-flowered form ('Flore Pleno') of the species was recorded by Handel-Mazzetti from Zhejiang in eastern China but, despite this, the species does not appear to be in cultivation at the present time. This is a pity for it is an attractive plant which comes close to the popular *C. florida* in general characteristics, differing primarily in its basically pinnate rather than ternate leaves and in the smaller blue rather than white flowers. The flower colour alone makes this a species well worthy of introduction.

82. Clematis viticella in cultivation. Photo: Raymond Evison

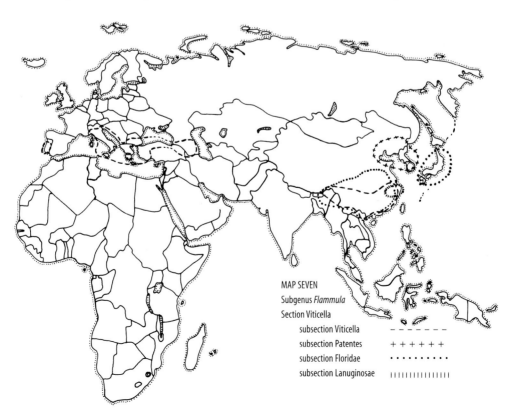

MAP SEVEN
Subgenus *Flammula*
Section Viticella
    subsection Viticella   – – – – – –
    subsection Patentes   + + + + + +
    subsection Floridae   • • • • • • • • • •
    subsection Lanuginosae | | | | | | | | | | | | | |

The recent 'Flora of Bhutan' (vol. 1, part 2, 1984) unaccountably links the species to *C. napaulensis*; the two species are completely different and could never be confused. It is also doubtful whether *C. cadmia* is actually native to Bhutan, being generally a species of more easterly locations.

▼ ▼ **Flowers nodding to half-nodding, with 4 (rarely 5) sepals (species 143–146)**
◆ **Flowers white or white flushed with lilac, violet or blue (species 143 & 144)**
❋ **Achenes without a plumose tail (species 143)**

143. *Clematis campaniflora* Brot.*
(syn. *C. viticella* var. *campaniflora* (Brot.) Willk. & Lange, *C. parviflora* DC., *C. revoluta* Desf.; *Viticella campaniflora* (Brot.) Spach)

DESCRIPTION. A very vigorous deciduous climber to 6 m (20 ft) with slender 6-ribbed stems, which are slightly downy when young, and pinnate or bipinnate rather glaucous leaves. Leaflets narrow-lanceolate to ovate, entire but often 2–3 lobed, to 75 mm (3 in) long, glabrescent. Flowers small and nodding, broad-campanulate, solitary or 2–3 on long slender stalks, 20–30 mm (0.8–1.2 in) across. Sepals 4, pale lilac or white flushed with violet or blue, oblong, to 20 mm (0.8 in) long and 8 mm (0.32 in) wide, with recurved somewhat twisted tips. Stamens with a few hairs towards the top of the filament, and cream anthers flushed with green. Achenes ovate, 6–7 mm (0.24–0.28 in) long with a very short, non-plumose style about the same length; style hairy in the lower third or two-thirds, not grooved.

DISTRIBUTION. Portugal and SW Spain.

HABITAT. Bushy places and hedges, occasionally over old walls; July–Sept.

This vigorous species is surprisingly dainty in flower and although the flowers are not particularly showy they do have a quiet charm, whilst at the same time they do appear over a comparatively long season. It can be extremely vigorous in gardens and shoots as long as 6–7 m (20–23 ft) are sometimes produced in a single season on established plants. It can look splendid when allowed to adorn a dark-leaved support such as a conifer (a *Chamaecyparis* or *Cupressus* perhaps). The species was introduced into cultivation as long ago as 1810. It is a close ally of the larger-flowered and brighter *C. viticella*. Although both are native to Europe they do not overlap in distribution in the wild.

Clematis campaniflora is sometimes listed as a subspecies or variety of *C. viticella* but they differ in a

number of respects. The flowers are a rather different shape, those of *C. campaniflora* being broader campanulate and with the sepals only narrowly flared towards the tip. In addition, the carpels are different, those of *C. campaniflora* being more densely hairy with the hairs covering the achene as well as the lower half or two-thirds of the style (especially easy to observe immediately after sepal fall) and the styles are ungrooved: in *C. viticella* the hairs are confined to the achene and the styles are distinctly grooved. I have no doubt that these two represent separate, although closely allied, species.

'Lisboa' has rather larger mauve-blue flowers to 50 mm (2 in) across. It was first collected as seed in the Lisbon Botanic Garden by Magnus Johnson and selected by him at his nursery at Södertälje in Sweden in 1993.

H6; P2

❋ ❋ **Achenes with a plumose tail (species 144)**

144. *Clematis huchouensis* Tamura

DESCRIPTION. A herbaceous perennial climber to 3 m (10 ft) with 5–6-furrowed stems. Leaves pinnate, rarely ternate, the leaflets ovate-elliptical to lanceolate, rather thin and papery, 20–50 mm (0.8–2 in) long and 10–40 mm (0.4–1.6 in) wide, finely pubescent on both surfaces, more densely so beneath, the apex acute to obtuse. Flowers in lateral cymes of 1–3, borne on bracted stalks to 80 mm (3.2 in) long, 20–30 mm (0.8–1.2 in) across, half-nodding. Sepals 4, white, ascending, oblong to lanceolate, 14–22 mm (0.55–0.87 in) long, 3–6 mm (0.12–0.24 in) wide, with an obtuse somewhat reflexed apex. Stamens about a quarter the length of the sepals. Achenes elliptic to ovate, 4–6 mm (0.16–0.24 in) long, finely appressed-pubescent, with a plumose style 40–60 mm (1.6–2.4 in) long.

DISTRIBUTION. E China (N Hunan, SE Jiangsu, N Jiangxi, N Zhejiang); c. 100 m (330 ft).
HABITAT. Grassy areas and banks, stream and lake margins; June–Aug.

◆ ◆ **Flowers blue, violet-blue to rose-purple or red (species 145 & 146)**
❋ **Flowers red, 20–35 mm (0.8–1.4 in) across (species 145)**

145. *Clematis calabrica* Grey-Wilson, nom. nov.
(syn. *C. campaniflora* sensu *Cavara*, non Brot., *C. scandens* Hutter, Porta & Rigo, non Borkh 1803, *C. viticella* subsp. *revoluta* (Desf.) Kuntze var. *scandens*

(Huter, Porta & Rigo) Kuntze and var. *scandens* (Huter, Porta & Rigo) Fiori)

DESCRIPTION. Similar to *C. viticella* but with pinnate to ternate leaves, the leaflets usually ternate or 3-lobed, and with smaller clear red flowers in leafy cymes of up to 12. Leaflets to 50 mm (2 in) long and 20 mm (0.8 in) wide. Flowers 20–35 mm (0.8–1.4 in) across, half-nodding. Sepals 4, oval to obovate, 15–20 mm (0.6–0.8 in) long and 5–8 mm (0.2–0.32 in) wide. Stamens one-third the length of the sepals.

DISTRIBUTION. S Italy (Calabria).

HABITAT. Bushy and rocky places, old walls; June–Aug.

The taxonomic position of this species is unclear and requires further field observations and data.

❀ ❀ **Flowers blue to purple or violet-blue, 30–60 mm (1.2–2.4 in) across (species 146)**

146. *Clematis viticella* L.* Virgin's Bower
(syn. *C. lugubris* Salisb., *C. viticella* subsp. *normalis* Kuntze; *Viticella deltoidea* Moench)

DESCRIPTION. A deciduous subshrubby climber to 4 m (13 ft) with slender ribbed stems that die down partway or almost to ground level each year to a woody base. Leaves pinnate with 5–7 primary divisions that are usually ternate; leaflets lanceolate to ovate, often 3-lobed, with an entire margin. Flowers solitary and terminal or 1–3 in lateral, short-stalked cymes, broadly campanulate, nodding or half-nodding, 30–60 mm (1.2–2.4 in) across. Sepals 4, blue, rose-purple or purple, obovate, with the margin expanded, somewhat undulate and recurved towards the tip. Stamens about one-quarter the length of the sepals. Achene compressed, 6–9 mm (0.24–0.35 in), appressed-hairy, with a short non-plumose tail only 5–10 mm (0.2–0.4 in) long; style glabrous, grooved.

DISTRIBUTION. S Europe (Italy eastwards to Greece and Crete, including S Bulgaria), the Caucasus (Armenia, Georgia, Azerbaijan), W & N Turkey, NW Iran; widely naturalized in parts of central and eastern Europe.

HABITAT. Bushy places, banks, old walls, often naturalized from cultivation or on abandoned cultivated land; June–Sept.

This is the showiest of the European species of clematis, although it also has a wide distribution in western Asia. It has certainly been cultivated since the

83. Clematis viticella', fruit

sixteenth century and probably earlier. The common name often applied to this species is Virgin's Bower. According to George Jackman and Thomas Moore who, in 1872 commented on some of the obscure names given to clematis, the origin of the common name was given to '…the first clematis brought back to England (*C. viticella*) was introduced in 1569 during the reign of Elizabeth I, the name Virgin's Bower might be intended to convey a compliment to that sovereign who, as is well known, liked to be called the Virgin Queen'.

Plants recorded in literature (see 'Flora Europaea' volume 1) from southern Italy and said to be transitional to *C. campaniflora* are almost certainly referable to *C. calabrica*.

84. Clematis viticella 'Etoile Violette'. Photo: Christopher Grey-Wilson

85. Clematis viticella 'Polish Spirit'. Photo: Christopher Grey-Wilson

The typical plant, as well as a double form, was grown by Gerard by 1797 who wrote that 'they grow in my garden at Holborn and flourish exceedingly.' Today the species is rarely seen in our gardens, which is a pity as it certainly has a poise and charm that few other clematis possess. It was much used at one time as a stock on which to graft other varieties and cultivars. The plant is very elegant in bloom with the nodding flowers held outwards on long elegant stalks. The wild plant is very variable, especially in the size of the flowers. However, it importance in the establishment of a whole race of different garden varieties should not be underestimated and this species had a profound effect on British gardens.

The viticellas, as they are popularly called, are a tribe of absolutely hardy, reliable and generally floriferous clematis which peak in performance in the late summer and autumn. They have a charm that is both captivating and enchanting and I would never be without them in the garden. For those who find the large and blowsy clematis cultivars fickle, wilt-prone and temperamental, then the viticellas offer considerable solace. Few clematis look more elegant when allowed to roam onto bushes in the garden. There is no problem about pruning them either, for a pair of shears in the late winter or early spring to lop them off close to the ground is all that is required. The old strands can then be easily pulled from the host bush and the cycle of growth is then repeated. If I could only have one group of clematis to grow in my garden it would undoubtedly be the viticellas. In recent years more and more viticella cultivars have appeared and many are absolutely first rate, easy and floriferous and with none of the wilt problems that afflict so many other cultivars. Admittedly many do not possess the elegance of *C. viticella* itself but they do offer a range of exciting cultivars for the garden, both in vigour, floriferousness and colour. Not only are they excellent for walls, pergolas and pillars, but are even more effective for scrambling up shrubs, both low and tall, or for sprawling over the ground. If growing the species in the garden make sure to select a good, well-coloured form for it can be extremely variable when seed-raised.

The cultivars include the following (many have 4–6 sepals); 'Abundance' (semi-nodding, saucer-shaped flowers, 50–70 mm (2–2.8 in) across, of wine-rose, with yellow anthers); 'Alba Luxurians'* (a vigorous English cultivar from around 1900, with pale rather glaucous-green foliage, and rather ungainly white nodding flowers 70–80 mm (2.8–3.2 in) across, with variable amounts of green towards the sepal tips, more prominent in the early rather than the late blooms); 'Betty Corning'* (nodding bell-flowers 50–60 mm (2–2.4 in) long, pale pinkish-blue, more mauve within, the sepal-tips elegantly recurved; believed to be a *C. crispa* × *C. viticella* hybrid); 'Blue Belle' (large deep violet-purple broad bells, 80–90 mm (3.2–3.5 in) across. on a vigorous plant); 'Carmencita' (a Swedish cultivar with 60 mm (2.4 in) carmine flowers with black anthers); 'Elvan' (semi-nodding 50 mm (2 in) flowers of violet-purple, rather similar to the wild type and borne on elegant slender stalks); 'Etoile Violette' AGM (an old and popular cultivar, vigorous and floriferous, violet-purple flowers, redder in bud, 70–80 mm (2.8–3.2 in) across.); 'Kermesina' (another old French cultivar, sometimes found under the name of 'Rubra', with deep velvety red flower 60 mm (2.4 in) across, the sepals with a green tip); 'Little Nell' (an early French cultivar with small 50 mm (2 in) mauvish-white flowers); 'Madame Julia Correvon' AGM (very popular and reliable old French cultivar with an abundance of 70–80 mm (2.8–3.2 in) rich velvety red flowers, pinker beneath); 'Margot Koster' (large 90–100 mm (3.5–4 in) flowers of deep mauve-pink, the sepals with characteristic rolled margins at maturity); 'Minuet'* AGM (another French cultivar with half-nodding flowers about 60 mm (2.4 in) across, which are white with purplish-red veining towards the margins of the sepals); 'Polish Spirit' (a wonderful recent Polish cultivar noted for its exquisite half-nodding rich purplish-blue satiny flowers, with deep reddish-black stamens, vigorous and very free-flowering); 'Purpurea Plena' (= 'Mary Rose'; a very early sixteenth-century cultivar with double smoky bluish-mauve nodding flowers without stamens); 'Purpurea Plena Elegans'* AGM (another sixteenth-century cultivar, finer than the previous with dusky violet-purple flowers, paler and greyer in bud and on the reverse, without stamens, very free-flowering and vigorous); 'Royal Velours'*AGM (a French cultivar from the early part of the twentieth century with sumptuous satiny dark velvet-purple flowers (the darkest of any), 60–80 mm (2.4–3.2 in) across; received an Award of Merit (AM) from the Royal Horticultural Society in 1934); 'Söldertälje'* (flowers half-nodding, pinkish-purple, 70–80 mm (2.8–3.2 in) across, the sepals with recurved tips, and pale green stamens; 'Tango'* (a fairly recent English cultivar with half-nodding 60–70 mm (2.4–2.8 in) flowers, greenish-cream with the sepal margins veined mauve); 'Venosa Violacea'* AGM (a French cultivar from the nineteenth century with half-nodding, relatively large, 90–100 mm (3.5–4 in) saucer-shaped flowers, white flushed and veined purple towards the sepal margins and darkest at the margins; sepals usually 5–6). All flower from mid-summer to the middle or end of the autumn and are generally 2.5–3.5 m (8–11.5 ft) tall at maturity. Some, especially the double-flowered types and those with very long flower-stalks, are excellent as cut flowers.

86. *Clematis viticella* 'Madame Julia Correvon'. Photo: Christopher Grey-Wilson

87. *Clematis viticella* 'Purpurea Plena Elegans'. Photo: Christopher Grey-Wilson

88. *Clematis viticella 'Royal Velour'*. Photo: Christopher Grey-Wilson

forma *albiflora* (**Kuntze**) **Rehd**., which is sometimes found in the wild with the normal-coloured plant, has pure white flowers.

H6; P2

Subsection Floridae
(THE FLORIDA GROUP)

Four species of Asian origin. They bear flowers that are borne on short leafy shoots directly from shoots of the previous year. Although all would be extremely desirable in cultivation, only *C. florida* is grown. It is without doubt one of the gems in the genus *Clematis*, and although perhaps not as easy to grow as some of the other species, it deserves every bit of attention that can be lavished upon it.

▼   **Achenes with a long plumose tail of 15–50 mm (0.6–2 in) (species 147 & 148)**

◆   **Flowers white, sometimes flushed purple, 50–95 mm (2–3.5 in) across; sepals usually 6 (species 147)**

147. *Clematis courtoisii* Hand.-Mazz.
(syn. *C. florida* sensu Courtois, non Thunb.)

DESCRIPTION. A herbaceous perennial climber to 2.5 m (8 ft) with 5-furrowed stems which are generally sparsely hairy when young. Leaves ternate to biternate, the leaflets papery, elliptic to ovate, 30–65 mm (1.2–2.6 in) long and 14–20 mm (0.55–0.8 in) wide, occasionally 3-lobed, otherwise undivided, finely pubescent on the veins above and beneath, with an entire margin. Flowers lateral and solitary with a pair of leaf-like bracts midway along the stalk, 50–95 mm (2–3.5 in) across. Sepals 6, white, often flushed with purple, elliptic, 27–55 mm (1.1–2.2 in) long, 10–28 mm (0.4–1.1 in) wide, spreading widely apart, with an acute apex, downy along the veins beneath. Stamens one-third the length of the sepals. Achenes obovate, 3.5–4.5 mm (0.14–0.18 in) long, sparsely pubescent, with a yellow plumose tail 12–35 mm (0.47–1.4 in) long.

DISTRIBUTION. CE & E China (S Anhui, S Henan, W Hubei, E Hunan, S Jiansu, N Zhejiang); 200–500 m (650–1650 ft).

HABITAT. Forested slopes and forest margins, streamsides.

◆ ◆   **Flowers blue-purple to reddish-purple, 30–50 mm (1.2–2 in) across; sepals usually 4 (species 148)**

148. *Clematis hancockiana* Maxim.
(syn. *C. florida* sensu Kuntze, non Thunb., *C. f.* var. *hancockiana* (Maxim.) Courtois, *C. tsengiana* Metcalf)

DESCRIPTION. Closely related to *C. florida*, but with 4-sepalled, bluish-purple to purple-red flowers, 30–50 mm (1.2–2 in) across. The sepals are narrow-oblong, 15–25 mm (0.6–1 in) long and 5–8 mm (0.2–0.32 in) wide, with an acute apex. In addition, the achenes are quite different with those of *C. hancockiana* densely hairy and with a long yellowish plumose tail, 35–50 mm (1.4–2 in) long, while the achenes of *C. florida* are very short-hairy with a short 6–8 mm (0.24–0.32 in) long tail which is hairy only in the base half, otherwise glabrous.

DISTRIBUTION. E China (SE Anhui, S Henan, SW Jiangsu, N & E Zhejiang); to 500 m (1650 ft).

HABITAT. Shrubberies and open part-wooded slopes; May–June.

This interesting plant would be an exciting addition to a collection of species clematis. Although the flowers are well coloured and a good size, the sepals are rather long and narrow.

▼ ▼ **Achenes with a short tail, 6–12 mm (0.24–0.47 in)
long (species 149 & 150)**
❊ **Stamens white with reddish-brown anthers
(species 149)**

149. *Clematis longistyla* Hand.-Mazz.
(syn. *C. florida* sensu Henry, non Thunb., *C. patens*
sensu Hance, non Morren & Dene)

DESCRIPTION. Very similar to *C. courtoisii* but the
achenes have a short tail only 8–12 mm (0.32–0.47 in)
long which is plumose (villous) only in the basal half.
In addition, the flowers are pure white, 50–70 mm
(2–2.8 in) across, with 4–6 sepals, and the leaflets can
often bear several small teeth along the margin.

DISTRIBUTION. CE China (S Henan, NW Hubei); c. 500
m (1650 ft).

HABITAT. Primarily shrubberies along stream margins
and adjacent slopes; May–June.

❊ ❊ **Stamens dark purple-black (species 150)**

150. *Clematis florida* Thunb.*
(syn. *Anemone japonica* Huttuyn; *Atragene florida*
(Thunb.) Pers.; *Clematis bracteata* (Roxb.) Kurz var.
leptomera (Hance) Kuntze, *C. japonica* sensu Makino,
non Thunb., *C. j.* var. *simsii* Makino, *C. leptomera*
Hance; *Viticella florida* (Thunb.) Spach)

DESCRIPTION. A semi-evergreen to deciduous climber
to 3 m (10 ft), occasionally more, with wiry, 6-ribbed
stems and biternate or pinnate, deep green, glossy
leaves. Leaflets usually 5–9, ovate to lanceolate, to 50
mm (2 in) long and 20 mm (0.8 in) wide, coarsely
toothed or somewhat lobed (less so and often entire in
cultivated forms), with an acute to somewhat cuspidate
apex, 3-veined, downy beneath. Flowers solitary,
45–80 mm (1.8–3.2 in) across (to 100 mm (4 in) in
cultivated specimens), borne on slender downy stalks
to 12 cm (4.7 in) long with a pairs of leaf-like bracts
(generally ternate or 3-lobed) near the middle. Sepals
4–8, frequently 6, white or cream, with a greenish
band on the reverse, oval, to 25–40 mm (1–1.6 in)
long and 10–25 mm (0.4–1 in) wide, 5-veined, with a
subacute apex, downy along the centre beneath.
Stamens dark purple-black, forming a prominent boss
in the centre of the flower, about a quarter the length
of the sepals, the filaments whitish towards the base.
Achenes obovate to almost rhombic, 3–4 mm
(0.12–0.16 in) long, with a short tail only 8–10 mm
(0.32–0.4 in) long, which is hairy (not plumose) only
in the lower half.

DISTRIBUTION. S & SE China (Guangdong, Guangxi,
Hunan, Jiangxi; possible still existing in Hubei),
naturalized in Japan; to 1700 m (5600 ft).

HABITAT. Shrubberies, thickets and streamsides;
Apr–early July.

Clematis florida has been long-cherished in Japanese
gardens and it was first known in the West from
cultivated specimens. It was first noted by Thunberg in
Japan and introduced in 1776. The ancestral form of
this Chinese species was not discovered until much
later when Ernest Henry Wilson came across it in the
early 1900s near Ichang in Hubei Province, but it has
been little seen since that date, although plants have
recently come into cultivation and it is listed by
Thorncroft Clematis Nursery near Norwich. In the
wild form stamens rather than petals or staminodes
represent the centre of the flower. The species is
sometimes allied to *C. patens*, indeed it has been
united by some authorities. The two, though, differ in
a number of respects: in *C. patens* the flower-stalks
are bractless and the leaves are simply ternate or
pinnate with 3 or 5 leaflets.

Clematis florida (in its various forms) is
undoubtedly one of the most exciting and dramatic
species and its cultivars are much sought-after,
although perhaps it is not always that easy to please in
the open garden. Failing this, they make excellent
subjects for container planting in conservatories,
provided that the pots do not become to hot or dry out
at any time. The species is rare in cultivation; however,
Ray Evison reports that both the prime forms in
cultivation, var. *plena* and var. *sieboldiana*, will
occasionally sport spontaneously to give seedlings
with flowers very similar to the wild type. 'Evison' is
a selected cultivar from such a reverted source, with
large 10–12 cm (4–4.7 in) flowers. Interestingly,
'Evison' seedlings either come more or less like the
parent cultivar or revert to var. *plena*. 'Pistachio' is an
'Evison' sport with 80 mm (3.2 in) flowers; these are
cream or greenish-cream, with pinkish-grey anthers,
the centre of the flower (the immature achenes) being
replaced by a tuft of green aborted ovaries. The
species is said to be rather more spindly in cultivation
than its cultivars and lacks their long and intermittent
flowering season.

The species and varieties require no pruning except
for the removal of weak, old flowering wood. Plants
can be killed to ground level during severe winters but
will often sprout afresh from below ground once the
weather relents in the spring.

Clematis florida is undoubtedly one of the
loveliest of all clematis and is freely available in two

89. *Clematis florida* var. *plena*. Photo: Christopher Grey-Wilson

varieties, var. *plena* and var. *sieboldiana*. Both are utterly delightful and anyone coming across them in flower for the first time cannot fail to be attracted by them. Although they are neither the easiest plants to cultivate, nor always particularly floriferous, they are utterly delightful and a must on the wants list of any budding clematis enthusiast.

var. *plena* D. Don (syn. *C. florida* sensu Jacq., non Thunb., *C. florida flore pleno* Lavallée, *C. f.* var. ß *flore-pleno* G. Don, 'Alba Plena', 'Flore Plena',

90. *Clematis florida* var. *sieboldiana*. Photo: Raymond Evison

'Plena') has 9–10 cm (3.5–4 in) flowers in which all the stamens have been transformed into petal-like staminodes; these are white or greenish, narrow-lanceolate, 10–12 mm (0.4–0.47 in) long and glabrous. Surprisingly, although well known in cultivation, this interesting variety is found in the wild, being restricted to widely isolated places in SW Yunnan and Zhejiang at c. 1700 m (5600 ft), where it inhabits thickets and streamsides, flowering in May–June. One can only imagine that it is able to set some seed, despite the lack of stamens; in fact in cultivated plants flowers sometimes bear a few central stamens and this is probably the case in the wild. In addition, plants will often sport back to var. *sieboldiana*.

This is one of the finest double clematis. It was initially a sport from var. *sieboldiana* but has been known in cultivation in Europe since 1835. It is a fine clematis in the garden being strongly recommended for growing through medium evergreen shrubs or as a container plant. It is rather thin-stemmed and can look gaunt on a wall or fence. The flowers, which are produced in quantity throughout the summer months, are good for cutting and last surprisingly long in water. It can look wonderful when planted as a climbing companion to a ceanothus. Having been quite scarce in the horticultural trade twenty years ago, it is now listed by many nurseries and even turns up in the better-endowed garden centres.

var. *sieboldiana* Morren (syn. 'Bicolor', 'Sieboldii', *C. sieboldii* Paxton and of Don, *C. f.* var. *bicolor* Lindl., var. *sieboldii* G. Don) is more widely available and has 9–10 cm (3.5–4 in) white flowers with the outer stamens at least transformed into small deep purple petal-like staminodes, filling the 'eye' of the flower. Both have been cultivated in gardens for many years. 'Sieboldii' was certainly long known in Japanese gardens and was introduced by Dr Phillipp von Siebold to the Botanic Garden in Leiden, reaching Britain in 1836.

It is not surprising that this lovely plant is much sought after by gardeners. At the same time it is a pity that it is not easier to please in cultivation. Well grown it is a glorious sight in full flower, but often plants sulk or do not perform particularly well, or worse still they simply shrivel away. It certainly requires a warm sheltered spot in the garden and is good trained up through medium-sized shrubs or grown as a container specimen. Both it and var. *plena* are excellent subjects for conservatories. The flowers are long-lasting, as are many 'double' clematis, and the common form in cultivation has sterile flowers with the sepals falling away to leave the boss of purple staminodes intact for a further week or so. The flowers, which are mainly borne in June and July, have a certain vague likeness to those of the Passion Flower, *Passiflora caerulea*, and indeed are sometimes mistaken for it. Var. *sieboldiana* will occasionally sport to var. *plena*. Both flower throughout the summer until autumn.

Another plant often placed under *C. florida* is the cultivar generally named **'Fortunei'** (syn. *C. florida* var. *fortunei* or *C. patens* var. *fortunei*). This interesting plant was introduced to the West by Robert Fortune from Japan where it had long been cultivated. The plant in question is similar to *C. florida* but has flowers up to 15 cm (6 in) across, which are fully double with numerous creamy white petals which can scarcely be differentiated from the sepals. This plant is sometimes placed under *C. florida*, or sometimes under *C. patens* but the plant in question may be of more complex origin that is almost impossible to resolve because of its long history of cultivation. However, 'Fortunei' proved a very important plant to breeders in the nineteenth century and gave rise to a vigorous 'race' of double clematis which are often classified as the Florida Group. These include cultivars such as 'Belle of Woking'. The Florida Group should not be confused with the species *C. florida*, for its origins encompasses a complex genetic ancestry which probably includes *C. patens* as well as *C. lanuginosa* and 'Fortunei' in its make-up. There is no compelling evidence that 'Fortunei' contains any 'blood' of *C. florida* at all, so its supposed involvement in the Florida Group of hybrids and cultivars may be wholly erroneous.

H6; P (little or none)

SUBSECTION PATENTES
(THE PATENS GROUP)

151. *Clematis patens* Morren & Decne.*
(syn. *C. azurea* Sieb. ex Steud., *C. a.* var. *grandiflora* Sieb. ex J. C. Loudon, *C. caerulea* Lindl., *C. florida* (Thunb.) Kuntze pro parte, *C. kasugunuma* Sieb., *C. luloni* Hort. ex Koch)

DESCRIPTION. A deciduous climber to 4 m (13 ft), with 6-ribbed stems, downy when young. Leaves ternate or pinnate with 3 or 5 ovate-lanceolate to ovate leaflets, each to 100 mm (4 in) long and 60 mm (2.4 in) wide, the lateral pair sometimes with 2 or 3 lobes, all with an entire margin and acute to subacute apex, downy beneath but sparsely and minutely hairy only on the veins above. Flowers solitary, upright, 70–120 mm (2.8–4.7 in) across,

91. *Clematis patens*, Gifu Prefecture, Honshu, Japan. Photo: Roy Lancaster

borne terminally on short lateral shoots on long downy, bractless, pedicels 46–120 mm (1.8–4.7 in), but occasionally up to 22 cm (9 in) long. Sepals usually 8, white flushed with violet, to violet-blue, occasionally pure white, ovate, to 35–70 mm (1.4–2.8 in) long and 15–35 mm (0.6–1.4 in) wide, acute-tipped, rather separated from one another and wide-spreading. Stamens one-third the length of the sepals, with reddish-purple anthers and white filaments. Achenes compressed, ovate, 3.5–5 mm (0.14–0.2 in) long, glabrous to appressed-pubescent, with a plumose tail to 50 mm (2 in) long which is more or less hairless at the base.

92. *Clematis patens*, violet-blue form in cultivation. Photo: Raymond Evison

93. Clematis 'Nelly Moser', a widely grown late-nineteenth-century
C. patens x *C. lanuginosa* hybrid. Photo: Christopher Grey-Wilson

DISTRIBUTION. NE China (E Shandong to Hebei and
SE Liaoning and S Jilin) and Korea but probably
naturalized in Japan; 200–1000 m (650–3300 ft).

HABITAT. Shrubberies, forest margins and grassy
slopes; May–June.

This important species has long been cultivated in
Japan; whether it is native there is uncertain, although
it is generally assumed to be naturalized. It was
introduced by von Siebold into European gardens in
1836 from a garden he had visited close to the city of
Yokohama. Some authorities have considered this
species to be merely a form of *C. florida*, but this
species can be always distinguished by possessing
biternate leaves, in having bracts on the 'pedicels' and
in usually possessing hairy achenes. *C. patens* has been
important in the breeding of some of the large-flowered
cultivars. For example 'Belle of Woking', 'Candida',
'Dr Ruppel', 'Elsa Späth', 'General Sikorski' and 'Mrs
Cholmondeley' all have *C. patens* in their 'blood'. The
form used by breeders was probably an old Japanese
garden variety introduced from Japan by Robert
Fortune in 1863 and today known as 'Standishii' (syn.
C. florida var. *standishii*, *C. f.* × *C. patens* 'Standishii',
C. patens 'Standishii', *C. patens* var. *standishii*). The
clematis associated with *C. patens* flower in early to
mid-summer on short shoots borne on the previous
year's stems. They generally require very little pruning
other than to remove old or diseased growth or to
shorten back those that have just flowered.

The wild form is cultivated still in gardens and is
available from a handful of sources in the nursery
trade. It is well worth while adding to a collection,
although only the better forms should be selected, as
seed-raised plants can be very variable in flower.

var. *tientaiensis* (M. Y. Fang) W. T. Wang has simple
or ternate leaves that are glabrous beneath, shorter
pedicels, usually 35–40 mm (1.4–1.6 in) long, and
flowers with 5 or 6 sepals. Similar habitats and
altitudes, but restricted to E Zhejiang.

H6; P3

SUBSECTION LANUGINOSAE (THE LANUGINOSUS GROUP)

152. Clematis lanuginosa Lindl.
(syn. *C. florida* Thunb. subsp. *lanuginosa* (Lindl.) Kuntze)

DESCRIPTION. A deciduous climber to 2 m (6.6 ft) with
slender downy, 6-ribbed stems. Leaves papery, simple
or occasionally ternate with heart-shaped leaflets, to
12 cm (4.7 in) long and 7.5 cm (3 in) wide, which are
entire and unlobed with an acute or subacute apex and
a characteristic down of soft grey hairs beneath.
Flowers large and upright, 8–15 cm (3–6 in) across.
(to 20 cm (8 in) in cultivated specimens), solitary at
the tips of the current year's shoots on woolly pedicels
50–100 mm (2–4 in) long, often supported by two
lateral flowers (opening subsequently) at the
uppermost node. Sepals 6, occasionally 7–8, pale lilac
or purplish to white, oval to obovate, 40–70 mm
(1.6–2.8 in) long and 30–60 mm (1.2–2.4 in) wide,
overlapping, spreading widely apart, downy beneath.
Stamens about one-third the length of the sepals,
glabrous, the anthers as long as the filaments. Achenes
rhombic, 4–8 mm (0.16–0.32 in) long, finely
appressed-hairy, with a yellowish plumose tail 40–80
mm (1.6–3.2 in) long.

DISTRIBUTION. E China (E Zhejiang); to 400 m (1300 ft).

HABITAT. Hill and valley shrubberies; May–June, then
intermittently until autumn.

This large-flowered and important species has a very
limited distribution in the wild in the province south
of Shanghai in eastern China. Although clearly allied
to *C. patens* and *C. florida* in Section Viticella, it is
readily identified on account of its woolly stems, the
equally woolly undersides of the leaves and by the

large overlapping sepals. Its rather dwarf habit is also distinctive. *C. lanuginosa* was first introduced into cultivation by Robert Fortune who found it near Ning-po in 1850. The species appear to be extinct in cultivation and a fresh introduction of seed would be highly valuable. Despite this, the importance of the species in the development of the familiar large garden hybrid clematises cannot be underestimated, for it infuses their 'blood'. The first crosses were made by Isaac Anderson-Henry in the middle of the nineteenth century, shortly after the introduction of *C. lanuginosa* from the wild. The resultant crosses (*C.* 'Lawsoniana' and *C.* 'Henryi' AGM, both with *C.* 'Fortunei' (see p.123) as the male (pollen) parent), laid the foundation for many of the fine large-flowered cultivars seen in our gardens today and generally referred to as the Lanuginosa Group, although their origins are often rather more complicated than this simple analysis reveals. Familiar cultivars of *C. lanuginosa* origin include 'Général Sikorski', 'W. E. Gladstone', 'Marie Boisselot' 'Mrs Cholmondeley', 'Nelly Moser', 'Prins Hendrik' and 'William Kennett'.

One of the most famous crosses involving *C. lanuginosa* is undoubtedly the popular garden plant *C.* 'Jackmanii' AGM*, produced by George Jackman of Woking in 1858. The plant was the result of a cross between *C. viticella* 'Atrorubens' and *C. lanuginosa* and bears sumptuous blooms to 15 cm (6 in) across of deep velvet-purple.

The Lanuginosa Group as a whole are characterized by producing their flowers in succession from the current season's shoots, generally on short lateral shoots from about late June onwards. They require enough pruning to remove weak, dead or unwanted growths, shortening the remainder back to the first good strong pair of buds. Hard pruning will simply delay flowering until later in the season.

H6; P3

SECTION PTEROCARPA

153. *Clematis brachyura* Maxim.*
(syn. *C. paniculata* Thunb. forma *pauciflora* Miq., *C. recta* subsp. *brachyura* (Maxim.) Kuntze, *C. spectabilis* Palib.)

DESCRIPTION. A deciduous semi-herbaceous species with erect 12-ribbed stems to 1 m, generally rather less. Leaves ternate to pinnate or simple, the leaflets oval, to 60 mm (2.4 in) long and 40 mm (1.6 in) wide, occasionally 3-lobed, with 3 or 5 veins from the base

94. *Clematis* 'Jackmanii'. Photo: Christopher Grey-Wilson

and an untoothed margin, generally a rather dull matt-green above, paler beneath. Flowers in lateral or terminal cymes, often of 3, green in bud but opening pure white, star-like, 16–35 mm (0.63–1.4 in) across, faintly scented. Sepals 4, occasionally 5, oblong, 8–16 mm (0.32–0.63 in) long and 3–4 mm (0.12–0.16 in) wide. Stamens about one-third to half the length of the sepals, with greenish-white or cream anthers. Achenes oval and rather compressed, widely winged, 6–7 mm (0.24–0.28 in) long, with a short pointed, non-feathery, tail just 3–4 mm (0.12–0.16 in) long at maturity.

DISTRIBUTION. SE Korea; c. 210 m (700 ft).
HABITAT. Open woodland and shrubberies; June–Aug.

A rare species in cultivation; it has rather pretty if sparse flowers and, although not difficult to cultivate, rarely produces enough flowers to make an impact. For this reason it is often consigned, perhaps unfairly, to species collections.

H6; P3

SECTION FRUTICELLA

A small section containing some ten species noted primarily for their shrubby or subshrubby habit and, apart from the Nepalese *C. phlebantha*, bearing relatively small, though often attractive, flowers.

SUBSECTION FRUTICELLA
(THE SHRUBBY GROUP)

Four species native to northern and western China and Mongolia. From the gardener's point of view *C. nannophylla* is by far the most desirable, forming a neat shrubby plant bearing numerous solitary yellow lantern-flowers; unfortunately it is still scarce in cultivation.

▼   Leaves simple, entire (species 154)

154. *Clematis canescens* (Turcz.) W. T. Wang & M. C. Chang

(syn. *C. fruticosa* forma *lanceifolia* Kozlova, *C. f.* var. *canescens* Turcz., and var. *tomentella* Maxim., *C. recta* subsp. *fruticosa* var. *canescens* (Turcz.) Kuntze)

DESCRIPTION. Closely related to both *C. fruticosa* and *C. nannophylla* but readily distinguished by possessing undivided rather leathery grey-green leaves with an entire margin, rarely with one or two small teeth towards the base, and grey-downy beneath. The flowers, borne in lateral and terminal clusters of 1–7 (generally 1–3), are yellow, 13–22 mm (0.5–0.87 in) across; sepals 9–16 mm (0.35–0.63 in) long and 3–8 mm (0.12–0.32 in) wide, finely hairy on the outside. Achenes elliptic, 4–5 mm (0.16–0.2 in) long, densely white-hairy (villous) with a plumose style to 20 mm (0.8 in) long.

DISTRIBUTION. W China (N & NW Gansu, SW Inner Mongolia, Ningxia and N Shaanxi); 1100–1900 m (3600–6200 ft).

MAP EIGHT

Subgenus *Flammula*

Section Flammula

    subsection Uncinatae   –·–·–·–·–·–·–

Section Fruticella

    subsection Songaricae   ············

    subsection Fruticella   + + + + + + +

    subsection Phlebanthae   ׀׀׀׀׀׀׀׀׀׀׀׀

Section Pterocarpa   – – – – – – – –

HABITAT. Rocky slopes and banks, sandy areas; late June–Aug.

This interesting species is not in cultivation, but it would make a good introduction. In the wild it is said to make a small bush of 0.5–1 m (20–40 in).

subsp. *viridis* W. T. Wang & M. C. Chang (syn. var. *viridis* (W. T. Chang & M. C. Chang) W. T. Wang) is a larger plant, sometimes attaining 2 m (6.6 ft), with thinner more papery leaves which are deep green and appear to be in fascicles. The flowers are solitary and terminal, the sepals larger, 12–26 mm (0.47–1 in) long and 5–13 mm (0.2–0.5 in) wide, scarcely hairy to glabrous on the outside. In addition, the achenes are hairy rather than villous and the plumose tails 20–32 mm (0.8–1.3 in) long. This subspecies is distributed further south than the typical plant (subsp. *canescens*), in SE Qinghai, NW Sichuan and E Tibet at 2700–3500 m (8850–11,500 ft), where it tends to favour rocky and scrubby slopes.

▼ ▼　**Leaves pinnate or at least lobed (species 155–157)**
◆　　**Flowers basically white, with usually 6 sepals, occasionally 4–5 (species 155)**

155. *Clematis delavayi* Franch.

DESCRIPTION. A twiggy shrublet to 1.5 m (5 ft), but often only 0.5 m (20 in) with ribbed stems that are silky when young; branchlets not spiny. Leaves pinnate; leaflets 7–13, unlobed, papery, oval to oblong with a rounded base, to 40 mm (1.6 in) long and 16 mm (0.63 in) wide, deep green above, silvery-white with silky hairs beneath. Flowers borne in 3-flowered cymes at the shoot tips (these together forming lax panicles), 15–25 mm (0.6–1 in) across. Bracts mainly ternate. Sepals usually 6, occasionally 4–5, white or cream, narrow-oval, 8–13 mm (0.32–0.5 in) long, 5–8 mm (0.2–0.32 in) wide, silvery-hairy outside, spreading widely apart. Achenes silky-hairy, with a silky plumose tail to 25 mm (1 in) long.

DISTRIBUTION. SW China (SW Sichuan, NW Yunnan); 1800–3300 m (5900–10,800 ft).

HABITAT. Dry rocky places, particularly sandstone cliffs, and stony slopes, scrub; July–early Sept.

This interesting species was introduced into cultivation by Ernest Henry Wilson from Sichuan but it is no longer in cultivation, although seed may have been brought back by recent expeditions to SW China. The species is more of botanical than horticultural interest.

It grows in dry rather hot places, often in deep valleys or gorges. It is common in the deep defiles of the Yangtse river and its tributaries, where little monsoon rain seems to percolate, despite the fact that the slopes high above receive abundant water during the summer months. This phenomenon of rain-shadow areas within the monsoon zone was noted by Frank Kingdon-Ward and others travelling in the Yunnan, Tibet, Sichuan border region. It is important in trying to understand the cultural requirement of plants like *C. delavayi* which inhabit such places. In gardens they require warm, sunny, sheltered spots, not the sort of place that would normally be reserved for a clematis.

Clematis delavayi is very variable in the wild and the following varieties are recognized:

var. *calvescens* Schneid. has non-spiny few-branched stems, and unlobed leaflets 8–20 mm (0.32–0.8 in) long which are scarcely hairy beneath and pale grey-green rather than silvery or white. Restricted to dry slopes in SW Sichuan (Muli region) and NW Yunnan.

var. *limprichtii* (Ulbr.) M. C. Chang (syn. *C. limprichtii* Ulbr.) is like the typical plant with non-spiny branches but with smaller lanceolate leaflets, which are not more than 17 mm (0.67 in) long and 12 mm (0.47 in) wide, often 2–3-lobed, silvery-hairy beneath. Grassy slopes and bushy places at similar altitudes in W Sichuan and NW Yunnan.

var. *spinescens* Balf. f. is a small twiggy bush with the stem tips spine-like after the first year; leaves with only 2–3 pairs of primary segments, the leaflets small and lanceolate, unlobed, to 10 mm (0.4 in) long and 3 mm (0.12 in) wide; sepals usually 4. Dry slopes, rocky areas and cliffs at 2000–3800 m (6500–12,500 ft) in the Jinsha Jiang of SW Yunnan and the neighbouring region of Tibet.

H5

◆ ◆　**Flowers yellow, with usually 4 sepals (species 156 & 157)**
✲　　**Leaf-segments with a few fine teeth (species 156)**

156. *Clematis fruticosa* Turcz.*
(syn. *C. fruticosa* forma *atriplexifolia* Kozlova and forma *chenopodiifolia* Kozlova, *C. f.* var. *lobata* Maxim. and var. *viridis* Turcz., *C. recta* subsp. *fruticosa* (Turcz.) Kuntze, *C. salsuginea* Bunge)

DESCRIPTION. A twiggy shrublet 0.5–1.2 m (20–48 in) high, with reddish-brown somewhat downy, 4–6-

95. *Clematis nannophylla*, photographed in Qinghai Province, NW China.
Photo: Rosemary Steele

ribbed stems. Leaves rather leathery, lanceolate to oblong, 15–60 mm (0.6–2.4 in) long, 5–22 mm (0.2–0.9 in) wide, pinnately lobed with 1–3 pairs of lateral lobes normally, deep green and somewhat shiny; lobes with a few coarse dentate teeth on each side or variously pinnatisect, slightly hairy above and beneath at first. Flowers terminal, solitary or 2–3, broad bell-shaped, nodding, 20–45 mm (0.8–1.8 in) across, borne on short 10–50 mm (0.4–2 in) long pedicels with leaves immediately below. Sepals yellow, 4, ascending, thick and rather fleshy, lanceolate, 10–25 mm (0.4–1 in) long, 5–12 mm (0.2–0.47 in) wide, sparsely grey-hairy outside. Stamens about two-thirds the length of the sepals, glabrous. Achenes oval, silky-hairy, with a silky plumose tail to 30 mm (1.2 in) long.

DISTRIBUTION. N China (C Gansu, Hubei, SW Inner Mongolia, N Shaanxi, Shanxi, E Qinghai) and S Mongolia; 800–2000 m (2600–6500 ft).

HABITAT. Dry rocky banks and scrubby hillsides, river gravels and cliffs; July–Sept.

Closely related to *C. nannophylla* and often inhabiting rather similar places. *C. nannophylla* has pinnatisect leaves and rather smaller flowers and is generally a far more densely twiggy species. Another difference can be observed in the stamens which are twice as long in *C. fruticosa*, with the anthers at least 3.5 mm (0.14 in) long, whereas in *C. nannophylla* they are never more than 2 mm (0.08 in) long. Lobed-leaved forms of

C. fruticosa have been distinguished in the past as var. *lobata* Maxim. but intermediate types occur frequently and the variety cannot be upheld.

An interesting but little-known plant in cultivation. Although not spectacular it would make an interesting subject for pot culture or for a raised bed or rock garden.

H6; P2

❀ ❀ **Leaf-segments pinnately lobed (species 157)**

157. *Clematis nannophylla* Maxim.

(syn. *C. recta* subsp. *nannophylla* (Maxim.) Kuntze)

DESCRIPTION. A small twiggy deciduous shrub to 1.2 m (4 ft) high, often wider, sometimes only 30 cm (12 in) tall, with the young stems 4–5-ribbed and with appressed grey hairs. Leaves deep grey-green and rather leathery, small, 5–20 mm (0.2–0.8 in) long, but more usually 10–14 mm (0.4–0.55 in), and 3–14 mm (0.12–0.55 in) wide, 3-lobed to pinnately lobed (with 2–3 (–4) pairs of lateral lobes), glabrous or almost so; lobes oblong and obtuse. Bracts similar to the leaves. Flowers solitary or 2–3 (rarely with cymes up to 7-flowered) at the ends of main shoots or short lateral shoots towards the stems tips, nodding, broad bell-shaped, to 12–24 mm (0.47–0.95 in) across. Sepals 4, golden-yellow, often suffused with brown outside, ascending, oval to elliptic, 8–16 mm (0.32–0.63 in) long and 4–8 mm (0.16–0.32 in) wide, hairy on the outside, especially along the margin, or glabrous except for the margin. Stamens reddish-brown, glabrous. Achenes elliptic, 3–4 mm (0.12–0.16 in) long, hairy, with a silky yellowish plumose tail to 20 mm (0.8 in) long.

DISTRIBUTION. N China (W & C Gansu, E Qinghai, Shaanxi); 1200–3200 m (3900–10,500 ft).

HABITAT. Dry rocky and earthy banks, loess and gravel slopes; late June–Sept.

This pretty little species is quite one of the most charming of the shrubby clematises. It is a pity that, until recently, it had been lost from cultivation, although it flourished for a number of years in a cool house at the Royal Horticultural Society's Garden at Wisley. It was first introduced from China by Reginald Farrer from Gansu during his 1914–15 expedition. More recently, some seeds and seedlings have been introduced from Ginghai Province by the Sino-British Qinghai Expedition (Chris Brickell, Ron McBeath et al.). *C. nannophylla* is perhaps the prettiest of the shrubby Fruticella Section. It grows in rather dry arid regions that are out of the summer monsoon or at least in an area not greatly affected by the monsoon. In this respect it closely matches the habitat conditions of Section Meclatis, whose members (typified by *C. orientalis*) also grow in drier conditions in the wild than most clematis, although the latter are primarily climbers rather than shrubs.

var. *foliosa* Maxim. is distinguished by its more leafy character (leaves 25–45 mm (1–1.8 in) long and 16–30 mm (0.63–1.2 in) wide) and larger flowers (sepals to 16 mm (0.63 in) long and 4–8 mm (0.16–0.32 in) wide); however, it has been noted that in cultivation at least, plants tend to produced larger leaves and the occurrence of such forms in the wild may be due solely to habitat conditions (i.e. those plants growing in moister or slightly shadier places bearing larger leaves and flowers). Var. *foliosa* is restricted to S Gansu, in similar habitats at 1200–1700 m (3900–5600 ft).

H7; P (little or none)

SUBSECTION SONGARICAE
(THE SONGARIA GROUP)

Four species from Central Asia and north-western China which are subshrubby or more or less herbaceous. The flowers are usually white and erect, borne in the summer and early autumn on the current year's shoots.

▼   **Leaves simple; sepals 4 or 6 (species 158 & 159)**
◆   **Leaves strictly opposite, with an entire margin (species 158)**

158. *Clematis lancifolia* Bur. & Franch.
(syn. *C. duclouxii* Lévl., *C. iochanica* Ulbr.)

DESCRIPTION. A shrublet or subshrub only 30–60 cm (12–24 in) tall, occasionally to 1 m (40 in), with appressed-hairy stems carrying up to five pairs of simple leaves. Leaves simple, linear-lanceolate to narrow-oval or elliptic, to 140 mm (6 in) long and 25 mm (1 in) wide, with a wedge-shaped or rounded base and an entire margin, 3-veined; petiole 4–25 mm (0.16–1 in) long. Flowers borne in long-branched terminal cymes, usually of 6–8, each flower 20–25 mm (0.8–1 in) across, the pedicels up to 50 mm (2 in) long, bearing one or two pairs of small lanceolate bracts. Sepals 4–6, white, often flushed pink, oblong to narrow-oblong, 10–13 mm (0.4–0.5 in) long, 3–5 mm (0.12–0.2 in) wide, with yellowish silky hairs on the margin outside. Stamens a half to two-thirds the

length of the sepals. Achenes ovate, 4–5 mm (0.16–0.2 in) long, silky-hairy, with a yellowish plumose tail to 25 mm (1 in) long.

DISTRIBUTION. SW China (W & SW Sichuan, N & NE Yunnan); 1500–1900 m (4950–6200 ft).

HABITAT. Grassy and rocky slopes and banks, river gravels and open forest; late June–Aug.

var. *ternata* W. T. Wang & M. C. Chang has distinctive ternate leaves with petioles more than 25 mm (1 in) long, the leaflets linear-lanceolate; otherwise it corresponds with the typical plant, var. *lancifolia*. It is confined to SW Sichuan (Miyi Xian) at c. 1100 m (3600 ft).

◆ ◆   **Leaves opposite and whorled, usually with a toothed margin (species 159)**

159. *Clematis songarica* Bunge*
(syn. *C. gebleriana* Bong., *C. recta* subsp. *songarica* (Bunge) Kuntze, *C. songarica* var. *integrifolia* Trautv. and var. *serratifolia* Trautv.)

DESCRIPTION. A subshrubby deciduous plant, with ridged glabrous downy stems, to 1.5 m (5 ft) tall, though generally less. Leaves smooth, grey- or blue-green, simple, lanceolate to linear, to 100 mm (4 in) long and 40 mm (1.6 in) wide, though often less, the margin often with coarse jagged teeth, sometime untoothed, with three prominent veins. Flowers borne in stalked lateral and terminal cymes (usually 3–7-flowered), these together forming a panicle-like inflorescence, each flower 18–35 mm (0.7–1.4 in) across, star-like, with a slender pedicel, hawthorn-scented. Sepals 4, occasionally 6, cream or pure white, narrow-oval, to 8–17 mm (0.32–0.67 in) long and 3–9 mm (0.12–0.35 in) wide, spreading widely apart, downy outside, glabrous or slightly downy inside. Stamens glabrous, with pale yellow anthers. Achenes ovate to obovate, 2.5–3.5 mm (0.1–0.18 in) long, hairy, with a plumose tail to 26 mm (1 in) long.

DISTRIBUTION. C Asia (Afghanistan, Kazakstan, Kyrgyzstan, Tadjikistan and S Siberia), NW China (Xinjiang) and Mongolia; 400–2500 m (1300–8200 ft).

HABITAT. Bushy or stony steppe, rocky hill-slopes, grassy places; June–Sept.

The species takes its name from the region of Dzungaria (Songaria) located in Kazakstan/Xinjiang border region (not as some publications report from the region of the river Sungari (Songhua), which is in north-eastern China's Helongjiang Province), where it is commonly found. It was sent to Kew in 1880 by E. Regel and has subsequently been introduced on a number of occasions. It is freely available today but is not a particularly garden-worthy species, although it can look reasonably well in the flower border: against a wall it may attain as much as 2 m (6.6 ft). The silky seedheads are perhaps more appealing than the bunches of flowers and extend the display well into autumn. In many ways it is a subshrubby counterpart of *C. orientalis*, with similarly coloured grey-green foliage, but this is simple rather than pinnate. It is often described in gardens as a 'low rambling shrub'.

Clematis songarica is widespread in Afghanistan, where I saw it on a number of occasions in 1971. It is particularly common in the centre of the country around Bamian where it grows on rocky slopes, often amongst other shrubs and various herbs.

Trautvetter (1860) attempted to divided the species on having entire or toothed leaves but this does not work as both types of leaf can sometimes be found on the same plant.

H6; P2

▼ ▼ **Leaves lobed or pinnate (lowermost sometimes undivided); sepals 4 (species 160 & 161)**
❋ **Stems glabrous; achene tails 15–20 mm (0.6–0.8 in) long (species 160)**

160. *Clematis asplenifolia* Schrenk
(syn. *C. asplenifolia* var. *boissieriana* (Korsh.) Krasch., *C. boissieriana* Korsh., *C. recta* subsp. *asplenifolia* (Schrenk) Kuntze, *C. songarica* var. *boissieriana* B. Fedtsch., *C. songarica* Bunge var. *asplenifolia* Trautv. and var. *intermedia* Trautv.)

DESCRIPTION. Very similar to *C. songarica* and included by some modern authors under that species as a variety. However, the species can be readily separated on account of its upper leaves which are divided and pinnately lobed, by the always glabrous inner surface of the sepals and by the longer anthers, 3–4 mm (0.12–0.16 in) (not 2–3 mm (0.08–0.12 in)) long.

DISTRIBUTION. C Asia (Afghanistan, Kazakstan, Kyrgyzstan, Tadjikistan), NW China (W Xinjiang) and NW Pakistan (Chitral, Gilgit); 500–2500 m (1650–8200 ft).

HABITAT. Similar dry habitats, but most frequent in dry gravelly places and along riverbanks;

❋ ❋ **Stems hairy; achene tails 30–40 mm (1.2–1.6 in) long (species 161)**

161. *Clematis ispahanica* Boiss.*
(syn. *C. pseudoorientalis* Kuntze, *C. recta* subsp. *ispahanica* Kuntze)

DESCRIPTION. A subshrub to 1.5 m (5 ft) tall, with the lower parts of the stems becoming woody. Leaves pinnate (with 5 or 7 leaflets normally), ternate, or the uppermost simple. Leaves or leaflets lanceolate to lanceolate-elliptic, to 80 mm (3.2 in) long and 30 mm (1.2 in) wide, generally much smaller, with an acute to subacute apex and an entire margin, rather leathery; the lower leaflets generally unlobed but the upper or terminal unlobed to 2–3-lobed, the lobes generally rather short and towards the base. Flowers solitary or 2–3 at the upper leaf-axils or terminal to the stem, 15–30 mm (0.6–1.2 in) across, borne on long slender stalks 5–15 cm (2–6 in) long; bracts simple, similar to the leaflets but unlobed. Sepals 4, white, lanceolate-elliptic, 10–13 mm (0.4–0.5 in) long and 3–5 mm (0.12–0.2 in) wide, spreading widely apart. Stamens about half the length of the sepals, with white anthers c. 2 mm (0.08 in) long, the connectives reddish-violet or purplish. Achenes elliptical, 3–4 mm (0.12–0.16 in) long, hairy, with a slender plumose tail 30–40 mm (1.2–1.6 in) long.

DISTRIBUTION. W & N Iran and Turkmenistan (Kopet Dagh); 1600–2400 m (5250–7900 ft).

HABITAT. Rocky and bushy places, ravines; July–Sept.

A rare species in cultivation: it makes a rather lax-growing open bush, sometimes sprawling, but without the flower size to make any real impact. It is sometimes placed in its own subsection, Ispahanicae Serov, but the species has so much in common with the members of Subsection Songaricae that I have decided to place them all together.

H6; P2

SUBSECTION PHLEBANTHAE

162. *Clematis phlebantha* L. J. H. Williams*

DESCRIPTION. A trailing shrub or more upright bush with stems to 2 m (6.6 ft) long, but often less than 0.5 m (20 in), with the young stems ribbed and covered in white down, later becoming brown and woody, the bark peeling away in strips. Leaves pinnate, deep and somewhat silky green above, silvery-silky beneath like the stems and petioles; leaflets 5–9, often 7, ovate to triangular, generally 3 or 5 lobed, sessile or almost so, heavily veined on the upper surface. Flowers more or less flat, terminal or, more generally on short lateral shoots, usually solitary, 25–45 mm (1–1.8 in) across. Sepals 5–7, white or yellowish with reddish-brown or reddish-purple veins, elliptic to obovate, to 20 mm (0.8 in) long and 10 mm (0.4 in) wide, with an acute or slightly mucronate tip, hairy outside. Stamens yellow. Achenes silky-hairy, with a silky plumose tail to 30 mm (1.2 in) long.

DISTRIBUTION. W Nepal; 2590–3660 m (8500–12,000 ft).

HABITAT. Cliffs and rocky hill-slopes, banks bordering cultivation; July–Sept.

This exceptional and very distinctive species looks almost like a briar rose at a distance. It has extremely attractive leaves which shimmer nicely in the slightest breeze. Although it will succeed outdoors in a warm sunny aspect in the garden (beneath a south- or west-facing wall is ideal) it rarely flowers as profusely as one might wish and in a cool wet summer may fail to flower altogether. It requires a light well-drained soil. In the warmer confines of a conservatory it will fair rather better, although the stems can get very long and ungainly. The stems are totally non-climbing and need to be tied into a framework in order to keep the plant within bounds; cultivated specimens can reach 2.5 m (8 ft) high when trained against a wall and twice as much across, with the peak flowering in cultivation in June and July; it certainly requires good ripening of the wood if it is to flower well the following season. This is a strikingly handsome species and it really should be tried in Mediterranean gardens or those with a similar climate. In the wild it grows within the rain-shadow of the Himalaya to the north-west of Mt Dhaulaghiri, on the north side of the main Himalayan Divide. Here the summer condition are hot and dry, with an occasionally heavy shower, whilst the winters are cold and snowbound. It grows in similar conditions to unrelated species such as *C. nannophylla* and *C. orientalis*.

Clematis phlebantha was first discovered in 1952 by the highly successful Polunin, Sykes and Williams expedition to West Nepal at 2500–3500 m (8200–11,500 ft) and seed was introduced under the number PSW 3436, the same year.

Phlebantha literally means 'grooved flower' which indicates the incised nature of the veins on the sepals. The flowers are very attractive in both shape and size

96. *Clematis phlebantha*, south of Pungmi, NW Nepal. Photo: Alan Dunkley

and remind one of *C. potaninii*, although that species is generally far easier to grow, more floriferous and has quite different foliage.

This is a fine species and it is to be hoped that better, more free-flowering clones can be introduced in the future. Its glistening silvery, silky foliage is one of its most distinguishing features. It received an Award of Merit (AM) when shown at the Royal Horticultural Society in 1968.

H7; P (little or none)

Subgenus Four *Archiclematis*

163. *Clematis alternata* Kitamura & Tamura

DESCRIPTION. A slender deciduous climber to 4 m (13 ft), though often less, with downy young stems. Leaves strictly alternate and simple, ovate, 3–5-lobed, 30–100 mm (1.2–4 in) long, 30–80 mm (1.2–3.2 in) wide, with a heart-shaped base and slightly toothed margin, silky-downy beneath, especially on the veins, sparsely appressed-pubescent above. Flowers usually solitary, occasionally 2–3, narrow urn-shaped, pendent on long slender pedicels which bear a pair of small bracts towards the base. Sepals 4, deep red, 18–28 mm (0.7–1.1 in) long and 6–10 mm (0.24–0.4 in) wide, with a strongly recurved tip, 3-ribbed, especially towards the base, sparsely downy all over, more densely so along the margins. Stamens two-thirds the length of the sepals, with hairy filaments and glabrous anthers. Achenes pubescent.

DISTRIBUTION. Central west Nepal and the neighbouring region of S Tibet (Gyirong Xian); 2200–2500 m (7200–8200 ft).

HABITAT. Forest margins and shrubberies, often amongst *Pinus*, *Picea* or *Larix*; June–July.

97. *Clematis alternata*, lower Marsyandi Valley, C Nepal.
Photo: Christopher Grey-Wilson

This is one of the most distinctive and readily recognized species of *Clematis*, in fact the only one which possesses alternate rather than opposite leaves. In addition, the leaves are simple and rather maple-like. The solitary flowers are reminiscent of some of the American or eastern Asian species of Section Viorna, but the resemblance is very superficial.

I have been fortunate enough to have seen *C. alternata* in flower on several occasions in the Marsyandi Valley of central Nepal. The flowers are not particularly easy to find but on each occasion the plants were spotted draped on overhead bushes along pathways. The Marsyandi Valley is about in the middle of the species' rather limited distribution. The species never seems to be common and has a rather narrow altitudinal range according to existing records. Unfortunately, *C. alternata* is not in cultivation; it would make an interesting, though by no means spectacular, garden plant. From a botanical point of view, however, live plants would be invaluable for comparative morphological studies.

Subgenus Five *Campanella*

With 76 species, *Campanella* is the largest subgenus in Clematis. The species, that are characterized by having alternate leaves in the seedling stage with predominantly campanulate flowers and hairy stamens, are scattered across Africa, with the majority of species in India, eastern and south-eastern Asia.

SECTION CAMPANELLA

(THE CONNATA GROUP)

A large and important section containing 43 species which, in the main, bear narrow- to broad-campanulate flowers in green, greenish-yellow or yellow, pink or reddish-brown. They are handsome more than spectacular in flower but add a whole new dimension to the general concept of the clematis, especially in cultivation. Although many of the species are not at present in cultivation they do include the popular, sweet-smelling, *C. rehderiana*, the charming and delicate *C. aethusifolia, C. connata* with its flanged petiole bases and the vigorous and rather striking half-hardy *C. buchananiana* and *C. grewiiflora*, with their rather furry blooms. In addition, the African *C. grandiflora*, which can be likened to an even more robust *C. grewiiflora*, bears very large fruitheads, perhaps the largest found in the genus overall.

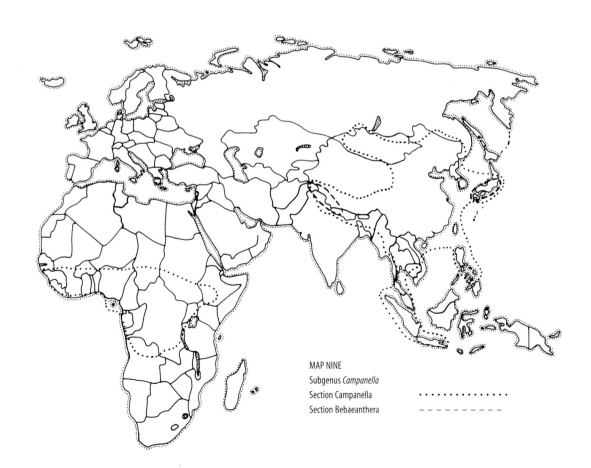

MAP NINE
Subgenus *Campanella*
Section Campanella · · · · · · · · · · · · · ·
Section Bebaeanthera – – – – – – – – –

98. Clematis ranunculoides; Bei-shui, N of Lijiang, NW Yunnan, China.
Photo: Martyn Rix

short hairy pedicels. Sepals 4, rose-pink to reddish-purple, oblong to lanceolate, to 7–15 mm (0.28–0.6 in) long and 4–6 mm (0.16–0.24 in) wide, erect to half-spreading, strongly recurved, with 2–3 prominent keels (wings) on the reverse. Stamens pinkish, about as long as the sepals, with glabrous anthers. Achenes compressed, narrow-elliptic to spindle-shaped, c. 3 mm (0.12 in) long, downy, with a short plumose tail to 13 mm (0.5 in) long.

DISTRIBUTION. SW China (NW Guangxi, W Guizhou, SW Sichuan, C & NW Yunnan); 500–3000 m (1650–9850 ft).

HABITAT. Open grassy or bushy places, open forest and shrubberies, stream margins; Sept–early Nov.

This interesting species was introduced into cultivation by George Forrest in the early 1900s from the Cangshan (Dali or Tali) range in NW Yunnan. It is very variable in the wild and plants can look very different, even in close localities. This is partly due to habitat conditions, for plants found in open grassy situations tends to be low and herbaceous, with upright stems sometimes only 30–60 cm (12–24 in) high, whereas in more confined shrubby situations the plants become scramblers or climbers with more substantial stems to 2 m (6.6 ft), occasionally more.

In cultivation it should be a fine plant for the herbaceous border but it has never proved long-lived or particularly hardy, which is surprising considering its distribution and habitat. However, its chief enemy in gardens appears to be not low temperatures but excessive winter wet. Given a warm sunny site and excellent drainage it may fair rather better than it has done to date in my garden.

▼ Plants herbaceous or subshrubby, not climbing (species 164 & 165)

164. *Clematis ranunculoides* Franch.*
(syn. *C. acutangula* Hook. f. & Th. forma *major* W. T. Wang, *C. a.* subsp. *ranunculoides* (Franch.) W. T. Wang, *C. philippiana* Lévl., *C. pterantha* Dunn. var. *grossedentata* Rehd. & Wils., *C. ranunculoides* var. *grossedentata* (Rehd. & Wils.) Hand.-Mazz. and var. *tomentosa* Finet & Gagn., *C. urophylla* var. *heterophylla* Lévl., *C. tenii* Ulbr.)

DESCRIPTION. An upright herbaceous perennial herb or scrambling deciduous subshrub to 2 m (6.6 ft), though often only 30-60 cm (12–24 in) tall, with 4–6 furrowed and angled stems, downy or glabrous when young. Leaves mid-green, variable, ternate to biternate, or pinnate with 5 primary segments, rarely simple on the same plant, the petiole to 15 cm (6 in) long, coiling strongly; leaflets ovate to obovate, to 70 mm (2.8 in) long and 60 mm (2.4 in) wide, coarsely toothed, sometimes 3-lobed, and generally hairy. Flowers campanulate, 10–20 mm (0.4–0.8 in) across, solitary or in terminal clusters, nodding on

var. *cordata* M. Y. Fang has ternate leaves with heart-shaped, unlobed, leaflets, to 70 mm (2.8 in) long and 60 mm (2.4 in) wide; margin entire or slightly crenate. Restricted to SW Sichuan.

var. *pterantha* (Dunn) M. Y. Fang (syn. *C. pterantha* Dunn) has glabrous stems and leaves, the latter ternate, the leaflets 7.5–12.5 cm (3–5 in) long, and white or pale rose flowers with 3–5-keeled sepals. The flowers are borne in larger lateral cymes of 7–12 normally. Restricted to S Yunnan (Pu'er Xian).

H8; P2

165. *Clematis pinchuanensis* W. T. Wang & M. Y. Fang
(syn. *C. ranunculoides* Franch. var. *tomentosa* Finet & Gagn.)

DESCRIPTION. Similar to *C. ranunculoides* but a subshrub with erect stems to 35 cm (14 in) tall with simple ovate leaves, 30–60 mm (1.2–2.4 in) long and wide, often 3-lobed, more densely pubescent beneath and often velvety. In addition, the anthers are hairy on the back of the connective and the achenes have short plumose tails rarely more than 10 mm (0.4 in) long.

DISTRIBUTION. SW China (Yunnan; Binchuan (Pinchuan) Xian).

HABITAT. Similar habitats to *C. ranunculoides* probably; Dec–Jan.

❀ ❀ **Plants climbing (species 166–206)**
◆ **Herbaceous climbers (species 166)**

166. *Clematis yuanjiangensis* W. T. Yang

DESCRIPTION. A herbaceous climber with slender 4-furrowed stems, closely related to *C. ranunculoides* but with more leathery ternate leaves, the leaflets narrow-ovate to elliptic, 27–80 mm (1.1–3.2 in) long and 10–28 mm (0.4–1.1 in) wide, with a more or less entire margin (usually with one small tooth on each side in the lower half). The flowers are larger, c. 18 mm (0.7 in) across, the spreading sepals pinkish, narrow-oblong, c. 18 mm (0.7 in) long and 4 mm (0.16 in) wide, with 3 keels on the back; stamens about two-thirds the length of the sepals.

DISTRIBUTION. SW China (S Yunnan); c. 1600 m (5250 ft).

HABITAT. Mountain shrubberies; Sept–Oct.

◆ ◆ **Evergreen or deciduous climbers (species 167–206)**
❇ **Flowers violet to purple, rose-purple or purplish-brown or reddish-brown (species 167–172)**
❀ **Leaves simple to ternate (species 167)**

167. *Clematis jinzhaiensis* Zh. W. Xue & Z. W. Wang

DESCRIPTION. Very similar to *C. pogonandra* in growth and in its solitary (occasionally 2–3) flowers borne on the current season's shoots. However, the leaflets are rather larger (usually ternate but sometimes simple) and clearly toothed, both peduncle (9–16 mm (0.35–0.63 in) long) and small linear bracts present. More obviously the flowers are purple, the sepals glabrous, not finely pubescent, inside. The sepals are 16–23 mm (0.63–0.9 in) long and 5–7 mm (0.2–0.28 in) wide. In both species the anthers bear hairy (villous) connectives on the outside.

DISTRIBUTION. E China (W Anhui; Jinzhai Xian); 800–1500 m (2600–4950 ft).

HABITAT. Rocky and bushy places; Aug–Sept.

99. Clematis yuanjiangensis, Stone Forest near Kunming, Yunnan, China. Photo: Martyn Rix

100. Clematis confusa in cultivation. Photo: Christopher Grey-Wilson

101. *Clematis pseudopogonandra*, Haba Shan, NW Yunnan, China.
Photo: Christopher Grey-Wilson

102. *Clematis dasyandra*, Wolong, Sichuan, China. Photo: Martyn Rix

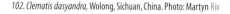

❀ ❀ **Leaves pinnate to bipinnate, occasionally biternate (species 168–172)**
❖ **Petioles fused round stem as a flat disc-like process (species 168)**

168. *Clematis confusa* Grey-Wilson*

DESCRIPTION. Similar to *C. connata* but with deeper green and normally 3-lobed leaflets and smaller reddish-brown flowers, with the sepals triangular-ovate, 12–20 mm (0.47–0.8 in) long and 5.5–7 mm (0.22–0.28 in) wide. In addition the connective of the anthers, like the filaments are hairy; in *C. connata* the connectives are glabrous.

DISTRIBUTION. Himalaya (E Nepal to Sikkim & Bhutan; possibly extending into adjacent regions of Tibet); 1830–2800 m (6000–9200 ft).

HABITAT. Mountain shrubberies, woodland margins and open woodland; late Aug–Oct.
This interesting species was only described in 1991. Although most of the material available for examination in herbaria are of recent origin, one sheet at Kew extends back to a collection of Joseph Dalton Hooker made in Sikkim in 1849. Like *C. connata*, *C. confusa* has a distinctive disc at each node uniting the base of adjacent pairs of leaves. The flower colour and size is quite different. *C. confusa* is in cultivation from a Bhutanese collection made by Keith Rushforth. I have one plant in my garden which has proved very hardy to date; although it will sprout readily from the previous years stems, after severe frost the plant is cut back close to ground level and new shoots arise from below ground. Unfortunately, it is rather late to come into flower and the buds can be easily damaged by early frosts. It is extremely vigorous and shoots up to 5 m (16.5 ft) long can be produced in a single season, on mature plants.

I have seen this species in the wild in the forests of east Nepal: on the Kew Edinburgh Kanchenjunga Expedition (KEKE) in September and October 1989 it was observed on several occasions in the region of the Surke Danda, above Suketar.

H6; P2

❖ ❖ **Petioles not fused round stem or scarcely so; not surrounding the stem disc-like (species 169–172)**
✳ **Leaves pinnate with 5 leaflets (species 169 & 170)**
✳ **Sepals 20–40 mm (0.8–1.6 in) long (species 169)**

169. *Clematis pseudopogonandra* Finet & Gagn.
(syn. *C. pseudopogonandra* var. *paucidentata* Finet & Gagn.)

DESCRIPTION. A small deciduous climber 1–3.5 m (3.3–11.5 ft), with slender downy, 4–6-furrowed stems and pinnate leaves. Leaflets usually 5, grey-green, sometimes flushed with purple, ovate to rounded, 18–40 mm (0.7–1.6 in) long, 10–30 mm (0.4–1.2 in) wide, generally 3–5-lobed, or sometimes ternate, with several coarse dentate teeth on each side, downy underneath, more sparsely so above. Flowers nodding, campanulate, solitary or 2–3, with two leaves borne on slender pedicels 3.5–11 cm (1.4–4.3 in) long, from the lateral buds of the previous year's shoots, pointed in bud. Sepals 4, purplish-brown, to dull deep purple or purple-maroon on the outside, generally paler and greenish-grey or yellowish-green inside, elliptic, 20–40 mm (0.8–1.6 in) long, 7–15 mm (0.28–0.6 in) wide, erect to half-spreading, densely downy inside but sparsely hairy and 3-ridged outside, with the margins often somewhat revolute. Stamens a half to two-thirds the length of the sepals, densely hairy; anthers yellow with the back of the connectives densely hairy. Achenes elliptical to ovate, 3–5 mm (0.12–0.2 in) long, hairy, with a reddish-brown or yellowish plumose tail to 35 mm (1.4 in) long.

DISTRIBUTION. SW China (W Sichuan, SE Tibet & NW Yunnan); 2700–4260 m (8850– 14,000 ft).

HABITAT. Forests, particularly of birch and rhododendron, scrub, stream banks, cliffs and screes; June–July. Var. *paucidentata* Finet & Gagn. is sometimes distinguished by having entire-margined leaflets or with 3 incised lobes (teeth). However, intermediates between these and the more clearly toothed leaf-forms can be found in the wild, especially in the Zhongdian region of NW Yunnan.

Although related to *C. pogonandra,* the two species are readily separated: *C. pogonandra* by its ternate leaves and entire leaf-margin, as well as its yellow flowers.

✳ ✳ **Sepals not more than 17 mm (0.67 in) long (species 170)**

170. *Clematis dasyandra* **Maxim.**

DESCRIPTION. Similar to *C. lasiandra* but a woody climber with the leaves strictly pinnate (with 5 ovate, sparsely toothed leaflets), and with the petiole base not expanded or fused with the opposing leaf-petiole. The flowers are solitary but pedunculate, the sepals purple, erect, oblong, 12–17 mm (0.47–0.67 in) long and 5–7 mm (0.2–0.28 in) wide, downy on the outside.

DISTRIBUTION. W China (S Gansu & NW Sichuan); c. 2400 m (7900 ft).

103. *Clematis lasiandra* in cultivation. Photo: Raymond Evison

HABITAT. Open forests, shrubberies and stream margins.

var. *polyantha* Finet & Gagn. has flowers in cymes of 3–9. Distributed in S Gansu, S Shaanxi and NE Sichuan at 1700–2000 m (5600–6500 ft).

✳ ✳ **Leaves usually bipinnate to biternate with 9 or more leaflets or segments (species 171 & 172)**

171. *Clematis acutangula* **Hook. f.**
(syn. *C. lasiandra* Maxim. var. *duclouxii* Finet)

DESCRIPTION. A deciduous climber to 5 m (16ft), with reddish-purple stems which are very sticky when young. Leaves bipinnate, to 22 cm (8.7 in) long, the primary divisions with 3 or 5 leaflets, deep shiny green with a purplish flush overall; leaflets oval to lanceolate, to 50 mm (2 in) long and 22 mm (0.87 in) wide, coarsely toothed or 2–3 lobed. Flowers in lateral cymes of 3–5, occasionally solitary, nodding, campanulate, borne on long, slender pedicels. Sepals 4, rarely 5, lilac or brownish flushed with lilac or yellow, ovate, to 16 mm (0.63 in) long and 6 mm (0.24 in) wide, with an acute, recurved, downy tip. Achenes pubescent, with a tawny plumose tail up to 25 mm (1 in) long.

DISTRIBUTION. NE Himalaya (Bhutan to Assam), W & SW China.

HABITAT. Open woodland and bushy places; Aug–Nov.

This species was introduced from western China by

Ernest Henry Wilson round about 1903. However, it has never become any more than a curiosity in gardens. Its rather demure flowers, which are rarely produced in profusion, and its late-flowering habit, often mean that the display is cut short by the first autumn frosts.

172. *Clematis lasiandra* Maxim.*
(syn. *C. nutans* var. *pseudo-connata* Pamp.)

DESCRIPTION. A moderately vigorous deciduous part-herbaceous climber 2–6 m (6.6–20 ft), with slender 4–6-grooved stems, glandular-hairy and sticky when young. Leaves bipinnate to biternate, occasionally pinnate, dark green and sparsely hairy above, paler and glabrous beneath or slightly hairy along the veins; leaflets ovate to lanceolate, 33–65 mm (1.3–2.6 in) long, 13–30 mm (0.5–1.2 in) wide, the lateral ones with an oblique base, sometimes 3-lobed, the apex acuminate and the margin coarsely and unevenly toothed. Flowers nodding, campanulate, 10–20 mm (0.4–0.8 in) across, borne in short lateral cymes, often 3-flowered, on the current season's shoots, occasionally in more substantial panicles of up to 9. Sepals 4, whitish to pale violet-purple or rose-purple, ovate-lanceolate to oblong, 12–25 mm (0.47–1 in) long, 5–8 mm (0.2–0.32 in) wide, somewhat recurved towards the apex, glabrous on the outside apart from the margin. Stamens with densely hairy filaments, almost as long as the sepals; anthers glabrous. Achenes narrow-elliptic to almost rhombic, 2–3.5 mm (0.08–0.14 in) long, short-hairy, rather velvety, with a plumose tail to 35 mm (1.4 in) long.

DISTRIBUTION. C & S China (S Gansu to Hubei, S Shaanxi and Zhejiang southwards, except for the tropical regions), southern Japan and Taiwan; 800–3000 m (2600–9850 ft).

HABITAT. Forest margins, shrubberies and open scrub; Sept–Nov.

This species was introduced into cultivation in 1900 by Ernest Henry Wilson. However, it is not showy and the late blooms often fall prey to autumn frosts and for these reasons it has never gained any appeal in gardens, except as a curiosity. The larger better-flowered forms are worth seeking out for collections.

var. *nagasawai* Hayata has ternate or pinnate leaves with 3 or 5 leaflets that are sometimes 3-lobed. The flowers are the palest purple, somewhat larger, the sepals to 23–29 mm (0.9–1.1 in) long and 7–8 mm (0.28–0.32 in) wide. Restricted to the mountains of central Taiwan at mid-altitudes.

H6; P2

✳ ✳ **Flowers basically white, cream, yellow or yellowish-green, occasionally slightly flushed with pink or purple, especially at the base of the sepals (species 173–206)**
✪ **Leaves pinnate to bipinnate (species 173–183)**
✤ **Petioles forming a large disc-like process around the stem (species 173)**

173. *Clematis connata* DC.*
(syn. *C. amplexicaulis* Edgew., *C. buchananiana* subsp. *connata* Kuntze, *C. b.* var. *trullifera* Franch., *C. gracilis* Edgew., *C. trullifera* (Franch.) Finet & Gagn., *C. velutina* Edgew., *C. venosa* Royle)

DESCRIPTION. A vigorous deciduous climber to 7 m (23 ft), sometimes more, with slightly 8–10-ribbed glabrous stems. Leaves pinnate, occasionally ternate, bright glossy green, sometimes glaucous beneath; leaflets 3 or 5, rarely 7, ovate, to 14 cm (5.5 in) long and 9.5 cm (3.7 in) wide, papery, coarsely toothed to 3-lobed, the base heart-shaped, the apex acuminate, sparsely hairy on the veins beneath, glabrous or almost so above. Base of each pair of petioles forming a fused thin, disc-like, flange around the stem at each node. Flowers bell-shaped, pendent on slender pedicels, borne in long-stalked many-flowered panicle-like cymes from the axils of the uppermost leaves, sometimes as few as 9 flowers per cluster, mildly fragrant. Sepals 4, pale yellow to ivory, oblong to oblong-lanceolate, 14–27 mm (0.55–1.1 in) long and 4–8 mm (0.16–0.32 in) wide, with an acute, somewhat recurved tip, downy inside and out, rarely subglabrous. Stamens about two-thirds the length of the sepals, the anthers. Yellow achenes ovate, 3–4 mm (0.12–0.16 in) long, hairy, with a plumose tail to 40 mm (1.6 in) long.

DISTRIBUTION. Himalaya (Kashmir to Bhutan), W & SW China (W Guizhou, W Sichuan, S & SE Tibet, N & NW Yunnan); 1800–3400 m (5900–11,150 ft). HABITAT. Forests at the mid-altitudes, but absent from the subtropical regions of the Himalaya, as well as the upper coniferous forest zone, especially along streams and rivers; late Aug–Oct.

Clematis connata varies considerably in leaf shape and hairiness and in the size of the flowers. The size of the petiole discs, which is a very useful diagnostic character in this species and its close allies, is also very variable.

This species is surprisingly hardy in cultivation and deserves to be more widely grown. The flowers appear late in the season, the first generally opening towards the end of September, and the waxy primrose blooms can be extremely attractive on a well-flowered specimen, although the whole show may be over in less than four weeks. Plants take a while to settle into the garden and can be rather invasive, with shoots extending sometimes to 6 m (20 ft) or more in the season. A sheltered warm sunny site and copious water during the growing season are its chief requirements. The flowers vary quite a lot in size and shape, some having narrow bell-shaped blooms, while in other the sepals spread more widely apart.

var. *bipinnata* M. Y. Fang. This variety, known from SW Sichuan and SE Tibet, is distinguished by its bipinnate foliage, or at least with the lower leaf divisions ternate; leaflets generally narrow-ovate and subglabrous, the base rounded or truncated, or only slightly heart-shaped; anthers puberulous on the connective outwards.

var. *lanceolata* Biswas is distinguished from the type by having smaller leaflets, 5–7 in number per leaf, but not more than 80 mm (3.2 in) long and 32 mm (1.3 in) wide, and smaller flowers with the sepals not longer than 16 mm (0.63 in). Restricted to northern India (Tehri Garhwal).

var. *trullifera* (Franch.) W. T. Wang (syn. *C. buchananiana* var. *trullifera* Franch., *C. connata* var. *sublanata* W. T. Wang, *C. coriigera* Lévl.) is like the typical plant, var. *connata*, but the leaflets are often 3-lobed and generally densely and finely silvery-hairy beneath; anthers like those of var. *bipinnata*. Similar habitats and altitudes, in SW China (W Guizhou, W Sichuan, N Yunnan).

H6; P2

❖ ❖ **Petioles not forming a large disc-like process around the stem (species 174–183)**
❖ **Leaves bipinnate (species 174–176)**

174. *Clematis roylei* Rehd.*
(syn. *C. nutans* Royle, *C. n.* var. *normalis* Kuntze)

DESCRIPTION. Very similar to *C. rehderiana* (p.141) and often confused with it; however, the leaves are usually bipinnate and the leaflets larger, to 13 cm (5 in) long and 8 cm (3.2 in) wide, with 3–7 main veins. In addition, the flowers are narrower and more tubular, cream rather than yellow or straw-coloured, the sepals 16–30 mm (0.63–1.2 in) long. The bracts are large and leaf-like.

DISTRIBUTION. Himalaya (N India to Nepal, Assam, S Tibet); 445–2140 m (1450–7000 ft).

104. *Clematis roylei* by Charkha, Dolpo, NW Nepal. Photo: Christopher Grey-Wilson

HABITAT. Shrubberies, hedgerows and old walls; July–Oct.

This species is quite widespread in the drier parts of the Himalaya. It is particularly common in the Dolpo region of north-western Nepal where it can be found often close to habitation, especially round field boundaries, sometimes growing in association with *C. tibetana* subsp. *vernayi*. It is quite as splendid as the closely related *C. rehderiana* and in some ways bolder with its larger flowers. It is, however, little-known in cultivation. Although it seems to inhabit a wide altitudinal range, certainly those from the higher elevations should prove to be hardy in temperate gardens. In the wild it does not overlap in distribution with *C. rehderiana*.

var. *patens* (Haines) Kapoor (syn. *C. nutans* var. *patens* Haines) has leaves with 5 leaflets and flowers with wide-spreading sepals. This variety is restricted to Bihar in India, at rather low elevations.

175. *Clematis veitchiana* Craib*

(syn. *C. nutans* Hort., non Royle, *C. n.* var. *thyrsoidea* Rehd. & Wils. pro parte, *C. rehderiana* sensu W. T. Wang, non Craib)

DESCRIPTION. Very similar to *C. rehderiana* (p.141) but leaves bipinnate, the leaflets often more than 20, smaller (to 60 mm (2.4 in) long), often 3-lobed. Bracts smaller and awl-shaped, only 4–6 mm (0.16–0.24 in) long. Flowers cream, rather smaller, 10–15 mm (0.4–0.6 in) long.

DISTRIBUTION. China: W Sichuan and the neighbouring part of Tibet; 3000–3300 m (9850–10,800 ft).

HABITAT. Shrubberies.

Clematis veitchiana was introduced into cultivation by Ernest Henry Wilson in 1904, but is not in cultivation today. It does not appear to have any advantage over the popular and widely cultivated *C. rehderiana* and the flowers are distinctly smaller.

H6; P2

105. *Clematis aethusifolia* wild in Qinghai Province, NW China.
Photo: Rosemary Steele

176. *Clematis aethusifolia* Turcz.* Parsley-leaved Clematis

(syn. *C. nutans* Royle subsp. *aethusifolia* Kuntze)

DESCRIPTION. A deciduous or sprawling climber to 2 m (6.6 ft), occasionally more, with slender, slightly 4–8-furrowed, pale green stems which are downy when young. Leaves 2–4-pinnately divided, to 20 cm (8 in) long, with 3–7 (often 4–5) primary divisions which are in turn ternate or deeply lobed; leaflets small, linear to narrow-oblong, coarsely and unevenly toothed, not more than 30 mm (1.2 in) long, downy; ultimate lobes not more than 1–5 mm (0.04–0.2 in) long and 0.6–2 mm (0.024–0.08 in) wide. Flowers nodding, narrow-campanulate, 10–18 mm (0.4–0.7 in) across, solitary and terminal or 3–5 in lateral cymes which make up large leafy 'panicles', each flower borne on a long slender pedicel, daphne-scented. Sepals 4, pale yellow, narrow-oblong, 12–20 mm (0.47–0.8 in) long and 4–8 mm (0.16–0.32 in) wide, glabrous or subglabrous overall, apart from the margin. Stamens about two-thirds as long as the sepals, with glabrous anthers. Achenes broad-elliptic, 3–5 mm (0.12–0.2 in) long, finely hairy, with a white plumose tail to 30 mm (1.2 in) long.

DISTRIBUTION. N & NW China (Gansu, Hebei, Inner Mongolia, Ningxia, E Qinghai, N Shaanxi, Shanxi, NE Tibet), S Mongolia; 300–3000 m (1000–9850 ft).

HABITAT. Shrubberies and rocky places, streamsides, sometimes sprawling over rocks and not climbing in the strict sense; July–Sept.

var. *latisecta* Maxim. (syn. *C. latisecta* (Maxim.) Prantl, *C. nutans* subsp. *latisecta* Kuntze) has larger broader, oblong to obovate, leaf-divisions, generally with a few coarse teeth or lobes; ultimate leaf-divisions 2–11 mm (0.08–0.43 in) long and 1–4 mm (0.04–0.16 in) wide (not 1–5 mm (0.04–0.2 in) long and 0.6–2 mm (0.024–0.08 in) wide). It is native to the north-east of the range of the typical plant (var. *aethusifolia*), in south-eastern Siberia (Amur and Ussuri), as well as the north-east of China (N Hebei, Inner Mongolia, N Shaanxi, N Shanxi) and northern Mongolia at 1500–2000 m (4950–6500 ft). *C. adrianowii* Maxim., described from the Tuva region of the Russian Federation and northern Mongolia, may well equate with *C. aethusifolia* var. *latisecta*.

Clematis aethusifolia is a delightful and dainty species that well deserves to be more widely known in gardens. The species was introduced into cultivation (to France initially) from northern China in 1861. It is very hardy and floriferous, once established, although young plants

106. Clematis aethusifolia in cultivation. Photo: Christopher Grey-Wilson

are vulnerable to attack from slugs and other predators in the garden. It is equally at home clambering over bushes or sprawling down a bank, where it makes an intricate entanglement. Unfortunately, its general rareness in gardens is due not so much to any problem with its general culture or hardiness, but the fact that it appears to be extremely difficult to raise from cuttings. In addition, young seed-grown plants are very slow to establish. Mature plants respond well to a hard prune in the early spring and will produce copious flowers on the new growth that ensues. A warm sunny position is preferable for, although plants will thrive in semi-shade, they rarely flower well in such places.

I have been fortunate enough to see this species growing in the wild in the grand setting of the Great Wall of China, not far from Beijing. In September the plants were still in full flower, growing on rocky slopes within a few metres of the Wall itself. It is a very distinctive species with its attractive, finely-cut foliage and narrow nodding flowers, and it is unlikely to be confused with any other.

H5; P2

❖ ❖ **Leaves pinnate (species 177–183)**
○ Flowers large; sepals 30–50 mm (1.2–2 in) long (species 177)

177. *Clematis grandiflora* DC.*
(syn. *C. chlorantha* Lindley, *C. longicaudata* Steud., *C. pseudograndiflora* Kuntze)

DESCRIPTION. A vigorous climber to 12 m (40 ft) with green, hairy, young stems, which become brown eventually. Leaves pinnate with 5 leaflets, rarely ternate, dark green above, paler and more yellowish beneath; leaflets ovate to elliptic leaflets, 5–14 cm (2–5.5 in) long, 2.5–8 cm (1–3.2 in) wide, the margin entire or somewhat serrate or dentate, sometimes 1–2-lobed (especially the upper leaves), 5–9-veined, hairy beneath, rarely subglabrous. Flowers few, borne in lateral cymes, occasionally solitary or terminal, broad nodding bells, 30–45 mm (1.2–1.8 in) wide. Sepals 4, thick, yellowish-green outside, buff-orange to pale yellow inside, oval to ovate, 30–50 mm (1.2–2 in) long, 15–25 mm (0.6–1 in) wide, 5–7-ribbed and densely downy on the outside, with the tip somewhat

107. *Clematis grewiiflora* in cultivation. Photo: Christopher Grey-Wilson

recurved. Stamens slightly shorter than the sepals, with greenish anthers. Achenes spindle-shaped, 4–5 mm (0.16–0.2 in) long, with a very long, silky plumose, tail to 11 cm (4.3 in) long, occasionally longer.

DISTRIBUTION. Tropical Africa (Sierra Leone and Guinea east to Liberia, Cameroon, Zaire, Angola, Uganda and S Ethiopia); 500–1493 m (1650–4900 ft).

HABITAT. Forest margins, thickets, secondary forest, ravines, river margins; Sept–Mar.

One of the most distinctive and most readily recognized African species, *C. grandiflora* has a wide distribution in western, central and north-eastern Africa, but avoiding much of east tropical parts of the continent. It is undoubtedly a very handsome climber and possesses some of the largest and most spectacular silky fruits found in *Clematis*. It certainly deserves to be more widely known and cultivated, especially in subtropical gardens.

In Sierra Leone putative hybrids between *C. grandiflora* and *C. hirsuta* have been reported. These seem unlikely as the two species have very different flowers and belong to distinct sections within the genus.

H10; P2

○ ○ **Flowers smaller; sepals 13–30 mm (0.5–1.2 in) long (species 178–183)**
● **Leaf-margins untoothed or remotely toothed (species 178 & 179)**

178. *Clematis hupehensis* Hemsl. & Wils.

DESCRIPTION. Closely related to *C. buchananiana*, *C. grewiiflora* and *C. rehderiana*, but differing from those species in its glabrous leaves and stems and untoothed leaf-margins, as well as in the normally solitary lateral flowers which are glabrous on the outside except for the sepal margins. The leaves are pinnate with 7 ovate leaflets, each 25–50 mm (1–2 in) long and 5–25 mm (0.2–1 in) wide. The sepals are plain yellow, ovate-oblong, c. 25 mm (1 in) long and 8 mm (0.32 in) wide and the anthers are glabrous.

DISTRIBUTION. C China (W Hubei); 1500–2100 m (4950–6900 ft).

HABITAT. Open forests and shrubberies.

179. *Clematis kakoulimensis* R. Schnell

DESCRIPTION. Very similar to *C. grandiflora* but a slenderer plant with narrower leaflets which are ovate-lanceolate, 25–60 mm (1–2.4 in) long, 7–25 mm (0.28–1 in) wide, with an entire or remotely toothed margin. Flowers smaller, the sepals only c. 18 mm (0.7 in) long and without recurved tips. Achenes with tails to 40 mm (1.6 in) long only.

DISTRIBUTION. French Guinea; endemic to Mt Kakoulima, as far as it is known.

HABITAT. Mountain shrubberies; Dec–Feb.

● ● **Leaf-margins coarsely toothed (species 180–183)**
▲ **Young stems densely downy to velvety (species 180 & 181)**
❋ **Leaf-undersurfaces and flowers densely velvety; flowers mainly in threes (species 180)**

180. *Clematis grewiiflora* DC.*

(syn. *C. buchananiana* subsp. *grewiiflora* Kuntze; often spelled grewiaeflora)

DESCRIPTION. Very similar to *C. buchananiana* but the whole plant, including the flowers, densely yellow- or brown-velvety; flowers urn- rather than bell-shaped usually solitary or in 3-flowered cymes, the sepals (10–30 mm (0.4–1.2 in) long) broader, 5–11 mm (0.2–0.43 in) broad, scarcely recurved at the apex, strongly ribbed. The leaves are pinnate with 5 leaflets, or sometimes ternate, the leaflets smaller 40–80 mm (1.6–3.1 in) long and as wide, occasionally larger. The stamens can be two-thirds the length of the sepals or equalling them, sometimes even slightly protruding from the mouth of the flower.

DISTRIBUTION. Himalaya (N India (Kumaon) and Nepal eastwards to Assam and N Burma) and SW China (S Tibet); 760–1830 m (2500–6000 ft).

HABITAT. Subtropical and warm broad-leaved forests and scrub, generally in rather dry places; Nov–Feb.

An attractive, primarily Himalayan species, which tends to flower in mid-winter and is for that reason of little use in any but the mildest, as well as subtropical, gardens. However, it can be grown successfully in a large conservatory. The whole plant, especially the young leaves and flowerbuds, are covered in an attractive yellowish-brown down which gives the plant a decidedly velvety appearance.

H8; P2

❋ ❋   **Leaf-undersurfaces and flowers hairy but not velvety; flowers usually many to a cyme (species 181)**

181. *Clematis buchananiana* DC.*

(syn. *C. b.* var. *rugosa* Hook. f. & Th.)

DESCRIPTION. A robust deciduous climber to 6 m (20 ft) with brownish-downy, 8–10-furrowed stems. Leaves pinnate with usually 5, occasionally, 7 leaflets, or sometimes ternate; leaflets ovate, 4–12 cm (1.6–4.7 in) long, 4–11 cm (1.6–4.3 in) wide, with a heart-shaped or rounded base and 3–7 main veins, the margin coarsely serrate, often 3–5-lobed, densely to sparsely downy beneath, more sparsely so above, but often densely furry when young; petioles narrowly winged at base, scarcely connate around the stem. Flowers borne in lateral, rarely terminal, cymes, many-flowered, panicle-like, nodding and narrowly bell-

108. *Clematis buchananiana* above Hatia in E Nepal. Photo: Roy Lancaster

shaped, 15–25 mm (0.6–1 in) across, narrow-oblong in bud. Sepals 4, greenish-yellow or creamy-yellow, ovate-lanceolate, 17–30 mm (0.67–1.2 in) long, 4–9 mm (0.16–0.35 in) wide, rarely wider, 3–5-ribbed, brownish appressed-downy on the outside, strongly recurved and diverging towards the tip. Stamens about three-quarters the length of the sepals, with hairy filaments and glabrous anthers. Achenes compressed, rhombic to elliptic, 3–5 mm (0.12–0.2 in) long, hairy, with a plumose tail to 50 mm (2 in) long.

DISTRIBUTION. Himalaya (from Kashmir to N Burma, including N India), SW China (SW Sichuan, SE Tibet,

109. *Clematis rehderiana* in cultivation. Photo: Christopher Grey-Wilson

almost glabrous foliage; var. *vitifolia* has thinly hairy stems and leaves.

Clematis buchananiana is often mistaken for *C. grewiiflora*, especially in cultivation. However, the two species are very different in the indumentum of the leaves and flowers. In *C. grewiiflora* the leaves are covered in a velvety indumentum of dense yellowish hairs, particularly beneath, and the flowers are similarly covered in a brownish-yellow velvet. In addition, whereas the cymes of *C. buchananiana* are usually many-flowered, those of *C. grewiiflora* are most often 3-flowered.

In cultivation *C. buchananiana* is a fine and impressive species but it tends to come into flower too late in the season and the flowers or buds can be easily spoiled by frost. However, in mild or subtropical gardens it can make a very impressive feature, dripping with its large furry blooms. It also makes an interesting feature for a large conservatory, for the plant can put on 4 m (13 ft) of growth in a single season. Even so, the various manifestations of the species in gardens vary a good deal in hardiness and those from higher altitude provenances are certainly more reliably hardy. In addition, it is wise to seek out the better-coloured forms; those with cream or yellow flowers being the best. It is sometimes dismissed in literature as being an inferior *C. rehderiana* type, but this is unjust, as those who have seen it in good flower will testify. If you want to grow it well then I suggest you move to the subtropics.

H7; P2

▲ ▲ Young stems sparsely hairy to glabrous
     (species 182–183)
✳   Flowers pale primrose-yellow; sepals 4–5
        (species 182)

182. *Clematis rehderiana* Craib* AGM
(syn. *C. buchananiana* Finet & Gagn., non DC., *C. b.* var. *vitifolia* Bois, *C. nutans* sensu Becket, non Royle, *C. n.* var. *thyrsoidea* Rehd. & Wils.)

DESCRIPTION. A moderately vigorous deciduous climber to 6 m (20 ft), with ribbed, downy stems. Leaves hairy and rather rough, pinnate, generally with 5, 7 or 9 yellow-green leaflets, somewhat hairy and puckered above but silky and prominently veined beneath, with 3 main veins; leaflets ovate to heart-shaped, to 80 mm (3.2 in) long and 55 mm (2.2 in) wide, often 3–5-lobed, coarsely toothed. Flowers nodding, campanulate, cowslip-scented, 15–18 mm (0.6–0.7 in) long, borne in lateral and terminal

Yunnan), N Vietnam (Tonkin); 460–3650 m (1500–12,000 ft).

HABITAT. Warm broad-leaved to cool mixed forests, forest margins, generally growing on small trees and bushes, occasionally over rocks along streams; July–Nov.
A very variable species. Several varieties have been recognized but are scarcely distinct when the overall characters of the species are analysed: var. *rugosa* Hook. f. & Th. is said to have more prominently veined leaves; var. *tortuosa* (Wall.) Hook. f. & Th. (syn. *C. tortuosa* (Wall.) C. E. C. Fischer) has

panicle-like cymes with up to 24 flowers. Bracts leaf-like, ovate, often 3-lobed, to 20 mm (0.8 in) long. Sepals 4, rarely 5, primrose-yellow, erect, narrow-oval to obovate, 13–20 mm (0.5–0.8 in) long and to 5–8 mm (0.2–0.32 in) wide, ribbed and velvety on the outside, the tips blunt and rolled back. Stamens about as long as the sepals, with hairy filaments and glabrous anthers. Achenes ovate to almost rounded, 3–4 mm (0.12–0.16 in) long, downy, with a plumose tail to 25 mm (1 in) long.

DISTRIBUTION. W China (S Qinghai, W & SW Sichuan, E Tibet, NW Yunnan); 2250–3200 m (7400–10,500 ft).

HABITAT. Shrubberies, scrubby slopes, streamsides, hedgerows and old walls; July–Sept.

This charming species was introduced to France in 1898 by Père Aubert from the Kangding (then Tatsien-lu) region of western Sichuan. The French misidentified the plant as *C. buchananiana* and later as *C. nutans* (*C. roylei*), both distinct Himalayan species. *C. rehderiana* was later introduced by Ernest Henry Wilson (1908) and Harry Smith (1935) and others, and it has remained a firm favourite ever since. Plants tend to take a year or two to settle down in the garden but, once established, put on a fine show of bloom each year. The best forms are delightfully and sweetly scented and have clear pale primrose-yellow flowers, without a masking flush of green. It is best when given enough space in the garden, such as a tall wall or fence, or simply allowed to roam into large shrubs or small trees. It is wholly delightful when in full flower but the flowers soon blemish and brown which does not add anything to its appeal; however, I would not be without it and on a warm summer's evening the scent wafts around the garden quite wonderfully. A vigorous specimen left unhindered will easily reach 8 m (26 ft) up a tree, larger than in the wild.

I have seen it growing in the wild in southern Sichuan where it often grows in association with *C. akebioides* inhabiting shrubberies, but more particularly growing in hedgerows. In the wild it comes into flower in July, rather earlier than it does in gardens. It seems to vary very little in its native haunts, although some certainly have paler flowers than others. In cultivation it seems to be more variable, at least in the size of the flowers.

Clematis rehderiana received an Award of Merit (AM) in 1936 when displayed at the Royal Horticultural Society.

H6; P2

✳ ✳ **Flowers golden-yellow to greenish-yellow; sepals 4 (species 183)**

183. *Clematis wattii* Drummond & Craib

DESCRIPTION. A vigorous climber with hairy young stems and pinnate leaves. Leaflets 5, papery, oblong to oval or lanceolate, 25–85 mm (1–3.3 in) long and 20–50 mm (0.8–2 in) wide, sometimes 2–3-lobed, with a few shallow to coarse teeth along the margin. Flowers up to 9, in lateral cymes, campanulate, 15–20 mm (0.6–0.8 in) long. Sepals 4, yellow, oval-lanceolate, 15–20 mm (0.6–0.8 in) long and 5–8 mm (0.2–0.32 in) wide, yellowish-brown downy on the outside but glabrous within or with a few hairs towards the top. Stamens three-quarters to as long as the sepals. Achenes elliptical, c. 4 mm (0.16 in) long, with a plumose tail to 30 mm (1.2 in) long.

DISTRIBUTION. NE India (Assam), Burma, Thailand; 1400–1800 m (4600–5900 ft).

HABITAT. Grassy and bushy places, streamsides; Nov–Jan.

✪ ✪ **Leaves simple to ternate (species 184–206)**
✛ **Flowers borne from lateral buds of last year's shoots, together with two leaves (species 184 & 185)**

184. *Clematis kilungensis* W. T. Wang & M. Y. Fang

DESCRIPTION. Very similar in general appearance to *C. pogonandra*, but flowers arising with a pair of leaves from lateral buds on stems of the previous year. In addition, the leaflets are obovate rather than lanceolate and the sepals (20–30 mm (0.8–1.2 in) long) are distinctly broader, 10–18 mm (0.4–0.7 in) wide, rather than 6–11 mm (0.24–0.43 in). See also *C. otophora*.

DISTRIBUTION. SE Tibet (Gyirong = Kilung); c. 3700 m (12,100 ft).

HABITAT. Forests and shrubberies; June–July.

185. *Clematis otophora* Finet & Gagn. ex Franch.
(syn. *C. otophora* var. *nanensis* K. Sun & M. S. Yan)

DESCRIPTION. Similar to *C. kilungensis* with yellow lateral flowers arising with a pair of leaves from the previous year's shoots, but a generally less woody climber (suffruticose) with shorter, 10–40 mm (0.2–1.6 in) long, glabrous pedicels (not 50 mm (2 in) long or more). In addition, the flowers are somewhat smaller, the sepals oblong, 18–27 mm (0.7–1.1 in)

110. *Clematis rehderiana* in cultivation. Photo: Christopher Grey-Wilson

long and 9–12 mm (0.35–0.47 in) wide, glabrous outside apart from the margin. The anthers bear dense yellowish hairs on the back of the connective.

DISTRIBUTION. WC China (S Gansu, W Hubei, E Sichuan); 1200–2000 m (3900–6500 ft).

HABITAT. Forests and forest margins, shrubberies; July–Aug.

✛ ✛ **Flowers borne laterally or terminally on the current season's shoots (species 186–206)**
✗   **Flowers solitary and lateral (species 186 & 187)**

186. *Clematis pogonandra* Maxim.
(syn. *C. faberi* Hemsl. & Wils., *C. prattii* Hemsl.)

DESCRIPTION. A small evergreen climber to 2.5 m (8 ft), with 4–6-furrowed stems, hairy when young. Leaves ternate, long-petioled, deep green and rather leathery; leaflets elliptical-lanceolate to ovate, 20–100 mm (0.8–4 in) long, 10–40 mm (0.4–1.6 in) wide, with an acute to acuminate apex and an entire margin, weakly 3- (occasionally 5-) veined in the lower half, glabrous on both surfaces or practically so. Flowers solitary and lateral, nodding narrow-campanulate, 20–30 mm (0.8–1.2 in) across, borne at the leaf-axils of the current year's shoots on bractless and glabrous pedicels. Sepals 4, yellow, often flushed with purple-brown or violet-purple, on the outside, especially towards the tip, elliptic, 16–30 mm (0.63–1.2 in) long, 5–11 mm (0.2–0.43 in) wide, erect to slightly spreading, glabrous outside but finely downy on the inside, not keeled but with a somewhat raised midrib. Stamens about a half to three-quarters the length of the sepals, with hairy filaments; anthers densely hairy on the back of the connective. Achenes narrow-obovate, 4–5 mm (0.16–0.2 in) long, hairy, with a plumose tail to 25 mm (1 in).

DISTRIBUTION. WC China (S Gansu, W Hubei, S Shaanxi, W Sichuan); 2200–3400 m (7200–11,150 ft).

HABITAT. Forest and forest margins, shrubberies, sometimes on limestone cliffs or alongside streams; late May–July.

var. *alata* W. T. Wang & M. Y. Fang has more oval leaflets that are finely toothed, while finely pubescent on the veins beneath, with pedicels finely pubescent and sepals with a narrow wing-like keel along the back. Restricted to SW Sichuan at 2400–3700 m (7900–12,100 ft).

var. *pilosa* Rehd. & Wils. has leaflets that are silky-hairy beneath and on the midrib above, finely pubescent pedicels and unkeeled sepals. Restricted to W Sichuan at 2500–3400 m (8200–11,150 ft).

187. *Clematis shenlungchiaensis* M. Y. Fang

DESCRIPTION. Similar to *C. pogonandra*, but leaflets finely downy on both surfaces (lamina and veins), as well as the pedicels. The flower colour of this species is apparently unknown but is probably yellowish or greenish-yellow. The flowers are about 25 mm (1 in) long.

DISTRIBUTION. WC China (W Hubei; Shennongjia Linqu = Tashenlungchia); c. 2900 m (9500 ft).

HABITAT. Rocky slopes; July.

✗ ✗ **Flowers in cymes, lateral or terminal, if solitary then terminal on the shoot (species 189–206)**

▶ **Leaves primarily simple, occasionally ternate (species 188–192)**

✖ **Anthers glabrous (species 188 & 189)**

188. *Clematis henryi* Oliver*
(syn. *C. hayatae* Kudo & Masamune, *C. henryi* var. *leptophylla* Hayata)

DESCRIPTION. An evergreen climber to 5 m (16ft), but often only 2–3 m (6.6–10 ft), with ribbed stems that are greyish-hairy when young. Leaves simple, large and subleathery, deep green, narrow-ovate to elliptic-lanceolate, 10–18.5 cm (4–7.3 in) long, 3–7.4 cm (1.2–3 in) wide, with an acuminate apex, entire to finely serrate margin, 5-veined from the base, glabrous to subglabrous above, with any hairs confined to the veins. Flowers solitary or 2–3 in the leaf-axils, 10–20 mm (0.4–0.8 in) across, borne on short-bracted pedicels 25–75 mm (1–3 in) long, nodding-campanulate, faintly fragrant. Sepals 4, creamy-yellow, occasionally whitish, sometimes with a pink flush on the outside, elliptic-oblong, 15–25 (–30) mm (0.6–1 (–1.2) in) long, 5–9 (–11) mm (0.2–0.35 (–0.43) in) wide, sparsely hairy on the outside. Stamens with very hairy filaments, about two-thirds the length of the sepals; anthers

111.*Clematis pogonandra*, Wolong, W Sichuan, China. Photo: Phillip Cribb

glabrous. Achenes oblong, 3–4 mm (0.12–0.16 in) long, finely hairy, with a plumose style to 40 mm (1.6 in) long.

DISTRIBUTION. Widespread in CW, C & E China (from S Shaanxi, Sichuan and Yunnan eastwards to S Anhui and Jiangsu, Fujian and Guangdong), Taiwan and N Vietnam; to 2500 m (8200 ft).

HABITAT. Forest margins, shrubberies and thickets, often in ravines, stream margins; Nov–Feb.

Clematis henryi is named after the Irish plant collector Augustine Henry.

var. *mollis* **W. T. Wang** has only simple leaves which are densely and finely pubescent above. Restricted to CS China (Guizhou, SW Hubei and NW Hunan), at 400–500 m (1300–1650 ft).

var. *morii* **(Hayata) Yang & Huang*** (syn. *C. henryi* var. *ternata* M. Y. Fang, *C. morii* Hayata) has distinguishing ternate leaves (the basal stem leaves occasionally simple, and then 3-lobed!), with the end leaflet twice the size of the lateral ones. Flowers usually solitary, sometimes 3, white changing to yellowish-brown, the sepals white-velvety outside but glabrous and often purplish within, 15–25 mm (0.6–1 in) long and 5–12 mm (0.2–0.47 in) wide. Endemic to Taiwan, primarily in the centre of the island (Hualien, Kaohsiung, Nantou, Taichung, Taitung, Taiyuan), between 1000 and 2500 m (3300 and 8200 ft), where it flowers between January and April.

This variety is treated as a distinct species, *C. morii* Hayata, in the 'Flora of China'. One interesting feature of this plant is that the leaves can be paired or in fours along the stems. Reports of ternate-leaved forms of *C. henryi* on mainland China might bring into question the validity of this variety, or at least make it doubtful that the taxon is indeed endemic to Taiwan. The presence of ternate leaves also throws into doubt the validity of Tamura's Subsection Henryanae, which is based on the single character of simple rather than compound leaves. The related *C. chiupehensis* and *C. jingdungensis* also have simple leaves, although ternate leaves are more common for the latter. For this reason I have therefore decided to abandon Subsection Henryanae.

H6; P2

189 *Clematis chiupehensis* M. Y. Fang

DESCRIPTION. Similar to *C. henryi* (above), but leaves rounded to broad-ovate, 9–14 cm (3.5–5.5 in) long and 8–12 cm (3.2–4.7 in) wide, with a more markedly toothed margin. In addition, the flowers are smaller and greenish, 8–10 mm (0.31–0.4 in) across, the sepals erect, elliptic to lanceolate, 10–12 mm (0.4–0.47 in) long and 3–4 mm (0.12–0.16 in) wide, densely downy on the outside. The achenes are narrow-ovate, c. 3 mm (0.12 in) long, with a plumose tail to 25 mm (1 in) long.

DISTRIBUTION. SW China (Yunnan; Qiubei Xian, Shuangbai Xian); 1500–2000 m (4950–6500 ft).

HABITAT. Open forests; Dec–Jan.

✖ ✖ Anthers hairy on the back (species 190–192)
✤ Flowers solitary, terminal, without bracts (species 190)

190. *Clematis yui* W. T. Wang

DESCRIPTION. Similar to *C. repens*, but flowers borne on the tip of the current season's shoots, or lateral on the same shoots, always solitary. Leaves simple elliptical to oval, to 90 mm (3.5 in) long and 54 mm (2.1 in) wide, with a rounded to wedge-shaped base, 5-veined. Flowers greenish-yellow or yellowish, the sepals lanceolate, 12–35 mm (0.47–1.4 in) long, 5–13 mm (0.2–0.5 in) wide, with a pointed apex, glabrous outside except for the margin. The anthers are hairy on the back of the connective.

DISTRIBUTION. SW China (SE Tibet (Myingchi Xian), Yunnan); c. 1600–2200 m (5250–7200 ft).

HABITAT. Forests and forest margins; Oct–Nov.
✤ ✤ Flowers lateral, with bracts (species 191 & 192)

191. *Clematis kweichowensis* Pei

DESCRIPTION. Very similar to *C. repens* (see below), but leaves rather more leathery and always simple, elliptic, sometimes 3-lobed, and with a wide wedge-shaped (cuneate) base, usually with an entire margin and 5 main veins, larger, to 17 cm (6.7 in) long and 8 cm (3.2 in) wide. Flowers greenish-yellow, the sepals oblong, 18–36 mm (0.7–1.4 in) long, and 7–10 mm (0.28–0.4 in) wide, hairy inside, but glabrous outside apart from the margin.

DISTRIBUTION. C, S & SW China (Sichuan to Hubei and Zhejiang southwards; not Fujian, S Guangdong or Hainan), Japan and Taiwan; 800–2800 m (2600–9200 ft).

HABITAT. Open forest and hillsides, shrubberies and streamsides; Aug–Oct.

192. *Clematis repens* Finet & Gagn.

DESCRIPTION. A deciduous climber with simple or ternate leaves. Leaves or leaflets papery, elliptic to elliptic-lanceolate, sometimes 3-lobed, with a rounded to slightly heart-shaped base, glabrous, the margin with a few dentate teeth, 3-veined. Bracts linear and small, 3–10 mm (0.12–0.4 in) long. Flowers campanulate, solitary and lateral, borne on pedicels 25–54 mm (1–2.1 in) long, with a small pair of bracts near the base. Sepals 4, pale yellow, lanceolate, 12–22 mm (0.47–0.87 in) long and 5–8 mm (0.2–0.32 in) wide, glabrous on the outside. Stamens about two-thirds the length of the sepals, with hairy filaments; anthers hairy on the outside of the connective. Achenes narrow-elliptic to ovate, 2.5–4 mm (0.1–0.16 in) long, hairy, with a silky plumose tail to 55 mm (2.2 in) long.

DISTRIBUTION. S & SC China (N Guangdong, N Guangxi, Guizhou); 1300–2500 m (4300–8200 ft).

HABITAT. Forests, often sprawling or clambering over rocks or stream banks; July–Sept.

❱❱ **Leaves compound, usually ternate, sometimes biternate (species 193–206)**
☆ **Anthers hairy (species 193 & 194)**
✺ **Stems densely hairy; flowers in cymes of 6 or more (species 193)**

193. *Clematis rubrifolia* Wright
(syn. *C. leschenaultiana* var. *rubrifolia* (C. H. Wright) W. T. Wang, *C. splendens* Lévl. & Vant.)

DESCRIPTION. Closely related to *C. leschenaultiana* but differing in the leaflets that have a finely toothed margin and are densely downy only beneath (rather sparsely so above), in the smaller flowers (sepals 12–15 mm (0.47–0.6 in) long and 4–7 mm (0.16–0.28 in) wide) and in the anthers which have the connectives sparsely hairy on the outside, rather than glabrous. The flowers are greenish-yellow or yellowish-white.

DISTRIBUTION. S & SW China (W Guangxi, S Guizhou, Yunnan); 800–2000 m (2600–6500 ft).

HABITAT. Bushy slopes and forest margins, streamsides; Nov–Jan.

✺✺ **Stems glabrous or slightly hairy; cymes 1–3-flowered (species 194)**

194. *Clematis pseudootophora* M. Y. Fang
(syn. *C. honanensis* S. Y. Wang & C. L. Chang, *C. pseudootophora* var. *integra* W. T. Wang)

DESCRIPTION. Similar to *C. repens* but bracts lanceolate and petiolate (not linear and sessile), 10–90 mm (0.4–3.5 in) long, and flowers more often in 3-flowered cymes rather than solitary. The leaves are always ternate and toothed. The yellow flowers have sepals 25–30 mm (1–1.2 in) long. The anthers are densely hairy along the back of the connective.

DISTRIBUTION. C & S China (Henan and Fujian southwards to Guizhou, Guangxi, C Hunan, Jiangxi and NW Zhejiang); 1300–1800 m (4300–5900 ft).
HABITAT. Forest and forest margins, shrubberies, streamsides; Aug–Sept.

var. *integra* W. T. Yang is distinguished readily by its entire leaflet-margins. This variety is distinct geographically, being found in Guizhou and Hunan provinces, to the west of the typical plant (var. *pseudootophora*).

☆ ☆ **Anthers glabrous (species 195–206)**
✺ **Sepals and buds yellow-brown velvety (species 195)**

195. *Clematis leschenaultiana* DC.
(syn. *C. acuminata* subsp. *leschenaultiana* (DC.) Brühl and subsp. *leschenaultiana* (DC.) Kuntze, *C. angustifolia* (Hayata) Hayata, *C. aurea* Bl., *C. caesariata* Hance, *C. fulva* Zoll. & Moritzi, *C. leschenaultiana* var. *angustifolia* Hayata, var. *denticulata* Merrill ex Groff, Ding & Groff, var. *grosseserrata* Miq. and var. *subglabrifolia* Merrill, *C. noronhiana* DC., *C. splendens* Lévl. & Van., *C. sumatrana* Ridl.)

DESCRIPTION. A vigorous evergreen climber to 8 m (26 ft) (occasionally as much as 15 m) with the younger stems and leaves covered in soft yellowish or tawny-coloured velvety hairs, 8–10-furrowed. Leaves ternate, papery; leaflets elliptic to ovate, sometimes 2–3-lobed, generally 60–110 mm (2.4–4.3 in) long and 25–60 mm (1–2.4 in) wide, with a rounded to heart-shaped base and entire margin, 3–5-veined, with a network of raised secondary veins beneath, golden- or tawny-pubescent all over, densely so beneath. Flowers up to 15, in lateral cymes, which together make up large leafy panicles, each flower bell-shaped, 15–30 mm (0.6–1.2 in) long; bracts small and linear. Sepals 4, brownish- or greenish-yellow or pale yellow, oblong-lanceolate, 15–30 mm (0.6–1.2 in) long, 5–10 mm (0.2–0.4 in) wide, covered in velvety rusty-brown or golden, velvety hairs on the outside, the tips often recurved. Stamens about two-thirds the length of the sepals, with glabrous anthers; filaments with long hairs along the margin, especially near the base. Achenes spindle-shaped, 3–6 mm (0.12–0.24 in) long, 2-ridged, hairy, with golden plumose tails to 70 mm (2.8 in) long, more often 30–50 mm (1.2–2 in) long.

DISTRIBUTION. S & SE China (SW Sichuan and Yunnan eastwards to Fujian and Guangdong, incl. Hainan), Taiwan, Vietnam, Philippines, Sumatra, Java, Bali & Lombok; at low and mid altitudes,

500–2200 m (1650–7200 ft), but up to 3000 m (9850 ft) occasionally.

HABITAT Forest and forest margins, thickets and shrubberies, stream margins; throughout the year depending on location, but Jan–Mar in the north of its range.

One of only a few species in the genus with a distribution in both the northern and southern hemispheres. The dense golden indumentum on most parts of the plant make it particularly easy to identify.

❦ Sepals not velvety (species 196–206)
☆ Leaflets linear-lanceolate to narrow-lanceolate (species 196)

196. *Clematis subfalcata* Pei ex M. Y. Fang

DESCRIPTION. A woody climber with 6–8-furrowed stems which are sparsely hairy only at the nodes, when young. Leaves ternate, net-veined, the leaflets narrow-lanceolate to linear-lanceolate, 7–11 cm (2.8–4.3 in) long and 15–25 mm (0.6–1 in) wide, more or less glabrous, with an entire or very finely toothed margin. Inflorescence a 1–8-flowered lateral cyme, sessile; flowers campanulate, nodding, 10–20 mm (0.4–0.8 in) across, borne on slender glabrous pedicels. Sepals 4, white, erect, oblong to ovate, 11–13 mm (0.43–0.5 in) long and 3.6–5.5 mm (0.14–0.22 in) wide, slightly hairy outside or glabrous overall. Stamens two-thirds to three-quarters the length of the sepals, with glabrous anthers. Achenes hairy.

DISTRIBUTION. SE Yunnan (Kaiyuan Xian); 2200–3100 m (7200–10,200 ft).

HABITAT. Forests and forest margins, shrubberies, slopes and streamsides; Oct–Feb.

var. *pubipes* W. T. Wang is like the typical plant but the young branches, petioles and pedicels are finely pubescent, sometimes densely so, and the leaves are finely pubescent on the veins, both above and beneath. Restricted to CN Yunnan (Wuding Xian) at c. 2300 m (7550 ft).

var. *stenophylla* (Hand.-Mazz.) W. T. Wang (syn. *C. clarkeana* var. *stenophylla* Hand.-Mazz., *C. angustifoliola* W. T. Wang) is distinguished by having linear-lanceolate, long-acuminate, leaflets, 40–140 mm (1.6–5.5 in) long and 6–22 mm (0.24–0.87 in) wide, by the presence of a prominent peduncle 10–40 mm (0.4–1.6 in) long, glabrous petioles and pedicels and by the larger flowers; sepals

16–21 mm (0.63–0.83 in) long and 5–6 mm (0.2–0.24 in) wide, finely appressed-hairy on both sides. Native to SW Sichuan and CN Yunnan in similar habitats and altitudes to the typical plant.

☆ ☆ Leaflets ovate to elliptical (species 197–206)
✱ Leaflets sessile or practically so (species 197)

197. *Clematis nukiangensis* M. Y. Fang

DESCRIPTION. Closely related to *C. acuminata*, but distinctive on account of its sessile or subsessile leaflets (in *C. acuminata* they have a distinct stalk) and virtually redundant peduncles which are never more than 2 mm (0.08 in) long. The erect sepals are white, flushed with reddish-purple at the base, ovate-oblong, c. 15 mm (0.6 in) long and 5 mm (0.2 in) wide.

DISTRIBUTION. SW China (NW Yunnan; Bijiang Xian); c. 2700 m (8850 ft).

HABITAT. Shaded or part-shaded shrubberies; Dec.

✱ ✱ Leaflets clearly stalked (species 198–206)
✿ Sepals glabrous on both surfaces (species 198)

198. *Clematis clarkeana* Lévl. & Vant.
(syn. *C. anshunensis* M. Y. Fang)

DESCRIPTION. Similar to *C. pogonandra* but flowers borne in 1–3-flowered bracteate cymes, white or yellowish flushed with purple, rather smaller, the sepals only 15–18 mm (0.6–0.7 in) long and 4–5 mm (0.16–0.2 in) wide, glabrous except for the velvety margins, and about the same length as the stamens. The anthers are glabrous.

DISTRIBUTION. SW China (S Guizhou); c. 2000 m (6500 ft).

HABITAT. Shrubberies and forest slopes; Sept–Nov.

✿ ✿ Sepals hairy on one or both surfaces (species 199–206)
■ Leaflets reticulately veined (species 199–201)

199. *Clematis acuminata* DC.
(syn. *C. acuminata* subsp. *wallichii* Kuntze, *C. a.* var. *wallichii* Hook. f. & Th., *C. trinervis* Buch.-Ham. ex DC.)

DESCRIPTION. (of var. *acuminata*). A slender climber to 5 m (16ft), with glabrous stems and ternate leaves. Leaflets dark green and somewhat shiny, rather leathery, oblong-ovate to elliptic-lanceolate, 60–120 mm (2.4–4.7 in) long, 15–45 mm (0.6–1.8 in) wide, with a distinctive tail-like (caudate) apex, with an entire or slightly toothed margin and 3, 5 or 7 main veins from the base, glabrous above, somewhat hairy beneath near the base, net-veined. Flowers in lateral cymes of 3 usually, sometime 4–5, nodding, bell-shaped, c. 10 mm (0.4 in) across. Sepals 4, erect, creamy-white or yellowish, ovate-lanceolate, 10–15 mm (0.4–0.6 in) long, 4–5 mm (0.16–0.2 in) wide, with an acute recurved tip, downy outside. Stamens three-quarters the length of the sepals, with hairy filaments but glabrous anthers. Achenes silky-hairy, with a plumose tail to 20 mm (0.8 in) long.

DISTRIBUTION. Himalaya (Nepal to Bhutan & Assam) and SW China (W & C Yunnan, SE Tibet); 200–2400 m (650–7900 ft).

HABITAT. Subtropical and warm broad-leaved forests, growing on small trees and shrubs, along streamsides; late Oct–Feb.

Another very variable species. Several varieties have been recognized, although their status requires further detailed investigation:

var. *andersonii* Brühl (syn. *C. acuminata* subsp. *andersonii* (Brühl) Kapoor) has larger more oval leaflets to 13.8 cm (5.4 in) long and 7.5 cm (3 in) wide and larger flowers, the sepals 23–27 mm (0.9–1.1 in) long. It is recorded from N Mayanmar and SW China (Yunnan).

var. *hirtella* Hand.-Mazz. (syn. *C. acuminata* subsp. *multiflora* Comber) is distinguished by having larger cymes with generally 10–20 flowers. Recorded from SW China (Yunnan) at 1500–2400 m (4950–7900 ft).

var. *longicaudata* W. T. Wang has narrow-ovate, rather leathery leaflets with a pronounced tail-like tip (caudate); sepals yellow, 14–17 mm (0.55–0.67 in) long, 4–5 mm (0.16–0.2 in) wide. Known only from Yunnan (Binchuan Xian).

var. *sikkimensis* Hook. f. & Th. (syn. *C. acuminata* subsp. *sikkimensis* (Hook. f. & Th.) Brühl, *C. sikkimensis* J. R. Drummond ex Burkill) has large leaflets like var. *andersonii* but glabrous beneath or practically so, and small flowers like var. *acuminata*, borne in 8–many-flowered cymes; sepals glabrous except at the margins. The stems and pedicels are also glabrous. It is recorded from Sikkim eastwards through Bhutan to N Mayanmar and SW China (W &

C Yunnan) at 1067–2400 m (3500–7900 ft). Two further (under the subsp. *sikkimensis* 'umbrella' varieties have been recorded (var. *clarkei* (Kuntze) Brühl (syn. *C. acuminata* var. *clarkei* Kuntze, *C. sikkimensis* var. *clarkei* (Kuntze) W. T. Wang) and var. *hookeri* Brühl but it would be difficult to uphold them as pubescence, leaflet size, flower numbers and size do not appear to correlate as stated by some authors). These require further investigation.

200. *Clematis qingchengshanica* W. T. Wang

DESCRIPTION. Very similar to *C. acuminata* (above), but flowers solitary, borne on a very short 3–4 mm (0.12–0.16 in) peduncle, and bracts tiny, narrow-triangular, c. 2 mm (0.08 in) long. The greenish-white sepals are slightly larger, 15–17 mm (0.6–0.67 in) long and 6–8 mm (0.24–0.32 in) wide.

DISTRIBUTION. China (W Sichuan; Qingcheng Xian, Guan Xian); 700–1400 m (2300–4600 ft).

HABITAT. Forests; Nov–Dec.

201. *Clematis jingdungensis* W. T. Wang

DESCRIPTION. Similar to *C. henryi* (p.144), but leaves usually ternate, rarely simple, the leaflets elliptic to elliptic-ovate and net-veined on both sides. In addition, the flowers are borne in clusters of 6 or more (sometimes as many as 25), each flower rather small, 10 mm (0.4 in) across; sepals white and erect, lanceolate, 10–18 mm (0.4–0.7 in) long and 2–5 mm (0.08–0.2 in) wide, downy on the outside. The stamens are as long as the sepals.

DISTRIBUTION. China (C & S Yunnan); 1700–2200 m (5600–7200 ft).

HABITAT. Forests margins and shrubberies; Mar–June.

■ ■ **Leaflets not reticulately veined (species 202–206)**
✔ **Stamens equal in length to the sepals (species 202 & 203)**

202. *Clematis yunnanensis* Franch.
(syn. *C. acuminata* DC. subsp. *yunnanensis* (Franch.) Brühl, *C. kockiana* Schneid., *C. yunnanensis* var. *brevipedunculata* W. T. Wang and var. *chingtungensis* M. Y. Fang)

DESCRIPTION. An evergreen climber, often rather bushy with 6–8-furrowed young stems which are finely hairy at first, becoming eventually reddish-brown and

112. *Clematis urophylla* in cultivation. Photo: Martyn Rix

DISTRIBUTION. SW China (W Guangxi, SW Sichuan, E Tibet, Yunnan); 1600–3000 m (5250–9850 ft).

HABITAT. Open forest and forest margins, bushy and rocky places, on mountain and hill-slopes and in ravines or along streamsides; Oct–Dec.

An extremely attractive species recently brought into cultivation.

H7; P2

203. *Clematis loasaefolia* DC.

DESCRIPTION. Similar to *C. grewiiflora* (p.139), but a less robust climber to 2.5 m (8 ft), with ternate, occasionally simple, leaves. In addition, the greenish-yellow flowers are not more than 20 mm (0.8 in) long. DISTRIBUTION. Himalaya (E Nepal, Sikkim & SE Tibet); 1700–2020 m (5600–6600 ft).

HABITAT. Similar places; Oct–Nov.

✔ ✔ **Stamens half to two-thirds the length of the sepals (species 204–206)**

204. *Clematis siamensis* Drummond & Craib

DESCRIPTION. A vigorous climber with sparsely hairy stems and ternate leaves. Leaflets oval to lanceolate, to 13.5 cm (5.3 in) long and 5.5 cm (2.2 in) wide, papery, with a rounded to wedge-shaped base, the margin usually sharply toothed. Inflorescence a lateral cyme, generally many-flowered, but sometimes reduced to 3–9, campanulate, to 23 mm (0.9 in) long. Sepals 4, greenish-yellow, oval-lanceolate, to 23 mm (0.9 in) long and 6 mm (0.24 in) wide, more or less glabrous on the outside. Stamens about two-thirds the length of the sepals.

DISTRIBUTION. N Thailand (Chiengmai, Doi Sutep); c.1300 m (4300 ft).

HABITAT. Probably shrubberies and forest margins.

205. *Clematis hainanensis* W. T. Wang

DESCRIPTION. Like *C. subfalcata* (p.146) but leaflets ovate to elliptic-lanceolate and the flowers rather larger, yellowish-white; sepals ovate, c. 23 mm (0.9 in) long and 8 mm (0.32 in) wide, densely downy on both surfaces. In addition, the flowers are borne singly.

woody. Leaves ternate, leathery; leaflets distinctly stalked (petioluled), lanceolate to narrow-ovate, 50–120 mm (2–4.7 in) long,15–50 mm (0.6–2 in) wide, 3-veined, the base rounded to somewhat heart-shaped, the apex acuminate, with a finely toothed margin. Flowers bell-shaped, borne in lateral cymes of up to 7. Sepals 4, white or yellowish, erect ovate-lanceolate, 12–17 mm (0.47–0.67 in) long and 4–6 mm (0.16–0.24 in) wide, finely downy outside, glabrous within. Stamens equalling or slightly shorter than the sepals, with hairy filaments and glabrous anthers. Achenes elliptic, c. 3 mm (0.12 in) long, hairy, with a silky plumose tail to 30 mm (1.2 in) long.

DISTRIBUTION. SE China (Hainan; Baisha Xian).

HABITAT. Forests; Jan–Feb.

206. *Clematis urophylla* Franch.*
(syn. *C. japonica* var. *urophylla* (Franch.) Kuntze,
C. urophylla var. *obtusiuscula* Schneid.)

DESCRIPTION. Very similar to *C. yunnanensis*, but
leaves thinner and usually with a serrate to denticulate
margin; flowers generally in cymes of 1–3, larger,
white, often suffused with greenish-yellow, the erect
sepals 20–29 mm (0.8–1.14 in) long and 5–9 mm
(0.2–0.35 in) wide, twice the length of the stamens.

DISTRIBUTION. SW China (N Guangdong, N. Guangxi,
Guizhou, SW Hubei, Hunan, Sichuan; doubtfully
recorded from SE Tibet and Yunnan); 500–2400 m
(1650–7900 ft).

HABITAT. Forests, forest margins and shrubberies; late
Oct–Dec.

A very beautiful species introduced from W China by
Martyn Rix. It received an Award of Merit (AM) when
shown at the Royal Horticultural Society in London in
1998. An excellent conservatory climber.

H7;P2

SECTION BEBAEANTHERA
(THE PARATRAGENE GROUP)

See p.29 for sectional description.

▼   **Pedicels without bracts; Himalayan plants
     (species 207)**

207. *Clematis barbellata* Edgeworth*
(Syn. *C. nepalensis* sensu Royle, non DC.)

DESCRIPTION. A deciduous climber to 4 m (13 ft), often
rather less, the young stems cylindrical, slightly ridged,
glabrous or almost so, often flushed with purple.
Leaves ternate, deep green, paler beneath. Leaflets
ovate-lanceolate, 50–110 mm (2–4.3 in) long, 15–45
mm (0.6–1.8 in) wide, the margin often lobed, sharply
toothed, with 3 or 5 veins from the base. Flowers
solitary or 2–3 borne in the axils of short lateral shoots,
pendent, bell-shaped, to 35 mm (1.4 in) long; pedicels
long and slender, without bracteoles. Sepals 4, dull

purple to violet-brown, lanceolate-elliptic, with an
acute, somewhat spreading, tip, 22–35 mm (0.87–1.4
in) long and 12–20 mm (0.47–0.8 in) wide, downy.
Stamens two-thirds the length of the sepals, with both
the filaments and anther connectives densely hairy to
give a felted appearance in the centre of the flower.
Achenes ovate to rhombic, glabrous or somewhat hairy,
with a plumose style to 50 mm (2 in) long.

DISTRIBUTION. Kashmir, N Pakistan (N Wazir), NW
India, W Nepal; 2130–3660 m (7000–12,000 ft).

HABITAT. Woodland, particularly of rhododendrons and
conifers, bushy places; May–Aug, occasionally earlier.

This species has a certain fascination, although the
flowers cannot be said to be spectacular. It is quite rare
in cultivation but deserves a quiet corner in more
gardens. It is often linked in literature with *C. alpina*
and its close cousins; however, the two are not closely
related and occupy different sections within the genus,
although admittedly they fall within the same
subgenus. 'Bletina'* has beetroot-coloured flowers.

H5; P2 (if at all)

▼ ▼ **Pedicels with a pair of small bracts, often near the
      middle; Japanese plants (species 208 & 209)**
◆   **Flowers reddish-purple to brownish-maroon
      (species 208)**

208. *Clematis japonica* Thunb.*

DESCRIPTION. A deciduous climber to 2 m (6.6 ft) with
ternate, rather pale green leaves. Leaflets oval to
elliptical, 50–80 mm (2–3.2 in) long and 25–40 mm
(1–1.6 in) wide, with serrated margins. Flowers
nodding bells, 20–30 mm (0.8–1.2 in) long, usually
solitary or 2–3, borne from the leaf-bud axils of the
previous season's shoots on slender pedicels which
bear a small pair of bracts towards the centre. Sepals 4,
rather fleshy and waxy, reddish-purple or maroon,
often with a brownish flush and a whitish margin,
yellowish–green inside flushed with purple, elliptical to
lanceolate, 20–30 mm (0.8–1.2 in) long and 5–8 mm
(0.2–0.32 in) wide, erect and with a slightly recurved
tip. Stamens about half the length of the sepals.
Achenes oval, 6–8 mm (0.24–0.32 in) long, thinly
hairy, with a plumose tail 30–35 mm (1.2–1.4 in) long.

DISTRIBUTION. Japan (Honshu, Kyushu).

HABITAT. Shrubberies; May–June.

113. *Clematis japonica* in cultivation. Photo: Martyn Rix

and the other plain green. Unfortunately, this interesting plant is rare in cultivation and certainly difficult to obtain. In addition, it is rather temperamental, with a tendency for the shoots to revert all too readily back to plain green; these must be removed if the variegated form is to be retained.

H6; P1

var. *purpureo-fusca* Hisauti ex Tamura (syn. *C. japonica* var. *brevipedicellata* Makino forma *purpureo-fusca* Hisauti) has distinguishing deep violet-purple flowers. It was described from Honshu where it is restricted to the Hondo region (Mt Mitutozhe in particular).

var. *villosula* Ohwi has yellow, almost golden, flowers that are somewhat downy on the outside. It may represent an intermediate between *C. japonica* and *C. tosaensis*.

var. *obvallata* Ohwi* (syn. *C. japonica* forma *obvallata* (Ohwi) Ohwi, *C. obvallata* Ohwi) has larger bracts, to 15 mm (0.6 in) long, which are situated immediately beneath the flowers. It is distributed on the island of Shikoku. *Clematis obvallata* var. *shikokiana* Tamura appears to represent an intermediate stage between the typical plant, var. *japonica*, and var. *obvallata*. As its varietal epithet implies it is, like the latter, restricted to Shikoku.

◆ ◆ **Flowers white or greenish-white (species 209)**

209. *Clematis tosaensis* Makino*
(syn. *C. japonica* var. *brevipedicellata* Makino ex Tamura)

DESCRIPTION. Similar to *C. japonica* but flowers white or greenish-white, somewhat smaller, the sepals generally 20–25 mm (0.8–1 in) long and 10–15 mm (0.4–0.6 in) wide, rather thinner and more flared towards the tip.

DISTRIBUTION. Japan (Honshu, Kyushu, Shikoku).

HABITAT. Open woodland, particularly with *Cryptomeria*, shrubberies; May–June.

A rare plant in cultivation but pretty and dainty in flower. A form with longer leaves and creamy-yellow flowers has been distinguished as var. *cremea* (Makino) Tamura (syn. *C. japonica* var. *cremea* Makino).

H6; P1

An interesting species perhaps more of curiosity than any real garden value and for that reason often dismissed as a plantsman's plant. Despite this, it should be more widely grown if just for its dainty qualities. The charming little flowers are borne from the axils of the previous year's shoots and are often partly hidden by the new foliage. Not easy to find but certainly not difficult to grow.

'Gokononosho'* is a rarity in clematis, being one of very few recorded with variegated foliage. The leaves are rather attractive and vary in the amount of variegation; this ranges from a generous splashing and mottling of creamy-white over the entire leaf surface, to leaflets in which one side is variegated

SECTION MECLATIS

This section contains two prime subsections; Subsection Meclatis is distributed from eastern Europe through Turkey and central Asia to China and Korea, while Subsection Africanae contains species only found in Africa, Madagascar and the Mascarene Islands. In this I have broadened Michio Tamura's original concept of the section to include the African species, assigned by Magnus Johnson to Subsection Africanae. Johnson ('Släktet Klematis', 1997) proposed the latter subsection, although he placed it, without explanation in Section Clematis. However, it clearly belongs close to Meclatis. The two subsections look very similar in many respects. On the whole Subsection Africanae has larger and thinner leaves and thinner-sepalled flowers. In addition, the stamen filaments are less dilated and usually hairy only at or near the base. In Meclatis the filaments are hairy for most of their lengths, broader and more markedly dilated, while the sepals are often thick and fleshy. Of the two subsections Meclatis is by far the most

important horticulturally, with quite a few species and numerous hybrids and cultivars in cultivation.

SUBSECTION AFRICANAE
(THE AFRICAN GROUP)

A group of mainly vigorous species restricted to the African continent and W India with marked affinities with Section Meclatis, tending to have thinner less fleshy sepals and more slender filaments, hairy generally only at the base and only slightly dilated. In addition, the leaves are always thin and papery, and green. The flowers tend to be greenish or greenish-yellow. Although rare or absent from cultivation, this group has considerable decorative value. *C. simensis* is in cultivation and has proved hardier than might be expected. Species like *C. hirsuta* and *C. welwitschii* have relatively large flowers and would make interesting introductions for warmer gardens.

Map 10
Subgenus Campanella
Section Meclatis
    subsection Meclatis   + + + + + + +
    subsection Africanae   · · · · · · · · · · · ·

▼ **Flowers unisexual; Madagascan plants (species 210)**

210. *Clematis ibarensis* Baker

DESCRIPTION. A dioecious climber. Leaves pinnate or bipinnate; leaflets 9–23, oblong-ovate to lanceolate occasionally 3-lobed, 12–40 mm (0.47–1.6 in) long, 6–20 mm (0.24–0.8 in) wide, with a slightly toothed or entire margin. Flowers borne in lateral or terminal leafy panicles, up to 30 cm (12 in) long, each flowers small, 10–15 mm (0.4–0.6 in) across, the flowers unisexual and borne on separate plants. Bracts ternate in male plants but entire in the female. Sepals 4, rarely 5, white, lanceolate to narrow-elliptic, 8–9 mm (0.32–0.35 in) long, 4 mm (0.16 in) wide, wide-spreading, downy on both surfaces or glabrous inside. Stamens about as long as the sepals. Achenes hairy, with a plumose tail 30–40 mm (1.2–1.6 in) long, the hairs absent from the lower quarter of the tail.

DISTRIBUTION. C, W & SW Madagascar; to 1000 m (3300 ft).

HABITAT. Forest margins and bushy places; Oct–Feb.

subsp. *edentata* (Baker) Perrier de la Bâthie

(syn. *C. bi-perrieri* Lévl., *C. edentata* Baker, *C. grata* sensu Hoffmann ex Kuntze, non Wall., *C. hoffmannii* Vatke, *C. insidiosa* Baill., *C. orientalis* subsp. *wightiana* var. *hoffmannii* Kuntze, *C. perrieri* Lévl., *C. saxicola* Hilsenb. & Bojer ex Baill.) has pinnate leaves with 5 larger, more oval, untoothed leaflets which often have a rounded or heart-shaped base, and with 3, occasionally 5, more prominent veins from the base. The larger flowers, 20–24 mm (0.8–0.95 in) across, are generally flushed with purple on the outside. Similar distribution and habitat; Oct–Apr.

▼ ▼ **Flowers hermaphrodite; African, S Indian and Madagascan plants (species 211–226)**
◆ **Flowers purple or violet-purple; Madagascan plants (species 211 & 212)**

211. *Clematis laxiflora* Baker

(syn. *C. mauritiana* subsp. *laxiflora* (Baker) Kuntze, *C. orientalis* subsp. *wightiana* Perrier de la Bâthie)

DESCRIPTION. Similar to *C. mauritiana* in general details but differing significantly in the smaller purple-violet flowers, only 15–16 mm (0.6–0.63 in) across, with very small anthers c. 1.3 mm (0.05 in) long (not 2–3 mm (0.08–0.12 in)).

DISTRIBUTION. Madagascar.

212. *Clematis microcuspis* Baker

(syn. *C. bathiei* Lévl., *C. orientalis* subsp. *simensis* sensu Perrier de la Bâthie (not *C. simensis* Fresen.), *C. orientalis* subsp. *thunbergii* var. *microcuspis* (Baker) Kuntze)

DESCRIPTION. Very similar to *C. laxiflora* and *C. mauritiana* but immediately separated on account of its pinnate rather than ternate leaves. The flowers are similar in size and colour to those of *C. laxiflora*. The anthers are 1–2 mm (0.04–0.08 in) long.

DISTRIBUTION. C Madagascar.

◆ ◆ **Flowers white, cream, greenish-yellow to yellow (species 213–226)**
❋ **Leaves ternate; Madagascan plants (species 213)**

213. *Clematis mauritiana* Lam.*

(syn. *C. mauritiana* var. *kelleriana* Kuntze, *C. sonneratii* Pers., *C. strigillosa* Baker, *C. triflora* Vahl)

DESCRIPTION. A climbing or sprawling evergreen, with hairy, sometimes densely woolly young stems. Leaves ternate, thick and deep green, rather holly-like, with a network of fine veins; leaflets oval to lanceolate, often with a heart-shaped base, 30–65 mm (1.2–2.6 in) long, 20–55 mm (0.8–2.2 in) wide, sparsely hairy to densely woolly beneath, with a sharply serrate margin, sometimes coarsely so, and 3–5 prime veins from the base. Flowers 1–3, in long-stalked lateral cymes, each flower 30–40 mm (1.2–1.6 in) across, rounded in bud. Sepals 4, occasionally 5, white, broad-oval to elliptic, 15–25 mm (0.6–1 in) long, 10–14 mm (0.4–0.55 in) wide, with an acute apex, downy on both sides, often with a rather truncated on slightly notched apex. Stamens a half to two-thirds the length of the sepals, the filaments hairy in the lower half. Achene oval, c. 3 mm (0.12 in) long, hairy with a plumose tail to 45 mm (1.8 in) long.

DISTRIBUTION. Madagascar, Mauritius, Reunion; 1270–2400 m (4200–7900 ft).

HABITAT. Forest margins, disturbed forest and bushy places, creeks and rocky places.

H8–9; P2

❋ ❋ **Leaves pinnate to bipinnate; African and S Indian plants (species 214–226)**
❋ **Leaves with a rusty-brown down beneath (species 214)**

214. *Clematis dolichopoda* Brenan
(syn. *C. hirsuta* var. *dolichopoda* (Brenan) Staner &
Léonard, *C. longipes* sensu Engl. non Freyn)

DESCRIPTION. Very similar to *C. hirsuta* and sometimes
treated as a variety of that species but readily
distinguished on account of the golden-brown downy
indumentum on the undersurfaces of the leaves, which
is particularly dense on the young leaves. In addition,
the flowers are rather larger, 30–50 mm (1.2–2 in)
across, and the achenes have a 50–60 mm (2–2.4 in)
long plumose tail.

DISTRIBUTION. Tropical East Africa (Rwanda, Burundi,
Tanzania & Uganda); 1067–3300 m (3500–10,800 ft).

HABITAT. Rocky and bushy places, bamboo thickets;
June–Sept.

✲✲　**Leaves with a whitish or greyish down or almost
　　glabrous beneath (species 215–226)**
❖　**Leaves bipinnate, occasionally pinnate on the same
　　plant (species 215 & 216)**
✳　**Sepals 10–12 mm (0.4–0.47 in) long, pure white
　　(species 215)**

215. *Clematis oweniae* Harvey
(syn. *C. brachiata* Thunb. forma Bremekamp &
Obermeyer, *C. orientalis* subsp. *thunbergii* var.
oweniae Kuntze)

DESCRIPTION. Similar to *C. hirsuta* but the leaves are
bipinnate (uppermost sometimes simple-pinnate) with
rather small leaflets that are deeply incised-toothed,
and the white flowers are small, not more than 25 mm
(1 in) across, the sepals 10–12 mm (0.4–0.47 in) long
and 4–6 mm (0.16–0.24 in) wide. In addition, the
anthers are small, not more than 1.5 mm (0.06 in) long
(1.5–2 mm (0.06–0.08 in) in *C. hirsuta*) and the
achenes bear a short 10–20 mm (0.4–0.8 in) long tail.

DISTRIBUTION. CS Africa (Botswana, Mozambique, S
Zimbabwe), Swaziland and South Africa (Natal to
Transvaal); to 1370 m (4500 ft).

HABITAT. Woodland and wooded grassland, shrubby
places; Feb–Apr.

✲✲　**Sepals 14–25 mm (0.55–1 in) long, white, often
　　flushed outside with pink or pale purple (species 216)**

216. *Clematis welwitschii* Hiern ex Kuntze
(syn. *C. kassneri* Engl., *C. thunbergii* sensu De Wild. &
Staner, non Steud., *C. thunbergii* var. *angustisecta* Engl.)

DESCRIPTION. A prostrate plant with trailing or
scrambling, ribbed stems, hairy when young, often
rather spindly in appearance with small leaves and long
internodes. Leaves bipinnate, with 5 or 7 prime
divisions, or sometimes ternate, then the leaflets 2–3-
lobed; leaflets oval to lanceolate to linear, 4–40 mm
(0.16–1.6 in) long, 2–20 mm (0.08–0.8 in) wide,
sometimes larger, with a cuneate to rounded base and
an acute apex, the margin entire to somewhat lobed or
serrate, downy beneath. Flowers scented, borne in very
lax lateral or terminal cymes of 1–7, each flower 25–50
mm (1–2 in) across. Sepals 4, white, generally flushed
with pale pink or purple on the outside, oblong to oval,
14–25 mm (0.55–1 in) long, 5–8 mm (0.2–0.32 in)
wide, wide-spreading, sparsely hairy beneath except
along the margin, densely downy inside. Stamens about
half the length of the sepals. Achenes spindle-shaped,
4–5 mm (0.16–0.2 in) long, hairy, with a yellowish
plumose tail to 40 mm (1.6 in) long.

DISTRIBUTION. Angola, Malawi, S Tanzania, E & S
Zaire, Zambia and Zimbabwe; 1000–1800 m
(3300–5900 ft).

HABITAT. Upland grassland and open grassy woodland,
occasionally in abandoned cultivated areas; Mar–Aug.

❖❖　**Leaves ternate, or pinnate, most often with 5
　　leaflets (species 217–226)**
✳　**Leaflets unlobed, rarely those of uppermost leaves
　　slightly lobed (species 217–220)**
✪　**Flowers small, the sepals not more than 15 mm
　　(0.6 in) long (species 217 & 218)**

217. *Clematis simensis* Fresen.*
(syn. *C. altissima* Hutch., *C. kissenyensis* Engl.,
C. orientalis var. *simensis* (Fresen.) Kuntze, var.
wightiana De Wild. & Staner, *C. sigensis* Engl.,
C. sigensis Engl., *C. simensis* var. *kilimandsharica*
Engl. and var. *ruwenzoriensis* De Wild., *C. stolzii*
Engl. (possibly a hybrid))

DESCRIPTION. A rather variable and vigorous climber to
20 m (66 ft), occasionally as much as 36 m (142 ft).
Leaves pinnate, with 5 ovate to ovate-lanceolate
leaflets, 4–13 cm (1.6–5 in) long and 1.5–9 cm
0.6–3.5 in) wide, which are rarely lobed (occasionally
1–2 lobes on those of the upper leaves), and with a
rounded to heart-shaped base, a short-acuminate tip
and an entire to regularly dentate margin, more or less
glabrous beneath, except along the veins, occasionally
downy; lower bracts leaf-like, with 1–3 leaflets or
trilobed. Flowers in lateral cymes or terminal panicles
up to 28 cm (11 in) long, although generally half that

114. *Clematis simensis*, Mt Kilimanjaro, c. 2600 m (8,500 ft) Photo: Phillip Cribb

specimen for a large conservatory, where it blooms can be the better appreciated in the depths of winter.

Clematis sigensis (see synonymy above), described from north-eastern Tanzania (Usambara Mountains) is sometimes separated out on account of its entire leaflets, while *C. simensis* var. *kilimanscharica* has broader and blunter heart-shaped leaflets, and var. ruwenzorensis is described as possessing densely hairy stems and leaves. However, none of these variations seems to hold up when the overall variation in the species over its entire range is examined.

H8 (possibly 7); P2

218. ***Clematis brachiata*** **Thunb.***
(syn. *C. brachiata* var. *burkei* Burtt Davy, *C. kerrii* Steud., *C. massoniana* DC. , *C. orientalis* subsp. *brachiata* (Thunb.) Kuntze, *C. stewartiae* Burtt Davy)

DESCRIPTION. Similar to *C. simensis*, but with relatively smaller more papery leaflets, not more than 70 mm (2.8 in) long and 50 mm (2 in) wide, finely toothed usually. The half-nodding flowers, 20–32 mm (0.8–1.3 in) across, are greenish-white or cream, the sepals 8–15 mm (0.32–0.6 in) long. Flowers fragrant. The anthers are only about a half to two-thirds the length of the sepals. The achenes have tails only 20–30 mm (0.8–1.2 in) long. As with *C. simensis* the flowers are borne rather late in the season on the current year's shoots.

DISTRIBUTION. CS Africa (Malawi, Mozambique and Zimbabwe) and South Africa; 500–1550 m (1650–5100 ft).

HABITAT. Woodland and wooded grassland; Mar–Apr (Sept–Oct in cultivation north of the equator).

This species is also closely related to the more widespread *C. hirsuta*, which it tends to replace in Zimbabwe and parts of Mozambique. However, the situation is not altogether clear and in parts of Angola and East Africa the two species are barely distinguishable. It is an attractive species in cultivation and often very free-flowering, although it is still rare in gardens and of those found under the name many prove to be *C. triloba*; the weakly scented flowers are like small Turk's-caps, the sepals recurving somewhat to expose the boss of yellow anthers. The species received an Award of Merit (AM) when shown at the Royal Horticultural Society in 1975. This is a species well worth persevering with, although it is unlikely to survive harsh winters outdoors in any but the warmest and most sheltered places.

H9; P2

length, each flower 15–28 mm (0.6–1.1 in) across. Sepals 4, white or cream, widely spreading to recurved, oblong to lanceolate, 8–14 mm (0.32–0.55 in) long, 3–5 mm (0.12–0.2 in) wide, white-hairy on both surfaces, more sparsely outside except for the margins. Stamens more or less the same length as the sepals, sometimes slightly shorter. Achenes elliptic, 2–3 mm (0.08–0.12 in) long, hairy, with a silky plumose tail 30–60 mm (1.2–2.4 in) long.

DISTRIBUTION. NE & E Africa (S Sudan and Ethiopia southwards through Kenya and Tanzania to Zimbabwe), Mozambique, Angola, Cameroon, Fernando Po and E Zaire; 500–2800 m (1650–9200 ft).

HABITAT. Forest fringes and evergreen bushy places; Aug–Jan.

An attractive species which is rare in cultivation. The flowers have the general appearance of *C. orientalis*, although larger, but the leaflets are far larger and green rather than glaucous. Outdoors, the latter flowers are generally spoilt by frost. The plant makes an admirable

✪ ✪ Flowers larger, the sepals 15–30 mm (0.6–1.2 in) long (species 219 & 220)

219. *Clematis tibestica* Quesel

DESCRIPTION. Similar to *C. simensis* and possibly only a variety of it, but differing primarily in its rather small lanceolate leaflets, not more than 60 mm (2.4 in) long and 30 mm (1.2 in) wide, and in the somewhat larger flowers 30–35 mm (1.2–1.4 in) across, the sepals 15–17 mm (0.6–0.67 in) long, broader, 7–8 mm (0.28–0.32 in) wide. The achenes have relatively short tails not more than 30 mm (1.2 in) long.

DISTRIBUTION. N Chad (Tibesti Mountains); 2100–2400 m (6900–7900 ft).

HABITAT. Open woodland and bushy places, particularly amongst acacias.

220. *Clematis commutata* Kuntze
(syn. *C. irangaensis* Engl., *C. keilii* Engl.)

DESCRIPTION. Similar to *C. welwitschii* but plant prostrate or climbing, the leaves pinnate to bipinnate or biternate generally, the leaflets narrow-ovate, to 14.5 cm (5.7 in) long and 8 cm (3.2 in) wide, often 2–3-lobed, generally asymmetrical, with a long-acuminate apex and coarsely serrate margin. The flowers are solitary or 2–3 together and slightly larger, 40–60 mm (1.6–2.4 in) across.; sepals greenish-yellow to cream, 18–30 mm (0.7–1.2 in) long and 8–15 mm (0.32–0.6 in) wide, densely yellowish-downy on the outside, as are the flowerbuds, but glabrous inside, spreading widely apart to somewhat recurved. The achenes bear a white plumose tail to 35 mm (1.4 in) long.

DISTRIBUTION. C & Tropical E Africa (Burundi, C Malawi, Rwanda, S Tanzania, E Zaire, N Zimbabwe) and Angola; 1400–2500 m (4600–8200 ft).

HABITAT. Upland grassland, open *Brachystegia* woodland and bushy places, secondary scrub; Feb–May.

Clematis commutata is one of the most attractive African species and would make an excellent introduction if seed could be obtained from the wild. In its better forms the flowers are large and starry and quite as attractive as some members of the *C. orientalis* group (Section Meclatis). Previous authors have often linked this species closely with *C. welwitschii* but although the habit of both is similar (they are primarily prostrate plants) they look quite different in leaves and flowers, besides which the flower colour of *C. welwitschii* is basically white rather than yellow and the sepals lack the dense tawny down on the reverse.

H8; P2

✳ ✳ Leaflets usually lobed (species 221–226)
❖ Flowers yellow or greenish-yellow; leaflets asymmetrical (species 221 & 222)

221. *Clematis wightiana* Wall.*
(syn. *C. orientalis* subsp. *wightiana* (Wall.) Kuntze, pro parte, *C. wightiana* var. *pseudobuchananiana* Kuntze)

DESCRIPTION. A vigorous climber with 6-ribbed hairy stems. Leaves pinnate to ternate; leaflets 3, 5 or 7 usually, oval to ovate or lanceolate, 20–90 mm (0.8–3.5 in) long and 20–65 mm (0.8–2.6 in) wide, often 2–5-lobed, with a heart-shaped base and a toothed margin, hairy on both surfaces, thinly so above. Inflorescences lateral or terminal, with usually numerous flowers to 65 mm (2.6 in) across. Sepals 4,

115. Clematis hirsuta, Kenya, N Kilimanjaro, at c. 1800 m (5,900 ft)
Photo: Phillip Cribb

116. *Clematis viridiflora*. in cultivation. Photo: John Gimshaw

pale yellow or greenish-yellow, oblong to oval, 15–30 mm (0.6–1.2 in) long and 7–15 mm (0.28–0.6 in) wide, spreading, yellow-downy on the outside. Stamens half the length of the sepals. Achenes hairy, oval to oblong, 3–4 mm (0.12–0.16 in) long, with a plumose tail to 35 mm (1.4 in) long.

DISTRIBUTION. S India; 1200–2600 m (3900–8500 ft).

HABITAT. Bushy places and forest margins; Jan–May.

This species is relatively common in the hill country of southern India, particularly in the Pulney and Nilgiri Hills and along the Western Ghats. This is the only species of Subsection Africanae to be found outside India and Malagasy. The large flowers of the finest forms make it an attractive plant for subtropical and Mediterranean gardens.

　　Apparent records, often cited in literature, of this species being native to Madagascar and to East Africa are wholly erroneous. The Madagascan plant is referable to *C. laxiflora* Baker and the African plant to *C. hirsuta* Guill., Perr. & Rich.

H6; P2

222. *Clematis viridiflora* Bertol.*
(syn. *C. zanzibarensis* Bojer ex Loudon, *C. zanzibarica* Sweet)

DESCRIPTION. Very like *C. hirsuta* but mature leaflets often rather asymmetrical and mostly 3-lobed with a pronounced acuminate tip, the flowers are similar in

size but pale yellow or greenish-yellow with very thin sepals. In addition, the achenes have a tail up to 70 mm (2.8 in) long.

DISTRIBUTION. Zanzibar, S Malawi and Mozambique; possibly E Tanzania (coastal region); low altitudes to c. 250 m (820 ft).

HABITAT. Forest margins, secondary woodland and bushy places, roadsides; July–Mar.

A little-known species. Interestingly, it is said that both the leaves and flowers have a strong smell of formaldehyde when crushed.

H8–9; P2

❖ ❖ 　**Flowers white to pale cream, occasionally flushed with pink or pale purple on the outside; leaflets symmetrical (species 223–226)**
❖ 　　**Leaflets untoothed (species 223)**

223. *Clematis thalictrifolia* Engl.
(syn. *C. kirkii* sensu De Wild, non Oliver)

DESCRIPTION. A prostrate plant similar to *C. welwitschii* (p.153), but with narrower entire leaflets, not more than 7 mm (0.28 in) wide, and often 2–3-lobed. The flowers are larger and generally solitary, 50–65 mm (2–2.6 in) across, the sepals white flushed with purple on the outside, 25–35 mm (1–1.4 in) long and 10–15 mm (0.4–0.6 in) wide.

DISTRIBUTION. S Tanzania, S Zaire & N Zimbabwe.

HABITAT. Open bushy savannah and *Brachystegia* woodland; Mar.

The distribution of this little-known species is imperfectly known due to confusion with *C. welwitschii*. The two species are clearly closely related, but *C. thalictrifolia* can always be distinguished on account of its larger, usually solitary, flowers and narrow leaflets.

❖ ❖ 　**Leaflets toothed (species 224–226)**
◯ 　　**Leaves pinnate to bipinnate or biternate; stamens 10–15 mm (0.4–0.6 in) long (species 224)**

224. *Clematis triloba* Thunb.*
(syn. *C. brachiata* Hort., in part, *C. orientalis* subsp. *thunbergii* (Steud.) Kuntze, *C. o.* subsp. *t.* var. *bolusiana* Kuntze, *C. thunbergii* Steud.)

DESCRIPTION. A deciduous climber to 3 m (10 ft), with stems hairy when young. Leaves pinnate to bipinnate, occasionally biternate. Leaflets deep green, usually 7, oval to lanceolate, 25–60 mm (1–2.4 in) long, 8–30 mm (0.32–1.2 in) wide, often 2–3-lobed, especially the lowermost pair, with a few sharp teeth on either side. Flowers in lateral cymes of up to 12, each 25–40 mm (1–1.6 in) across, nodding to half-nodding, scented. Sepals 4, white, elliptical-lanceolate, 12–18 mm (0.47–0.7 in) long and 4–10 mm (0.16–0.4 in) wide, spreading widely apart to somewhat recurved, sparsely hairy inside, more densely so outside and in bud. Stamens three-quarters the length of the sepals. Achenes hairy with a plumose tail.

DISTRIBUTION. South Africa (described from Cape Province).

HABITAT. Open forests and bushy places; Apr–July.

An attractive species, perhaps better known under the name *C. thunbergii*, which deserves to be more popular in gardens. The flowers are quite large and deliciously scented. Many plants in cultivation as *C. brachiata* are in fact *C. triloba*.

var. *congensis* (A. Chev.) M. Johnson
(syn. *C. thunbergii* var. *congensis* A. Chev.) described from central Zaire has smaller more bell-shaped flowers and also differs in various characters of the leaves. It seems unlikely that it is anything to do with *C. triloba*, especially when its extreme disjunct distribution is taken into account. The plant requires further more detailed investigation.

H9; P2

○ ○ **Leaves strictly pinnate; stamens 6–10 mm (0.24–0.4 in) long (species 225–226)**

225. *Clematis hirsuta* Guill., Perr. & Rich.
(syn. *C. atunesii* Engl., *C. brachiata* sensu F. White, non Thunb., *C. burgensis* Engl., *C. chariensis* Chev., *C. friesiorum* Ulbr., *C. glaucescens* Fresenius, *C. grata* sensu Oliver, non Wall., *C. inciso-dentata* Rich., *C. longicaudata* Steud., *C. orientalis* subsp. *wightiana* auct. non Wall., *C. petersiana* Klotzsch, *C. simensis* sensu Staner, non Fresenius, *C. wightiana* auct. non Wall., *C. wightiana* var. *gallaeensis* Engl.)

DESCRIPTION. A vigorous climber, occasionally prostrate, to 15 m (50 ft) with ribbed stems that are usually downy, especially when young. Leaves pinnate with 5–7 leaflets that are sparsely hairy beneath, pale green to rather silvery beneath, contrasting with the deep green upper surface. Leaflets ovate, 15–100 mm (0.6–4 in) long,

117. Clematis triloba in cultivation. Photo: Daan Smit

15–90 mm (0.6–3.5 in) wide, with a heart-shaped base and subacute apex, rarely slightly acuminate, the margin serrate or crenate, often 3-lobed; lowest bracts generally leaf-like but ternate or trilobed. Flowers numerous in lateral or terminal panicles up to 40 cm (16 in) long, each flower 16–40 mm (0.63–1.6 in) across. Sepals white or cream, sometimes becoming pinkish with age, elliptic-oblong to lanceolate, 8–20 mm (0.32–0.8 in) long, 4–7 mm (0.16–0.28 in) wide, widely spreading, grey- or white-downy on both surfaces. Stamens about half the length of the sepals. Achenes rounded to elliptical, 2–3 mm (0.08–0.12 in) long, hairy, with a silky plumose tail to 40 mm (1.6 in) long, occasionally longer.

DISTRIBUTION. Most of Tropical Africa (Senegal and Gambia eastwards to Ethiopia and southwards to Kenya, Tanzania, Angola and Mozambique), Arabia; to 2200 m (7200 ft).

HABITAT. Forest and forest margins, bushy and grassy places, rocky outcrops and fences; July–Mar (depending on latitude).

var. *glabrescens* Chev. (syn. *C. orientalis* subsp. *thunbergii* Steud. var. *glabrescens* Kuntze, *C. o.* var. *triloba* (Thunb.) Williams subvar. *glabrescens*)

226. *Clematis djalonensis* Chev.

DESCRIPTION. Similar to *C. hirsuta*, but flowers generally rather small, 18–22 mm (0.7–0.9 in) across, rounded rather than oblong in bud, and with very short

5–8 mm (0.2–0.32 in) long pedicels (10–70 mm (0.4–2.8 in) long in *C. hirsuta*), strongly scented. In addition, the bracts are often 3-lobed and the filaments yellowish-brown or reddish-brown.

DISTRIBUTION. W Africa (SW Mali, N Guinea); 1300–1400 m (4300–4600 ft).

HABITAT. Rocky and bushy places; Sept–Nov.

Two additional varieties are recognized: var. *latipaniculata* Chev., described from Guinea, has almost glabrous leaves and large inflorescences to 25 cm (10 in) long, with flowers 32–36 mm (1.3–1.4 in) across; var. *hirsutissima* Chev., described from Mali (Mt Loura) also has larger inflorescences, but more densely downy leaves. The range and variation of *C. djalonensis* is not properly understood and the species requires further careful field analysis.

SUBSECTION MECLATIS
(THE ORIENTALIS GROUP)

This group consists of those wonderful small-flowered species with yellow nodding or semi-nodding blooms. They are charming and easy to grow and very distinct. In fact the subsection encompasses a group of closely related species which are some of the few bright yellow-flowered hardy wild clematis and for this reason they have a special place in the garden. In addition, they are among the hardiest and most drought-tolerant group of clematis. This is scarcely surprising considering where they come from for they are native to dry mountain ranges in eastern Turkey, eastwards through Iran and much of central Asia, the dry northern slopes of the Himalaya and the drier mountain regions of western and northern China, north-east as far as Mongolia and Korea. Their typical habitat is rocky places along valley bottoms, especially along riverbanks, walls and hedgerows, sometimes climbing into bushes or small trees but often just sprawling on the ground or over a rock. They flower on the current season's shoots, generally from mid-summer to early autumn in the wild.

Members of the Orientalis Group have pinnate or bi-pinnate leaves that often have five prime divisions. The leaflets can be toothed or untoothed or variously lobed, their colour ranging from green to markedly glaucous. In fact the glaucous-leaved species tend to have thicker more waxy leaflets. The flowers are generally lateral but they may be terminal, solitary or, more often, in groups of three or more, or many in a large panicle-like inflorescence. They always have four sepals which are generally rather thick and without obvious veins, the sepals scarcely to widely spreading or occasionally reflexed; they may be yellow or greenish-yellow, sometimes flushed or speckled with purplish brown on the outside. The stamens have hairless anthers but the purplish-red to maroon filaments are dilated and hairy towards the base, the hairs sometimes covering the entire surface of the filaments. The achenes are generally hairy and the styles are hairy to the top, up to 55 mm (2.2 in) long in fruit.

The Orientalis Group has, over the years, proved a major problem to the horticulturist and gardener and species delineating has been no less a problem to botanists. In horticulture only three species were generally recognized, the familiar and well-known *C. tangutica*, the lesser known *C. serratifolia*, and a blanket species encompassing a wide range of different plants called *C. orientalis*. In the mid-1980s I did a considerable amount of research on the group and established that ten distinct species could be recognized based on various characters of the plant (especially the habit of the plant and the details of leaves and petals, as well as the actual flower shape). Of these only one, *C. pamiralaica*, is not in cultivation, although several of the others are rare in cultivation; however, since then the Chinese have added several additional species which have not yet filtered their way into cultivation. The main problem in horticulture has been the long-term usage of the name *C. orientalis* for a number of disparate elements, a problem confounded by the fact that in cultivation the species and their forms are extremely promiscuous and few seedlings come true to type unless the species are well isolated from one another in the garden.

Unfortunately, the horticultural press has confounded the problem and even, dare one say, that great gardener and writer Christopher Lloyd in his fine book 'Clematis' (revised edition, 1989) makes a complete hash of both naming and identification in this group (it's wonderful when a botanist can have a dig at gardeners for causing nomenclatural confusion!) declaring of *C. orientalis* and *C. tangutica* that '…the latter is often considered as a mere variety of the former (and I find myself, in many instances, hard put to it to say which is which).' Lloyd includes a mish-mash under *C. orientalis*, including *C. graveolens*, some forms of *C. tangutica* and the lovely Ludlow and Sherriff (L & S 13342), which is in fact *C. tibetana* subsp. *vernayi*. Anyone who has seen the true *C. orientalis* in the wild or in cultivation would never confuse it with either *C. tangutica* or *C. tibetana*. Although the former is widespread in the wild, it does not overlap with the other two. The confusion is confounded still further by the inclusion of the very distinctive *C. graveolens* as a synonym of

C. orientalis. The situation is likely to be perpetuated by the horticultural trade's insistence on still selling many of these plants under the name *C. orientalis*, although thank goodness the latest edition of 'The RHS Plant Finder' has got it correct.

Most of the members of the *C. orientalis* group are fully hardy and they are amongst the most drought-tolerant of any clematis, but that is not to say that they will tolerate long periods of desiccation. However, they will thrive in drier and sunnier parts of the garden than most of their kin. They are excellent for walls and fences, for scrambling over bushes or simply allowed to form a low entanglement over a bank. They can be pruned hard back in the late winter if desired (to 30 cm (12 in) of the ground if necessary) and will, as a consequence, put on a good deal of lush vigorous young growth. This will certainly delay flowering to later in the season; plants allowed to ramble freely and unpruned will start into flower considerably earlier and continue, in many instances, right into the autumn.

118. *Clematis orientalis* var. *daurica* in cultivation. Photo: Christopher Grey-Wilson

▼ **Species with glaucous, lobed or unlobed, often untoothed leaves (species 227–234)**
◆ **Sepals recurved (species 227)**

227. *Clematis orientalis* L.*

DESCRIPTION. Climber or scrambler to 8 m (26 ft), though generally less and often only 2–3 m (6.6–10 ft). Stems ridged, greyish or whitish-green, often flushed with purplish-red, hairless or slightly hairy at first. Leaves glaucous; leaflets 5–7, rather leathery, lanceolate to oblong, occasionally linear, unlobed to trilobed, but often unevenly bilobed, with or without a few small uneven teeth along the lower margin, generally hairy on both surfaces. Bracts and bracteoles similar to the leaves or trifoliate or reduced to a single leaflet. Peduncle always present, at least 10 mm (0.4 in) long, often much longer. Flowers yellow to greenish-yellow, sometimes flushed with reddish or brownish-purple on the outside, in lateral many-flowered clusters, occasionally reduced to three flowers. Sepals lanceolate to elliptical 8–23 mm (0.32–0.9 in) long and 3–7 mm (0.12–0.28 in) wide, acute to subacute, spreading to strongly reflexed, silkily hairy inside, less so to almost glabrous outside.

Clematis orientalis has a wide distribution from the Greek islands of Kos and Tinos eastwards through Turkey and Iran to Pakistan (Chitral) and the neighbouring regions of the CIS to the north, east as far as W Xinjiang in China. It is by far the most widespread species in the Orientalis Group and, as might be expected, it is very variable and a number of subspecies can be recognized based on details of the leaves and inflorescence. Any treatment of *C. orientalis* in the wide sense is bound to be controversial and I am certain that the last word on the subject has yet to be written. However, the following subdivision of *C. orientalis* which I proposed in 1989 still seems to hold good and helps to resolve the variations observable through the geographical range of the species. In broad terms the variability increases markedly to the east of the range. It is perhaps significant that in the extreme east in Chitral and Kashmir, where the variation is most marked, *C. orientalis* overlaps in distribution with both *C. graveolens* and *C. tibetana*. Natural hybridization and introgression in the wild can account for some of this variation, although this still has to be established on scientific data. Clearly further field research would prove valuable. As this is such a complicated and, in many ways, controversial, species I have in this instance separated out var. *orientalis* from the matrix description in order to clearly point out the differences between it and the other varieties.

var. *orientalis* (syn. *C. albida* Klotzsch, Klotzsch & Garcke, *C. flava* Moench, *C. glauca* var. *angustifolia* Ledeb., *C. graveolens* sensu Hook., non Lindley, *C. longecaudata* Ledeb., *C. orientalis* subsp. *orientalis* var. *flava* (Moench) Kuntze, *C. o.* subsp. *o.* var. *normalis* & var. *albida* (Klotzsch) Kuntze, *C. o.* subsp. *wightiana* (Wall.) Kuntze var. *longecaudata* (Ledeb.) Kuntze; *Meclatis orientalis* (L.) E. Spach). Leaflets very variable in shape from lanceolate to elliptical or ovate, often with one or two lateral lobes but sometimes unlobed, especially immediately below the flowers, generally rather obtuse, up to 55 mm (2.2 in) long and 35 mm (1.4 in) wide. Inflorescence a many-flowered cyme,

119. *Clematis orientalis* var. *robusta*, Badakhshan, NW Afghanistan.
Photo: Christopher Grey-Wilson

occasionally reduced to 3 flowers; peduncle 5–60 mm (0.2–2.4 in) long. Sepals 8–15 mm (0.32–0.6 in) long, usually hairy outside. It is found almost throughout the range of the species: Greece (Kos and Tinos), Turkey, N Iraq, W & N Iran, W, C & N Afghanistan, N Pakistan, Georgia, Turkmenistan, Uzbekistan, Kazakstan, NW China (NW Gansu, Qinghai, N Tibet, Xinjiang).

Var. *orientalis* is rather rare in cultivation, although it has certainly been in and out of cultivation for a number of years. Various collections were made in the boon years of plant collecting in the Middle East, particularly by Paul Furse in Turkey and Iran during the 1960s and 1970s. Since then various other introductions have been made, particularly that of Dick and Rosalind Banks from Hergest Croft in Hereford, who collected seed in Turkey in the early 1980s. It has been grown at the Royal Botanic Gardens, Kew, from a Furse collection, for a number of years. The typical form of the plant has rather small, thin-sepalled flowers in which the sepals are strongly reflexed: they look very different to most other species of the *C. orientalis* association. Although not nearly as spectacular in flower as the related *C. tangutica* or *C. tibetana*, it has a charm all of its own. The foliage is

very attractive and very glaucous in some forms and the flowers are followed by a significant display of fluffy seedheads. It is wise to propagate the best forms from cuttings, as the seedlings are extremely variable, particularly in flower size and leaf and flower coloration.

H6; P2

var. *hindukushensis* Grey-Wilson has leaflets that are lanceolate to lanceolate-ovate, with 1–2 rather long lateral lobes towards the base (up to half the length of the leaflet), to 60 mm (2.4 in) long and 30 mm (1.2 in) wide. Inflorescence a 7-many-flowered cyme; peduncle 6–11 cm (2.4–4.3 in) long. Sepals 6–22 mm (0.24–0.87 in) long, hairy to almost hairless on the outside. Afghanistan, central Hindu Kush (Bamian and Ghorat Provinces).

var. *robusta* Grey-Wilson has leaflets that are ovate to lanceolate with 1–2 large lateral lobes as well as several acute teeth in the lower half, to 75 mm (3 in) long and 45 mm (1.8 in) wide. Inflorescence many-flowered, panicle-like ; peduncle robust, 7.5–12 cm (3–4.7 in) long (to 20.5

cm (8 in) long, including the rachis). Sepals 16–20 mm (0.63–0.8 in) long, silky hairy on the outside. NE Afghanistan (Badakhshan Province).

var. *baluchistanica* **Grey-Wilson** has leaflets that are linear to linear-lanceolate, unlobed or with 1–2 short lateral lobes near the base, acute, to 37 mm (1.5 in) long and 4 mm (0.16 in) wide. Inflorescence a cyme, usually 3–9-flowered; peduncle 10–35 mm (0.4–1.4 in) long. Sepals 8–11 mm (0.32–0.43 in) long, silky hairy on the outside. Pakistan (Baluchistan); possibly also the neighbouring regions of Afghanistan.

var. *tenuifolia* **(Royle) Grey-Wilson*** (syn. *C. tenuifolia* Royle) has leaflets that are linear-lanceolate, unlobed or with 1–2 short lateral lobes towards the base or with several acute teeth, to 40 mm (1.6 in) long and 6 mm (0.24 in) wide. Inflorescence a cyme, 3–many-flowered; peduncle 20–67 mm (0.8–2.6 in) long. Sepals 13–18 mm (0.5–0.7 in) long, slightly hairy to glabrous outside. C Afghanistan (Bamian Province), N Pakistan (Gilgit) and NW India (Kashmir).

Clematis baltistanica Qureshi & Chaudhri would seem to be an extreme of this variety with rather small flowers, the sepals only 7–12 mm (0.28–0.47 in) long; this requires further investigation. It is recorded in the Flora of Pakistan to be restricted to N Pakistan, to the regions of Chitral and Gilgit.

var. *latifolia* **Hook. f. & Th.** (syn. *C. globosa* Royle, *C. orientalis* var. *globosa* (Royle) Mukerjee) has leaflets ovate to almost suborbicular, often almost as broad as long, generally lobed or toothed from just below the apex, obtuse. Inflorescence a cyme, 3–many-flowered; peduncle 15–60 mm (0.6–2.4 in) long. Sepals 10–13 mm (0.4–0.5 in) long, glabrous outside. NW India (Himal Pradesh and Ladakh).

var. *daurica* **(Pers.) Kuntze*** (syn. *C. dahurica* (Pers.) DC., *C. daurica* Pers., *C. davurica* Ledeb., *C. glauca* Willd., *C. orientalis* subsp. *orientalis* var. *daurica* (Pers.) Kuntze forma *persoonii* Kuntze, *C. o.* var. *glauca* Maxim., *C. o. obtusifolia* sensu Trautv., non Hook. f. & Th., *C. o.* var. *obtusifolia* forma *oblongifolia* E. Regel) has leaflets that are lanceolate-elliptic to oblong or oval, usually unlobed, sometimes fused with the adjacent leaflet(s) at the base, obtuse to subobtuse. inflorescence a 3–7-flowered cyme, occasionally reduced to a solitary flower; peduncle 10–42 mm (0.4–0.17 in) long. Sepals 17–23 mm (0.67–0.9 in) long, hairy outside. E Kazakstan and probably the neighbouring regions of Russia (Dzungaria) and NW China (Xinjiang Province).

Var. *sinorobusta* W. T. Wang (syn. *C. orientalis* var. *robusta* sensu W. T. Wang, non Grey-Wilson) is very similar to var. *orientalis* differing according to the author in its longer and thicker pedicels (37–76 mm (1.5–3 in) long, rather than 14–55 mm (0.55–2.2 in)). However, it may not be distinguishable from var. *daurica*; the two apparently grow in W & SW Xinjiang; var. *sinorobusta* is described from the Yecheng Xian region of SW Xinjiang at c. 3800 m (12,500 ft).

Var. *uniflora* Tamura described from the Mustang region of CN Nepal (Syang 2650 m (8700 ft) and Muktinath 3300 m (10,800 ft)) is almost certainly synonymous with *C. tibetana* subsp. *vernayi*, which is common in the region.

H6

◆ ◆ **Sepals erect to spreading but not recurved (species 228–234)**

❊ **Flowers usually solitary, terminal (species 228 & 229)**

228. *Clematis caudigera* W. T. Wang

DESCRIPTION. Similar to *C. tibetana* but flowers strictly terminal and solitary, the sepals drawn out distally into a 3–6 mm (0.12–0.24 in) long tail-like projection. The leaves are similar to *C. tibetana* but the flowers are generally larger, the sepals 23–42 mm (0.9–1.7 in) long and 8–11 mm (0.32–0.43 in) wide, densely downy on the inside.

DISTRIBUTION. NW China (S Xinjiang); 3000–3700 m (9850–12,100 ft).

HABITAT. Rocky valley slopes; June–July.

In the best forms this species has flowers that are larger than those of the much admired *C. tangutica* and for this reason alone it would be an interesting introduction into cultivation.

229. *Clematis corniculata* W. T. Wang

DESCRIPTION. Similar to *C. tibetana*, but flowers always solitary and terminal, the sepals plain yellow and with a characteristic horn-like appendage, to 2.5 mm (0.1 in) long, at the tip; sepals narrow-ovate, not more than 8 mm (0.32 in) wide, glabrous except for a downy margin. The leathery leaflets are simple, 3-lobed or sometimes ternate, with an entire margin, occasionally with a single small tooth on each side.

DISTRIBUTION. NW China (SW Xinjiang; Qira Xian, Yecheng Xian); 2800–2900 m (9200–9500 ft).

120. *Clematis akebioides* in cultivation. Photo: Christopher Grey-Wilson

HABITAT. Grassy slopes; Aug–Sept.

The status of this species and *C. caudigera*, both described by W. T. Wang in the 1990s requires further close investigation. Both come from S Xinjiang and bear a tail or horn-like extension to the sepals.

❊ ❊ **Flowers usually clustered, mostly lateral (species 230–234)**
❖ **Sepals notched at the apex (species 230)**

230. *Clematis graveolens* Lindley, non Hook.*
(syn. *C. orientalis* subsp. *graveolens* (Lindl.) Kuntze, *C. o.* subsp. *g.* var. *aitchisonii* Kuntze, *C. o.* subsp. *thunbergii* (Steud.) Kuntze var. *intricata* (Bunge) Kuntze, *C. parviflora* Edgeworth)

DESCRIPTION. Climbing or scrambling plant to 3–4 m (10–13 ft). Stems pale green, often whitish when older. Leaves bipinnate, glaucous-green with 5–7 prime divisions, oblong to elliptical or lanceolate, to 37 mm (1.5 in) long and 3–14 mm (0.12–0.55 in) wide, untoothed but generally with 1–3 small lobes on each side towards the base, and occasionally unlobed. Bracts similar to the leaves but smaller and with 1 or 3 leaflets. Peduncle 20–90 mm (0.8–3.5 in) long; pedicels slender, 1.5–10.8 cm (0.6–4.3 in) long. Flowers yellow nodding and broadly lantern-shaped, 25–40 mm (1–1.6 in) across, generally in groups of 3–5, occasionally solitary and terminal. sepals spreading widely apart, thick, oblong to elliptical, 11–18 mm (0.43–0.7 in) long and 5–10 mm (0.2–0.4

in) wide, with a truncated or more normally notched apex, glabrous outside except for a thick band of marginal hairs, silky with hairs inside. Stamens with purplish-brown anthers and reddish filaments.

DISTRIBUTION. E & NE Afghanistan, Pakistan (Baluchistan, Hazara, N Punjab), NW India (Kashmir, N Punjab, Himal Pradesh), W Nepal (Tibricot region) and probably SW Tibet; 900–2850 m (3000–9350 ft).

HABITAT. Dry hill-slopes, banks and hedgerows, occasionally on screes; June–Oct.

Rare in cultivation, although some of the larger-flowered forms would make an excellent introduction. This species requires a warm sunny position in the garden if it is to flower well. 'Gravetye Variety' is the best clone available at present, with rather bright green foliage and 50–60 mm (2–2.4 in) flowers.

H7; P2

❖ ❖ **Sepals with a pointed, not notched, apex (species 231–234)**
✳ **Sepals hairless except for the margins (species 231 & 232)**

231. *Clematis akebioides* (Maxim.) Veitch*
(syn. *C. glauca* var. *akebioides* (Maxim.) Rehd. & Wils., *C. orientalis* var. *akebioides* Maxim., *C. o.* var. *potaninii* Kom.)

DESCRIPTION. Climber or scrambler to 4 m (13 ft); stems 6–10-furrowed, pale green when young, often flushed with red or purple, hairy to glabrous. Leaves glaucous and rather leathery; leaflets 5–7 usually, oval to oblong, the margin crenate-dentate, to 46 mm (1.8 in) long and 21 mm (0.83 in) wide. Bracts generally reduced to a single leaflet, often trilobed and untoothed, occasionally entire. Peduncle short or absent, never more than 15 mm (0.6 in) long; pedicels slender, 40–125 mm (1.6–5 in) long. Flowers bell-shaped and nodding, in clusters of 3–7 at the leaf-axils. Sepals yellow, generally tinged or speckled with green, bronze or purple on the outside, narrowly to broadly ovate with an acute tip, quite thick and fleshy, slightly recurved at the tip, 13–27 mm (0.5–1.1 in) long and 6–13 mm (0.24–0.5 in) wide, glabrous on both surfaces except for the margin. Anthers greenish-brown. Achenes obovate to elliptic, c. 3 mm (0.12 in) long, with a plumose tail to 40 mm (1.6 in) long.

DISTRIBUTION. W China (SW, W & N Gansu, SW Inner Mongolia, S Qinghai, W Sichuan and NW Yunnan; E Tibet); 1200–3600 m (3900–11,800 ft).

widely apart, glabrous outside; anthers 1.6–2 mm
(0.06–0.08 in) long. Distributed in N India (Uttar Pradesh;
Kumaon) and SW Tibet (Gê'gyai); 3300–5000 m
(10,800–16,400 ft). A rare subspecies in cultivation and
scarcely the rival of subsp. *vernayi*. Most of the plants
sold under the name are in fact referable to subsp. *vernayi*.
The flowers tend to be greenish-yellow, but the foliage is
attractive and markedly glaucous in the best forms. The
specific name has often been corrupted in the horticultural
literature to *thibetianus* or worse still to *thibetanicus*.

subsp. *vernayi* (C. E. C. Fischer) Grey-Wilson* (syn. *C.
chrysantha* Ulbrich var. *brevipes* Tamura, *C. orientalis* var.
uniflora Tamura, *C. tenuifolia* sensu Ling, non Royle, *C.
tibetana* sensu Hara & Williams, *C. tibetana* var.
lineariloba W. T. Wang and var. *vernayi* (C. E. C. Fischer)
W. T. Wang, non Grey-Wilson, *C. vernayi* C. E. C.
Fischer) has very thick (like citrus peel) and leathery,
ovate to oblong sepals, 15–35 mm (0.6–1.4 in) long, 8–17
mm (0.32–0.67 in) wide, acute to shortly acuminate,
usually forming an open bell-shaped flower, usually
glabrous outside; anthers 2.4–4 mm (0.1–0.16 in) long.

Three distinct varieties can be recognized of which var.
vernayi is by far the most common and widespread.

var. *vernayi* has linear-lanceolate to oblong leaflets,
2–10 mm (0.08–0.4 in) wide, occasionally wider,
untoothed, mostly with 1–2 short lobes near the base.
Sepals glabrous outside. W & N Nepal (rarely east of
the Marsyandi Valley), C & S Tibet (especially close
to Lhasa, between Gyantse and Shigatse and the
region of the upper Tsangpo) and SW Sichuan;
1850–4800 m (6100–15,800 ft).

This clematis has been the most confused and
misidentified clematis in cultivation. For many years it
has been called *C. orientalis* or *C. glauca*, *C. glauca* var.
akebioides or even *C. orientalis* var. *akebioides*, all of
which are patently wrong. Under the *C. orientalis*
umbrella it has been frequently described and illustrated
in journals and gardening magazines far too numerous to
include here. Suffice it to say that in the 8th edition of
W. J. Bean's 'Trees and Shrubs Hardy in the British
Isles' the plant photographed as *C. orientalis* (Pl. 52) and
described as *C. glauca* var. *akebioides* is in fact *C.
tibetana* var. *vernayi*. This is the so-called 'Orange Peel
Clematis'. It was introduced from the Tibet (near Lhasa)
in 1947 by Ludlow, Sherriff and Elliott under the
number LSE or L & S 13342* (sometimes misquoted as
13372!) and has been popular in gardens ever since, for
its fine show of flowers from August onwards until late
autumn. This is a very beautiful plant with attractive
finely dissected foliage and exceptionally thick-sepalled

125. *Clematis tibetana* subsp. *vernayi* (corresponding to var. *lineariloba*), SE of
Lhasa, Tibet. Photo: Roger Long

126. *Clematis tibetana* subsp. *vernayi* (corresponding to var. *lineariloba*), a
particularly dark-flowered form; SE of Lhasa, Tibet. Photo: Roger Long

127. Clematis ladakhiana in cultivation. Photo: Raymond Evison

flowers in a delightful lemon shade. Conscientious nurserymen sell plants grown from cuttings from the original stock but, unfortunately, others sell seed-raised stock and sell it quite wrongly under the number; in my experience all seed-raised plants are inferior. Plants sold as 'Orange Peel' are a mixed bunch of rather dubious origin in most instances, but you may get a good plant.

Subsequently, various other collections have been introduced from the wild, especially from central and western Nepal. These show the variety to be extremely variable in both flower size and colour and in the amount of leaf lobing. As with many members of the Meclatis Section the flowers, which are basically yellow, can become suffused with brownish-purple or blackish-purple on the exterior. This suffusion is generally in the form of specks or mottling and, in extreme forms, can be so pronounced that the buds appear to be almost black. Such forms rarely live up to their expectations in cultivation, the results generally disappointing if not dowdy. The original LSE 13342 is still the finest manifestation of var. *vernayi* in cultivation; it has rather globular-shaped flowers with the sepals gradually spreading with age; they are pure yellow and unspeckled and so thick and fleshy that this clone is often referred to as the 'Orange Peel Clematis'.

Plants with linear or linear-lanceolate leaflets have been distinguished as var. *lineariloba* W. T. Chang but they fall well within the range of var. *vernayi*; individuals within populations often display such narrow leaflets and occasionally both broad and narrow leaflets can be found on the same plant.

var. *laciniifolia* Grey-Wilson* has lanceolate to ovate leaflets, 16–28 mm (0.39–1.1 in) wide, lobed and

toothed, the lobes and teeth all acute. Sepals glabrous outside. W Nepal (Kali Gandaki and Bheri valleys); 1800–3700 m (5900–12,100 ft).

var. *dentata* Grey-Wilson (syn. *C. tangutica* var. *pubescens* M. C. Chang & P. P. Ling) has lanceolate-oblong leaflets, 5–14 mm (0.2–0.32 in) wide, shallowly lobed in the lower half, dentate. Sepals somewhat hairy outside. Restricted to NW China (SW Gansu, C & S Qinghai and NE Tibet); 1300–3600 m (4300–11,800 ft), growing on open slopes on riverbanks, sometimes in open forest. The position of this variety is not clear-cut. In the 'Flora of China' it is placed under *C. tangutica* as var. *pubescens* by Chang and Ling but if this were the case then the epithet *dentata* Grey-Wilson would be valid. For the presence the evidence seems to me to favour inclusion under *C. tibetana*.

H5; P2

234. *Clematis ladakhiana* Grey-Wilson*
(syn. *C. orientalis* subsp. *orientalis* var. *daurica* (Pers.) Kuntze (incl. forma *persoonii* Kuntze and forma *thomsonii* Kuntze), *C. o.* var. *acutifolia* Hook. f. & Th., *C. o.* var. *longecaudata* sensu Mukergee, non Ledeb.)

DESCRIPTION. Clambering or sprawling deciduous climber to 2–3 m (6.6–10 ft), occasionally more. Stems pale green, often flushed with purplish brown. Leaves glaucous-green; leaflets narrow-lanceolate, to 27 mm (1.1 in) by 4–20 mm (0.16–0.8 in), caudate (drawn out into a long pointed tip), untoothed but often with 1–2 short pointed lobed towards the base. Bracts similar to the leaves but smaller and generally with 3–5 leaflets. Peduncles 6–47 mm (0.24–2.9 in) long; pedicels 15–120 mm (0.6–4.7 in) long. Flowers yellow or orange-yellow, often flushed or spotted with purplish or reddish-brown on the outside. Sepals narrow-lanceolate to elliptic, 15–25 mm (0.6–1 in) long and 4–10 mm (0.16–0.4 in) wide, usually spreading rather widely apart, with an acute to somewhat acuminate tip, hairless or almost so outside but densely hairy inside.

DISTRIBUTION. NW India (Ladakh; especially in the regions around Leh, Piti and Askole) and probably the neighbouring part of Tibet; 2800–3850 m (9200–12,600 ft).

This species is well established in cultivation and readily recognized by its finely pointed foliage. The flowers cannot be described as eye-catching at a distance but they have a subtle beauty all of their own when viewed close-up. Cultivated forms tend to have flowers of 'old gold finely speckled with dark red'. Like various other members of the Orientalis Group, *C. ladakhiana* needs an open airy site and plenty of sunshine if it is to flower well, although it is late to come into flower, being at its best in gardens in September usually. Its hardiness is not in question and in my garden it has certainly withstood −17°C (0°F) unscathed. It is rather less rampant than most other members of the *C. orientalis* association. The usual forms in gardens have yellow or orange-yellow flowers flecked finely all over with red.

H6, P2

▼ ▼ **Species with green leaves, generally sharply toothed along the margin, and with terminal as well as lateral flowers (species 235–240)**
✳ **Subshrubs, not climbing (species 235)**

235. *Clematis pamiralaica* Grey-Wilson

DESCRIPTION. A subshrub, woody towards the base, 15–45 cm (6–18 in) tall; stems finely hairy when young, 6-furrowed. Leaves bright green, ternate to pinnate; leaflets lanceolate to elliptic, to 8–30 mm (0.32–1.2 in) long and 5–20 mm (0.2–0.8 in) wide, often with 1–2 small lobes towards the base, the margin serrate. Peduncle, when present, 2–20 mm (0.08–0.8 in) long; pedicels 9–21.5 cm (3.5–8.5 in) long. Flowers yellow, often flushed with greenish-brown outside, nodding bell-shaped, solitary, terminal, rarely lateral. Sepals papery, ascending, narrow-lanceolate to elliptical, 17–33 mm (0.67–1.3 in) long and 6–12 mm (0.24–0.47 in) wide, acute to subacute, finely silkily hairy on both surfaces, more densely so inside. Achenes elliptic, hairy, with a plumose tail to 40 mm (1.6 in) long.

DISTRIBUTION. Pamir Mountains (Tadjikistan and W China (SW Xinjiang; Tagdumbash Pamir)); 3000–4600 m (9850–15,100 ft).

HABITAT. Grassy and rocky slopes, cliffs; late June–early Aug.

✳ ✳ **Climbing plants (species 236–240)**
✳ **Sepals glabrous inside except for the margin (species 236 & 237)**

236. *Clematis tangutica* (Maxim.) Korsh*
(syn. *C. alpina* sensu Gupta, non Miller, *C. chrysantha* Ulbr., *C. eriopoda* sensu Koehne, non Maxim., *C. orientalis* var. *tangutica* Maxim.)

DESCRIPTION. Climbing or sprawling shrub; stems 6–8-furrowed, green and slightly hairy when young. Leaves bright green, generally pinnate but occasionally more

128. Clematis tangutica in Qinghai, N W China. Photo: Rosemary Steele

or less bipinnate; leaflets lanceolate to narrow-elliptic or oblong, to 57 mm (2.3 in) long and 16 mm (0.63 in) wide, unlobed or with 1–2 lobes near the base, with an acute tip and serrate margin with up to 7 acute teeth on each side. Bracts like the leaves but smaller and with 3 leaflets or one trilobed leaflet. Peduncle 6–30 mm (0.24–1.2 in) long; pedicels 4.3–32 cm (1.7–12.6 in) long. Flowers lemon-yellow, occasionally flushed with brown or purplish-brown on the outside, nodding bell-shaped, 2–3 together in the leaf axils or solitary and

128. Clematis tangutica in cultivation (Jack Drake form). Photo: Christopher Grey-Wilson

129. *Clematis tangutica*, fruit. Photo: Christopher Grey-Wilson

terminal. Sepals moderately thick but fairly soft to the touch, lanceolate-elliptic to oblong, 18–40 mm (0.7–1.6 in) long, 7–16 mm (0.28–0.63 in) wide, erect to ascending, acute to acuminate or cuspidate, silky with hairs outside but glabrous inside. Achenes obovate, 3.5–4.5 mm (0.14–0.18 in) long, finely hairy, with a plumose tail to 55 mm (2.2 in) long.

DISTRIBUTION. E Kazakstan, NW India (Kashmir; Rupshu) and W & NW China (W & S Gansu, Qinghai, S Shaanxi, NW Sichuan, W & N Tibet (especially the Kunlun), Xinjiang); 1300–5400 m (4300–17,700 ft).

HABITAT. Scrub, grassy, rocky and gravelly areas, river and lake banks; June–Sept.

The introduction of this fine, popular and widely grown species into cultivation is generally credited to the Imperial Gardens of St Petersburg (1898), from where plants filtered their way into Western Europe. But there are indications that the species was in fact in cultivation in France in the 1880s for it was written about in the *Revue Horticole* by Francisque Morel in 1902, who states quite clearly that plants had been received some 15 years earlier. However, its dissemination in Britain and much of western Europe came primarily from a later introduction made by William Purdom in western Gansu in 1911: seed was sent to the Royal Horticultural Gardens at Wisley and the resultant home-reared seed and seedlings were widely distributed. Plants sold under the *C. tangutica* 'umbrella' today are very variable, some being of hybrid origin, others simply misidentified. The

best forms are excellent and free-flowering with long lantern-shaped flowers with fine-tipped sepals in which the stamens are scarcely visible. The form sold by Jack Drake's nursery at Inshriach in the Scottish Highlands is the finest in cultivation, with exceptionally long lantern flowers and looks more like the plant referred to by Morel in France than the dumpier smaller-flowered forms that resulted from Purdom's introductions. Apart from its flowers, the species is well worth growing for its fine display of relatively large fruits, a character it shares in common with many of its hybrid offspring such as 'Bill MacKenzie'. Certainly if you want to grow a good yellow-flowered species then this or *C. tibetana* are the ones to go for.

The species name refers to the home of the Tangut peoples of Asia (in north-western China).

Two hybrids of different origins had *C. tibetana* subsp. *vernayi* L & S 13342 as the seed parent and *C. tangutica* as the pollen or male parent. 'Burford Variety' was a chance seedling in late John Treasure's garden (Burford House) at Tenbury Wells. 'Bill MacKenzie' the superior of the two and far more widely available, has foliage the shape and colour of *C. tangutica*, although a trifle coarser and attractive, relatively large yellow flowers which open lantern-shaped and gradually expand as the sepals spread widely apart. Judging by the open habit of the flowers one would expect that the pollen parent was in fact *C. tangutica* subsp. *obtusiuscula*. It was named after the retired Keeper of the Chelsea Physic Garden who died fairly recently, although the plant actually originated at the Waterperry School of Horticulture in 1968. It was presented to the Royal Horticultural Society in September 1976 when it received an Award of Merit (AM). Few nurseries and garden centres seem to sell the genuine plant, with many being inferior seed-raised plants in circulation. My advice is to go to a reliable nursery and ask if the plants are raised from cuttings; if not leave them well alone.

The flowers are often said to be sweetly scented, although I have to say that I have never detected a scent of any note, but that is not to say that scented forms do not exist.

subsp. *obtusiuscula* (Rehder & Wilson) Grey-Wilson* (syn. *C. atragenoides* Batalin, *C. tangutica* var. *obtusiuscula* Rehd. & Wils.) has leaflets with up to 7 acute teeth on each side, to 38 mm (1.5 in) long and 20 mm (0.8 in) wide. Flowers saucer-shaped, the sepals spreading widely apart, obtuse to subobtuse, glabrous inside. China (SW Gansu, S Qinghai, W Sichuan (Kangding region, primarily in the Minya Konka Range) E Tibet); 2600–4300 m (8500–14,100 ft). Introduced into cultivation by Ernest Henry Wilson in 1908 from western Sichuan.

This subspecies is more compact in growth than the

lankier forms of subsp. *tangutica* and perhaps, for that reason, better suited to smaller gardens. However, the flowers are more rounded and less lantern-shaped than subsp. *tangutica*, with the sepals spreading more widely apart, and they scarcely have the same charm. It was introduced into cultivation from gatherings made in Sichuan and Gansu in China in 1908 by Ernest Henry Wilson and in 1910 by William Purdom. It won an Award of Merit (AM) when shown at the Royal Horticultural Society in 1913 by Frederick C. Stern. In the *Proceeding of the Royal Horticultural Society* in 1921 Reginald Farrer extols the virtues of this subspecies …'it unfurls a coil almost as long as its name over the river-shingles of all the streams above Jo-ni, ascending to about 10,000 ft on the fringes of the alpine coppice. In August it is all a dancing carillon of big, yellow bells like gay golden fritillarias, succeeded in November by the most voluminous fluffs of soft silver that I know among these clematids.' 'Gravetye Variety'* has rather smaller flowers, but is not particularly distinguished.

subsp. *mongolica* **Grey-Wilson** has leaflets with 9–13 acute teeth on each side, to 52 mm (2.1 in) long and 11 mm (0.43 in) wide. Flowers bell-shaped, the sepals scarcely spreading, long acuminate. Known only from N Mongolia (NE of Ulan Batour and probably elsewhere).

Various cultivars are credited with *C. tangutica* in their 'blood'. Most of these plants, which are of hybrid origin, have green, serrated, or partially serrated leaflets. It is often difficult to be sure of their true parentage, although certainly *C. serratifolia* and *C. tibetana* have been involved. However, some are clearly of more complex hybrid origin. The following are a sample of the most popular and are excellent and easy garden plants, very floriferous when given a bright sunny position in the garden: 'Aureolin'* (a Dutch variety with large 'cowbell' yellow flowers 50 mm (2 in) across, followed by large fruitheads); 'Bill MacKenzie'* AGM (very popular English cultivar with nodding flowers which open widely at maturity, 60–70 mm (2.4–2.8 in) across, an attractive yellow with reddish stamens; many plants sold under the name are inferior seedlings; see above under *C. tangutica* subsp. *tangutica*); 'Burford Variety'* (another English cultivar with shorter more rounded flowers than *C. tangutica*, its seed parent, which are about 40 mm (1.6 in) long and freely produced, as are the attractive fruitheads); 'Corry'* (a Dutch cultivar with exceptionally large deep yellow flowers, to 70 mm (2.8 in) across, the sepals spreading widely apart, but not always free-flowering); 'Helios'* (a compact Dutch cultivar of recent origin with broad saucer-shaped nodding pale yellow flowers 40–60 mm (1.6–2.4 in) across; will flower easily in the first year from seed and look very effective grown on the ground

130. *Clematis tangutica* fruit. Photo: Christopher Grey Wilson

without support); 'Lambton Park'* (an English cultivar with large 'cowbells' of buttercup yellow, 50 mm (2 in) across, freely produced; said to smell of coconut).

Interestingly, although all the species of Subsection Meclatis hybridize freely with one another I have no record of them hybridizing with other species. One might, for instance expect them to cross with the members of Subsection Africanae.

H5; P2

131. *Clematis* Orientalis Group 'Helios'. Photo: Christopher Grey-Wilson

132. Clematis hilariae, Badakhshan, NE Afganistan. Photo: Christopher Grey-Wilson

237. *Clematis zandaensis* W. T. Wang

DESCRIPTION. Closely related to *C. tangutica,* but the flowers are said to be always lateral and never terminal, borne in cymes of 1–3. The flowers are small and plain yellow, the sepals 9–17 mm (0.35–0.67 in) long and 5–8 mm (0.2–0.32 in) wide, finely pubescent only on the margin and inside. Achenes elliptic, 3 mm (0.12 in) long, pubescent, with a c. 30 mm (1.2 in) long plumose tail.

133. Clematis serratifolia in cultivation. Photo: Christopher Grey-Wilson

DISTRIBUTION. W China (W Tibet; Zanda Xian); c. 3500 m (11,500 ft).

HABITAT. Open forest, rocky slopes, river margins; June–July.

Very like a small-flowered version of *C. tangutica* and probably without the general appeal of that species as a potential garden plant.

✳ ✳ **Sepals silky-hairy inside (species 238–240)**
✪   **Leaflets slightly and unevenly toothed, often lobed (species 238 & 239)**

238. *Clematis hilariae* Kovalevskaja*
(syn. *C. chrysantha* Ulbr. var. *monantha* and var. *paucidentata* Tamura, *C. orientalis* var. *roschanica* Korsh.)

DESCRIPTION. Climbing or scrambling shrub to 3–4 m (10–13 ft); stems greenish white, sometimes flushed with reddish purple. Leaves deep green, pinnate or bipinnate, with 5–7 prime divisions; leaflets narrow-elliptic to lanceolate, to 40 mm (1.6 in) long and 4–10 mm (0.16–0.4 in) wide, apex acute, the margin usually with 1–4 acute teeth on each side. Bracts like the leaves but smaller and with 1–3 lobes. Peduncle 4–60 mm (0.16–2.4 in) long; pedicels 4.5–12 cm (1.8–4.7 in) long. Flowers lemon yellow, star-shaped, mostly lateral, solitary or up to 7 in a cluster. Sepals rather thin, spreading widely apart or slightly reflexed, lanceolate to narrow-ovate, 17–28 mm (0.67–1.1 in) long and 6–9 mm (0.24–0.35 in) wide, acute, sparse with silky hairs outside, more densely so inside.

DISTRIBUTION. Pamir Mountains (S Tadjikistan and NE Afghanistan (Badakhshan, especially the Wakhan Corridor)); 2400–3400 m (7900–11,150 ft).

H5; P2

239. *Clematis sarezica* Ikonn.

DESCRIPTION. Very similar to *C. hilariae,* but the flowers brownish flushed with deep purple on the outside and rather smaller, the sepals 15–19 mm (0.6–0.75 in) long and 5–8 mm (0.2–0.32 in) wide.

DISTRIBUTION. NE Afghanistan (Badakhshan), Tadzjikistan.

This species inhabits the same general regions as *C. hilariae* and it seems to me to be doubtfully distinct. Many species in the *C. orientalis* group vary a great deal in flower size from one plant to another, often in the same population. In addition, the first flowers to open are often the largest. Forms in which the yellow of the sepals is flushed or flecked with brownish-purple or purple are not uncommon, especially in *C. tibetana* and *C. intricata*, the flowers sometimes appearing to almost black, especially in bud. *C. sarezica* may well represent such an extreme case, but this requires further investigation.

✪ ✪ **Leaflets evenly toothed, not lobed (species 240)**

240. *Clematis serratifolia* Rehder*

(syn. *C. intricata* Bunge var. *serrata* (Maxim.) Kom. and var. *wilfordii* (Maxim.) Kom., *C. orientalis* var. *serrata* Maxim., *C. o.* var. *wilfordii* Maxim., *C. serrata* (Maxim.) Kom., *C. serratifolia* Rehder forma *wilfordii* (Maxim.) Kitagawa, *C. wilfordii* (Maxim.) Kom.)

DESCRIPTION. Climbing or scrambling shrub to 3–4 m (10–13 ft); stems 6–8-furrowed, green, sometimes flushed with reddish-purple. Leaves deep green and papery, pinnate; leaflets usually 5, the lowermost pair often 3-lobed or trifoliate, lanceolate to ovate with a serrate margin, 30–72 mm (1.2–2.9 in) long and 7–28 mm (0.28–1.1 in) wide, sparsely hairy on both surfaces. Bracts similar to the leaves but smaller, usually simple, lanceolate to linear. Peduncle 5–41 mm (0.2–1.6 in) long; pedicels slender, 36–65 mm (1.4–2.6 in) long. Flowers star-shaped, solitary or 3 together, mostly lateral but occasionally terminal, nodding. Sepals creamy-yellow, rather thin, ascending to spreading widely apart, narrow-lanceolate to elliptic, 15–27 mm (0.6–1.1 in) long and 5–10 mm (0.2–0.4 in) wide, acute, glabrous outside except for the margin, silky-hairy inside. Achenes elliptic, c. 3 mm (0.12 in) long, hairy, with a plumose tail to 40 mm (1.6 in) long.

DISTRIBUTION. N Japan, N Korea, NE China (Manchuria; E Jilin, Liaoning) and extreme SE Russia (Primorsky Province; Far East Region); to 400 m (1300 ft).

HABITAT. Forests and forest margins, hedgerows and old walls, rocky and gravelly slopes, riverbanks; Aug–Oct.

An attractive late-flowering clematis which has a great charm in full bloom. Unlike the other members of Section Meclatis, the flowers are more creamy than yellow and the sepals spread widely apart to form a star shape and are sweetly lemon-scented. It was introduced into cultivation from Korea round about 1918. In gardens it is vigorous and, given a good sunny position, free-flowering, although it is generally not as showy as *C. tangutica* or *C. tibetana*. In

134. Clematis serratifolia in cultivation. Photo: Jack Elliott

addition, the flowering season only lasts three or four weeks. The distinctive leaves are the largest in the *C. orientalis* association. The fluffy fruitheads are attractive in the autumn and often borne in profusion. This species occasionally self-sows in the garden, although it will hybridize with other members of the association if they are close by. The better, larger-flowered forms are well worth seeking out.

H6; P2

135. Clematis Orientalis Group 'Bill Mackenzie'. Photo: Christopher Grey-Wilson

Subgenus Six Atragene (The Atragene Group)

This is one of the most distinctive groups within *Clematis*. The species of the Atragene Section are unlikely to be confused with any others in the genus. Carl Linnaeus in 1753 recognized *Atragene* as a genus distinct from *Clematis*. This distinction rests upon a single character and that is the possession in *Atragene* of prominent petaloid staminodes that encircle the stamens. In the type species of the genus, *C. alpina*, and the majority of species in the section, the staminodes are scarcely longer than the stamens and distinctly shorter than the sepals, though they may be the same colour as the sepals or a contrasting colour. In *C. macropetala*, in contrast, the outer staminodes are about the same length as the sepals, although narrower, and this gives the flowers a distinctly 'double' look. In effect the petaloid staminodes are usually transitional to stamens: the outer staminodes are the largest and most petal-like, while the inner are increasingly more stamen-like, often with vestiges of anthers at their tip. The staminodes generally bear nectaries towards the base on the inner surface.

Horticulturally, the species of this section are very important and have given rise to a whole host of colourful and exciting cultivars which include some of the earliest clematis to flower in our gardens. They are all early-flowering and bear charming little nodding or half-nodding lantern flowers which are delightfully formed. Although in the majority of the species most of the flowers are produced from the axil buds of the previous season's shoots, some flowers are often borne at the fresh shoot tips later in the year. They will thrive under a variety of garden conditions, in shade or part-sun, on a

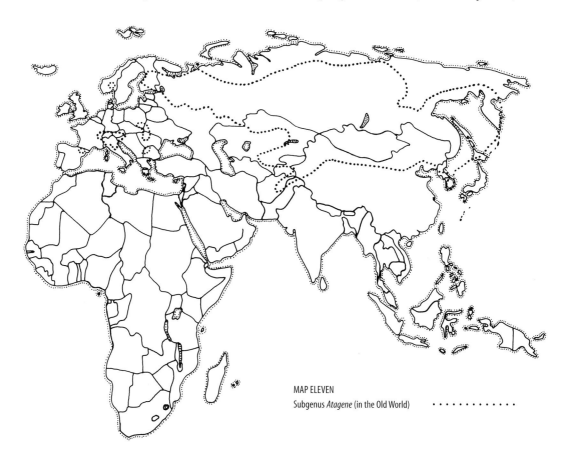

MAP ELEVEN

Subgenus *Atagene* (in the Old World) · · · · · · · · · · · ·

176

wall or draped over a shrub. Birds can sometimes prove bothersome, pecking out the potential flowerbuds in late winter before they have had a chance to expand.

Section Atragene contains some 17 species that are scattered in a broad band right across the temperate northern hemisphere from Scandinavia and central Europe to Korea and Japan and North America. They are essentially plants of cool montane forests and scrub, occasionally venturing out into more exposed rocky habitats, sometimes above the tree line. They are absent from the monsoon-rich regions of the Himalaya and western China. All the species are deciduous and although the majority are climbers, several are low and tufted and without climbing stems. All possess flowers with four sepals, although the occasional flower with five or six sepals can be found, especially in cultivated specimens. In the majority, the margin teeth of the leaflets occupy only the central portion, with the basal and apical margin being more or less entire.

The species are broken down into two subsections according to Magnus Johnson. The majority of species fit in Subsection Atragene, characterized by flowers that are borne in the leaf-axils or at the shoot tips. Subsection Brachyblasti M. Johnson ('Släktet Klematis', 1997) contains just three species (*C. dianae*, *C. iliensis* and *C. moisseenkoi*) which have flowers borne on short congested lateral shoots or brachyblasts. However, these distinctions are not always clear-cut and both the familiar *C. alpina* and *C. macropetala* seem sometimes to conform to the latter condition. In this work the two subsections are not recognized.

136. *Clematis macropetala* in cultivation. Photo: Christopher Grey-Wilson

▼ **Flowers with both sepals and 'petals' (species 241)**

241. *Clematis macropetala* Ledeb.*
(syn. *Atragene macropetala* (Ledeb.) Ledeb., *A. macropetala* sensu Meyer, *A. ochotensis* Pall. subsp. *macropetala* (Ledeb.) Kuntze; *Clematis alpina* var. *m.* var. *rupestris* Turcz. ex Kuntze, *C. alpina* var. *macropetala* (Ledeb.) Maxim., *C. alpina* var. *m.* subvar. *rupestris* Maxim., *C. macropetala* var. *rupestris* * Turcz. ex Kuntze) Maxim.)

DESCRIPTION. Climber 2–4 m (6.6–13 ft), occasionally more, with slender, 4–6-angled, somewhat downy stems and biternate leaves. Leaflets ovate to lanceolate, 20–50 mm (0.8–2 in) long and 10–45 mm (0.4–1.8 in) wide, with an acute apex and a coarsely, and rather unevenly, serrate margin, sometimes with one or two lobes towards the base. Flowers solitary, nodding, lantern-shaped, 30–60 mm (1.2–2.4 in) across, with the sepals half-spreading to almost horizontal, borne on green or purplish slender pedicels up to 12 cm (4.7 in) long. Sepals blue, violet-blue or purplish-blue, lanceolate to elliptical, 30–48 mm (1.2–2 in) long and 10–20 mm (0.4–0.8 in) wide, with an acute apex. Staminodes transitional, the outermost similar in colour and length to the sepals but narrower, often narrow-lanceolate to linear-lanceolate, the innermost paler or whitish, linear-lanceolate to linear, about half the length of the sepals; all staminodes softly hairy all over. Achenes obovate, 3–4 mm (0.12–0.16 in) long, sparsely pubescent, with a plumose tail to 45 mm (1.8 in) long.

DISTRIBUTION. SE Siberia (from Irkutsk to Ussuri), Mongolia, N China (from E Qinghai and Gansu eastwards Shaanxi and Shanxi, Inner Mongolia, Liaoning, Jilin and Heilongjiang); 900–2000 m (3000–6500 ft).

HABITAT. Open woodland and shrubberies, occasionally growing over rocks; June–Aug (generally May–June in cultivation, with a few flowers later in the season).

137. *Clematis tenuiloba* in cultivation. Photo: Christopher Grey-Wilson

This extremely pretty member of the *C. alpina* association was first introduced into cultivation by William Purdom (presumably from Gansu) and first flowered in 1912 at the Coombe Wood Nursery. It was subsequently introduced by Reginald Farrer. However, its discovery goes back considerably earlier to 1742 when it was first collected north of Peking by d'Incarville whose named is splendidly commemorated in another striking and familiar Chinese genus, *Incarvillea*, several species of which

138. *Clematis alpina* in cultivation. Photo: Christopher Grey-Wilson

are well known in our gardens. The plump flowers are so full of petal-like staminodes that they appear to be double and the fruits that follow add to the decorative value of the plant from mid-summer onwards. As with *C. alpina*, the occasionally bloom will be borne on the current season's shoots through the summer months. Like *C. alpina* its extreme hardiness make it a useful plant for many locations in the garden. It is perhaps most decorative when allowed to scramble over a shrub or arch. It pays to cut it hard back after flowering every third year or so, otherwise plants become very scraggy in time.

The species received an Award of Merit (AM) from the Royal Horticultural Society in April 1923.

The following varieties have been described from the wild: **var. *albiflora* (Maxim.) Hand.-Mazz.** (syn. *C. alpina* subsp. *macropetala* var. *albiflora* Maxim. ex Kuntze, *C. a.* var. *m.* subvar. *albiflora* Maxim.) described from N China (Ningxia (Helan Shan) and Shanxi (Guandi Shan)) at 1700–2000 m (5600–6500 ft) has white flowers with oblong-lanceolate sepals; **var. *punicoflora* Zhao** from Inner Mongolia has red flowers. In addition, **var. *rupestris* (Turcz.) Hand.-Mazz.** (see synonymy above) has been recorded from several localities in northern China (Shaanxi to Inner Mongolia in particular) and has small violet flowers with the sepals not more than 25 mm (1 in) long, and smaller leaflets.

Clematis macropetala has given rise to some beautiful cultivars in a wide range of colours (particularly blues, pinks and purples), some with exceptionally large and fine flowers: 'Alborosea' (pinkish-blue with paler staminodes); 'Anders' (lavender-blue); 'Ballet Skirt'* (large full-looking flowers of deep pink); 'Blue Bird' (mauve-blue, the sepals rather narrow and somewhat contorted, with paler staminodes within); 'Celesta' (Wisteria-blue flowers with a hint of purple); 'Floralia'* (pale blue, small flowers); 'Harry Smith'* (small pale lavender-blue, in profusion); 'Jan Lindmark'* (small mauve-purple flowers, early); 'Lagoon'* (large deep blue late flowers); 'Lincolnshire Lady' (large dusky-blue flowers with paler staminodes); 'Maidwell Hall'* AGM (an early 1930s cultivar with deep pink flowers set against rather pale green foliage); 'Markham's Pink' (good sized blooms of rosy-mauve with a hint of purple); 'Paloma' (Lobelia-blue, rather small flowers); 'Pauline'* (large flowers with deep blue sepals and staminodes, freely produced); 'Rosy O'Grady' (large pinkish-mauve flowers with somewhat paler staminodes); 'Veronica' (violet-blue moderately large flowers); 'White Moth'* (often listed as *C. sibirica* 'White Moth', has rather small creamy-white flowers and pale green foliage, late and of a somewhat weak constitution, although one of the loveliest in the Atragene Section; 'White Swan'* (creamy-white flowers set against pale green foliage; slow to establish); 'White Wings'* (creamy-white of good size and freely produced, against pale green foliage; the best of the whites). For further details and the history of the *C. macropetala* hybrids see Magnus Johnson's 'Släktet Klematis'.

H5; P1

- ▼ ▼ **Flowers with sepals and much shorter non-petal-like staminodes (species 242–258)**
- ◆ **Flowers blue, violet or purple (species 242–251)**
- ✳ **Leaves biternate (species 242–248)**
- ❖ **Dwarf, non-climbing plants (species 242 & 243)**

242. *Clematis nobilis* Nakai

DESCRIPTION. Similar to *C. ochotensis* but a dwarf plant with ascending stems only 50–60 mm (2–2.4 in) long, the leaves biternate with small leaflets, without twisting petioles or petiolules. Flowers violet-blue with the sepals up to 38 mm (1.5 in) long, the staminodes whitish, about one-third the length of the sepals.

DISTRIBUTION. North Korea (Waigalbon); 2000–2200 m (6500–7200 ft).

HABITAT. Granitic mountain rocks; July.

This interesting species, which is not in cultivation, is probably a dwarf ecotype of *C. ochotensis* and as such it bears the same relationship to that species as the American *C. tenuiloba* does to *C. columbiana*.

243. *Clematis tenuiloba* (A. Gray) Hitchcock*
Matted Purple Virgin's Bower
(syn. *Atragene occidentalis* var. *chalicodocolus* Clements & Clements; *Clematis alpina* var. *occidentalis* subvar. *tenuiloba* A. Gray, *C. alpina* var. *tenuiloba* (A. Gray) A. Gray, *C. columbiana* var. *tenuiloba* (A. Gray) Pringle, *C. occidentalis* Barr, *C. pseudoalpina* var. *tenuiloba* (A. Gray) A. Nelson, *C. pseudoatragene* subsp. *subtriternata* Kuntze).

DESCRIPTION. A low tufted and suckering plant forming open mats, with stems above ground not more than 20 cm (8 in) long but spreading considerably further underground. Leaves ternate to biternate, the leaflets lanceolate to ovate, entire to incisely lobed, generally finely divided. Flowers solitary, nodding-campanulate, with the sepals spreading widely apart, terminal or lateral on long slender, green or purple-tinged pedicels to 13 cm (5 in) long. Sepals pale to deep violet-blue, occasionally

139. Clematis alpina Val d'Isere, E France. Photo: Brinsley Burbidge

pinkish or white, lanceolate-elliptical, 20–35 mm (0.8–1.6 in) long and up to 9 mm (0.35 in) wide, often somewhat recurved towards the acute tip. Staminodes white tinged with purple or violet, narrow-oblanceolate, subacute, about half the length of the sepals. Achenes with a plumose tail to 45 mm (1.8 in) long.

DISTRIBUTION. W USA, primarily in the Rocky Mountains (Montana and Idaho east as far as the western Dakotas and south as far as Utah, Colorado and N Arizona; 2200–2700 m (7200–8850 ft).

HABITAT. Mountain rocks, especially cliffs and rock crevices; June–July.

This interesting and very pretty little clematis is one of the smallest members of the genus. It is a true alpine and can be found in the wild growing with other choice alpines such as *Androsace montana*, *Aquilegia jonesii* and *Boykinia jamesii*. It taxonomic position has long been disputed as can be seen from the accompanying synonymy. The plant is clearly derived from *C. columbiana* and probably represents an ecotype evolved to more open, rocky and exposed habitats.

This is a delightful little plant for growing in a pan in an alpine house or an unheated glasshouse, where it must never be allowed to dry out. It will succeed outdoors on a raised bed given a nice gritty sand humusy, freely drained compost. In my experience the resting buds, which lie at or close to the soil surface, tend to rot during the winter if they get too moist, although plants generally shoot from below the surface in the spring should this happen; however, by then much of the bloom for the year will have been lost. Seedlings tend to be very variable and some have decidedly pale and washy flowers, while others are far finer. There is a beautiful pure white form in cultivation.

H4; P1

❖ ❖ **Tall climbing or scrambling plants (species 244–248)**

❑ **Staminodes spoon-shaped; European & western Asian plants (species 244)**

244. *Clematis alpina* (L.) Miller* AGM
(syn. *Atragene alpina* L., *A. austriaca* Scopoli, *A. clematidis* Crantz; *Clematis alpina* subsp. *normalis* Kuntze)

DESCRIPTION. Deciduous climber to 2–3 m (6.6–10 ft), occasionally more, with biternate leaves, the primary segments stalked, the lateral with usually 3 but sometimes 2 leaflets. Leaflets lanceolate to more or less elliptical, to 50 mm (2 in) long, with an acute tip and a coarsely serrate margin, short-stalked to sessile. Flowers nodding, lantern-shaped, with the sepals half-spreading to widely spreading apart, borne on pedicels up to 10 cm (4 in) long. Sepals blue to violet-blue, 40–50 mm (1.6–2 in) long, elliptical with an acute apex which is flat or very slightly recurved. Staminodes white or pale cream, occasionally with a flush of blue or violet on the outermost, spoon-shaped, about one-third the length of the sepals, with a ciliate margin. Achenes with a plumose tail up to 40 mm (1.6 in) long.

DISTRIBUTION. Mountains of central and southern Europe; primarily the Alps, northern Apennines and Carpathians (including the south-west Ukraine), with isolated stations in the central French Pyrenees and western Bulgaria; to 2900 m (9500 ft).

HABITAT. Rocky woodland, both deciduous and coniferous, and mountain scrub, occasionally on cliffs; late May–July.

Several varieties have been described from the wild: var. *kraettliana* Schroeter from eastern Switzerland

(Graubnden) has flowers often with 5 fringed sepals; var. *pallida* Ausserdorfer from the eastern Austrian Alps has pale rose sepals; var. *wenderothii* (Schlecht.) Kuntze (= *Atragene cordata* Wenderoth, *A. wenderothii* Schlecht.; *C. austriaca* Lodd., *C. wenderothii* (Schlecht.) Steud.) has leaves reduced to three leaflets. In addition, var. *lactea* Beck, described from cultivated material, has white flowers.

This very beautiful and widely grown species has had a long history in cultivation, as might be expected; it was introduced into gardens certainly by 1792, where it was often referred to as the 'Alpine Virgin's Bower'. As with *C. macropetala* and its allies, the flowers are produced directly from the lateral buds on the previous year's stems so that pruning at any time except immediately after flowering will certainly reduce the flowering display for the following season. When growing the wild species from seed it is wise to select and keep only the best coloured forms when they come into bloom, for seedlings can vary a great deal, even from a single seed source; most have sepals in various shades of blue or mauve.

Clematis alpina, sometimes called the 'Alpine Clematis', makes a fine plant for the rock garden where it will drape itself attractively over large rocks or shrubs, where the dainty flowers will dance enticingly in spring breezes. It is a remarkably hardy species, withstanding temperatures as low as –35°C (–32°F) and will withstand quite exposed positions in the garden, especially if it is scrambling amongst shrubs. Few clematis are as valuable for their charming display of flowers early in the season. The species received an Award of Merit (AM) from the Royal Horticultural Society as long ago as 1894.

In cultivation *C. alpina* flowers at the same time as its eastern cousin *C. macropetala* and the two hybridize readily. The offspring can be very fine plants but many are, in my experience, inferior to the parent species. Many of the so-called *C. alpina* types of gardens are of such origin and plants should be bought from a reputable source for unfortunately many mongrels appear in garden centres. However, having said this there are some very fine and large-flowered cultivars of *C. alpina* from which to make a selection: 'Albiflora' (white, 50 mm (2 in) long flowers); 'Bluebell' (Cambridge-blue, 50 mm (2 in) long flowers); 'Blue Dancer' (pale blue, 50–70 mm (2–2.8 in) long flowers with narrow twisted sepals); 'Burford White'* (cream, 50 mm (2 in) long flowers); 'Candy' (rose-pink with red veins, paler inside, 40–50 mm (1.6–2 in) flowers); 'Columbine'* (pale blue, 50 mm (2 in) flowers); 'Constance'* (Purple-pink, 50 mm (2 in) long flowers, very freely produced); 'Cyanea' (deep blue, with paler petals within as well as whitish staminodes, 50 mm (2 in) long flowers); 'Ernst Lindmark' (gentian blue, 50–60 mm (2–2.4 in) long flowers); 'Foxy'* (pale pink with pink staminodes, 50 mm (2 in) long flowers); 'Frankie'* (Mid-blue with the outer staminodes blue-tipped, freely produced 50 mm (2 in) long flowers); 'Jacqueline du Pré'* (pale pink-veined maroon, especially towards the sepal base, 50 mm (2 in) long flowers); 'Magnus Johnson' (gentian-blue, 50–65 mm (2–2.6 in) long flowers); 'Orchid Purple' (purple, 40–50 mm (1.6–2 in) flowers); 'Pamela Jackman'* (deep blue rather small 40 mm (1.6 in) long flowers, freely produced); 'Rodomax' (deep reddish-purple with a pale margin, 60 mm (2.4 in) long flowers); 'Ruby'* (pinkish-purple to reddish-mauve, 40–50 mm (1.6–2 in) long flowers); 'White Columbine'* AGM (pure white, 40–50 mm (1.6–2 in) long flowers); 'Willy'* (clear pale pink flowers, paler inside, 40–50 mm (1.6–2 in) long flowers). All flowering from mid to late spring and mostly 2–3 m (6.6–10 ft) tall.

H4; P1

❏ ❏ **Staminodes spatula-shaped or oblanceolate; North American and eastern Asian plants (species 245 & 248)**

245. *Clematis columbiana* (Nutt.) Torrey & Gray*
Columbia Virgin's Bower, Bellrue
(syn. *Atragene columbiana* Nutt., *A. diversiloba* (Rydb.) Rydb., *A. pseudoalpina* (Kuntze) Rydb., *A. pseudoalpina* var. *diversiloba* Rydb., *A. repens* (Kuntze) Rydb.; *Clematis alpina* var. *occidentalis* sensu A. Gray, *C. alpina* subsp. *occidentalis* var. *repens* Kuntze, *C. occidentalis* var. *albiflora* Cockerell, *C. pinetorum* Tideström & Kittell, *C. pseudoalpina* (Kuntze) A. Nelson, *C. pseudoatragene* subsp. *wenderothioides* Kuntze)

DESCRIPTION. Scrambling plant or climber 1–3 m (3.3–10 ft) , although occasionally less, with biternate leaves. Leaflets lanceolate to narrow-ovate, generally with a few incised serrate teeth or lobes, sometimes clearly 3-lobed. Flowers campanulate, with the sepals half-spreading, terminal or lateral. Sepals violet-blue to rosy-purple or lavender, lanceolate, 40–63 mm (1.6–2.5 in) long. Staminodes oblanceolate, subacute, about one-third the length of the sepals, hairy towards the base.

DISTRIBUTION. Western USA (primarily in the Rocky Mountains) from Montana, Wyoming and Idaho southwards to Colorado, Arizona and northern New Mexico and north-west Texas; 800–2700 m (2600–8850 ft).

HABITAT. Rocky woodland and scrub, often on steep mountain slopes; late Apr–July.

140. *Clematis alpina* 'Burford White'. Photo: Christopher Grey-Wilson

This species is very similar to *C. alpina*, indeed it can be likened to the American counterpart of it, but it is scarcely as good a garden plant both in habit or floriferousness and is certainly more challenging to grow. For that reason it is seldom seen in cultivation, although it is certainly represented in some specialist collections. The flowers have a laxer appearance, with thinner more pointed sepals which, in the best forms, are a delightful clear blue, although a purple-blue is more common.

H4; P1

141. *Clematis alpina* 'Willy'. Photo: Christopher Grey-Wilson

142. *Clematis ochotensis*, Changbai Shan, NE China. Photo: Roy Lancaster

143. *Clematis ochotensis* in cultivation. Photo: Raymond Evison

246. *Clematis ochotensis* (Pall.) Poir.* (syn. *Atragene ochotensis* Pall., *A. alpïna* var. *ochotensis* (Pall.) Regel & Til., *A. ochotensis* subsp. *caerulescens* Kom., *A. platysepala* Trautv. & Mey.; *Clematis alpina* subsp. *ochotensis* (Pall.) Kuntze, *C. alpina* subsp. *ochotensis* var. *ochotensis* Shimizu, *C. alpina* var. *chinensis* Maxim., *C. a.* var. *ochotensis* (Pall.) S. Wats., *C. nobilis* Nakai, *C. platysepala* (Trautv. & Mey.) Hand.-Mazz., *C. sibirica* var. *ochotensis* (Pall.) S. H. Li & Y. H. Huang).

DESCRIPTION. Climber to 3 m (10 ft), with biternate leaves very similar to *C. alpina*, but the leaves often a more yellow-green, and the flowers with broader sepals (12–24 mm (0.47–0.95 in) as opposed to 10–15 mm (0.4–0.6 in)). In addition, the staminodes are quite different: in *C. ochotensis* they are spatula-shaped, up to 20 mm (0.8 in) long but not more than 3 mm (0.12 in) wide, whereas in *C. alpina* they are pronouncedly spoon-shaped, not more than 15 mm (0.6 in) long but about 6 mm (0.24 in) wide at the widest. The flower colour ranges from bright indigo blue to violet-blue or purple (rarely white) with contrasting whitish staminodes which are about one-third the length of the sepals.

DISTRIBUTION. NE Asia: E Siberia (including Kamtchatka, Sakhalin, Ussuriland, Kuril Islands), N Korea, NE China (N Hebei, E Jilin and Heilongjiang, E Inner Mongolia, N Shanxi), N Japan, (Hokkaido); to 1200 m (3900 ft).

HABITAT. Rocky deciduous or coniferous woodland (often mixed), primarily of pine, maple or birch and scrub, occasionally growing over more exposed rocks; May–July.

Although clearly closely related to *C. alpina*, *C. ochotensis* occupies a very distinct and easterly geographical area. It has been much confused in the past as can be witnessed by its messy synonymy. It is also closely allied to *C. sibirica*, which is readily distinguished on account of its white flowers. Interestingly, *C. ochotensis* replaces *C. sibirica* entirely in extreme eastern Asia and although the two come close geographically further west, they do not appear to overlap in distribution.

Its deeply coloured and attractive flowers, larger than those of *C. alpina*, in it best forms, make it a potentially valuable garden plant as well as in a breeding programme. Indeed, the popular cultivar 'Francis Rivis' (syn. 'Blue Giant') AGM, which dates back to the 1960s from the garden of Sir Cedric Morris in Suffolk, with large 50–60 mm (2–2.4 in) long flowers of a charming gentian-blue, is probably of such hybrid origin (*C. alpina* × *C. ochotensis*). More recent authenticated hybrids with a similar parentage, primarily raised by Magnus Johnson, in Sweden, include: 'Helsingborg'* AGM (purple-blue flowers with dark purple staminodes, 50 mm (2 in) long flowers) and 'Tage Lundell'* (Deep rose-purple, 50–60 mm (2–2.4 in) long flowers). It is to be hoped that these and other hybrids do not eclipse the true species in our gardens, for they are equally appealing. Two *C. ochotensis* cultivars are 'Carmen Rose'* (pale rose-pink with long undulate sepals, 50–60 mm (2–2.4 in) long flowers) and 'Chastity' (white, 60–70 mm (2.4–2.8 in) long flowers).

var. *grandidentata* Nakai from S Hokkaido, Japan, has unusually coarsely toothed foliage; **var. *tenuifolia* (Nakai) Tamura** (syn. *C. subtriternata* Nakai, *C. t.* var. *tenuifolia* Nakai) from the Changbai Shan (North Korea and Jilin Province, NE China) has narrow, often lobed leaflets and reddish-purple flowers with noticeably acuminate tips. In addition, var. *ochotensis* forma *rubicunda* Freyn has been described, having flowers of rose-carmine.

H5; P1

247. *Clematis crassisepala* Ohwi*

DESCRIPTION. Closely related to *C. ochotensis* from which it differs in being generally smaller, the leaflets not more than 30 mm (1.2 in) long, and the sepals violet-blue, 20–25 mm (0.8–1 in) long. The staminodes are no more than 8 and are just over half the length of the sepals.

DISTRIBUTION. S North Korea (endemic to Mt Myokosan).

HABITAT. Rocky and wooded places; June–July

H5; P1

248. *Clematis fusijamana* (Kuntze) M. Johnson*
(syn. *C. alpina* subsp. *ochotensis* var. *fusijamana* Kuntze, *C. alpina* subsp. *ochotensis* var. *japonica* (Nakai ex Hara) T. Shimizu, *C. ochotensis* var. *japonica* Nakai ex Hara)

DESCRIPTION. Similar to *C. fauriei* but the leaves are biternate and deeply incised serrate or sometimes with additional lobes. The flowers are smaller but a similar colour, although rather deeper, the sepals noticeably thicker and less undulate, not more than 35 mm (1.4 in) long and 17 mm (0.67 in) wide. The staminodes are whitish and often flushed with violet-purple towards the rounded apex, slightly more than half the length of the sepals, narrow spatula-shaped.

DISTRIBUTION. Endemic to NC Honshu, Japan; c. 1100 m (3600 ft).

HABITAT. Open woodland in shaded or semi-shaded places; May–June.

This interesting species, formerly included under subspecies or varieties of *C. alpina,* is distinctive with its thick sepals which are reminiscent of those of members of the *C. orientalis* complex (Section Meclatis) but quite distinct in their coloration. *C. fusijamana* is rare in cultivation.

H5; P1

144. *Clematis* 'Francis Rivis'. Photo: Christopher Grey-Wilson

145. *Clematis koreana* in cultivation. Photo: Raymond Evison

❀ ❀ **Leaves ternate (species 249–251)**
❀ **Leaflets toothed; Asian plants (species 249 & 250)**

249. *Clematis fauriei* (Boissieu) M. Johnson*

(syn. *C. alpina* var. *fauriei* Boissieu, *C. alpina* var. *japonica* Hort., *C. alpina* subsp. *ochotensis* var. *fauriei* Shimizu, *C. alpina* subsp. *ochotensis* var. *fusijamana* forma *fauriei* (Boissieu) Tateishi, *C. ochotensis* var. *fauriei* (Boissieu) Murai, *C. ochotensis* var. *ternata* Nakai)

DESCRIPTION. Climber to 2 m (6.6 ft), often less, with trifoliate leaves, occasionally trilobed. Leaflets ovate with a coarsely serrate margin, sometimes 3-lobed, the apex acuminate. Flowers solitary, campanulate with the sepals half-spreading, borne on green pedicels up to 10 cm (4 in) long, terminal or on short lateral shoots. Sepals plum-purple to violet-purple, narrow-ovate, 25–42 mm (1–1.7 in) long and up to 23 mm (0.9 in) wide, long-acuminate and somewhat recurved towards the tip. Staminodes a similar colour to the sepals or paler or whitish, spatula-shaped, half the length of the sepals, with hairs towards the apex and along the margin. Achene with a plumose tail to 30 mm (1.2 in) long.

DISTRIBUTION. Endemic to N Honshu, Japan (Tohoku District); 1000–1850 m (3300–6100 ft).

HABITAT. Rocky and wooded places; June–July.

H5; P1

250. *Clematis koreana* Kom.*

(syn. *Atragene koreana* Kom.; *Clematis alpina* var. *koreana* (Kom.) Nakai, *C. komaroviana* Koidz., *C. komarovii* Koidz.)

DESCRIPTION. Climber to 5 m (16.5 ft) with 6-angled glabrous stems and trifoliate leaves. Leaflets papery, ovate to ovate-elliptical, 50–90 mm (2–3.5 in) long and 30–85 mm (1.2–3.3 in) wide, the terminal leaflet sometimes 3-lobed, the lateral sometimes 2-lobed, usually with a few coarse serrate teeth along the margin, the apex subacute to somewhat acuminate. Flowers nodding-campanulate, 30–35 mm (1.2–1.4 in) across, borne on purple-violet flushed pedicels up to 12 cm (4.7 in) long, on the previous or current season's shoots, generally solitary in the former case. Sepals violet-blue to reddish-violet, sometimes greenish towards the tip, narrow-ovate, 35–50 mm (1.4–2 in) long, 7–12 mm (0.28–0.47 in) wide, with an acuminate, spreading widely apart eventually, with a slightly recurved apex and with 3–5 keel-like ridges outside, each with a short spur-like blunt appendage at the base. Staminodes pale yellow, cream or whitish, spatula-shaped, subacute, pubescent, about one-third the length of the sepals. Achenes narrow-obovate, 4–5 mm (0.16–0.2 in) long, finely pubescent, with a plumose tail to 45 mm (1.8 in) long.

DISTRIBUTION. NW China (E Jilin, E Liaoning), E Siberia (Ussuriland), North and South Korea except for the coastal regions; 1000–1900 m (3300–6200 ft).

HABITAT. Mixed coniferous-deciduous woodland, often with rhododendrons, firs, maples, oaks and various deciduous shrubs; late May–early Aug.

The following varieties have been recognized from the wild: **var.** *biternata* **Nakai** from North Korea (Kanhoku and Kâgen) has biternate leaves; **var.** *fragrans* **M. Johnson*** from South Korea (Seorak) has larger reddish-purple or violet-purple narrowly campanulate, fragrant, flowers, with more obvious 'shoulders', the colour particularly intense and shiny in bud (it was introduced into cultivation in 1976 by the Nordisk Arboretum in Sweden); **var.** *lutea* **(Rehd.) M. Johnson*** (syn. *C. koreana* forma *lutea* Rehd.), first collected by Komarov in 1901 and 1904 has attractive yellow flowers, the sepals often purple- or violet-flushed at the base; **var. *umbrosa* Nakai** (syn. *C. ochotensis* var. *triphylla* Ohwi) from NE North Korea (Mt Kanâbâh) is subshrubby with reddish-purple flowers. All flower in cultivation in late spring and early summer.

H5; P1

❋ ❋ **Leaflets untoothed: North American plants (species 251)**

251. *Clematis occidentalis* (Hornem.) DC.* Western Blue Clematis
(syn. *Atragene occidentalis* Hornem., *A. americana* Sims; *Clematis alpina* var. *occidentalis* (Hornem.) A. Grey, *C. alpina* subsp. *occidentalis* (Hornem.) Kuntze, *C. alpina* subsp. *occidentalis* var. *verticillaris* (DC.) Kuntze, *C. hexagona* Eaton, *C. pseudoatragene* Kuntze, *C. verticillaris* DC., *C. verticillaris* var. *cacuminis* Fernald, *C. verticillaris* var. *grandiflora* Boivin).

DESCRIPTION. Climber to 3 m (10 ft), occasionally more, with ternate leaves. Leaflets lanceolate to ovate with an entire margin, to 10 cm (4 in) long. Flowers solitary wide-campanulate. Sepals violet to violet-purple or blue-purple, lanceolate to elliptical or almost ovate, to 50 mm (2 in) long and 15 mm (0.6 in) wide (plants with larger flowers, the sepals up to 60 mm (2.4 in) long and 25 mm (1 in) wide, have been described as var. *grandiflora* Boivin), borne on a green or purplish pedicel to 12 cm (4.7 in) long. Staminodes narrow-elliptical with a subacute apex, hairy in the lower part. Achenes with tails up to 70 mm (2.8 in) long, though generally 30–50 mm (1.2–2 in).

DISTRIBUTION. E North America: Canada (S Ontario and S & SE Quebec); USA (Wisconsin east to New England, and south to the Appalachians of Virginia and North Carolina.

HABITAT. Damp generally mixed deciduous and coniferous woodland; May–July.

The ternate rather than biternate leaves are a useful distinguishing character of this species which otherwise looks very similar to the European *C. alpina*. In its typical form (subsp. *occidentalis*) as described above the leaflets are untoothed, which further serves to distinguish it. The species was introduced into cultivation in 1797 but is rare in gardens today. In the wild it is quite common in the Niagara Falls region and the Blue Ridge Mountains of North Carolina and Virginia.

H6; P1

subsp. *grosseserrata* (Rydb.) Grey-Wilson, stat. nov. (syn. *Atragene columbiana* forma *albescens* E. H. Kelso, *A. grosseserrata* Rydb.; *Clematis obliqua* Douglas ex Hooker, *C. occidentalis* var. *grosseserrata* (Rydb.) Pringle; *C. verticillaris* var. *columbiana* sensu A. Gray).

DESCRIPTION. Distinguished by its generally serrately toothed or sometimes 2–3-lobed leaflets and rather larger violet-blue flowers with wide-spreading sepals 50–60 mm (2–2.4 in) long. White-flowered forms are also known in the wild.

DISTRIBUTION. W North America: Canada (Yukon Territory southwards to British Columbia); USA (Idaho and Montana south to Colorado).

var. *dissecta* (C. L. Hitchcock) Pringle* (syn. *C. columbiana* var. *dissecta* C. L. Hitchcock)

DESCRIPTION. A generally smaller plant with stems up to 0.5 m (20 in), occasionally as much as 1 m (40 in), with ternate to biternate leaves, the leaflets smaller and incisely lobed. Flowers rather small, violet-blue to reddish-violet, the sepals to 40 mm (1.6 in) long.

DISTRIBUTION. NW USA (Washington and Oregon); primarily in the Cascades and the Wenatchee Mountains.

H3; P1

◆ ◆ **Flowers white to cream or pale yellow (species 252–258)**
❋ **Leaves biternate (species 252–254)**
✪ **Flowers large, the sepals 55–75 mm (2.2–3 in) long (species 252)**

252. *Clematis robertsiana* Aitch. & Hemsl.

DESCRIPTION. Scrambling or climbing plant to 3 m (10 ft), generally less, with biternate leaves, the central segment generally with 3 leaflets, the lateral with 2. Leaflets ovate-lanceolate, to 75 mm (3 in) long and 22 mm (0.87 in) wide, with a serrate margin. Flowers large, nodding, terminal or lateral. Sepals lemon-yellow, lanceolate, 55–75 mm (2.2–3 in) long and 15–22 mm (0.6–0.87 in) wide, with an acuminate tip, sparsely hairy on the outside.

DISTRIBUTION. Endemic to E Afghanistan (Nagarhar, north of Jallalabad) and CN Pakistan (Kurram Valley); c. 3300–3500 m (10,800–11,500 ft).

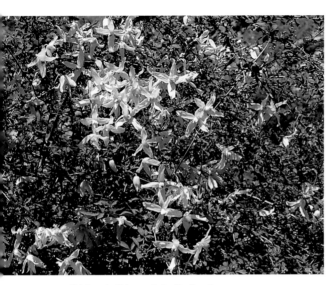

146. *Clematis sibirica* near Medeo, Tien Shan, Kygyzystan.
Photo: Christopher Grey-Wilson

HABITAT. Rocky scrub and cliffs; May–July.

A rare and little-known species, scarcely seen since it was first collected by J. E. T. Aitchison in 1879. In more recent times few expeditions have ventured into this politically sensitive region and it has not been re-collected. This is a great pity because it would be excellent to get this species into cultivation for it has the largest flowers of any atragene and the colour would certainly also be a bonus in a group where yellow scarcely exists.

147. *Clematis sibirica* near Medeo, Tien Shan, Kygyzystan.
Photo: Christopher Grey-Wilson

❂ **Flowers smaller, the sepals not more than 45 mm (1.8 in) long (species 253 & 254)**

253. *Clematis dianae* **Serov**

DESCRIPTION. Trailing plant or climber with biternate leaves, the central segment generally with 3 leaflets, the lateral with two. Leaflets lanceolate to narrow-ovate, 18–35 mm (0.7–1.4 in) long, with a serrate margin and acute tip. Flowers wide-campanulate, solitary, borne on very short lateral shoots from the previous season's growth. Sepals white, sometimes with a hint of violet, lanceolate, 26–35 mm (1–1.4 in) long and 10–17 mm (0.4–0.67 in) wide. Staminodes variable, the outer petal-like, about the same length and colour as the as the sepals but less than half the width, narrow-lanceolate, the inner about half the length of the sepals and not more than 5 mm (0.2 in) wide.

DISTRIBUTION. N China (E Xinjiang, N Qinghai, N Gansu, W Inner Mongolia).

HABITAT. Rocky and bushy places; May–July.

254. *Clematis sibirica* **(L.) Miller***
(syn. *Atragene sibirica* L., *A. alpina* Pall., non L., *A. alpina* var. *sibirica* Regel & Til., *A. spectabilis* Weinm.; *Clematis alpina* subsp. *sibirica* (L.) Kuntze, *C. alpina* var. *alba* Davis, *C. alpina* var. *sibirica* Maxim., *C. sibirica* var. *tianzhuensis* M. S. Yan & K. Sun).

DESCRIPTION. Very similar in overall proportions to *C. alpina*, although often with rather longer petioles and pedicels. The prime difference is seen in the flower colour, those of *C. sibirica* being white or creamy-white overall, the sepals very rarely tinged with pale violet. The sepals appear to be thinner with a somewhat recurved margin often, narrow-lanceolate to narrow-oblong, 30–45 mm (1.2–1.8 in) long and 10–16 mm (0.4–0.63 in) wide, with an apiculate or acuminate apex. The staminodes, which are about one-third the length of the sepals, are spoon-shaped with a slightly emarginate apex.

DISTRIBUTION. W Russia and most of Siberia except for the extreme north, east and south-east (east as far as Yakutsk), with isolated stations in S Norway and Finland, south as far as the Tien Shan, N & NW Xinjiang in China and NW Mongolia; to 2000 m (6500 ft). Records in the 'Flora of China' for Gansu, Inner Mongolia and Heilongjiang seem to me to be wholly erroneous; specimens from the former two, at least, would seem to be referable to *C. dianae*.

HABITAT. Rocky woodland (deciduous or coniferous)

and woodland margins, shrubberies and rocky places; May–July.

var. *tianschanica* (**Pavlov**) **M. Johnson*** (syn. *Atragene tianschanica* Pavlov) described from the eastern Tien Shan (Kungei Tau, south of Almaty, on the Kazakstan/Kyrgyzstan frontier) has larger flowers with the sepals 50–60 mm (2–2.4 in) long and staminodes less than one-third their length.

This is a very attractive species in its best and larger-flowered forms. I have been fortunate to see it growing in profusion on steep rocky shrubberies close to Medeo, south of Almaty, where it flowers in May. Both large- and small-flowered forms were present in the same colony, in the same colony, and one has to doubt the validity of the variety *tianschanica*. In all its forms the foliage tends to be a rather pale green. It is very hardy and is known to resist temperatures in the wild in Norway as low as –30°C (–22°F). 'Flavia' has pale yellow flowers which are about 50 mm (2 in) long.

H4; P1

✳ ✳ **Leaves ternate (species 255–258)**
❖   **Sepals prominently keeled on the outside, spurred at the base (species 255)**

255. *Clematis chiisanensis* Nakai*

(syn. *C. alpina* var. *carunculosa* Gagn. ex S. Mottet, *C. chiisanensis* var. *carunculosa* Rehd., *C. koreana* Kom. in part, *C. koreana* var. *carunculosa* (Gagn.) Tamura)

DESCRIPTION. A deciduous climber to 3.5 m (11.5 ft) with ternate leaves. Leaflets ovate to lanceolate, 25–65 mm (1–2.6 in) long, with a few coarse serrate teeth on each side, the apex acute to somewhat acuminate, with petiolules up to 25 mm (1 in) long. Flowers 1–3, nodding, campanulate, with the sepals half spreading, borne on red-violet or purple-flushed pedicels up to 12 cm (4.7 in) long, on both the previous as well as the current season's shoots. Sepals pale lemon-yellow to cream or brownish-orange, sometimes flushed or speckled with purple, narrow-ovate, 30–50 mm (1.2–2 in) long, with an acuminate, slightly recurved, apex and with 3–5 prominent keel-like ridges on the outside, each ending at the base in a short blunt spur. Staminodes white or cream, spatula-shaped, pubescent, about half the length of the sepals. Achenes with a plumose tail 30–40 mm (1.2–1.6 in) long.

DISTRIBUTION. Endemic to South Korea (Chisan region) and the nearby island of Cheju-do; 1300–1900 m (4300–6200 ft).

148. *Clematis chiisanensis* (showing spurs at base of sepals) in cultivation
Photo: Christopher Grey-Wilson

HABITAT. Coniferous or deciduous woodland, generally a mixture of firs, yew, rhododendrons, rowans and various deciduous shrubs; June–July.

Clematis chiisanensis is unaccountably linked with *C. tangutica* in some horticultural publications. Apart from the general flower colour and flower shape, the two could not be more different. Cultivated plants vary somewhat in flower colour. In the best forms the sepals are a clear pale yellow, but seedlings may produce flowers of brownish-yellow or those with a slightly orange hue. The strongly ribbed sepals with their clearly spurred base, coupled with the ternate leaves make this an easy species to identify. Although scarcely as attractive as either *C. alpina* or *C. macropetala*, this Korean species has a certain charm which will endear it to the plantsman. A mature plant can be a most attractive sight in fruit with its large silky seedheads. In gardens it thrives on attention and is not always the easiest to please; a cool humusy soil is to be recommended. The usual form seen in cultivation has pale lemon-yellow flowers with a hint of purplish-red outside towards the base of the strongly ribbed sepals. The flowers are borne on both the previous as well as the current season's stems.

H5; P1

❖ ❖ **Sepals not keeled or spurred (species 256–258)**
❖   **Sepals small, not more than 35 mm (1.4 in) long and 8 mm (0.32 in) wide (species 256)**

256. *Clematis moisseenkoi* Serov

DESCRIPTION. Similar to *C. dianae* but with ternate rather than biternate leaves, the leaflets ovate with a truncated or heart-shaped, rather than rounded, base. In addition, the flowers are about the same size but with pale yellow tepals 25–35 mm (1–1.4 in) long, but only 5–8 mm (0.2–0.32 in) (not 10–17 mm (0.4–0.67 in)) wide. The outer staminodes are more or less petal-like, spoon-shaped and about two-thirds the length of the sepals.

DISTRIBUTION. China: W Xinjiang (Boro Chora).

HABITAT. Rocky and wooded places, shrubberies; June–July.

The relationship of this species to *C. dianae* requires further detailed investigation. Neither species is in cultivation. In addition, they both seem to come close to *C. turkestanica* in general morphology, indeed they overlap in distribution. *C. dianae*, *C. iliensis* and *C. moissenkoi* are placed in their own subsection by Magnus Johnson, the Brachyblasti, due to the fact that the flowers are borne on very reduced shoots on the previous season's growth. However, this character is by no means clearcut in the Atragene Section as a whole and I have not followed this subdivison of Atragene.

❖ ❖ **Sepals larger, more than 35 mm (1.4 in) long and 11 mm (0.2 in) wide (species 257 & 258)**

257. *Clematis iliensis* Y. S. Hou & W. H. Hou*
(syn. *C. sibirica* var. *iliensis* (Y. S. & W. H. Hou) J. G. Liu)

DESCRIPTION. Very similar to *C. dianae* but the leaves are ternate, the leaflets oval, to 70 mm (2.8 in) long and 30 mm (1.2 in) wide. The flowers are larger, 40–70 mm (1.6–2.8 in) across, with yellow sepals 36–50 mm (1.4–2 in) long and 11–30 mm (0.43–1.2 in) wide, while the outer staminodes are only half the length of the sepals and spatula-shaped with a pointed apex.

DISTRIBUTION. China: W Xinjiang (Gong Liu Xian); at about 1600 m (5250 ft).

HABITAT. Forests, particularly of *Picea*, forest margins, streamsides; June–July.

Differs from *C. koreana*, which also has ternate leaves, in its consistently larger yellow flowers, and sparsely hairy stems.

H5; P1

258. *Clematis turkestanica* M. Johnson*

DESCRIPTION. Climber to 3 m (10 ft), occasionally more, with basically ternate leaves, those towards the shoot tips usually sub-biternate, with the end leaflet trilobed and the lateral leaflets usually bilobed. Leaflets narrow-ovate to almost lanceolate, with a truncated or shallow heart-shaped base, to 80 mm (3.2 in) long and 50 mm (2 in) wide, but those of the upper leaves half that size or less, the margin finely serrate; leaves dull green above, shiny and paler beneath. Flowers solitary, borne at the tips of short lateral branches of the previous year on slender pedicels to 15 cm (6 in) long, broadly campanulate, with the sepals spreading widely apart and somewhat recurved at the tip, fragrant. Sepals pale creamy yellow, oblanceolate, 35–40 mm (1.4–1.6 in) long and 17–20 mm (0.67–0.8 in) wide, acute. Staminodes narrow spoon-shaped with an acute or subacute apex, the inner narrower, linear-lanceolate, about half the length of the sepals. Achenes with a plumose tail to 45 mm (1.8 in) long.

DISTRIBUTION. Centred on the Tien Shan, Pamir, NE Hindu Kush and Karakorams (Kazakstan east to Kyrgyzstan and W & N Xinjiang in NW China, south to NE Afghanistan and N Pakistan); 1370–3000 m (4500–9850 ft).

HABITAT. Open coniferous or deciduous woodland; May–June.

It is perhaps surprising that this species was not recognized and described until 1997. The description was based upon material collected in fruit and latter cultivated at the Gothenburg Botanic Garden and collected in 1983 by the Swedish Expedition to Gilgit in northern Pakistan. The plant in question was certainly known before this time but had always been named *C. alpina* subsp. (or var.) *sibirica*, or *C. sibirica*. Specimens were collected as early as 1878 by Dr A. Regel in 'Turkestan', but dried collections from other sources also exist.

The species has a wide and scattered distribution covering the extreme dry western end of the Himalaya and all the mountains to the north and north-east (NE Hindu Kush, Pamir, Tien Shan) eastwards into north-western China.

subsp. *kirgizica* M. Johnson* has sparser leaflets with a rounded to cuneate base, and more narrowly campanulate flowers, while the staminodes are only about one-third the length of the sepals and bear a slight notched apex. The subspecies is restricted to Kyrgyzystan and was described from live material that originated from Moscow Botanic Garden.

H5; P1

Subgenus Seven Tubulosae (The Heracleifolia Group)

This subgenus contains eight species that are either subshrubs or herbaceous perennials and as such they have a special place in the flower garden. They form a distinctive group within *Clematis* with their pronouncedly tubular flowers, with only the tips of the sepals spreading apart. The flowers are borne on the shoots of the current year, generally in the late summer and autumn. They are native primarily to northern China, Mongolia, and Japan. Although they appear to cross readily with one another, few hybrids with species outside the subgenus have been recorded. On the other hand, few crosses outside the subgenus have probably been tried.

▼   **Flowers solitary and terminal, borne on long slender stalks (species 259)**

259. *Clematis tsugetorum* Ohwi

DESCRIPTION. Readily distinguished from the other species in Subgenus *Tubulosae* by its often pinnate (with 5 leaflets), or ternate leaves with small leaflets which are only 25–40 mm (1–1.6 in) long and 25–35 mm (1–1.4 in) wide and by the flowers which are solitary and terminal, borne on longer, slender stalks. The leaves are rather variable from simple to ternate or pinnate (with 5 leaflets). The sepals are bluish to purple, narrow-oblong, 10–20 mm (0.4–0.8 in) long and 3–7 mm (0.12–0.28 in) wide; anthers c. 2.5 mm (0.1 in) long.

DISTRIBUTION. N Taiwan; 3400–3600 m (11,150–11,800 ft).

MAP TWELVE
Subgenus *Tubulosae*   – – – – – – – –
Subgenus Archiclematis   • • • • • • • • • • •

149. Clematis heracleifolia form in cultivation. Photo: Christopher Grey-Wilson

HABITAT. Open forests, particularly of *Tsuga formosana*, and hill-slopes, over limestone; July–Sept.

A very distinctive member of the *Tubulosae* but scarcely of great garden value. A curiosity for the clematis connoisseur.

▼ ▼ **Flowers in long- or short-stalked clusters at the nodes (species 260–266)**
◆ **Leaves pinnate, occasionally biternate (species 260)**

260. *Clematis tatarinowii* Maxim.
(syn. *C. pinnata* Maxim. var. *tatarinowii* (Maxim.) Kuntze)

DESCRIPTION. Similar to *C. heracleifolia* but leaves pinnate to biternate, the leaflets not larger than 100 mm (4 in) long and 78 mm (3.1 in) wide; bracts linear-lanceolate to rhombic, simple to 3-lobed, only 3–4 mm (0.12–0.16 in) long. In addition, the flowers are smaller, the sepals oblong-obovate, 11–16 mm (0.43–0.63 in) long and 4–5 mm (0.16–0.2 in) wide and the anthers 2–3 mm (0.08–0.12 in) long.

DISTRIBUTION. NE China (Hebei, N Shaanxi, environs of Beijing).

HABITAT. Bushy places and stony slopes, open woodland; July–Sept.

◆ ◆ **Leaves ternate (species 261–266)**
✳ **Flowers nodding or half-nodding, long-stalked (species 261–265)**
✳ **Flowers in lax whorls at the upper nodes (species 261–263)**

261. *Clematis heracleifolia* DC.*
(syn. *C. heracleifolia* subsp. *normalis* (incl. var. *tubulosa* Kuntze & var. *maxima* Kuntze), *C. h.* var. *hookeri* Makino and var. *ichangensis* Rehd. & Wils., *C. hookeri* Decne., *C. tubulosa* Turcz., *C. t.* var. *hookeri* (Decne.) Hk .f.)

DESCRIPTION. A patch-forming subshrub to 1 m (40 in), often 30–60 cm (12–24 in), with erect simple or somewhat branched, ribbed stems, brownish-red or brownish-violet, downy when young, sometimes partly herbaceous, but generally woody in the lower third. Leaves ternate, dark green, long-stalked, with the end leaflet larger than the lateral; end leaflet rounded to ovate with a somewhat truncated or heart-shaped base, 8–16 cm (3.2–6.3 in) long and wide, often somewhat lobed, finely appressed-pubescent on both surfaces, with a bristle-toothed margin and a long petiolule, the lateral leaflets half the size and with a very short petiolule. Flowers fragrant or not, 15–20 mm (0.6–0.8 in) across, nodding to half-nodding, borne in a terminal branched inflorescence composed of a number of flower clusters (mainly 3–5-flowered whorl-like cymes), unisexual but usually with male and female flowers on the same plant (monoecious), hyacinth-shaped, to 25 mm (1 in) long, downy outside. Sepals 4, deep blue or violet-blue, occasionally mauve or pink, narrow oblong, 15–30 mm (0.6–1.2 in) long and 3–7 mm (0.12–0.28 in) wide, somewhat expanded and frilled at the apex, strongly recurved in the upper third, but forming a close tube below which is slightly swollen at the base, unscented. Stamens almost reaching the mouth of the sepal-tube, the anthers 3.2–5 mm (0.13–0.2 in) long. Achenes elliptic, 3–5 mm (0.12–0.2 in) long, hairy, with a short plumose tail to 25 mm (1 in) long.

DISTRIBUTION. C & E China (Shaanxi, Hubei and Hubei eastwards to Zhejiang and Shandong and north-eastwards to Jilin and Liaoning, including S Inner Mongolia); to 2000 m (6500 ft).

HABITAT. Scrub, bushy slopes, forest margins; July–early Oct.

This widely cultivated species, often referred to as the 'Hyacinth-flowered Clematis', is well known to gardeners and can provide a notable feature in the flower border, or the shrub border, during the late summer and autumn. In addition, the invasive fragrance attracts late butterflies into the garden. The species was introduced into cultivation in 1837. The robust leafy stems are semi-herbaceous and die back to a woody base that can become quite substantial in time, although in severe winters the plant may be cut to ground level; however, in such instances it will sprout from below the ground once warmer weather returns.

Seed-raised plants, especially those of wild origin, often produce rather inferior forms than those long-established in gardens. On the whole pale-leaved seedlings produce pale flowers and the darker leaved seedlings the deeper coloured finer forms. It is an excellent plant for the flower border, although some will no doubt find it too coarse and leafy, mixing well with many different herbaceous plants, but equally effective in a shrubbery. A well-flowered specimen is worth waiting for and the flowering stems cut rather well, if sufficient quantities can be produced.

'Fulton's Variety'* rarely grows more than 30 cm (12 in) tall and bears rather larger deep hyacinth-blue flowers. Var. *ichangensis* Rehd. & Wils. from western China, is sometimes distinguished on account of its leaves which have a more rounded base and are densely downy beneath, and the flowers which are silvery-hairy on the outside, whilst dark blue within.

H3; P2

262. *Clematis psilandra* Kitagawa*
(syn. *C. heracleifolia* var. *taiwanica* Suzuki & T. Hosokawa)

DESCRIPTION. Similar to *C. heracleifolia*, but leaflets glabrous above and bracts entire, triangular, silky-pubescent like the flower-stalks, only 3–6 mm (0.12–0.24 in) long (not 3-lobed or toothed), while the flowers smaller and pinker, the sepals 14–20 mm (0.55–0.8 in) long and 4–10 mm (0.16–0.4 in) wide, silky with hairs on the outside. In addition, the leaves are generally smaller, rarely being more than 80 mm (3.2 in) long and generally only 40–50 mm (1.6–2 in).

DISTRIBUTION. S Taiwan; 1000–2500 m (3300–8200 ft).

HABITAT. Open slopes; July–Sept.

H4; P2

263. *Clematis urticifolia* (Nakai) Kitagawa
(syn. *C. heracleifolia* var. *tubulosa* Turcz, *C. tubulosa* sensu Nakai, non Turcz.)

DESCRIPTION. Close to *C. heracleifolia*, but distinguished by being a generally larger plant, to 2 m (6.6 ft) sometimes, and by its distinctive urn-shaped flowers, with broader, markedly 3-ribbed blue sepals. The flowers have a bulbous tube and rather short recurved lobes.

DISTRIBUTION. South Korea.

HABITAT. Open mixed woodland and shrubberies; Aug–Oct.

forma *rosea* (Nakai) Nakai (syn. *C. tubulosa* var. *rosea* Nakai, *C. urticifolia* var. *carnea* Nakai) has rose-pink flowers.

✳✳ Flowers in clusters at branch tips (species 264 & 265)

264. *Clematis stans* Sieb. & Zucc.*
(syn. *C. heracleifolia* DC. subsp. *lavallei* Kuntze (incl. var. *lanceolata* Kuntze & var. *kousabotan* Kuntze), *C. h.* var. *savatieri* Kuntze, *C. h.* subsp. *stans* Kuntze (incl. var. *decaisneana* Kuntze, var. *maximowicziana* Kuntze and var. *savaterioides* Kuntze), *C. heracleifolia* sensu Huth, non DC., *C. h.* DC. var. *lavallei* Decne ex Huth, *C. kousabotan* Decne., *C. lavallei* Decne., *C. l.* var. *foliosa* Decne., *C. savatieri* Decne., *C. stans* var. *monoica* Lav., *C. s.* var. *typica* Schneid. (incl. var. *kousabotan* Schneid. & var. *lavallei* Schneid.), *C. maximowiczii* Decne. ex Rehd. & Wils.)

DESCRIPTION. A deciduous subshrub, sometimes with scandent stems to 2 m (6.6 ft) long, tending to die back almost to the base in the winter; stems 6-ribbed, downy when young. Leaves ternate; leaflets ovate to almost triangular, 5–15 cm (2–6 in) long and almost as wide, the terminal one usually 3–5-lobed, the outer unlobed or somewhat 3-lobed, but all coarsely and unevenly toothed, and with prominent veins. Flowers fragrant, borne on branched stalks (peduncles to 25 cm (10 in) long), in whorls from the axils of small leaf-like bracts (to 10 mm (0.4 in) long, ternate or 3-lobed to entire); each flower to 10–20 mm (0.4–0.8 in) long, narrow tubular-bell shaped like those of the hyacinth, male or female on the same or on different plants. Sepals whitish to pale lavender-blue, obovate, 13–25 mm (0.5–1 in) long and to 5 mm (0.2 in) wide, with a strongly recurved, acute tip, downy outside. Stamens about half the length of the sepals. Achenes downy,

150. *Clematis tubulosa* in cultivation. Photo: Raymond Evison

151. *Clematis* 'Crépuscule' (*C. tubulosa* x *C. stans*). Photo: Christopher Grey-Wilson

with a plumose tail to 30 mm (1.2 in) long.
DISTRIBUTION. Japan (Honshu).

HABITAT. Open grassy places and scrub; July–Sept.

This species is closely related to *C. heracleifolia* but it can be distinguished on account of its laxer more scandent habit, more downy stems and distinctly smaller and narrower paler flowers. It was introduced to France from Japan by Von Siebold round about 1860 and has been in cultivation ever since, although it has never been as popular as its cousin. The form often distinguished under the cultivar name 'Lavallei' (more correctly var. *lavallei* Decne ex Huth) is exceptionally vigorous monoecious plant with gardenia-scented flowers, but it fits well within the general variation found within the species.

In gardens, *C. stans* scarcely has the impact of its brighter-coloured cousin *C. heracleifolia*, but it is pretty enough and the flowers, which are often produced in profusion, are followed by attractive seedheads. Christopher Lloyd dismisses it as 'carrying flowers of a spiteful non-contributory off-white, skimmed-milk colouring' which will successfully put off all potential growers. He should, I cry, try 'Lavallei' for even if the posture and colour were dismissed the scent would surely seduce him.

var. *austrojaponensis* **(Ohwi) Ohwi** (syn. *C. austrojaponensis* Ohwi) differs in its smaller anthers that are only 3 mm (0.12 in) long, not 4–7 mm (0.16–0.28 in). A southerly distributed variety that is restricted to the islands of Kyushu and Shikoku.

H4; P2

265. *Clematis speciosa* Makino
(syn. *C. heracleifolia* var. *speciosa* Makino, *C. tubulosa* sensu Koidz., non Turcz.)

DESCRIPTION. Similar to *C. stans* but the leaves generally rather narrower and regularly toothed. In addition, the stamens are only one-third the length of the sepals, the anthers c. 3 mm (0.12 in) long (not 4–7 mm (0.16–0.28 in)).

DISTRIBUTION. S Japan (E Kyushu & W Shikoku).

❀ ❀ **Flowers ascending to erect, sessile or almost so (species 266)**

266. *Clematis tubulosa* Turcz.*
(syn. *C. davidiana* Decaisne ex Verlot, *C. davidiana* sensu Schneider ex Nakai, *C. heracleifolia* sensu Finet

& Gagn., non DC., *C. heracleifolia* DC. var. *davidiana* Kuntze, var. *davidiana* Decne ex Nakai, var. *davidiana* (Verlot) Hemsl. and var. *tubulosa* Turcz., *C. tubulosa* Turcz. var. *davidiana* Franch.)

DESCRIPTION. A herbaceous perennial or subshrub to 1.5 m (5 ft), though often less, dioecious. Leaves ternate with elliptical to oval leaflets, each up to 20 cm (8 in) long and 12 cm (4.7 in) wide, the terminal leaflets somewhat larger than the lateral, the margin evenly toothed and often slightly lobed. Flowers borne in tight clusters at the upper nodes, ascending to erect, 20–35 mm (0.8–1.4 in) across, very fragrant. Sepals 4, blue, narrow in the lower 'tubular' third, but expanding widely and spreading towards the apex, to 28 mm (1.1 in) long and 13 mm (0.5 in) wide overall. Stamens under half the length of the sepals, to 13 mm (0.5 in) long, the anthers twice the length of the filaments in the male flowers.

DISTRIBUTION. NW China (Shanxi to Liaoning) eastwards to North Korea.

HABITAT. Similar to *C. heracleifolia*, although the two species only overlap in distribution in the west of the range of *C. tubulosa*; July–Sept.
A much confused and misunderstood species which is often absorbed without comment into *C. heracleifolia*. In fact the majority of plants grown in gardens, especially under cultivar names are referable to *C. tubulosa* and not *C. heracleifolia*. *C. tubulosa* is the so-called 'Hyacinth-flowered Clematis'. It looks very different to *C. heracleifolia* with its large upright flowers that are bunched together at the nodes. Contrast the airy sprays of *C. heracleifolia* with its narrow, nodding or half-nodding flowers. Fundamental differences can be also observed in the flower structure, in the short stamens of *C. tubulosa* and by the fact that the male and female flowers are borne on different plants; in *C. heracleifolia* they are borne on the same plant.

The plant widely grown as *C. heracleifolia* var. *davidiana* (Verlot) Hemsl. is wholly herbaceous with thicker, more leathery leaves, and pale blue, very fragrant (described by Christopher Lloyd as 'hair-oil scent') flowers, opening widely to 40 mm (1.6 in) across. It represents little more than a herbaceous form of *C. tubulosa* and is difficult to distinguish on any other botanical features. Introduced into cultivation from north-eastern China in 1863 by Père David from the environs of Peking (now Beijing), this plant has been popular ever since. Its attractive powder-blue flowers have a scent reminiscent of hyacinths. Var. *davidiana* is an excellent subject for the flower border,

especially with other herbaceous perennials. It is patch-forming, spreading by means of underground rhizomes that make propagation a fairly simple task. Interestingly, the foliage is also scented when it dries in the autumn. 'Wyevale'* AGM is similar but has darker blue, equally fragrant, flowers; this cultivar dates back to the 1950s and was given an Award of Merit (AM) when exhibited at the Royal Horticultural Society in September 1976.

The flowers of *C. tubulosa* are much loved by butterflies, no doubt attracted to the plants by the strong fragrance that pervades the flower border in the late summer.

Clematis tubulosa has been involved with other species in Subgenus Tubulosae to produce some very interesting garden hybrids. Of these the finest are: 'Bryzgi Morja'*, 'Chance' and *C.* x *jouiniana** (all *C. tubulosa* × *C. vitalba*). Of these the latter is best known and more widely available. 'Bryzgi Morja' has almost the same vigour as the previous. 'Chance' is more like *C. tubulosa* in size and habit and with pleasing lavender-violet flowers 30 mm (1.2 in) across.

'Campanile'* (*C. tubulosa* × *C. stans*) is subshrubby like its parents, to 1.5 m (5 ft), bearing hermaphrodite mid-blue flowers that are densely clustered on the upper stems.

'Côte d'Azur'* is very similar to 'Campanile' and 'Praecox' (both *C. tubulosa* × 'Jouiniana'). The latter is very similar to 'Jouiniana' but comes into flower a full six weeks earlier.

'Crépuscule'* (*C. tubulosa* × *C. stans*) is not unlike *C. tubulosa* but is a more compact plant with smoother leaves. Often listed as 'Bonstedtii Crépuscule' which presumably is the same thing.

'Edward Pritchard'* (*C. tubulosa* var. *davidiana* × *C. recta*) is of Australian origin and is a thin-stemmed herbaceous plant to 1 m (40 in), occasionally more, with pinnate leaves each with 5 leaflets, bearing clusters of pale mauve, attractively scented, flowers, (30–40 mm (1.2–1.6 in) across) in the late summer and autumn. It is of less robust constitution and requires careful placing in the flower garden if it is to do its best.

'Mrs Robert Brydon'* (*C. tubulosa* × *C. virginiana*) is a rather ungainly scrambling plant to 3 m (10 ft), with coarse ternate leaves and clusters of 30 mm (1.2 in) bluish-white untubed flowers with prominent white stamens, borne from mid-summer until the late autumn; the sepals spread widely and curl back characteristically at the tips. It is not self-supporting and is best when tied to a support, but it can be attractive in full flower and the bees and butterflies

152. *Clematis* 'Mrs Robert Brydon' (*C. tubulosa* x *C. virginiana*)
Photo: Christopher Grey-Wilson

153. *Clematis* x *jouiniana* (*C. tubulosa* x *C. vitalba*).
Photo: Christopher Grey-Wilson

seem addicted to it. It is usually listed incorrectly as *C. × jouiniana* Hort. 'Mrs Robert Brydon'; this hybrid is a cross between *C. tubulosa* and *C. vitalba* and does not, to my knowledge at least, have a Latin name. Although the plant generally lacks quality and the flowers are often described as dull or dingy, it can look effective when sprawled over a wall where it has no distractors.

This brings me to *C. × jouiniana* Hort.* (syn. *C.* 'Jouiniana') named after E. Join who was manager of the Simon-Louis nurseries at Metz. It is an interesting hybrid as it involves *C. tubulosa* and our own native *C. vitalba* (in fact the only hybrid involving this latter species). The plant is vigorous and non-climbing with a woody base to a metre from which the stems arise and die back to annually. They may reach 2–3 m (6.6–10 ft) and bear numerous coarse and not particularly attractive pinnate leaves of a very average clematis green. What makes this an exciting plant are

the large garlands of small (25–30 mm (1–1.2 in)) near-white flowers which are flushed with violet on the outside, the 4 sepals spreading widely apart. The flowers have a very faint scent that at least the bees and butterflies seem to appreciate. This plant requires plenty of space and can look equally effective fixed to a wall (it has to be tied in as it cannot climb, although it will scramble up and between wires) or attached to a pillar at the back of a herbaceous border. It can also be used as ground cover. Like many of the more vigorous clematis, this is a greedy plant requiring a rich soil, with plenty of feeds and mulches, if it is to do its best. In the typical plant the flowers are borne in late summer (late August) and autumn but in 'Praecox' the flowers first appear in July and continue on into early autumn.

H4; P2

Subgenus Eight Pseudanemone (The Clematopsis Group)

For a discussion of the genus *Clematopsis* see p.21. The members of Subgenus *Pseudoanemone* are erect subshrubs without climbing stems and this makes them look very different to all the other clematis species in Africa, which are vigorous climbers. This habit combined with the imbricate nature of the sepals clearly convinced early authors that the species involved should be treated as a separate genus. However, the habit of the species involved is not unique. Outside Africa there are quite a few herbaceous and subshrubby non-climbers as well, e.g. *C. heracelifolia, C. integrifolia, C. recta, C. stans* and *C. fremontii* for instance. Neither is the imbricate nature of the sepals a unique feature and it is to be found in the New Zealand species, several Australian ones as well as the Japanese *C. williamsii*, all of which are climbers. Despite this, the species of Subgenus Pseudoanemone do form a distinctive group of species restricted to Africa and Madagascar and they cannot be confused with any others in the genus *Clematis*. They are delightful plants little known in gardens. If they were hardier (they are all frost-tender as far as it is known) they would undoubtedly make highly desirable plants for the flower garden with their elegant nodding relatively large flowers. Several (notably various forms of *C. villosa*) have been crossed with different species of climbing clematis in recent years, but the results are as yet uncertain. If a hardier race of non-climbing hybrids could be produced, then a whole new range of possibilities in the production of garden clematis would certainly result.

The members of this section would undoubtedly make fine plants for Mediterranean gardens and would also do well in those subtropical gardens which have a marked dry season. In the wild they come into flower late in the year and in the new year during the wet season, while the fruits ripen several months later during the prolonged dry season.

MAP THIRTEEN
Subgenus *Pseudanemone* – – – – – – – –

154. *Clematis uhehensis* Rungwe Mts., S. Tanzania.
Photo: Christopher Grey-Wilson

▼ **Species with undivided, unlobed or slightly lobed leaves; see also *C. homblei*, species 274, which can have simple as well as pinnate leaves, but the simple leaves are usually deeply lobed (species 267–270)**

◆ **Anthers 4–5 mm (0.16–0.2 in) long (species 267)**

267. *Clematis uhehensis* Engl.
(syn. *Clematis villosa* subsp. *uhehensis* (Engl.) Brummitt; *Clematopsis scabiosifolia* subsp. *uhehensis* (Engl.) Brummitt, *C. simplicifolia* Hutch. & Summerh., *C. uhehensis* (Engl.) Hutch. ex Staner & Léonard, *C. villosa* subsp. *uhehensis* (Engl.) J. Raynal & Brummitt)

DESCRIPTION. A subshrub with erect stems to 0.9 m (3 ft), often only half that height, with strongly ribbed stems which are densely hairy (villous). Leaves simple, ovate, to 90 mm (3.5 in) long and 55 mm (2.2 in) wide, sessile or almost so, the upper smaller than the lower, the margin coarsely and irregularly toothed, occasionally somewhat lobed, with scattered hairs on both sides, especially on the veins beneath. Flowers usually solitary and nodding, 65–120 mm (2.2–4.7 in) across, campanulate. Sepals usually 4, white flushed with rose, mauve or lilac on the reverse, oval to almost rounded, to 32–58 mm (1.3–2.3 in) long and 30–50 mm (1.2–2 in) wide, with an acute to somewhat acuminate apex, softly hairy all over. Stamens about one-third the length of the sepals, the anthers 4–5 mm (0.16–0.2 in) long.

DISTRIBUTION. Malawi & N Mozambique to S Tanzania & E Zambia; 1800–2800 m (5900–9200 ft).
HABITAT. Upland grassland and open woodland; Dec–Apr.

On the Kitulo Plateau in southern Tanzania, where I have observed this species growing in large scattered colonies, the plants are quite uniform in appearance, especially in the leaf and flower characters, although the plants can vary quite a lot in height. However, reports from the those who have observed it on the Nyika Plateau further south in Malawi, indicate that it often grows in association with different forms of *C. villosa* and that intermediate stages between the two species are readily observable. These may represent hybrids or introgressions of some sort. Clearly this requires further detailed fieldwork and analysis.

◆ ◆ **Anthers 6–8 mm (0.24–0.32 in) long (species 268–270)**

268. *Clematis grandifolia* (Stanner & Léonard) M. Johnson
(syn. *Clematopsis grandifolia* Staner & Léonard)

DESCRIPTION. Very similar to *C. uhehensis*, but the leaves are generally larger, 11–16 cm (4.3–6.3 in) long and 4.5–9 cm (1.8–3.5 in) wide, sparsely hairy to practically glabrous, and with a regularly toothed (dentate) margin, rather than with fewer irregular teeth. In addition, the leaf base is often half-clasping (semi-amplexicaule) the stem. The solitary flowers are relatively small, the sepals 25–30 mm (1–1.2 in) long and 18–20 mm (0.7–0.8 in) wide.

DISTRIBUTION. Zaire (Katanga).

HABITAT. Grassy savannah and bushy places or open woodland; Dec–Feb.

269. *Clematis spathulifolia* (Kuntze) Prantl
(syn. *Clematis villosa* subsp. *spathulifolia* Kuntze; *Clematopsis spathulifolia* (Kuntze) Staner & Léonard)

DESCRIPTION. Similar to *C. uhehensis* but the leaves tend to be obovate with a distinctly cuneate (wedge-shaped) base and a coarsely toothed margin, to 10 cm (4 in) long and 4 cm (1.6 in) wide, subglabrous. The flower details are unknown.

DISTRIBUTION. S Zaire (between the Kasai and Kwango rivers).

HABITAT. Bushy savannah.

270. *Clematis teuczii* (Kuntze) Engler
(syn. *C. villosa* subsp. *spathulifolia* var. *teuczii* Kuntze, *C. spathulifolia* var. *teuczii* (Kuntze) Th. Durand & Schinz; *Clematopsis speciosa* Hutch., *C. teuczii* (Kuntze) Hutch.)

DESCRIPTION. Similar in general appearance to *C. uhehensis*, but the leaves are distinctly rough (scabrid), not smooth, to the touch and the achenes are noticeably narrowly winged along the margin. The leaflets are narrow fan-shaped with a wedge-shaped lower half and a toothed upper half. A form in which the leaves are whorled in fours has been described as forma *verticillata* Kuntze, but this feature is common to many of the specimens observed.

DISTRIBUTION. N & W Angola.

HABITAT. Bushy savannah.

Clematis angolana M. Johnson (syn. *Clematopsis speciosa* Hutch.; not to be confused with *Clematis speciosa* Makino) described from Angola is doubtfully distinct. The leaves are similar in size and shape to *C. uhehensis*, but the flowers can be very large, to 15 cm (6 in) across, the sepals to 70 mm (2.8 in) long and 30 mm (1.2 in) wide. In addition, the anthers are about 8 mm (0.32 in) long.

▼▼ **Species with divided (pinnate) leaves (species 271–274)**
❈ **Anthers 3–5 mm (0.12–0.2 in) long; flowers usually numerous, in broad branched cymes (species 271)**

271. *Clematis villosa* DC.*
(syn. *C. scabiosifolia* DC., *C. villosa* subsp. *scabiosifolia* (DC.) Hutch., *C. v.* var. *scabiosifolia* (DC.) Hiern; *Clematopsis scabiosifolia* (DC.) Hutch., *C. villosa* (DC.) Hutch.)

DESCRIPTION. An erect subshrub to 1.5 m (5 ft) though often shorter, sometimes only 0.5 m (20 in), with ribbed stems that are usually silky-hairy, although sometimes almost glabrous. Leaves pinnate to bipinnate, occasionally ternate, the leaflets variable from narrow- lanceolate to lanceolate or ovate, sometimes 3-lobed, usually rather coarsely toothed. Flowers nodding to half-nodding, generally several in a branched bracteate inflorescence, rarely solitary, 35–70 mm (1.4–2.8 in) across, sweetly scented. Sepals 4, occasionally 5–6, variable in colour from white to cream, pale pink, mauve or lilac, elliptical to oval, 17–40 mm (0.67–1.6 in) long and 10–25 mm (0.4–1 in) wide, spreading widely apart, softly hairy all over. Stamens a half to two-thirds the length of the sepals, the anthers c. 5 mm (0.2 in) long. Achenes oval, 5–10 mm (0.2–0.4 in) long, hairy, with a plumose tail to 50 mm (2 in) long, borne in heads up to 10 cm (4 in) across.

DISTRIBUTION. Angola, E Tanzania, E Uganda, Zaire, Zambia; 1000–2300 m (3300–7550 ft).

HABITAT. Primarily upland grassland and *Brachystegia* woodland; Nov–Apr.

In its best forms this is a highly desirable plant, bearing stiff stems carrying many flowers which, in those I have seen in the wild, are nearly always white or cream. Plants are occasionally offered in the horticultural trade under the name *Clematopsis scabiosifolia* but it is scarcely at all seen in gardens.

subsp. *kirkii* (Oliv.) Brummitt (syn. *C. kirkii* Oliv., *C. scabiosifolia* DC. Group C sensu Exell, Léonard & Milne-Redhead, *C. villosa* subsp. *normalis* var. *kirkii* (Oliv.) Kuntze; *Clematopsis costata* Weimarck, *C. kirkii* (Oliv.) Hutch., *C. kirkii* sensu Weimarck, *C. scabiosifolia* (DC.) Hutch. subsp. *kirkii* (Oliv.) Brummitt, *C. villosa* subsp. *kirkii* (Oliv.) Raynal & Brummitt) is like subsp. *oliveri*, but stems with many flowers and leaves with rounded segments, with the hairs confined mainly to the veins. The flowers are rather small, 35–50 mm (1.4–2 in) across, occasionally larger, generally with 4 sepals, and the anthers are 4–5 mm (0.16–0.2 in) long. Distributed in Malawi, Mozambique, S Tanzania and the neighbouring parts of Zaire.
   Clematis stuhlmannii Hieron. (syn. *Clematopsis scabiosifolia* DC., *C. scabiosifolia* DC. Group C sensu Exell, Léonard & Milne-Redhead, *C. stuhlmannii* (Hieron.) Hutch.) described from Tanzania (Kagehi) is almost certainly another manifestation of this subspecies with more densely hairy, almost silky leaflets, with the hairs practically concealing most of the veins, especially on the undersurface of the leaf. Uganda and Tanzania (not Zanzibar) to Zimbabwe and Angola.
   Likewise *C. goetzii* Engl., described from Tanzania (Uhehe) is probably conspecific with *C. villosa* subsp. *kirkii*, differing primarily in its long-acuminate sepals.
   Clematis argentea (Kuntze) Durand & Schinz (syn. *C. villosa* subsp. *argentea* Welw. ex Kuntze, *C. villosa* var. *argentea* forma *acutiloba* Welw. ex Hiern.; *Clematopsis argentea* (Kuntze) Hutch., *C. argentea* (Welw.) Hutch., *C. scabiosifolia* DC. Group E sensu Exell, Léonard & Milne-Redhead) is very similar to *C. stuhlmannii* in the silky nature of its leaves, but the leaflets are narrow-elliptic, rather than suborbicular, certainly more than 3 times longer than broad. It was described from Angola.

subsp. *oliveri* (Hutch.) M. Johnson (syn. *Clematis chrysocarpa* var. *stipulata* (Kuntze) Dur. & Schinz, *C. oliveri* (Hutch.) M. Johnson, *C. villosa* subsp. *chrysocarpa* var. *stipulata* Kuntze; *Clematopsis lineariloba* Hutch. & Summerh., *C. nigerica* Hutch., *C. oliveri* Hutch., *C. o.* forma *lineariloba* (Hutch. &

155. *Clematis villosa* subsp. *oliveri*, Dedza Mt, S Tanzania.
Photo: Christopher Grey-Wilson

Summerh.) Stanner & Léonard, *C. scabiosifolia*
(DC.) Hutch. subsp. *oliveri* (Hutch.) Brummitt, *C. s.*
Group D of Exell, Léonard & Milne-Redhead, *C.
villosa* subsp. *oliveri* (Hutch.) J. Raynal &
Brummitt) has pinnate leaves with broad segments
which are not more than 3 times longer than broad
and the flowers are often solitary, or 2–3 per stem.
Distributed from Nigeria to Cameroon, Zaire, S
Sudan, Burundi, Uganda, Kenya, Tanzania (not
Zanzibar) & N Malawi.

subsp. *stanleyi* (Hook.) Kuntze* (syn. *Clematis busseana*
Engl., *C. lugnigu* De Wild., *C. stanleyi* Hook., *C. s.* var.
hirsuta (Kuntze) Durand & Schinz, var. *pubescens* (Kuntze)
Th. Durand & Schinz, & var. *tomentosa* (Kuntze) Durand
& Schinz, *C. villosa* subsp. *stanleyi* (Hook.) Kuntze, *C. v.*
subsp. *schinziana* Kuntze, *C. v.* subsp. *s.* var. *hirsuta*
Kuntze, & var. *tomentosa* Kuntze; *Clematopsis pulchra*
Weimarck, *C. scabiosifolia* (DC.) Hutch. subsp. *stanleyi*
(Hook.) Brummitt, *C. s.* Group A & B of Exell, Léonard &
Milne-Redhead, *C. stanleyi* (Hook.) Hutch., *C. villosa*
subsp. *stanleyi* (Hook.) Raynal & Brummitt) has bipinnate,
occasionally pinnate, leaves with narrow linear to narrow-
elliptical segments, often 5 times longer than wide, or more.
The flowers are 35–60 mm (1.4–2.4 in) across, with small
3–4 mm (0.12–0.16 in) long anthers. Distributed from S
Angola & E Namibia to S Zaire, Zambia, Zimbabwe, S
Tanzania, Botswana and South Africa (Transvaal).
Occasionally cultivated as a conservatory plant, but far
from common and only occasionally available.

H10; P2

❇❇   **Anthers 5–9 mm (0.2–0.35 in) long; flowers often
solitary or few (species 272–274)**
❇   **Achenes covered in golden-brown hairs (species 272)**

272. *Clematis chrysocarpa* Welw. ex Oliver
(syn. *C. villosa* subsp. *chrysocarpa* (Welw. ex Oliv.)
Kuntze, *C. v.* subsp. *c.* var. *angolensis* (Kuntze) Th.
Durand & Schinz, *C. v.* subsp. *c.* var. *angolensis*
Kuntze and var. *stipulata* Kuntze; *Clematopsis
chrysocarpa* (Welw. ex Oliv.) Hutch.)

DESCRIPTION. A subshrub to 80 cm (32 in) tall with erect,
ribbed and silky-hairy stems. Leaves pinnate (with up to 7
primary divisions) to ternate, the leaflets narrow-oval to
lanceolate, to 60 mm (2.4 in) long and 20 mm (0.8 in)
wide, the margin toothed to entire, thinly hairy on both
surfaces. The flowers are solitary and nodding to half-
nodding, 50–70 mm (2–2.8 in) across, white, borne on
peduncles up to 40 cm (16 in) long. Sepals 4 (–6), elliptical,
to 30 mm (1.2 in) long and 20 mm (0.8 in) wide, spreading,
softly hairy all over. The stamens are about two-thirds the
length of the sepals, the anthers 5–9 mm (0.2–0.35 in) long.
Achenes c. 8 mm (0.32 in) long, adorned, like the c. 60 mm
(2.4 in) long plumose tail, with golden-brown hairs.

DISTRIBUTION. Angola, Malawi, N Mozambique,
S Tanzania, S Zaire, Zambia.

HABITAT. Upland grassland and bushy places; Dec–Apr.

The golden-brown achene hairs are very distinctive
and serve to distinguish this species from the others
in Subgenus *Pseudoanemone*.

❇❇   **Achenes not covered in golden-brown hairs, the
hairs whitish or greyish usually (species 273 & 274)**
❖   **Leaves more or less triangular in outline with 3 or
more primary divisions; leaflets long-petioluled;
Madagascan plants (species 273)**

273. *Clematis bojeri* Hook.
(syn. *C. pimpinellifolia* Hook., *C. villosa* subsp.
emirnensis Kuntze, *C. villosa* subsp. *normalis* var. *bojeri*
(Hook.) Kuntze, *C. villosa* subsp. *oligophylla* var.
hildebrandtii Kuntze, *C. villosa* subsp. *pimpinellifolia*
(Hook.) Kuntze, *C. villosa* subsp. *stanleyi* var. *hirsuta*
Kuntze, *C. villosa* subsp. *trifida* (Hook.) Kuntze;
Clematopsis bojeri (Hook.) J. Raynal, *C. pimpinellifolia*
(Hook.) Hutch., *C. trifida* Hook.)

DESCRIPTION. A subshrub with erect to spreading stems
to 45 cm (18 in), occasionally more, ridged and hairy.
Leaves pinnate, occasionally ternate, stalked, mid- to
deep green on both sides, the uppermost pair often

subentire and coloured like the sepals. Leaflets usually 5, occasionally 3, ovate to broad-elliptical, sharply toothed to deeply lobed, slightly hairy to almost glabrous. Flowers nodding, 40–50 mm (1.6–2 in) across, often 3–9 at the branched stem tips, occasionally solitary, scented. Sepals 4, occasionally 5 or 6, white, lanceolate, with an acute or somewhat acuminate apex, softly hairy all over. Stamens about one-third the length of the sepals. Achenes hairy with a plumose tail to 50 mm (2 in) long.

DISTRIBUTION. C & CE Madagascar (Antananarivo to Andringitra).

HABITAT. Dry grassy and rocky places, generally on calcareous soils; Oct–Jan.

var. *anethifolia* (Hook.) M. Johnson (syn. *C. anethifolia* Hook., *C. villosa* subsp. *anethifolia* (Hook.) Kuntze; *Clematopsis anethifolia* (Hook.) Bojer ex Hutch., *C. bojeri* var. *anethifolia* (Hook.) J. Raynal) is readily distinguished by its finely cut much dissected bi- or tripinnate foliage reminiscent of Dill (*Anethrum*), with numerous linear, thread-like, segments, and by its long-stalked flowers, the pedicels up to 40 cm (16 in) long. Distributed in C & CE Madagascar (Ankaratra massif to Andringitra). This variety overlaps with the typical plant, var. *bojeri* and var. *oligophylla* over much of its range, but only with var. *macrophylla* in the south.

var. *macrophylla* (J. Raynal) M. Johnson (syn. *Clematopsis bojeri* var. *macrophylla* J. Raynal) has ternate leaves with broad ovate to lanceolate, shallowly and rather regularly toothed, but not markedly lobed, leaflets. Only found in a few localities in the south of the range of the species (Andrinitra at 1800–2000 m (5900–6500 ft)).

var. *oligophylla* (Hook.) M. Johnson (syn. *C. oligophylla* Hook., *C. villosa* subsp. *bakeri* Kuntze and subsp. *olighophylla* (Hook.) Kuntze; *Clematopsis bojeri* var. *oligophylla* (Hook.) Raynal, *C. oligophylla* (Hook.) Hutch.) has pinnate to bipinnate with small narrow-elliptical incisely-lobed and toothed segments; all the leaves are equally green. Almost throughout the range of the species except for the south (Ankaratra massif primarily).

var. *pseudoscabiosifolia* (H. Perrier) M. Johnson (syn. *C. pseudoscabiosifolia* H. Perrier; *Clematopsis bojeri* var. *pseudoscabiosifolia* (H. Perrier) J. Raynal) has pinnate leaves with 5 rather small ovate, incisely toothed leaflets which are silky-hairy beneath; the uppermost leaves are often subentire and sepal-like. Restricted to the centre of the range of the species (Ambatofangena, at c.1400 m (4600 ft)).

H10

156. *Clematis villosa* subsp. *oliveri*, Kitulo Plateau, S Tanzania.
Photo: Christopher Grey-Wilson

❖ ❖ Leaves oblong in outline, with up to 3 primary divisions; leaflets sessile to short-petioluled; African plants (species 274)

274. *Clematis homblei* De Wild.
(syn. *C. chrysocarpa* auct. non Welw. ex Oliv., *C. chrysocarpoides* De Wild., *C. katangensis* (Hutch.) M. Johnson, *C. sapinii* De Wild., *C. villosa* subsp. *chrysocarpa* (Welw. ex Oliv.) Kuntze var. *poggei* De Wild.; *Clematopsis homblei* (De Wild.) Staner & Léonard, *C. katangensis* Hutch., *C. sapinii* (De Wild.) Staner & Léonard)

DESCRIPTION. Looks rather similar to *C. villosa* subsp. *oliveri*. It has few (sometimes solitary), larger flowers, generally 60–90 mm (2.4–3.5 in) across, the sepals 30–45 mm (1.2–1.8 in) long and 15–35 mm (0.6–1.4 in) wide, and anthers 5–9 mm (0.2–0.35 in) long. In addition, the flowers usually have very many more stamens overall, 250 or more as opposed to 75–200 for *C. villosa*; carpels 300–600 (50–200 in *C. villosa* usually). The leaves in this species are extremely variable between specimens, but sometimes also on the same plant: they can be simple with a toothed and deeply pinnately lobed margin (sometimes with just a pair of lobes towards the base), partly pinnate or pinnately lobed to fully pinnate, with up to 7 leaflets.

DISTRIBUTION. Angola to S Zaire (Kasai; Bas Katanga) and Zimbabwe; 1300–1500 m (4300–4950 ft).

HABITAT. *Cryptosepalum* woodland and bushy places. The position and synonymy of this species are not clear-cut and require further more detailed investigation.

Subgenus Nine *Viorna*

Subgenus Viorna contains a large majority of the North American species of *Clematis*. Only three species of the subgenus are found outside the region: *C. fusca* and *C. ianthina* in eastern Asia and *C. integrifolia* in Europe, western and central Asia. The species are herbaceous perennials or subshrubby (suffrutescent) perennials with the stems dying part-way or most of the way down to a woody base each season. The woody base can become quite substantial in time and is similar to that found in *C. viticella*. The herbaceous types tend to be free-standing non-climbing plants, whereas the suffrutescent ones generally possess climbing stems with the usual twinning leaf-petioles, although in some the end leaflet can be modified into a tendril-like process. The leaves can be simple or compound and with an entire or sometimes toothed margin. The flowers are solitary and terminal or 1–few in lateral cymes; they are usually nodding and with 4 (occasionally 5) thick, erect sepals that are held close together for most of their length, although the tip may be

strongly recurved. The stamens generally have a hairy margin to the filaments. The achenes are compressed and generally have a pronounced rim and a plumose tail.

SECTION VIORNA

SUBSECTION VIORNA
(THE VIORNA GROUP)

The section comprises those species that are subshrubby climbers (with the exception of *C. addisonii* that is more bushy), with pinnate, occasionally ternate, leaves, that terminate in a simple tendril-like appendage; in the majority the upper pair of leaflets of the leaf are much smaller than the lowermost pair. The nodding flowers are borne in lateral cymes, 1–few-flowered; they have thick sepals that are held close together (connivent) and usually only slightly expanded or recurved at the tip.

Most of the species in Subsection Viorna come away readily from seed, if it can be obtained. They tend not to hybridize in the garden freely, which makes the seedlings more reliable than those of some of the other groups of clematis. However, *C. texensis*, in particular, has been of great importance in the breeding of a hybrid race of excellent garden clematis, primarily involving *C. viticella* or *C. lanuginosa* in their genetical makeup: see below under *C. texensis*.

▼   **Leaves glaucous (species 275–278)**
◆   **Flowers scarlet-red (species 275)**

275. *Clematis texensis* Buckl.*
(syn. *C. coccinea* Engelm. ex Gray, *C. c.* var. *major* Beissner, var. *parviflora* Beissner and var. *segreziensis* Beissner, *C. pitcheri* sensu Carr., non Torr. & Gray, *C. texensis* subsp. *coccinea* Kuntze, *C. t.* subsp. *coccinea* var. *parvifolia* Kuntze and var. *segreziensis* Kuntze, *C. t.* var. *parviflora* Lavall. and var. *typica* Lavall., *C. viorna* var. *coccinea* Gray; *Viorna coccinea* Small)

DESCRIPTION. A slender climber with glabrous stems which are glaucous, especially close to the nodes. Stem leaves pinnate with 4 or 5 pairs of primary leaflets,

MAP FOURTEEN
Subgenus *Viorna*
    subsection Integrifoliae   + + + + +
    (in North America)
Section Hirsutissima   – – – –
Section Viorna
    subsection Viorna   · · · · · ·

terminating in a slender tendril, glabrous, green above but glaucous beneath; leaflets rounded to ovate, simple, 2–3-lobed or ternate, often with a somewhat heart-shaped base, the tip rounded to emarginate, net-veined. Flowers borne in lateral cymes of 2–7, sometimes solitary, urn-shaped, 20–30 mm (0.8–1.2 in) long. Sepals scarlet, but cream or yellowish inside, glabrous and somewhat glaucous on the outside, ovate-lanceolate, 20–30 mm (0.8–1.2 in) long, 6–12 mm (0.24–0.47 in) wide, the acute tip slightly recurved. Stamens about three-quarters the length of the sepals. Achenes rounded, 6–7 mm (0.24–0.28 in), with a prominent rim and a yellowish-brown plumose tail to 50 mm (2 in), occasionally 70 mm (2.8 in), long.

DISTRIBUTION. S USA (CS & NE Texas; especially in the region of Edwards Plateau north-eastwards).

HABITAT. Woodland and stream margins, in moist humusy soils, often over limestone; June–Sept.

An attractive and exciting as well as much-sought-after species, particularly in its deep scarlet-red forms. However, it is not always the easiest of plants to please in the garden and may take several years to settle down, but a specimen in good flower can be very appealing. Plants can be subject to attacks of powdery mildew in the open garden, especially in mid and late summer. In cultivation, at least in the British Isles (it was introduced as long ago as 1868), it often behaves as a semi-herbaceous plant, the stems dying back to the thicker woodier growths towards the base of the plant.

Clematis texensis has played an important role in the production of some excellent and popular garden hybrids. Although some of these have been produced in recent years, most date back to the late 1800s and early 1900s. Hybridizers were not only attracted by the flower colour but also by the shape of the flowers. The hybrids mostly have attractive rather waxy blooms that can be upright or nodding; they are often referred to as tulip-flowered clematis because of their shape. They can fall prey to clematis wilt, but this should not deter anyone for trying one or two of these lovely and unusual clematis in the garden.

Unfortunately, the species is by no means easy to propagate from cuttings and seeds are not always available. It and many of the texensis cultivars are prone to devastation from mildew, which can attack foliage and flowerbuds alike and with equal vigour.

The old nineteenth-century cultivar 'Star of India', with its large purple flowers banded with reddish-purple, played an especially important role; it was a cross between *C. lanuginosa* and *C.* 'Jackmanni' (itself a *C. lanuginosa* × *C. viticella* hybrid). Crossed with *C.*

157. *Clematis texensis* in cultivation. Photo: Daan Smit

texensis in the late nineteenth century it gave rise to the following cultivars: 'Admiration', 'Countess of Onslow'* (the original had bright violet-purple flowers with a broad flash of scarlet down the centre of each sepal, but plants sold under the name today are paler and less exciting), 'Duchess of Albany'* AGM (a vigorous plant with upright 50–60 mm (2–2.4 in) flowers of deep candy-pink with a deeper band down each sepal), 'Duchess of York', 'Grace Darling' (the form available

158. *Clematis* Texensis Group 'Duchess of Albany'. Photo: Christopher Grey-Wilson

159. *Clematis* Texensis Group 'Etoile Rose'. Photo: Christopher Grey-Wilson

today seems to be identical with 'Duchess of Albany') and 'Sir Trevor Lawrence'* (50–60 mm (2–2.4 in)) flowers which are pink or whitish pink outside and cherry-red with a central band of scarlet inside down each of the 4–6 sepals. A cross with 'Bees Jubilee'* AGM gave rise to 'Ladybird Johnson'* (deep purple-red flowers about 40 mm (1.6 in) long, with a crimson band down each sepal) and 'Princess Diana'* = 'Princess of Wales' (6 cm (2.4 in) flowers of luminous pink, even

160. *Clematis addisonii* in cultivation. Photo: Raymond Evison

deeper along the centre of each sepal); crossed with 'Ville de Lyon'* gave rise to 'Madame Lerocher'; crossed with 'Comtesse de Bouchaud'* AGM gave rise to 'Madame Moret'; crossed with 'Gipsy Queen'* AGM gave rise to 'Madame Raymond Guillot'. Strangely enough, *C. texensis* has not be much crossed with other 'pure species' to notable effect, the one exception being *C.* 'Clocheton' (*C. texensis* × *C. integrifolia*).

Other cultivars with a good proportion of *C. texensis* 'blood' in them include the popular and much admired 'Etoile Rose'* (nodding flowers 50–60 mm (2–2.4 in), deep satiny pink outside but darker and more scarlet within), 'Gravetye Beauty'* (upright 60–80 mm (2.4–3.2 in) flowers of rich red; a fine cultivar introduced from Morel of Lyon by William Robinson in 1914, which received an Award of Merit (AM) from the Royal Horticultural Society in 1935) and 'Pagoda'* (an 'Etoile Rose' × *C. viticella* cross; large nodding 60–80 mm (2.4–3.2 in) flowers of basically creamy-pink, but the sepals banded with purplish-mauve on the outside).

H5; P2

◆ ◆ **Flowers not red; generally pink to purple, lavender, greenish or greenish-yellow (species 276–278)**
❖ **Leaflets reticulately (net) veined; flowers lavender or greenish (species 276)**

276. *Clematis versicolor* Small*
(syn. *C. troutbeckiana* Spingarn; *Viorna versicolor* Small)

DESCRIPTION. Similar to *C. texensis* but net-veined leaflets with an obtuse to rounded tip (never notched), and flowers lavender with greenish tips, sometimes violet-purple towards the base, or greenish all over. The leaves generally have 3 or 4 pairs of simple or sometimes 3-lobed leaflets. Sepals 13–25 mm (0.5–1 in) long, 5–10 mm (0.2–0.4 in) wide. Achenes with usually pale yellow tails 30–60 mm (1.2–2.4 in) long.

DISTRIBUTION. C USA (Oklahoma eastwards to Missouri and Arkansas, Kentucky and Tennessee).

HABITAT. Pine barrens and stony woodland; June–Aug.

Clematis versicolor and *C. texensis* can be readily confused when out of flower, or as herbarium specimens. The latter tends to have more numerous and often divided leaflets which are frequently emarginate at the tip, and larger flowers. There is some evidence that the two hybridize in the wild, especially in the region south of the Ozark Plateau.

H5; P2

✼ ✼   **Leaflets not reticulately (net) veined; flowers reddish-purple to bluish-purple (species 277 & 278)**

✼   **Leaves simple to pinnate with not more than 7 leaflets (species 277)**

277. *Clematis addisonii* Britton*

(syn. *C. ovata* Torr. & Gray; *Viorna addisonii* Small)

DESCRIPTION. A bushy subshrub with erect to ascending, much-branched slender stems which are rounded and scarcely ridged, glabrous and glaucous. Leaves non-clinging, basically pinnate with 2 or occasionally 3 pairs of leaflets, but on the lower part of the stems and on young plants the leaves are simple; leaflets oval to ovate, with an obtuse, sometime apiculate, tip, glabrous, green above and glaucous beneath, generally only one pair large. Bracts leaf-like, simple. Flowers solitary, terminal or at the end of short lateral shoots, urn-shaped, 10–25 mm (0.4–1 in) long. Sepals rosy-purple or bluish-purple, cream within and along the margins, narrow-ovate, with slightly recurved, acute tips. Stamens with cream anthers, about three-quarters the length of the sepals. Achenes rounded to quadrangular, pubescent, with a yellow or yellowish-brown plumose tail to 35 mm (1.4 in) long.

DISTRIBUTION. E USA (N Georgia, NW North Carolina, SW Virginia).

HABITAT. Wooded and bushy riverbanks; June–Sept.

Closely related to *C. glaucophylla* but unique in its mixture of simple and compound leaves. *C. addisonii* is restricted to the region of the Blue Ridge Mountains. In cultivation this is a pretty but in no way spectacular species which is useful in the flower border. The stems are thin and require some support such as pea-sticks or wire hoops, otherwise they will flop ungainly over other plants or on the ground.

H7; P2

✼ ✼   **Leaves pinnate with 9 or 11 leaflets, these often ternate (species 278)**

278. *Clematis glaucophylla* Small*

(syn. *Clematis addisonii* sensu Gray, non Britton, *C. viorna* sensu Gray, non L.; *Viorna glaucophylla* (Small))

DESCRIPTION. Similar to *C. addisonii* but a climbing plant with all the leaves (not bracts) pinnate and with 4 or 5 pairs of ovate, glabrous leaflets; leaflets, especially the lower pairs, ternate or 3-lobed, but all more or less heart-shaped at the base and with an acute to subobtuse apex, more prominently, (but not net-), veined, conspicuously glaucous beneath. Bracts simple, variable in size but sometimes as large as the leaflets. Flowers rather larger, 20–25 mm (0.8–1 in) long, generally in 1–3-flowered lateral cymes. Sepals reddish-purple. Achenes with a yellowish-brown plumose tail to 40 mm (1.6 in) long.

DISTRIBUTION. CS & SE USA (Arkasas and Tennessee NE to Virginia and south to Florida).

HABITAT. Woodlands or riverbanks in moist leafy soils; June–Aug.

In the wild this species is sometimes found to intergrade with *C. viorna* and such hybrid swarms need further investigation. The absence of glaucous undersurfaces to the leaves is a useful characteristic to distinguish *C. viorna*, especially when the plants are not in flower. The related *C. texensis* and *C. versicolor* can be distinguished by their clearly net-veined (reticulate) leaves.

H5; P2

▼ ▼   **Leaves not glaucous (species 279–283)**

❖   **Leaves not noticeably net-veined (species 279)**

279. *Clematis viorna* L.* Leather Flower, Vase Vine

(syn. *C. gattingeri* Small, *C. viorna* subsp. *normalis* Kuntze, *C. v.* var. *flaccida* (Small) Erickson and var. *viorna* Steyerm.; *Viorna gattingeri* Small, *V. ridgwayi* Stadl., *V. urnigera* Spach, *V. viorna* Small)

DESCRIPTION. A subshrub with 6–12-ribbed stems to 3 m (10 ft), generally hairy at least below the nodes. Leaves pinnate with 3 or 4 pairs of primary segments, occasionally ternate; leaflets ovate, entire to 3-lobed or sometimes ternate, 3- or 5-veined, with an acute to acuminate apex, usually downy beneath, not net-veined. Bracts simple to 3-lobed. Flowers 1–7, urn-shaped, pendent, 15–25 mm (0.6–1 in) long, borne in small lateral cymes. Sepals reddish-purple to violet-purple with a woolly margin 2–3 mm (0.08–0.12 in) thick and leathery, otherwise slightly downy on the outside, with a recurved tip and creamy margins. Achenes hairy, elliptical to rounded, 3–6 mm long (0.12–0.24 in), with a yellowish or brownish plumose tail to 30 mm (1.2 in) long.

DISTRIBUTION. EC, NE & S USA (Indiana, S Ohio, S Pennsylvania and Delaware south-westwards to Georgia, SE Missouri and N Mississippi).

HABITAT. Wooded riverbanks and scrub; June–Sept.

161. *Clematis viorna* in cultivation. Photo: Raymond Evison

A reasonably attractive species but rarely performing at its best in cultivation and often rather sparsely-flowered; although the flowers are small, a well-flowered specimen can make a very interesting spectacle in the garden. It certainly could never be described as spectacular but can be guaranteed to enthral the curious. The little urn-shaped flowers are very thick and fleshy, with the margins of the sepals held closely together. In addition, the fruitheads borne in the late summer and autumn can also be very attractive and it is worth growing for these alone; they are at first a very pleasing pale apple-green. It is wise to select out the best-coloured forms from batches of seedlings. Plants perhaps look best when allowed to scramble up shrubs in the garden.

var. *flaccida* (**Small**) **Erickson** (syn. *C. flaccida* Small ex Rydb.) is sometimes distinguished on account of its thinner leaves which are velvety pubescent beneath, and the flowers which are paler, lavender with greenish tips. It was described from Warren County in Kentucky. Likewise, *C. gattingeri* Small, described from Tennessee (Davidson and Franklin Counties) has been distinguished

on account of its smaller (10–13 mm (0.4–0.5 in) long) purple flowers and rather smaller leaves which are densely downy beneath. However, taking into consideration the wide range of variability found within the species, these are very doubtfully distinct, although they may warrant recognition horticulturally.

H4; P2

❖ ❖ **Leaves conspicuously net-veined (species 280–283)**
✳ **Achenes with plumose (feathery) tails (species 280 & 281)**

280. *Clematis beadlei* (**Small**) **Ericks**
(syn. *Viorna beadlei* Small)

DESCRIPTION. Similar to *C. reticulata*, but differing primarily in the leaflets which are thinner, with finer more distant reticulate veining, and with acute to acuminate tips. The species has reddish-brown stems. The flowers are always solitary.
DISTRIBUTION. CS USA (Arkansas, N Georgia, Mississippi, Tennessee, Texas).

HABITAT. Bushy places.

A little-known species, recorded from a number of scattered localities across the southern United States.

281. *Clematis reticulata* **Walt.** *
(syn. *C. versicolor* forma *pubescens* Steyerm., *C. viorna* subsp. *reticulata* Kuntze, *C. v.* subsp. *r.* var. *flavida* Kuntze; *Viorna reticulata* Small, *V. subreticulata* Harbison)

DESCRIPTION. A climber to 3 m (10 ft) with 6-ribbed, reddish stems which are somewhat hairy at the nodes. Leaves pinnate with 3 or 4 pairs of lateral leaflets, terminating in a simple tendril or very reduced leaflet, green on both surfaces; leaflets leathery, elliptical to ovate, 20–60 mm (0.8–2.4 in) long, usually entire but occasionally 2–3-lobed, with a rounded and mucronate tip to an acute tip, with a well marked reticulate pattern of veins on both surfaces. Flowers solitary or 2–3 on short lateral peduncles, urn-shaped, 15–25 mm (0.6–1 in) long, pendent. Sepals greenish-yellow with a flush of purple, especially as the flowers age, narrow-ovate, 20–22 mm (0.8–0.8 in) long, 5–10 mm (0.2–0.4 in) wide, with a slightly recurved acute tip, usually covered on the outside by a yellowish down (canescent). Stamens slightly shorter than the sepals. Achenes oval, 4 mm (0.16 in), short-pubescent, with a pale yellow-brown plumose tail to 60 mm (2.4 in) long.

DISTRIBUTION. S & SE USA (E Texas and S Arkansas eastwards to Tennessee, South Carolina and Florida).

HABITAT. Fields, thickets and open bushy places, generally on rather light sandy soils; May–Aug.

✽ ✽ **Achenes with glabrous or silky but not plumose (feathery) tails (species 282 & 283)**

282. *Clematis pitcheri* Torr. & Gray*
(syn. *C. coloradensis* Buckl., *C. pitcheri* var. *lasiostylis* Gray and *leiostylis* Gray, *C. pitcheri* var. *sargentii* Davis ex Bailey, *C. p.* var. *sargentii* Rehd., *C. sargentii* Lavall., *C. simsii* sensu Kuntze, non Sweet, *C. s.* subsp. *lobata* Kuntze and subsp. *normalis* Kuntze, *C. s.* subsp. *pitcheri* Kuntze, *C. s.* subsp. *p.* var. *chrysocarpa* Kuntze and var. *micrantha* Kuntze, *C. s.* var. *lasiostylis* (Gray) Kuntze and var. *leiostylis* (Gray) Kuntze, *C. viorna* subsp. *reticulata* Kuntze, *C. v.* subsp. *r.* var. *obtusifoliola* Kuntze and var. *sargentii* Kuntze, *C. v.* var. *pitcheri* James; *Viorna pitcheri* Britton & Brown, *V. simsii* Small)
DESCRIPTION. A deciduous or semi-herbaceous climber to 4 m (13 ft), occasionally more, with downy 6-ribbed young stems. Leaves ternate to pinnate, with 3 or 5 ovate leaflets, each 2.5–10 cm (1–4 in) long, with a rounded to slightly heart-shaped base, entire to 2–3-lobed, the terminal leaflet often modified into a short tendril. Flowers solitary, or 2–7, in lateral cymes, pitcher- to urn-shaped, to 20 mm (0.8 in) long, 10–15 mm (0.4–0.6 in) across, nodding on long downy stalks to 10 cm (4 in) long, 1–7 borne at the shoot tips. Sepals 4, purplish-blue to purplish-violet, to brick red outside, violet-purple to greenish-yellow within, ovate, to 20–30 mm (0.8–1.2 in) long, with 5–7 veins, the pointed tip slightly recurved, downy only on the thick margins. Stamens about three-quarters the length of the sepals. Achenes rounded, 6–8 mm (0.24–0.32 in), with a broad and thick rim, appressed-hairy, with a slightly downy to almost glabrous, occasionally silky, but not feathery, tail to 30 mm (1.2 in) long.

DISTRIBUTION. C & S USA (Nebraska eastwards to W Indiana and south-westwards to Texas, but rare in Arkansas and Tennessee and absent from Louisiana).

HABITAT. Open bushy places and shrubberies, riverbanks; June–Sept.

Clematis pitcheri is one of the most distinctive and attractive members of the Viorna Section. It was introduced into cultivation in 1878, being first grown at the Royal Botanic Gardens, Kew. Although it never puts on a spectacular display of bloom, it does flower over an extended season, to provide a dignified charm through much of the summer and autumn. Sometimes confused with *C. texensis*, which has redder flowers, it is readily distinguished by its non-plumed styles. In addition, the plant is less herbaceous and the stems scarcely die back during the winter months, but will sprout higher up the following season if left unpruned. *C. pitcheri* is best when grown through other shrubs, especially those close to a protecting wall. The spiky fruits are attractive and are produced from late summer onwards.

In the wild it is quite a variable species and for this reason it has acquired a rather formidable synonymy. The variation is in some ways clinal: plants to the north of the range have leaflets that are larger and less divided and the sepals scarcely (if at all) expanded towards the tip, whereas in the south the leaflets are more divided and often more markedly pubescent beneath, while the sepals are expanded towards the tip, sometimes pronouncedly so. Despite this, one variety is worthy of distinction:

var. *dictyota* (Greene) Dennis (syn. *C. dictyota* Greene, *C. filifera* var. *incisa* Hemsl., *C. pitcheri* var. *filifera* (Benth.) Robins., *C. simsii* subsp. *filifera* Kuntze; *Viorna dictyota* Heller, *V. filifera* Wooton & Standley) has pinnate to bipinnate leaves with 3–4 pairs of primary leaflets; leaflets leathery with prominently net-veined, usually 2–3-lobed, pubescent beneath. Sepals with expanded margins above the middle and with the tip more strongly recurved. Achenes silky-hairy.

This interesting variety is distributed in northern Mexico, southern New Mexico and the neighbouring regions of Texas. It is generally easily recognized by its far more dissected leaves.

H4–5; P2

283. *Clematis morefieldii* Kral

DESCRIPTION. Similar to *C. pitcheri* but a more rampant climber to 5 m (16.5 ft) with larger leaves bearing 9–11 pairs of primary leaflets, these 5–10 cm (2–4 in) long, entire to 2–3-lobed. Flowers urn-shaped, 20–25 mm (0.8–1 in) long. Sepals narrow-oval to lanceolate, green flushed with red, 20-25mm long. Achenes oval, 7–9 mm (0.28–0.35 in), with a brownish silky tail to 35 mm (1.4 in) long.

DISTRIBUTION. SE USA (Alabama; restricted to Madison County).

HABITAT. Mixed woodland and shrubberies; July–Aug.

H4; P2

SUBSECTION CRISPAE

The prime distinguishing character of this section is in the cylindrical-campanulate flowers in which the sepals are greatly expanded, frilled and recurved in the upper half. The one species, *C. crispa*, is a climber, which readily distinguishes it from members of the Subsection Integrifoliae, whose members are exclusively herbaceous perennials.

284. *Clematis crispa* L.*

(syn. *C. cordata* Sims, *C. crispa* C. Moench, *C. crispa* L. var. *walteri* Gray, *C. c.* var. *typica* Schneid., *C. cylindrica* Sims, *C. divaricata* Jacq., *C. lineariloba* DC., *C. simsii* Sweet, *C. viticella* subsp. *crispa* Kuntze, *C. v.* subsp. *c.* var. *pilostylis* Kuntze and var. *leiostylis* Kuntze, *C. v.* subsp. *walteri*, *C. v.* subsp. *w.* var. *lineariloba* Kuntze, *C. walteri* Pursh; *Viorna crispa* Small, *V. c.* var. *walteri* Small, *V. obliqua* Small; *Viticella crispa* Bercht. & Presl)

DESCRIPTION. A deciduous, semi-woody climber to 2.5 m (8 ft), often less, with the stems dying back part-way each season, sometimes close to ground level; stems slender, 6- or 12-ribbed, slightly downy. Leaves thin and glabrous, ternate to pinnate with 2–5 pairs of primary segments; leaflets broad-ovate to lanceolate, entire to unevenly 2–3-lobed, more rarely ternate, untoothed leaflets, to 75 mm (3 in) long and 38 mm (1.5 in) wide, 3-veined. Flowers solitary and pendent, semi Turk's-cap shaped (sepals forming a close urn-shaped tube in the lower half, but spreading widely apart in the upper), 25–40 mm (1–1.6 in) long, borne on a slender violet-flushed bractless pedicels to 80 mm (3.2 in) long. Sepals bluish-purple or violet-purple or pale blue, whitish towards the base and margins, lanceolate, widely flared and strongly recurved in the upper half and with a frilled (crisped) margin, to 35 mm (1.4 in) long and 1.2 mm (0.05 in) wide. Stamens just under half the length of the sepals. Achenes rounded to squarrish, 6–9 mm long (0.24–0.35 in), somewhat silky to almost glabrous, with a short slender non-plumose tail, not more than 30 mm (1.2 in) long.

DISTRIBUTION. E & S USA (the Atlantic and Gulf States from N Virginia and southwards to Tennessee, Florida and Texas (rare in Mississippi), Arkansas, SW Kentucky, W Tennessee and S Illinois).

HABITAT. Swampy habitats; late June–Aug, sometimes later.

This pretty species was introduced into cultivation from North America as long ago as 1726. It is placed in the Viorna Section together with about twenty other American species. However, it is accorded its own subsection because of the distinctive flared and frilled nature of the sepals. It is certainly one of the most attractive of the North American species, but is sadly, perhaps surprisingly, overlooked in gardens; indeed plants sold under the name often prove to be other species or hybrids. Despite this, its attractive characteristics have been used to good effect in hybridization with other species: 'Anne Harvey' (*C. crispa* × *C. pitcheri*), 'Betty Corning' (*C. crispa* × *C. viticella*) and 'Simsii' (*C. crispa* × *C. viorna*). The species is less often seen in gardens than it deserves, although it is often represented by a clone 'Distorta' (syn. *C. crispa* Sims, non L., *C. distorta* Lav.) with larger flowers of a charming rosy-purple, although these are rarely produced in profusion. Cultivated plants are not reliable hardy during severe winter weather; a protection of straw or wood chippings round the crown of the plant will help fend off the worst effects of frost. Unfortunately, many plants sold under the name prove to be misnamed or often of hybrid origin. Treasures of Tenbury Wells listed a white-flowered form at one time.

In the wild it is a species distributed in the low-lying regions of the Atlantic and Mexican Gulf states but ventures well north to Illinois along the Mississippi valley. As might be expected it is quite variable in the wild but no subordinate taxa have been recognized that have been upheld by subsequent authors. The variation in leaflet shape and size (particularly width) is very marked but this appears to show no correlation with its natural distribution, indeed markedly different leaflets can sometimes be found on the same plant.

Clematis crispa is a very distinctive American species without obvious allies amongst the other members of Section Viorna; however, some authors have suggested that perhaps its affinities lie in fact with the European/western Asian *C. integrifolia* or even *C. viticella*. This requires further careful research.

H5; P2

SUBSECTION FUSCAE
(THE FUSCA GROUP)

Two species of eastern Asian origin which look superficially like those of Subsection Viorna, but the flowers are produced laterally as well as terminally on the stems and the flowers have a rather dingy appearance, often being enshrouded in a dark felt of hairs.

▼ **Flowers downy outside, often densely so; leaves terminating in a small leaflet; flowers borne on stalks usually 20–40 mm (0.8–1.6 in) long (species 285)**

285. *Clematis fusca* **Turcz.***
(syn. *C. fusca* subsp. *normalis* Kuntze, *C. f.* var. *kamtschatica* (Regel & Tiling) Nakai and var. *typica* Schneid., *C. kamtschatica* Bong. & Meyer)

DESCRIPTION. A semi-herbaceous climber to 2 m (6.6 ft) (occasionally more) with angled 4–8-furrowed stems which are downy at first. Leaves pinnate, with 5–9 ovate to lanceolate leaflets, these to 90 mm (3.5 in) long and 50 mm (2 in) wide, with a rounded or somewhat heart-shaped base and an acuminate apex, entire, generally unlobed, often downy beneath. Flowers solitary terminal or lateral, nodding pitcher- (urn-) shaped, the lateral flowers with a pairs of simple leaf-like bracts towards the top, borne on thick often purplish-brown or violet-brown, rather stiff, downy peduncles to 40 mm (1.6 in) long; pedicels downy. Sepals 4, rarely 5–6, erect, greenish or reddish-brown, often flushed with violet-purple or cream inside, thick, ovate, 14–30 mm (0.55–1.2 in) long and 7–12 mm (0.28–0.47 in) wide, with an acute or subacute, somewhat recurved apex, brownish-downy on the outside, thick and fleshy. Achenes broad-obovate to elliptic, 5–7 mm (0.2–0.28 in) long, usually appressed-pubescent, with a tawny plumose tail to 40 mm (1.6 in) long.

DISTRIBUTION. N & NE China (Heilongjiang, E Jilin, E Liaoning, E Shandong), Japan (Hokkaido, Kuril Is.) Korea, Mongolia, E Russia (Kamchatka, Sakhalin, E & SE Siberia); to 1200 m (3900 ft).

HABITAT. Shrubberies and open bushy places; July–Sept.

Although not a particularly showy or beautiful species this is a fascinating one and it is generally quite easy to grow and sets plenty of seed. The short, thickened downy pedicels and dark, rather

162. Clematis fusca in cultivation. Photo: Raymond Evison

sombre, downy flowers are very characteristic of the species as a whole. In cultivation it tends to form a rather gaunt woody frame unless pruned fairly hard on a regular basis; as plants flower on the current season's shoots fairly late in the year, pruning in early spring is best advised. Certainly a plant of botanical curiosity and for the connoisseur's collection. Many plants sold in the nursery trade under this name prove to be *C. japonica*.
A number of varieties have been recognized in the wild, which is scarcely surprising considering its distribution; a number of these variants almost certainly represent island races:

var. *ajanensis* **Regel & Tiling** is a herbaceous perennial, the leaves with 3–5 pairs of lateral leaflets that can be entire to 3-lobed, the leaf often terminating in a small tendril rather than the usual leaflet. Sepals 20–30 mm (0.8–1.2 in) long, 10–14 mm (0.4–0.55 in) wide. Achenes with a tail not more than 20 mm (0.8 in) long. Restricted to eastern Siberia (Kamchatka).

163. Clematis ianthina in cultivation. Photo: Daan Smit

var. *amurensis* (Kuntze) M. Johnson (syn. *C. fusca* subsp. *amurensis* Kuntze, *C. fusca* var. *mandschurica*, sensu Nakai, non Regel) has heart-shaped leaflets not more than 15 mm (0.6 in) wide and with a heart-shaped base and sepals with ciliate margins. Described from SE Siberia (Amur).

var. *coreana* (Lévl.) Nakai ex T. B. Lee* (syn. *C. coreana* Lévl.) is a herbaceous perennial to 80 cm (32 in), primarily with ternate or 3-lobed leaves up to 10 cm (4 in) long and 5–10 cm (2–4 in) wide, often with a heart-shaped base. Flowers borne on pedicels up to 40 mm (1.6 in) long, the sepals lanceolate, to 30 mm (1.2 in) long and 8 mm (0.32 in) wide. Achenes with tails to 35 mm (1.4 in) long. Restricted to Korea (described from Soraksan at 1700 m (5600 ft) in NE South Korea). This is probably the so-called 'dwarf form' of *C. fusca* that is occasionally seen in cultivation. Like var. *ajanensis* and var. *kamtschatica*, this variety is fully herbaceous and does not form any woody stems.

var. *glabricalyx* Nakai (syn. *C. fusca* var. *yesoensis* Miyabe apud Nakai) has flowers which are purple-violet

flushed with red (often described as a metallic bronze-purple overall), not downy on the outside of the sepals but appressed-pubescent. Restricted to Japan (Hokkaido).

var. *kamtschatica* Regel & Tiling* (syn. *C. fusca* sensu Turcz., non Thunb., *C. f. kamtschatica* (Regel & Tiling) Takeda, *C. f.* var. *yezoensis* sensu Hara, non Miyabe) is a herbaceous perennial to 80 cm (32 in) with pinnate leaves, each with 2–3 pairs of ovate lateral leaflets, the terminal leaflet usually 3-lobed. Flowers deep blackish-brown, the sepals oblong-lanceolate, 30–35 mm (1.2–1.4 in) long, 10–14 mm (0.4–0.55 in) wide, borne on peduncles to 40 mm (1.6 in) long. Native from E Siberia (Kamchatka, Amur, Ussuri) to Korea and N Japan (Hokkaido and the Kuril Is.)

var. *mandshurica* Regel* (syn. *C. fusca* sensu Maxim., non Thunb., *C. f.* forma *manshurica* Regel, *C. f.* subsp. *violacea* (Maxim.) Kitag. var. *mandshurica* (Regel) Kitag., *C. f.* var. *mandshuricum* Maxim., *C. ianthina* var. *mandshurica* (Regel) Nakai) is a climber to 2 m (6.6 ft) with pinnate leaves terminating in a short tendril and with 2–5 pairs of ovate to lanceolate lateral leaflets which are usually lobed. Flowers small, brownish, but greenish-white within, the sepals only 15–17 mm (0.6–0.67 in) long and 6–10 mm (0.24–0.4 in) wide. Achenes with a tail not more than 25 mm (1 in) long. E Siberia (Amur, Sachalin, Ussuri), Korea and the neighbouring regions of NE China (Manchuria; Heilongjiang, E. Jilin, E Liaoning).

var. *obtusifoliola* (Kuntze) M. Johnson (syn. *C. ianthina* var. *mandshurica* forma *obtusifoliola* (Kuntze) Nakai) is a climber with small leaves with 2–3 pairs of ovate to rounded lateral leaflets. Flowers medium sized, the sepals 25–30 mm (1–1.2 in) long and 10 mm (0.4 in) wide. Apparently restricted to NE China (Manchuria; Heilongjiang, E. Jilin, E Liaoning).

var. *tomentosa* Nakai is similar to var. *kamtschatica* but is non-herbaceous and the leaves are clothed beneath with a brownish indumentum. Restricted to N Japan (Hokkaido; Iburi Province).

var. *yezoensis* Miyabe is a herbaceous perennial to 2 m (6.6 ft), the leaves with 3–4 pairs of lateral leaflets, the lowest of which are often 3-lobed. The flowers are borne on short peduncles 10–20 mm (0.4–0.8 in) long, the sepals about 20 mm (0.8 in) long and not more than 9 mm (0.35 in) wide, brown tinted with violet. Restricted to N Japan (Hokkaido); possibly also in Sakhalin.

H5; P2

▼▼ **Flowers glabrous outside or practically so; leaves terminating in a tendril; flowers borne on very short stalks generally less than 15 mm (0.6 in) long, often only 3–8 mm (0.12–0.32 in) (species 286)**

286. *Clematis ianthina* Koehne*

(syn. *C. fusca* forma *violacea* (Maxim.) Korsh., *C. f.* subsp. *violacea* (Maxim.) Kitagawa, *C. f.* var. *violacea* Maxim., *C. ianthina* var. *violacea* (Maxim.) Nakai, *C. viorna* subsp. *violacea* (Maxim.) Kuntze)

DESCRIPTION. Very similar to *C. fusca* and often mistaken for it but the leaves terminate in a small tendril and the flowers are somewhat larger, 30–40 mm (1.2–1.6 in) long, violet-blue or purple-blue, borne on short peduncles not more than 20 mm (0.8 in) long, with small (c. 4–5 mm (0.16–0.2 in)) bracts close to the base, in the leaf axils. The plant is a deciduous climber to 4 m (13 ft), the leaves pinnate, with 2–4 pairs of lateral leaflets that are entire or the lowermost may be trilobed. The flowers are a very similar shape to those of *C. fusca* and 20–30 mm (0.8–1.2 in) long, borne on glabrous pedicels, apricot-scented; sepals not more than 10 mm (0.4 in) wide, but glabrous or practically so, on the outside.

DISTRIBUTION. N & NE China (E. Heilongjiang, SE Jilin), Korea, E Siberia (Amur, Ussuriland).

HABITAT. Shrubberies and other bushy places; July–Sept.

This species comes very close to *C. fusca*; however, it can also be separated on account of its short-stalked flowers with small bracts close to the base of the stalks and by the more violet-coloured flowers. In *C. fusca* the bracts are larger and leaf-like and borne in the upper part on appreciably longer stalks. The presence of leaf-tendrils is also a useful clue in distinguishing *C. ianthina* but tendrils do occur sometimes in the *C. fusca* complex, for instance in *C. fusca* var. *ajanensis*.

In cultivation it is frequently sold under the name *C. fusca* forma or var. *violacea*. The fruit clusters are attractive in late summer and autumn, being large and orange-flushed when ripe.

Magnus Johnson (1997) recognized a distinct new variety of *C. ianthina*:

var. *kuripoensis* M. Johnson* has 4–5 pairs of lateral leaflets which are often lobed, frequently 3-lobed, especially on the lower leaves, and somewhat larger flowers (sepals 25–35 mm (1–1.4 in) long, 12–16 mm (0.47–0.63 in) wide) borne on very short peduncles only 5–15 mm (0.2–0.6 in) long. In addition, the sepals are significantly thick and spongy, the margin 2–3.5 mm (0.08–0.14 in) wide. This interesting variety comes from South Korea (Kuripo).

H5; P2

MAP FIFTEEN
Subgenus *Viorna*
Section Viorna
   subsection Fuscae   — · — · — · —
Section Integrifolia
   subsection Integrifolia   + + + + + +
   (in Europe and Asia)

164. *Clematis integrifolia* in cultivation. Photo: Christopher Grey-Wilson

165. *Clematis integrifolia* 'Rosea'. Photo: Raymond Evison

SECTION INTEGRIFOLIAE

SUBSECTION INTEGRIFOLIAE
(THE ENTIRE-LEAVED GROUP)

This section contains the herbaceous species of the Viorna complex. Although some of the species are genuinely herbaceous most develop a woody base to the stems and it is from these that the new shoots usually arise; these bear the current season's flowers during the summer months. The sepals are clearly expanded towards the recurved tip.

The eight species are, except for the European and Western Asian *C. integrifolia*, North American in origin.

▼ **Flowers deep purple, blue or mauve, the sepals 30–50 mm (1.2–2 in) long, not held closely together along their margins as in Section Viorna; leaves always untoothed; European and Asian plants (species 287)**

287. *Clematis integrifolia* L.*
(syn. *C. inclinata* Scop., *C. integrifolia pratensis* Neilr., *C. i.* var. *latifolia* Kuntze and var. *normalis* Kuntze, *C. nutans* sensu Crantz, non Royle; *Viorna integrifolia* Spach)

DESCRIPTION. A herbaceous perennial or subshrub, with the stems dying back to a woody base each season; stems to 1 m (40 in), but generally only about half that height, slender, 6-ribbed, often flushed with violet or purple, downy when young. Leaves undivided and sessile, ovate to lanceolate, 5–14 cm (2–5.5 in) long and 1.8–11 cm (0.7–4.3 in) wide, with an entire margin and 3–5 prominent veins, generally downy beneath, the upper leaves generally smaller than the lower. Flowers solitary, nodding, broad-campanulate from a rather narrow base, terminal, or lateral at the uppermost nodes (but rarely more than 5 flowers per stem), borne on slender downy pedicels to 20 cm (8 in) long. Sepals 4, violet, mauve or blue, rarely white, lanceolate to elliptical, to 30–50 mm (1.2–2 in) long and 10–15 mm (0.4–0.6 in) wide, half-spreading, strongly recurved in the upper half and often somewhat twisted. Stamens with the filaments hairy towards the top, and the anthers hairy on the back of the connective. Achenes narrow-obovate, 6–10 mm (0.24–0.4 in) long, hairy, with a shiny silvery plumose tail to 50 mm (2 in) long, occasionally longer.

DISTRIBUTION. C & E Europe (Poland and the Czech Republic, Balkans and Turkey) eastwards to S Russia and the Ukraine, the Caucasus, the Tien Shan (Kazakstan and Kyrgyzstan in particular) and Altai, in China restricted to N Xinjiang; primarily 500–1200 m (1650–3900 ft), rarely above 2000 m (6500 ft).

HABITAT. Bushy places and meadows, river and stream banks; June–early Aug, occasionally also in the autumn.

This attractive species has long been grown in our gardens; it makes an excellent cottage garden flower as well as an imposing plant for the herbaceous border, both in flower and fruit. It is of interest botanically in being the only member of the Viorna Section (whose members are primarily to be found in North America) native to Europe. It was introduced into cultivation in Britain as early as 1573. Horticulturally, *C. integrifolia* has proved to be of great importance as a parent of a whole range of exciting and garden-worthy hybrids, particularly with *C. viticella* as the second parent, but other more complex hybrids with *C. integrifolia* and various cultivars or hybrids also exist. Familiar garden plants such as *C.* × *eriostemon* AGM (*C. integrifolia* × *C. viticella*) and its cultivars such as 'Blue Boy' and 'Hendersonii' as well as *C.* × *durandii* AGM (*C. integrifolia* × *C.* 'Jackmanii') belong here.

Clematis integrifolia var. *latifolia* Kuntze is occasionally distinguished from the typical plant but the differences are by no means clear-cut. It is said to be a taller plant (to 1.3 m (4.3 ft)) with somewhat larger 7-veined leaves and rather larger flowers but intermediates can often be found and it would be difficult to uphold this variety. It is reported from the Altai Mountains.

In its own right, *C. integrifolia* is an altogether charming and graceful garden plant and one of the best for the herbaceous border. Plants take some time to settle in once planted, but after a few years can be expected to produce numerous shoots and a fine display of flowers. The stems are often not very strong and a few pea-sticks placed around the plant as the stems extend will help to keep the plant in order; it looks awful tied up! There are a number of interesting cultivars of the species that primarily extend the colour range:

'Alba'* (probably the same as var. *albiflora*) has, or should have, pure white, attractively scented, flowers, 60–90 cm (24–36 in) tall (unfortunately many plants sold under the name are inferior seedlings, often with some hint of mauve or purple in the sepals); 'Hendersonii'* (sometimes regarded as hybrid with *C. viticella*), has extra large dusky purple-violet flowers with wide-spreading sepals to 80 mm (3.2 in) long, the plant, 60–90 cm (24–36 in) tall, received an Award of Merit (AM) in May 1965 from the Royal Horticultural Society when it was exhibited at the Chelsea Flower

166. *Clematis x eriostemon.* Photo: Christopher Grey-Wilson

167. *Clematis fremontii.* Photo: Mike Ireland

Show; 'Monika'* has rather small violet-blue flowers on stems to 70 cm (28 in); 'Pangbourne Pink'* is a large-flowered selection with deep pink flowers and distinct from 'Rosea'; 'Pastel Blue'* flowers powder-blue on stems to 60 cm (24 in); 'Pastel Pink'* flowers soft pale pink, to 60 cm (24 in) tall; 'Rosea'* charming flowers of sugar-pink with a darker band on the outside, pleasantly scented, the sepals with a rather wavy margin, 0.7–1.2 m (28–48 in) tall (unfortunately plants sold under this name are often inferior seedlings, or are more lilac than pink, so it is best sought from a reliable source); 'Tapestry'* has large rich mauve-red flowers on stems to 90 cm (36 in)

The cultivar 'Olgae'*, known since the 1930s, is often listed under *C. integrifolia*. However, it is almost certainly of hybrid origin (*C. integrifolia* × *C. viticella*). The plant is rather lanky, to 1.5 m (5 ft), although sometimes only half that height. The flowers are produced in lax clusters; they are larger than *C. integrifolia* and an eye-catching mid-blue, with the bonus of being wonderfully scented. The sepals have a delightful twist to them.

C. × *eriostemon* Hort. (the name never seems to have been validly published; syn. *C. bergeronii* Hort., *C. chandleri* Hort., 'Eriostemon', C. 'Hendersonii' (not to be confused with *C. integrifolia* 'Hendersonii')) covers all the hybrids between *C. integrifolia* and *C. viticella*. The plants are not climbing but will scramble up through shrubs to 2–3 m (6.6–10 ft), dying part back to a woody base. The leaves are pinnate, with the leaflets occasionally lobed and the flowers generally look rather small and out of proportion to the size of the plant. However, they are produced in sufficient numbers to make it interesting; they are various shades of blue or violet-blue, 30–35 mm (1.2–1.4 in) long, and nod attractively like those of *C. integrifolia*, although the flair at the sepal margins is more reminiscent of those of *C. viticella*. 'Blue Boy'* has rather larger flowers of a lovely shade of hyacinth-blue.

H3; P2

▼ ▼ **Flowers whitish, yellowish or greenish, sometimes with a purple or lavender flush, then generally green-tipped, the sepals 15–38 mm (0.6–1.5 in) long; leaves often toothed; North American plants (species 288–292)**

◆ **Achenes without feathery (plumose) tails (species 288)**

288. *Clematis fremontii* S. Wats.*

(syn. *C. integrifolia* subsp. *fremontii* Kuntze, *C. ochroleuca* var. *fremontii* James; *Viorna fremontii* Heller)

DESCRIPTION. Herbaceous perennial with rather stout stems 15–40 cm (6–16 in) tall, occasionally taller; stems simple or somewhat branched, villous, particularly at the nodes. Leaves simple, leathery, broad-ovate to rounded, 6–10 cm (2.4–4 in) long, sessile, with strong reticulate veins, an obtuse apex and entire to coarsely serrate margin, becoming glabrescent at maturity; leaves of lateral stems smaller. Flowers nodding to half-nodding, solitary and terminal, narrow-urn-shaped, 19–38 mm (0.75–1.5 in) long. Sepals 4, purple or pale bluish-lavender with greenish tips, pale greenish or yellowish within, narrow-lanceolate, 19–40 mm (0.75–1.6 in) long, 5–13 mm (0.2–0.5 in) wide, glabrous to sparsely pubescent, the margins slightly expanded towards the recurved tip. Stamens half the length of the sepals. Achenes rounded, 5–6 mm (0.2–0.24 in), slightly compressed and with a broad rim, tomentose, the tail to 30 mm (1.2 in) long, not plumose but tomentose at the base and glabrous towards the tip.

DISTRIBUTION. C USA (NC Kansas, S Nebraska).

HABITAT. Prairies; June–Aug.

A charming little species which is unaccountably rare in cultivation. The narrow bell-shaped flowers are rather appealing, although they are never produced in large numbers. Given a warm and sheltered spot in the garden, where the plants can be guarded from too much winter wet this plant will succeed. Some alpine gardeners have been successful with it grown in a pot in an unheated glasshouse.

var. *riehlii* Erickson is a larger and laxer plant to 70 cm (28 in) tall (occasionally only 35 cm (14 in)), with usually branched stems and narrower elliptic-lanceolate to elliptic-ovate leaves, 7–14 cm (2.8–5.5 in) long on the main stems. Woodland glades in a small region of the Ozarks, W Missouri.

This interesting variety is geographically isolated from the typical plant (var. *fremontii*) and the difference in the habit of the two taxa is quite pronounced; var. *fremontii* has a much squatter appearance with more crowded leaves.

H4; P2

◆ ◆ **Achenes with feathery (plumose) tails (species 289–292)**

✳ **Sepals glabrous; achene tails reddish-brown (species 289)**

289. *Clematis viticaulis* Steele

DESCRIPTION. Similar to *C. albicoma* and *C. ochroleuca*, but the plant profusely branched and with small narrower, lanceolate, somewhat glossy, leaves, not more than 60 mm (2.4 in) long. In addition, the flowers are somewhat smaller, 15–25 mm (0.6–1 in) long, and the achenes scarcely compressed, almost rimless and with a reddish-brown plumose tail. The flowers are violet-purple with a slight greenish tinge, contrasting with the pale greenish-white inside.

DISTRIBUTION. E USA (Virginia; restricted to Bath County); only known from the type locality.

HABITAT. Shale barren; June–July.

❀ ❀   **Sepals downy; achene tails pale, whitish or yellowish (species 290–292)**

❀   **Plant with simple or few-branched stems; achenes tails pale yellowish-brown or reddish-brown (species 290)**

290. *Clematis ochroleuca* Aiton*
(syn. *C. integrifolia* subsp. *ochroleuca* (Aiton) Kuntze and subsp. *ovata* (Pursh) Kuntze, *C. ochroleuca* Torr. & Gray, *C. o.* var. *ovata* Wherry, *C. ovata* Pursh, *C. sericea* sensu Michx., non Humboldt *et al.*; *Viorna ochroleuca* (Aiton) Small)

DESCRIPTION. A herbaceous perennial to 60 cm (24 in) tall with erect, 6- or 12-ribbed stems which are downy at least at the nodes, simple or few-branched. Leaves simple, narrow- to broad-ovate, subsessile, with an entire to coarsely serrate margin, 60–120 mm (2.4–4.7 in) long, white-downy beneath when young, sometimes very densely so, but becoming glabrescent at maturity. Flowers solitary and nodding, narrow-urn-shaped, 15–25 mm (0.6–1 in) long. Sepals whitish-green tinged with yellow, often also flushed with purple towards the base and on the pedicels, narrow-lanceolate, somewhat spreading and markedly recurved towards the obtuse tip, silky-hairy on the outside. Stamens about half the length of the sepals. Achenes oval to spindle-shaped, scarcely compressed, 3–4 mm long (0.12–0.16 in), with a narrow rim, somewhat hairy in the upper half, with a yellowish or brownish plumose tail to 50 mm (2 in) long.

DISTRIBUTION. E USA (New York south-west to Georgia).

HABITAT. Piedmont region growing in bushy and grassy places on light sandy soils; June–July.

H6; P2

168. *Clematis coactilis* in cultivation. Photo: Raymond Evison

❀ ❀   **Plant with much-branched stems; achenes tails pale yellow or whitish (species 291 & 292)**

291. *Clematis albicoma* Wherry*
(syn. *C. ochroleuca* sensu James, non Aiton, *C. ovata* sensu Britton ex Vail, non Pursh; *Viorna albicoma* (Wherry) Moldenke, *V. ochroleuca* Small, *V. ovata* Small)

DESCRIPTION. Very similar to *C. ochroleuca* but plant silky-pubescent with white hairs, and with much-branched 6-ribbed stems. Flowers not more than 20 mm (0.8 in) long, yellowish flushed with purple towards the base. Achenes with white or pale yellow plumose tails.

DISTRIBUTION. E USA (Virginia and West Virginia; restricted to the Allegheny Mountains).

HABITAT. Shale barrens; June–Aug.

In both *C. albicoma* and *C. coactilis* the flowers tend to be held below the uppermost pair of leaves, whereas in *C. ochroleuca* they are usually held well above on longer stalks.

H5; P2

292. *Clematis coactilis* (Fernald) Keener*
(syn. *C. albicoma* var. *coactilis* Fernald, *C. carrollii* Wherry, *C. ochroleuca* var. *sericea* (Michx.) Wherry)

DESCRIPTION. Similar to *C. albicoma*, but leaves velvety-pubescent below (not glabrous or slightly downy), the stems 6- or 12-ribbed, and the flowers

169. Clematis bigelovii. Photo: Martyn Rix

DESCRIPTION. A herbaceous perennial with slender, simple stems 30–60 cm (12–24 in) tall, sometimes with two short branches from the uppermost leaf pair. Leaves few (1–3 pairs on the main stems) ovate-lanceolate and undivided or deeply cleft into linear segments, glabrous, the margin entire and the veins inconspicuous. Flowers terminal, 1–3 on slender pedicels to 25 cm (10 in) long, nodding, tubular-campanulate, glabrous outside apart from the densely downy margins. Sepals 4, lavender-blue, linear-lanceolate, 20–25 mm long (0.75–1 in), the margins widely expanded and undulate (crisped) towards the strongly recurved tips. Achenes rounded to ovoid, not compressed, rimmed and with a pale yellow plumose tail to 80 mm (3.2 in) long.

DISTRIBUTION. SE USA (Peninsular Florida).

HABITAT. Flatwoods, growing on light sandy soils; Feb–Apr.

H7; P2

294. *Clematis socialis* Kral

DESCRIPTION. Related to *C. baldwinii* but differing in the leaves which can be simple to pinnate, 4–12 cm (1.6–4.7 in) long, 5–10 mm (0.2–0.4 in) wide, occasionally larger, with 3 or 5 leaflets. The flowers are 20–25 mm (0.8–1 in) long, violet-blue with a yellowish-green interior. The achenes have a short hairy but non-plumose tail, not more than 20 mm (0.8 in) long.

DISTRIBUTION. SE USA (Alabama).

HABITAT. Bushy and herb communities; probably Mar–May.

larger, the sepals 19–34 mm (0.75–1.3 in) long, white slightly flushed with green or pale purple.

DISTRIBUTION. E USA (South Virginia).

HABITAT. Bushy places and shale barrens; June–Aug.

Clematis coactilis is rare in cultivation but it is a pleasing, if quiet, plant that will make a dense clump in time. The rather pale green foliage and whitish flowers give the plant a particularly distinctive appearance. It deserves to be more widely grown in gardens and is particularly suitable for the front of the herbaceous border.

H5; P2

SUBSECTION BALDWINIANAE
(THE BALDWIN GROUP)

293. *Clematis baldwinii* Torr. & Gray* Pine-hyacinth
(syn. *Viorna baldwinii* (Torr. & Gray) Small)

SECTION HIRSUTISSIMA
(THE ROCKY MOUNTAINS GROUP)

This is perhaps the most distinctive section within Subgenus *Viorna*, indeed one of the most distinctive sections in the whole of *Clematis*. It contains just two North American species that are clump-forming herbaceous perennials which more resemble a pasque-flower (*Pulsatilla*) in flowers than a clematis. However, this appearance is purely superficial and the leafy stems with their paired leaves are typically those of a clematis.

▼ Achenes with a glabrous to somewhat hairy, but not plumose, tail; flowers small, not more than 25 mm (1 in) long; leaves with 15–23 leaflets (species 295)

295. *Clematis bigelovii* Torr.
(syn. *C. pitcheri* var. *bigelovii* Robins ex Gray; *Viorna bigelovii* Heller)

DESCRIPTION. A herbaceous perennial to 50 cm (20 in) tall, with simple stems which sometimes are branched at the upper nodes; stems slender and usually more or less glabrous. Leaves pinnate with 7–11 primary segments that are 3-lobed or ternate; leaflets ovate, generally 2–5-lobed. Flowers solitary at shoot tips, urn-shaped to sub-campanulate, 15–25 mm (0.6–1 in) long. Sepals 4, purplish, broad-lanceolate, slightly expanded at the recurved apex, sparsely pubescent outside, more densely so along the margins. Stamens slightly shorter than the sepals. Achenes rounded to obovate, 4–5 mm (0.16–0.2 in), slightly rimmed, hairy, with a 30 mm (1.2 in) long tail that is glabrous or somewhat hairy, but not plumose.

DISTRIBUTION. SW USA (E Arizona and W & C Texas).

HABITAT. Rocky bushy places in canyons; May–June.

The exact status of this plant is unclear. In many ways it fits in well in Section Hirsutissimae, with obvious links with *C. palmeri* in its habit and leaf-dissections. However, in flower and fruit details it more closely matches *C. pitcheri* in Section Viorna. The fact that this species may be of hybrid origin does not seem to have been considered: *C. bigelovii* certain grows in close proximity in some of its localities with *C. palmeri*, although apparently not with *C. pitcheri*; however, the two varieties of *C. pitcheri* are found just to the west (var. *dictyota*) and east (var. *pitcheri*) of *C. bigelovii*.

▼ ▼ Achenes with a plumose, tail; flowers larger, generally 25–40 mm (1–1.6 in) long; leaves with up to 13 leaflets (species 296 & 297)
◆ Leaflets narrow, often lanceolate to linear-lanceolate, hairy, often densely so, when young (species 296)

296. *Clematis hirsutissima* Pursh* Sugarbowl, Old Man's Whiskers, Vase Flower
(syn. *Anemone hirsutissima* MacMillan, *A. patens* var. *hirsutissima* Hitchcock; *Clematis bakeri* Greene, *C. douglasii* Hook., *C. d.* forma *pulsatilloides* Kuntze, *C. d.* subsp. *jonesii* Kuntze, subsp. *normalis* Kuntze

170. *Clematis hirsutissima* in NW Wyoming, USA. Photo: Phil Phillips

and subsp. *wyethii* Kuntze, *C. d.* var. *bigelovii* sensu Jones and var. *rosea* Cockerell, *C. eriophora* Rydb., *C. jonesii* Rydb., *C. scotii* var. *eriophora* Tidestr., *C. wyethii* Nutt.; *Pulsatilla hirsutissima* Britton, *P. patens* subsp. *hirsutissima* Zamels; *Viorna bakeri* Rydb., *V. douglasii* Cockerell, *V. eriophora* Rydb., *V. hirsutissima* Heller, *V. jonesii* (Rydb.) Rydb., *V. wyethii* Rydb.)

DESCRIPTION. A very variable tufted herbaceous perennial, 15–60 cm (6–24 in) tall; stems with 2–5 leaf pairs, simple or with up to 4 sterile lateral branches. Leaves green to bluish-green, 2–3-pinnatifid with 7–13 leaflets which are themselves divided into 2–many lanceolate to linear segments, sparingly to densely pilose, but usually becoming glabrescent at maturity. Flowers solitary, terminal, nodding, cylindrical-campanulate, 25–40 mm (1–1.6 in) long, borne on slender pedicels to 15 cm (6 in) long. Sepals 4, rarely 5, thickish but not leathery, deep dull purple or purple-red inside, paler, more lavender and silky-hairy on the outside, the margin somewhat expanded towards the acute, slightly recurved, tip. Stamens a half to two-thirds the length of the sepals. Achenes spindle-shaped, 3–4 mm (0.12–0.16 in), scarcely compressed and not rimmed, the tail 25-40cm (1–1.6in) long, yellow to pale brown or silvery plumose.

DISTRIBUTION. Mountainous western USA (Rocky Mountains of S Washington, E Oregon and SW Montana, southwards to Arizona and New Mexico; not in California or Nevada); to 2440 m (8000 ft).

HABITAT. Moist areas in upland plains, hills and mountains; late Apr–July.

Clematis hirsutissima is one of the most distinctive species in the genus. The fact that it has been placed in both *Anemone* and *Pulsatilla* by earlier authors, as well as in the genus *Viorna*, shows that there was no general agreement as to the exact status of the plant. The fact that the flowers looked very pulsatilla-like and produced pulsatilla-like fruits must have been perplexing, especially as at the time the 'boundaries' of the genus *Clematis* were not properly understood. However, today no one would argue that this plant was not a species of *Clematis*, indeed a distinctive member of Section *Viorna*. The most important character that places this species in *Clematis* is the possession of opposite pairs of stem leaves, a character never found in *Anemone* and *Pulsatilla*. The 4-sepalled nodding flowers are very typical of Subgenus *Viorna*, although the tufted, unbranched habit is very distinctive.

The species has been used traditionally by local Indian tribes for medicine.

Clematis hirsutissima should make a fine and attractive neat-foliaged garden plant but it has rarely proved to easy in gardens and it is more usually seen as a pot plant in an alpine house or cold frame. It would be well worth while gathering seed from various locations in the wild, especially from the higher elevations, in order to ascertain whether easier forms could be introduced into gardens. It would seem to have an excellent potential as a parent employed in a programme to breed a range of good small herbaceous clematis that could readily rival those of *C. integrifolia* for popularity. Although available in the horticultural trade, this intriguing species seldom performs well in cultivation. It is often listed in catalogues under its synonym, *C. douglasii*.

Although *C. hirsutissima* is very variable over its range (plants in the north of its range tend to be significantly hairier) two variants from the typical and widespread form can be recognized:

var. *arizonica* (Heller) Erickson (syn. *C. arizonica* Heller, *C. bigelovii* var. *arizonica* Tidestr.; *Viorna*

arizonica (Heller) Heller) has stems with only 2–3 pairs of leaves that are 2–3-pinnate with filiform segments only 1 mm (0.04 in) wide. Confined to the Flagstaff region of CN Arizona.

var. *scottii* (Porter) Erickson* (syn. *C. plattensis* A. Nels., *C. douglasii* var. *scottii* Coulter, *C. scottii* Porter & Coulter; *Viorna scottii* Rydb.) is like the typical plant (var. *hirsutissima*) but leaves pinnate, with undivided to 5-lobed, distinctly petioluled, wider leaflets, which are rather sparingly hirsute. Primarily in N & C Colorado, but also in N New Mexico, N Utah (Salt Lake County) and SW South Dakota (Bad Lands and Black Hills). An attractive plant, rather easier than the ordinary species in the garden. The purple-blue flowers are followed by attractive heads of fruit. Being only 45 cm (18 in) tall in flower it is a subject for the front of the flower border or for the rock garden. 'Rosea' has rose-pink flowers in mid to late summer. This is rather 'easier' in cultivation than the typical plant, but easier needs to be taken with some caution. Plants do well in some gardens and fail in others, including mine; I wish I could say that I had thriving clumps all round the garden. I have grown it from seed on a number of occasions and got to the one- to two-year plant stage and then disaster, the plants generally collapse or do not like being planted out. Still I will try again for this is an attractive and unique clematis.

H6; P2

◆ ◆ **Leaflets broad, usually ovate, glabrous or ractically so when young (species 297)**

297. *Clematis palmeri* Rose
(syn. *C. bigelovii* sensu James, non Torr., *C. douglasii* var. *bigelovii* Jones; *Viorna palmeri* Wooton & Standley)

DESCRIPTION. Similar to *C. hirsutissima* but a more robust plant to 1 m (40 in) tall, the stems becoming stouter, red and woody towards the base, bearing 5–6 pairs of pinnate leaves; leaflets broad, 3–5-lobed to ternate, 30–70 mm (1.2–2.8 in) long, scarcely hairy. Details of flowers and fruits very similar to *C. hirsutissima*, but stems sometimes with a terminal as well as several lateral flowers.

DISTRIBUTION. SW USA (E Arizona and W New Mexico).

Clematis palmeri has a distinctive distribution to *C. hirsutissima* and the two are never found growing together to my knowledge. However, *C. palmeri* often grows in the same vicinity as *C. bigelovii*.

Glossary

Achene: a single-seeded fruit that does not split but falls from the plant in one piece; often borne in clusters.

Acuminate: tapering to an abrupt point; as the tip of a leaf or leaflet.

Adpressed: same as appressed.

Anther: the part of the stamen that bears the pollen.

Apiculate: ending abruptly in a small point or apiculum.

Apiculum: see apiculate.

Appressed: pressed closely to or lying flat against; often refers to hairs on stems or leaves.

Axil: the angle between two organs such as the leaf and the stem.

Axillary: arising in the axils; flowers or whole inflorescences are said to be axillary or lateral (as opposed to terminal), when they arise at the leaf-axils.

Bipinnate: pinnate leaves in which the primary divisions are themselves pinnate; often referred to as twice-pinnate or 2-pinnate.

Bisexual: in this context are plants that bear both male and female organs in the same flowers, the same as hermaphrodite.

Biternate: the equivalent of bipinnate, in which the primary divisions of a ternate leaf are themselves ternate; often referred to as twice-ternate or 2-ternate.

Bracts: the leaf-like or scale-like organ found at the base of a flower-stalk (pedicel) where it joins the stem.

Bracteoles: in cymes and other compound inflorescences, are secondary bracts or bracteoles that are often found at each branch of the inflorescence.

Campanulate: bell-shaped.

Connective: in reference to stamens, is that part of the anther which connects the two parallel halves together; in some instances the connective, that runs down the centre of the anther, protrudes beyond the top of the anther as a small appendage.

Crenulate: with tiny rounded teeth along the margin.

Cuneate: with a wedge-shaped base; often refers to leaf and petal shapes.

Cyme: an inflorescence in which each branch is terminated by a flower that opens before those of the supporting, and subsequent, lateral branches.

Dioecious: having both sexes separated, and borne on different plants, so that plants in the same species are either male or female.

Emarginate: with a notched margin or apex.

Entire: with an untoothed margin; generally refers to leaf-margins.

Filament: the stalk of the stamen.

Forma: a subdivision of a variety: a forma generally only differs consistently in a single character found in wild populations and mixed with ordinary individuals; many white-flowered plants (albinos) found in normally coloured populations are distinguished as formas.

Glabrous: without hairs.

Glaucous: bluish- or greyish-green.

Hermaphrodite: containing both sexes, male and female, in the same flower.

Imbricate: overlapping; refers in this book to sepals that overlap in bud.

Indumentum: any adornments such as hairs and scales on the surface of leaves, stems, flowerbuds etc.

Internode: the areas on the stem between the nodes.

Lamina: the blade part of the leaf.

Lanceolate: lance-shaped; elliptical but broadest about a third of the distance from the base.

Lateral: to the side; same as axillary.

Leaflet: leaf-like subdivision of a compound leaf; ternate leaves have three leaflets.

Monoecious: have the sex organs separate and borne on the same plant, so that plants are hermaphrodite but with separate male and female flowers.

Node: the specific points on the stem where leaves and branches arise.

Oblanceolate: like lanceolate but reverse; i.e. elliptical but widest two-thirds from the base.

Obovate: reversed egg-shaped; broadest towards the top.

Ovate: egg-shaped, broadest towards the base.

Pedate: foot-like or hand-like; refers in this context to compound or lobed leaves in which the leaflets or lobes all arise from the same point.

Pedicel: the stalk of a single flower.

Peduncle: the stalk of an inflorescence which is often many-flowered; the peduncle generally refers to the stalk from the stem to the first flower, thereafter the axis which bears the flowers is called the rachis.

Peltate: leaves or leaflets in which the petiole or petiolule is attached to the centre or lower half of the lamina, rather than at its base as in the vast majority of plants.

Petaloid: petal-like; both sepals and staminodes can resemble petals; in *Clematis* the sepals are petaloid.

Petals: the large and colourful organs seen in most flowers; generally the secondary whorl of the flowers with the smaller, less conspicuous, outer organs being the sepals. Some plants lack petals.

Petiole: the stalk of a leaf that attaches it to the stem.

Petiolule: the stalk of a leaflet; in effect a secondary petiole.

Pinnate: compound leaves with two or more pairs of leaflets arise along a common axis or rachis; an additional leaflet generally terminates pinnate leaves, sometimes a tendril.

Plumose: feather-like.

Procumbent: spreading over or lying on the ground.

Revolute: with the margins rolled under.

Sepals: the outermost whorl of most flowers, consisting of small, often whitish or greenish organs, generally smaller than the petals within; in *Clematis* the sepals are large, conspicuous and petal-like.

Sessile: unstalked; sessile leaves bear no petiole.

Simple: undivided; simple leaves have a single undivided lamina.

Solitary: single or one on its own; flowers that arise singly along a stem are said to be solitary.

Stamen: the male organ of flowering plants that consists usually of a stalk or filament, and the anther that bears the pollen.

Subgenus: a major subdivision of a genus; subgenera generally differ in a number of important characters not possessed by the other subgenera.

Subsessile: almost sessile.

Subshrub: a shrub-like plant in which only the basal part becomes woody; in some *Clematis* the upper non-woody parts of the stems die back annually to a basal framework of woody branches.

Subspecies: a prime subdivision of a species; subspecies usually differ in two or more characters from the typical plant and are, at the same time, geographically distinct.

Terminal: at the end of a stem or shoot, terminating it; often refers to flowers or inflorescences.

Ternate: compound leaves with three leaflets.

Valvate: held with the margins touching but not overlapping; the majority of *Clematis* have valvate sepals.

Variety: the subdivision of a species or subspecies differing from the typical plant in one or two characters, but usually found in the same geographical range, or at least in a part of it.

Bibliography

ALLAN H. H. 'Clematis', in the *Flora of New Zealand*, Wellington, 1961, pp. 162–172.

BEAN, W. J., *Trees and Shrubs Hardy in the British Isles*, 8th edition, John Murray, 1973.

CHITTENDEN, F. J., 'Clematis', in vol. 1 of *The Royal Horticultural Society Dictionary of Gardening*, Oxford University Press, 1951, pp. 498–503.

DE CANDOLLE, A. P. AND A. DE, *Prodromus*, 1824, pp. 2–10.

ERICKSON, R. O., 'Taxonomy of Clematis section Viorna', in *Annals Missouri Bot. Gard.*, vol. 30, no. 1, 1943, pp. 1–60.

EVISON, R. J., *Making the most of Clematis*, 3rd edition, Floraprint, 1995.

EVISON, R. J., *The Gardener's Guide to Growing Clematis*, David & Charles, 1988.

FINET AND GAGNEPAIN, *Contributions à la Flore de l'Asie Orientale*, vol. 1 no. 27, 1905.

FISK, J., *Success with Clematis*, Thomas Nelson & Sons, 1962.

FISK, J., *Clematis, the Queen of Climbers*, revised edition, Cassel, 1994.

FRETWELL, B., *Clematis*, Collins, 1989.

FRETWELL, B., *Clematis as Companion Plants*, Cassel, 1994.

GOOCH, R., *Clematis, the Complete Guide*, Crowood Press, 1996.

GREY-WILSON, C., 'Clematis orientalis, a much confused species', in *The Plantsman*, vol. 7, no. 4, Royal Horticultural Society, 1986, pp. 193–204.

GREY-WILSON, C., 'Clematis orientalis (Ranunculaceae) and its Allies', in *Kew Bulletin*, vol. 44 no. 1, Her Majesty's Stationery Office, 1989, pp. 33–60.

GREY-WILSON, C. AND MATTHEWS, V., *Gardening on Walls*, Collins, 1983.

GREY-WILSON, C. AND MATTHEWS, V., *Gardening with Climbers*, Harper Collins, 1997.

HILLIER, *Manual of Trees and Shrubs*, David & Charles, 1973, pp. 428–433.

HOWELLS, J., *A Plantsman's Guide to Clematis*, Ward Lock, 1990.

HULTÉN, E., 'Flora of Kamtchatka and the adjacent islands', in *Kungl. Sv. Vetenskapsakademiens* Handlingar, vol. 5 no. 2, 1927–30, pp. 117–119.

HUXLEY, A. ed., 'Clematis', in *The New Royal Horticultural Dictionary of Gardening*, vol. 1, Macmillan, 1992, pp. 640–652.

JOHNSON, M., *Släktet Klematis*, Södertälje, Sweden, 1997.

KUNTZE, O., 'Monographie des Gattung Clematis', in *Verh. Bot. Ver. Prov. Brandenb.*, vol. 26, 1885, pp.83–202.

KRÜSSMANN, G., *Handbuch der Laubgehölze*, Paul Parey, 1976, pp. 365–382.

LING, P., 'Ranunculaceae', in *Flora Reip. Pop. Sinicae*, vol. 28, 1988, pp. 80–81 and 139–147.

LLOYD, C., *Clematis*, Collins, 1977.

LLOYD, C. AND BENNETT, T., *Clematis*, Viking, 1989.

LOURTEIG, A., 'Ranunculaceas de Sudamerica Templada', in *Darwinia*, vol. 9, nos. 3–4, 1949, pp. 397–421.

MILNE-REDHEAD, E. AND TURRILL, W. B., 'Ranunculaceae', in the *Flora of Tropical East Africa*, 1952, pp. 1–8.

MOORE, T. AND JACKMAN, G., *The Clematis as a Garden Flower*, 2nd edition, John Murray, 1877.

PERRIER DE LA BÔTHIE, H., 'Ranonculacées', in *Flore de Madagascar et des Comores*, famille, vol. 76, 1950, pp. 1–23.

PRANTL, K., 'Beiträge zur Morphologie und Systematik der Ranunculaceen', in *Engler Bot. Jahrb*, vol. 9, 1880, pp. 225–273.

PRANTL, 'Ranunculaceae', in Engler & Prantl, *Die natürlichen Pflanzenfamilien*, vol. 3 no. 2, 1891, pp. 43–66.

RAYNAL, J., 'Clematopsis, genre Africano-Malgache: types biologiques et taxonomie', in *Adansonia* vol. 18 no. 1, 1978, pp. 3–18.

RECHINGER, K. H., 'Clematis' in *Flora Iranica*, vol. 171, 1992, pp. 229–239.

ROBINSON, W., *The Virgin's Bower Clematis*, John Murray, 1912.

STANER, P. AND LÉONARD, J., 'Ranounculacées', in *Flore du Congo Belge et du Ruanda-Urundi*, vol. 2, 1951, pp. 167–201.

SNOEIJER, J. F. & W., *Clematis Index*, Boskoop, Holland, 1991.

TAMURA, M., 'Systema Clematidis Asiae Orientalis', in *Sci. Rep. Osaka Univ.*, vol. 4, 1955, pp. 43–55.

TAMURA, M., 'Notes on Clematis of Eastern Asia', in *Acta Phytotax. Geobot.*, vol. 16 no. 3, 1956, pp. 79–81.

TAMURA, M., 'Morphology, ecology and phylogeny of the Ranunculaceae', in *Sci. Rep. Osaka Univ.* vol. 7, 1968, pp. 21–43.

TAMURA, M. , Ranunculaceae in Engl.– Prantl Pflanzenfamilien, 17, IV, 1995

TIE, XIAN LIAN SHU, 'Clematis' for the *Flora of China*, 1998 in mss!

WEBB, C. J., SYKES, W. R., & GARNOCK-JONES, P. J., 'Clematis' in the *Flora of New Zealand*, 1988, pp. 1005–11

Index

- Names in **bold** signify principal names, not synonyms
- Page numbers in **bold** signify main entry for species
- Page numbers in *italic* signify illustrations

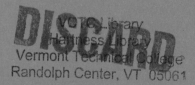